Quality Instruction and Intervention for Elementary Educators

Quality Instruction and Intervention for Elementary Educators

Edited by
Brittany L. Hott and Pamela Williamson

ROWMAN & LITTLEFIELD
Lanham • Boulder • New York • London

Published by Rowman & Littlefield
An imprint of The Rowman & Littlefield Publishing Group, Inc.
4501 Forbes Boulevard, Suite 200, Lanham, Maryland 20706
www.rowman.com

86-90 Paul Street, London EC2A 4NE

Copyright © 2024 by The Rowman & Littlefield Publishing Group, Inc.

All rights reserved. No part of this book may be reproduced in any form or by any electronic or mechanical means, including information storage and retrieval systems, without written permission from the publisher, except by a reviewer who may quote passages in a review.

British Library Cataloguing in Publication Information available

Library of Congress Cataloging-in-Publication Data Available

ISBN 978-1-5381-8698-5 (cloth : alk. paper) | ISBN 978-1-5381-8699-2 (pbk. : alk. paper) | ISBN 978-1-5381-8700-5 (ebook)

∞™ The paper used in this publication meets the minimum requirements of American National Standard for Information Sciences—Permanence of Paper for Printed Library Materials, ANSI/NISO Z39.48-1992.

This book is dedicated to the little ones in our lives. Thank you, Asher Lowry, Henry Abbas, Lucy Belle, Luke Taleb, Saleh Joseph, Sylvie Anne, and Yara June for making our world so much brighter.

Instructor Resources

PowerPoint Slides. For each chapter in the text, there is a PowerPoint slide that can be edited to meet instructor needs. These slide decks are appropriate for online and in-person course delivery. The PowerPoint slides are available to adopters for download on the text's webpage at **https://rowman.com/ISBN/9781538186985**. Instructions to access the PowerPoint slides can be found by selecting the "Resources" tab on the webpage.

Contents

Acknowledgments ... ix

1 **Introduction to Quality Instruction and Intervention** ... 1
Brittany L. Hott and Bailey D. Smith

2 **Reading Instruction Methods for Elementary Students** ... 4
Andrea K. W. Smith, Jodi Arroyo Nagel, Hanna Moore, and Pamela Williamson

3 **Reading Intervention for Elementary Students** ... 27
Pamela Williamson, Andrea K. W. Smith, Jodi Arroyo Nagel, and Hanna Moore

4 **Core Mathematics Instruction** ... 48
Corey Peltier, Garret Hall, and Casey Hord

5 **Quality Mathematics Intervention for Elementary Students** ... 68
Corey Peltier and Scott Dueker

6 **Quality Writing Instruction for Students in the Elementary Grades** ... 88
Alyson A. Collins, Hope Rigby-Wills, and Stephen Ciullo

7 **Quality Writing Intervention for Students with Disabilities in the Elementary Grades** ... 107
Stephen Ciullo, Sagarika Kosaraju, Alyson A. Collins, and John W. McKenna

8 **Modeling in Elementary Science** ... 128
Kelly Feille and Stephanie Hathcock

9 **Inclusive Instruction and Intervention in Elementary Science Education** ... 141
Maria B. Peterson-Ahmad and Randa G. Keeley

10 **Social Studies in the Elementary Grades** ... 168
David A. Brunow

11 **Inclusive Social Studies Instruction** ... 191
Caroline Fitchett and Jacquelyn Purser

12 **Setting Up the Physical Environment for Elementary General Education Classrooms** 207
Jasmine Justus, Julie Atwood, and Bre Martin

13 **Elementary Instruction and Intervention** 226
Kathleen M. Randolph, Julie Atwood, Glenna Billingsley, and Kevin T. Muns

14 **Technology** 251
Theresa Cullen

15 **Executive Functioning Skills** 259
Pamela Williamson

Index 267
About the Authors 280
About the Editors 285

Acknowledgments

WE ARE GRATEFUL TO all of the children, families, and teachers who have taught us many lessons over the years about the value and importance of each individual to our collective society. When everyone is included, society is better for it. We are thankful for our partners (Joe Williamson and Jeff Zadeh) and our families, who fully support this work.

Thank you to Nathan Davidson, acquisitions editor of Rowman & Littlefield, who stood by us and served as a powerful thought partner in this work. This book would not have been possible without the support of the Rowman & Littlefield team. They are top notch! We also appreciate the reviewers who generously gave of their time to provide feedback as we conceptualized this project. This book is better as a result.

We are most appreciative of the support from Ms. Bailey Smith, coauthor and graduate research assistant at the University of Oklahoma. Bailey drafted all of the PowerPoints that can be used as a companion to our text. We are also thankful to Ms. Julie Atwood, coauthor and research scientist at the University of Oklahoma. Julie drafted the supplementary materials that can be used with our text. Their work was integral to this project.

1

Introduction to Quality Instruction and Intervention

Brittany L. Hott and Bailey D. Smith

EFFECTIVE TEACHING STARTS WITH quality instruction and most students respond well to it. However, about 35% of students require specialized and more intensive instruction or intervention to meet academic and behavioral standards. According to the US Department of Education, approximately 7.5 million students (15%) between three and twenty-one years old received special education and related services during the 2022–23 school year (National Center for Education Statistics, 2024). This is a significant increase from the 2009–10 academic year when approximately 6.3 million (13%) of US children received special education and related services. The increasing numbers of children receiving special education services vary by locale, student ethnicity, and family income level. For example, fewer students in Southern regions of the United States receive special education services than their Northern East Coast peers, which suggests under identification of students in some locales and overidentification in others. Further, the largest number of students receiving special education and related services identify as American Indian or Alaska Native (19%) or Black (17%), and the fewest identify as Asian (8%) or Pacific Islander (11%) (National Center for Education Statistics, 2024). This disproportionality leads to inequities in the quality of education for students of color, students living in poverty, and students with disabilities (Kramarczuk Voulgarides et al., 2024).

To address disproportionality and the quality of education students receive, greater attention must be placed on effective core instruction. Further, students with disabilities who are eligible to receive special education and related services require, deserve, and are legally entitled to quality intervention. Students who are placed at risk due to circumstance such as poverty or locale should also be able to access quality intervention to support their development. Most general education methods books focus on academic subject matter and do not address specialized instruction and interventions that are needed by approximately 35% of the school-aged population. Conversely, the majority of special education texts focus solely on interventions with little attention to quality general education instruction, including the development of teacher knowledge of academic subject matter. This text is the second book in a series dedicated to evidence-based instruction and intervention to support educators in meeting student academic, social, emotional, and behavioral needs.

The chapter authors are from diverse backgrounds, bringing perspectives from numerous positions including teachers, behavior analysts, school administrators, technology specialists, and education researchers. Many are also parents of school-aged children. Theses authors are leaders in their respective areas and serve locales from rural and remote schools to large urban districts. The instruction chapters are led by those with strong backgrounds in general education and the intervention chapters are led by educators who have training in school-based intervention. Because there is no replacement for the professional wisdom that comes from teaching students, each chapter includes a practitioner who is working directly with students at the elementary level. The authors worked collaboratively to ensure cohesive chapters that include instruction and intervention, illustrating how to integrate intervention within core content areas. Researchers and specialists provide the theoretical frameworks and evidence that support effective practice with the hope of bridging the research-to-practice gap that ultimately impacts the quality of both instruction and intervention that students receive. Regardless of the frameworks illustrated, both instruction and intervention are grounded in evidence-based practice centering on direct instruction and explicit instruction, presenting a unifying theme across all content areas.

Dedicated chapters focus on core academic content including reading, mathematics, and writing as well as social studies and science. Classroom management and behavioral intervention chapters introduce student social, emotional, and behavioral instruction and intervention. This book concludes with executive functioning and technology integration chapters that impact both academic and content area instruction.

Each team has selected a framework to guide their work. For example, the reading and social, emotional, and behavioral instruction chapters present concepts within a multi-tiered system of supports (MTSS) framework. Smith and colleagues focus on core reading instruction so that all students have access to evidence-based reading services implemented with fidelity. Essential components of literacy instruction include general knowledge, linguistic and writing systems knowledge, phonological awareness, phonics, fluency, vocabulary, and comprehension. Due to the wide variety of curricula and practices available to teach these skills, it is important to stress the importance of selecting an evidence-based core curriculum. MTSS frameworks are tiered models that focus on evidence-based core instruction and interventions that meet the needs of students. For example, Tier 1 focuses on the core components of reading. If implemented correctly, approximately 90% of students should respond to quality general education instruction and make adequate progress. Tier 2 instruction addresses the needs of 5 to 10% of students who require more specialized instruction, typically provided in small-group setting. Tier 3 instruction supports 1 to 3% of students requiring individualized instruction. Due to the large nature of the reading block, teachers have the ability to design multiple forms of daily instruction allowing for successful implementation of MTSS at the classroom level. This may include small-group and large-group instruction as well as an opportunity for students to independently practice a skill.

Like Smith and colleagues, Atwood et al. share the essential components of a classroom environment to facilitate learning. Randolph et al. provide examples of behavioral interventions that can be provided to students who need additional supports beyond a structured classroom environment. Instruction can be provided within a small group setting: Tier 2, to teach strategies such as goal setting or be more individualized; and Tier 3, to provide support such as behavioral contracts. These interventions go beyond classroom set up and evidenced-based instructional practices including behavior-specific praise and precorrection.

Collings and colleagues share a universal design for learning (UDL) framework that centers student choice and voice in writing (Center for Applied Special Technologies [CAST], 2024). Examples of UDL may include using multiple means of engagement, strategic lesson planning, and advanced planning of student groupings and supports. The revised writer(s)-within-community (WWC) model (Graham, 2019) is one instructional method that aligns well with the UDL framework. The WWC model asserts that student writing communities shape the types of writing that occur within that community. WWC provides teachers a unique opportunity to foster creativity while providing writing instruction through "Big Ideas." Some students may need additional supports beyond evidence-based core writing instruction. Cuillo et al. focus on identifying and prioritizing long-term and short-term goals, which involves developing goals that are both measurable and specific to provide effective intervention. Within a UDL framework, there is room to provide explicit instruction that provides clear step-by-step directions; teachers present skills or concepts in small, unambiguous steps.

Like Cuillo et al., Peltier and colleagues emphasize the importance of centering explicit instruction in both core mathematics instruction as well as intervention. Conversely, the science and social studies chapters focus on constructivist approaches to science and social studies instruction. Both Fitchett and Purser and Brunow illustrate how explicit instruction can be incorporated into constructivist methods of teaching to meet individual student learning needs.

Williamson shares the importance of understanding student executive functioning and how to address areas of student need. Finally, Cullen provides an overview of responsible technology integration across content areas.

The author teams have selected and presented a variety of frameworks to illustrate quality instruction and intervention. These frameworks can be applied across content areas to ensure students receive the instruction and intervention needed to make meaningful progress. The goal is not to adopt a specific framework but, rather, to view the frameworks as ways of establishing core instructional components. Many can be implemented simultaneously and across content areas. We hope this text provides both an introduction to quality instruction and intervention and also prompts further learning and discovery.

REFERENCES

Center for Applied Special Technologies (2024). Until learning has no limits. https://www.cast.org/

Graham, S. (2019). Writers in community model: 15 recommendations for future research in using writing to promote science learning. *Theorizing the Future of Science Education Research*, 43–60.

Kramarczuk Voulgarides, C., Jacobs, J., Lopez, D., & Barrio, B. L. (2024). Moving beyond compliance and toward equity to address racial disproportionality. *Intervention in School and Clinic*, 0(0), https://doi.org/10.1177/10534512241258721

National Center for Education Statistics. (2024). Students with disabilities. *Condition of education*. US Department of Education, Institute of Education Sciences. Retrieved from https://nces.ed.gov/programs/coe/indicator/cgg

2

Reading Instruction Methods for Elementary Students

Andrea K. W. Smith, Jodi Arroyo Nagel,
Hanna Moore, and Pamela Williamson

LEARNING TO READ IS one of the most significant accomplishments of elementary school for most students and is too important to be left to chance. In fact, children who do not read proficiently at the end of third grade are four times as likely as proficient readers to leave school without earning a diploma (Hernandez, 2011). Teachers are responsible for retraining brain parts to translate symbols into sounds and meaning. Fortunately, we have research on what works best for teaching reading, and many schools are required to provide materials aligned with this research. The National Reading Panel (2000) has shown that instruction in phonemic awareness, phonics, fluency, vocabulary, and reading comprehension strategies is essential for building comprehension and becoming a proficient reader.

Reading is often given the largest block of time during the instructional day, providing elementary teachers the unique opportunity to work with students in varied groups and formats to address the many components of reading. Though primary teachers expect to teach children to read, intermediate teachers should also know how to teach foundational reading skills, as some students require additional instruction and intervention.

We know that students need well-designed instruction on how to read, but how do we provide that? This chapter will begin to show you what is involved in elementary reading instruction. We will explore the theoretical foundations of reading instruction and what the research tells us about how to teach reading most effectively. We will also examine the legal foundations for reading instruction. We will look at how teachers can use formative and summative assessment to guide reading instruction and how they can differentiate that instruction to meet student needs. From there, we will consider components of reading instruction, including general knowledge, oral language, phonological awareness, phonics, fluency, vocabulary, and comprehension. Ultimately, this chapter will help you answer the following guiding questions:

1. What are the policies, standards, theories, and research that inform high-quality core reading instruction in inclusive elementary classrooms?

2. How can assessments guide instructional planning and decision-making?
3. What does high-quality core reading instruction look like in inclusive elementary classrooms?
4. Which evidence-based methods and practices can teachers use to meet the needs of a diverse range of learners?

UNDERLYING POLICIES, STANDARDS, THEORIES, AND RESEARCH

Educational Policy

In 1965, Congress passed the Elementary and Secondary Education Act (ESEA) as part of President Lyndon B. Johnson's Great Society program. It expanded the federal government's role in education, which had previously been left to the states in the Constitution. ESEA (1965) created Title 1, a federal funding source that school districts depend upon to support intervention for struggling learners. By tying compliance to these funds, ESEA dramatically increased the federal government's role in guiding education. In 2002, the No Child Left Behind Act (NCLB) was signed into law as a continuation of ESEA, kicking off decades of high-stakes testing with the intention of guaranteeing each child in the United States a quality education in reading and math. The law mandated highly qualified teachers, standardized state assessments for grades 3 through 8 and in high school, and 100% proficiency on these tests for every state by 2014. NCLB also offered families options if their child's school did not make adequate yearly progress (AYP) regarding overall test scores and growth or scores for specific subgroups (NCLB, 2002).

The federal and state governments have a vested interest in mandating strong reading instruction due to the critical role of literacy. Over decades of reading instruction, a disagreement developed between whole language advocates (i.e., those who believe that children learn to read best through an emphasis on meaning-making and exposure to oral language and real literature) and phonics or "back to the basics" advocates (i.e., those who believe that reading is a complex skill that should be taught systematically and explicitly) (Preston, 2022). The United States Congress commissioned the National Reading Panel in 1997 to address what became known as the reading wars. Their April 2000 report synthesized the findings of hundreds of research articles and recommended reading education focusing on phonemic awareness, phonics, fluency, vocabulary, and comprehension (National Reading Panel, 2000). Despite the report, the reading wars continued with disagreements about how students should be cued when they misread a word. Recently, scholars have recognized that reading is a science, though they continue to debate precisely which elements are critical and how they should be taught (Goldberg & Goldenberg, 2022).

Academic Standards

In 2012, the Obama administration began granting waivers for some NCLB requirements in exchange for states enacting high standards and creating a plan to shrink or close gaps. In 2015, President Obama signed the Every Student Succeeds Act (ESSA), replacing NCLB and further codifying options for closing the gap and mandating rigorous state standards. Forty-six states adopted the Common Core State

Standards (CCSS) for literacy created by the Council of Chief State School Officers (CCSSO) and the National Governors Association (NGA) to make education more uniform across the country. However, more than a dozen states later modified or replaced the CCSS (EdGate, 2023).

State standards typically address reading, writing, and communication, though how they do so varies substantially from state to state among those who do not use the CCSS. Well-designed standards are threaded through the grade levels, with teachers able to trace the vertical alignment as students build their skills with a given standard from year to year. Standards utilize a coding method to make it easy for teachers to document them in lesson plans and to see how they connect across the grade level and throughout the grades. It is important to remember that reading is an inclusive act that requires many skills to be implemented at once, so a reading lesson may address several standards. The standards are often taught best in combination with other literacy or content-area standards.

Foundational Theories

For many years, a debate has raged between whole language advocates who choose to teach reading using exposure to real literature with the expectation that students will learn how to read by making meaning of language and those who choose to teach reading through explicit, systematic phonics instruction, believing that making the process of reading more visible to students will help them master the skills (Preston, 2022). Though these reading wars raged for decades and continue to some degree, recent research has provided strong evidence that students need explicit instruction in decoding with a strong foundation in phonics, as well as opportunities to apply their phonics learning in real reading situations (National Reading Panel, 2000; Torgerson et al., 2019). Recognizing the importance of decoding and comprehension, scholars have attempted to create theoretical frameworks and models to explain this interaction. We will examine three such frameworks here.

Gough and Tunmer (1986) proposed the simple view of reading (SVR). They believe that reading ability comes down to a formula based on its components, which means that reading equals decoding times comprehension ($R = D \times C$). In this model, comprehension refers to linguistic comprehension or the understanding of language. If a student has fully developed grade-level decoding skills (measured as 1) and fully developed grade-level comprehension skills (measured as 1), then his reading ability will be complete ($1 \times 1 = 1$). However, suppose both decoding and comprehension are halfway developed to grade level. In that case, the student's reading ability will be only one-quarter of what is needed for that grade level ($1/2 \times 1/2 = 1/4$). Having either skill only halfway to mastery for the grade level, even with the other skill completely developed, will result in reading success at about one-half ($1/2 \times 1 = 1/2$). In extreme cases, we would see a student with dyslexia who understands language but cannot decode at all being unable to read because $0 \times 1 = 0$ and a student with hyperlexia having exceptional decoding skills but no comprehension and, likewise, being completely unable to read for meaning because $1 \times 0 = 0$. Though this view is simple, as its name states, it provides an essential insight into the importance of building up decoding and comprehension and identifying which deficit needs support for each student. However, it also assumes that listening and reading comprehension are interchangeable skills, which has not been borne out by research (Shanahan, 2020), so we need to consider how to explicitly teach reading comprehension to increase the outcome of the equation.

Building on the SVR, Scarborough (2001) has developed her reading rope to expand the concepts of decoding and comprehension. She uses a diagram of five strands of warm colors braided together and then entwined with three strands of cool colors braided together to create a strong rope. The upper five strands represent the components of language comprehension: background knowledge, vocabulary, language structure, verbal reasoning, and literacy knowledge. As these strands are strengthened and used together, reading becomes increasingly strategic because students have more from which to draw as they attempt to understand what they read. Meanwhile, the bottom three strands represent aspects of word recognition: phonological awareness, decoding, and sight recognition. Reading grows more automatic as these three strands develop and are used together. Reading becomes more skilled when both word recognition and language comprehension become fluent and coordinated.

Subsequently, Perfetti and Stafura (2014) have proposed the reading systems framework (RSF). This model was developed in response to concerns that simplified models of the reading process lead to a deemphasis on essential aspects of reading, such as making inferences during reading, and the importance of general knowledge, including text forms (e.g., genre, text structures). Thus, the RSF framework "reintroduces a wide-angle view of reading comprehension" to account for progress made in understanding the process of reading comprehension (p. 22). Notably, the model retained the importance and complexity of word knowledge from earlier models.

In the RSF model, top-down and bottom-up processes inform reading. The reading processes draw from three classes of knowledge sources: linguistic knowledge, orthographic knowledge, and general knowledge of the world and text forms. The bottom-up aspects of reading include the orthographic system and the linguistic system (phonology, syntax, morphology). Top-down processes include general knowledge, including students' knowledge of text forms (e.g., text structures, story grammar, genre). Reading processes (e.g., decoding, word identification, meaning retrieval, sentence parsing, inferencing, and comprehension monitoring) use these three classes of knowledge in constrained and interactive ways. For example, decoding uses phonological and orthographic knowledge but not general knowledge, whereas inferences require interactive processes that use both general knowledge and knowledge parsed from sentences. Further, these processes are situated within a system of cognition that includes perceptual and memory systems with limited resources (e.g., short-term memory). For teachers of students with a wide variety of backgrounds, including students with disabilities, this model supports developing more detailed hypotheses about potential sources of reading difficulties than earlier models (e.g., executive functioning skills, background knowledge of text forms, inference making) could.

Guiding Research

As reading research continues, teachers have access to a wealth of information about how to teach reading. Unfortunately, some of this information conflicts with other studies or the curricular materials purchased by schools. Teachers are tasked with becoming wise consumers of information, able to recognize what their students need to succeed. Gone are the days when students sit in rows and complete worksheets while the teacher conducts reading groups focused on reading a story aloud and then answering the questions back at student desks. Teachers today are responsible for organizing whole-group and small-group instruction and differentiating the instruction to meet the diverse needs of students with and without disabilities, some of whom may be learning English as a second or third language and some of whom may be gifted or in need of academic enrichment. As such, we are fortunate to have meta-analyses that highlight themes threaded through the research on reading instruction.

The National Reading Panel (2000) and the National Early Literacy Panel (2008) have synthesized multiple studies and reinforced the importance of explicitly teaching phonemic awareness, as well as phonics, to help children break the code of written language and become readers. Gentry and Ouellette (2019) have clarified the role of phonics as one key element of building what they call "brain words" or "a dictionary in each child's brain" (p. 2), positing that one critical responsibility of teachers is to help students become fluent readers by helping them come to recognize thousands of words by sight. This is accomplished by helping them use phonics to decode and giving them frequent exposure to words, so they come to own those words and seldom need to slow down to decode an individual word, thereby allowing students to focus their working memory on comprehension, the real purpose of reading. Rasinski (2017) lent his support to the critical importance of building foundational decoding skills through daily word work in the early grades, but he also proposed that fluency is a critical component of reading that leads to understanding and should be taught and practiced daily. We know that robust vocabulary instruction is integral to building strong readers, as text does not make sense when we do not understand the words deeply enough to determine the applicable meaning (Beck et al., 2002). Uccelli and colleagues (2015) have narrowed down the influence of vocabulary knowledge on reading comprehension. They highlight the importance of building proficiency with cross-disciplinary academic language for multilingual learners. Though comprehension depends on decoding, fluency, and vocabulary skills, it also requires a set of cognitive strategies. Strong readers have mastered a set of strategies and can choose among them and utilize them in appropriate combinations to comprehend texts. These strategies include activating background knowledge, asking questions of the text, searching the text for information, summarizing, graphically organizing information from the text, and determining the text structure and its aspects (Guthrie et al. 2004). Additionally, students need motivation for reading, which may come from learning content information (Guthrie et al., 2004).

ASSESSMENTS AND INSTRUCTION IN THE ELEMENTARY LANGUAGE ARTS CLASSROOM

Elementary teachers are tasked with planning and providing instruction to a class of perhaps seventeen to thirty students. As students have varying instructional needs, teachers must be thoughtful and thorough in their planning to meet all needs through diverse supports and differentiation. Teachers can use data-based decision-making (DBDM) to plan their lessons strategically. DBDM is the process of using data to identify students' patterns of strengths and weaknesses as they relate to instructional goals and using the data to plan instruction that facilitates student achievement of those instructional goals (Dunn et al., 2013). Though each district or state will have access to different tools, assessments that teachers can use class-wide or with individual students include STAR Reading, STAR Early Literacy, i-Ready, the Dynamic Indicators of Basic Early Literacy Skills (DIBELS), and the Diagnostic Assessment of Reading (DAR). Speech language pathologists and reading coaches often have access to additional assessment tools they can administer to individual students or loan to teachers.

Mr. Miller, a first-grade teacher, gives a summative reading assessment each Friday to help students review what they learned that week. He also uses the results to diagnose reading challenges and determine groups for the next week. Mr. Miller frequently administers quick formative assessments before, during, and after his lessons to gauge how well the students are learning and what he may need to address. For example, he has students share background knowledge on a topic with a partner while he listens in, asks students to agree or disagree with their classmates' answers, and listens to each student read aloud for one minute or asks a question or two about what each student is reading during independent reading time.

Ms. Johnson, the school's special education teacher, visits Mr. Miller's room a few times a week to support all students, including students with disabilities. While she is there or during their shared planning time, she helps Mr. Miller analyze data from both classroom assessments and school-wide progress monitoring assessments given every quarter to identify students who may need extra support. She and Mr. Miller share the task of identifying and providing evidence-based intervention for these students. Often, Ms. Johnson pulls a few students without disabilities into her small groups or teaches the class while Mr. Miller supports students who need additional explanation.

Using student data, teachers like Mr. Miller and Ms. Johnson adapt instruction and plan lessons to provide explicit instruction in the skills for which students need the most support. Combining this targeted instruction with universal design for learning (UDL) is a critical foundation for successful classroom instruction and implementation of multi-tiered system of supports (MTSS).

Explicit Instruction

Explicit instruction is a research-supported approach used to design and deliver instruction that reduces the students' cognitive load through purposeful, clear, concise, and engaging instruction (Hughes et al., 2017). The Institute for Educational Sciences recommends explicit instruction for students with and without disabilities (Foorman et al., 2016). Explicit instruction is guided by six principles and 16 elements (Archer & Hughes, 2011). The principles include optimizing engaged time or time on task, promoting high levels of success, and scaffolding instruction. Examples of explicit instruction elements include sequencing skills logically, reviewing prior skills and knowledge before beginning instruction, providing step-by-step demonstrations, providing guided and supported practice, providing immediate feedback, and delivering the lesson at a brisk pace.

Differentiated Instruction

Differentiated instruction (DI) is a framework that allows teachers to adjust their instruction to meet the needs of every learner in the classroom—students who are gifted and talented, students with disabilities, multilingual learners, other diverse learners, and neurotypical learners on grade level. DI is not a set of instructional strategies but a set of principles that emphasizes student needs and curriculum content (Tomlinson & Imbeau, 2013). Differentiation involves adjustment of the content (what students are expected to learn), process (how students are expected to learn the content), and product (how students are expected to show their learning) while considering student affect (how students' emotions and feelings impact their learning), preparedness for the learning, and interest (what engages the student's attention and excitement) concerning the present learning aims (Tomlinson & Imbeau, 2013). A teacher differentiating instruction continually considers her students' performance and interests to develop curricular content that maximizes their academic growth. Affect is most often influenced by adaptations to the learning environment, which are best situated within a universal design for learning.

Universal Design for Learning

Universal design for learning (UDL) is a framework to guide instruction that is accessible and challenging for all (CAST, 2018). Rather than try to change the learner to meet the needs of instruction, UDL aims to change the instructional environment to meet all learners. This change in environment can be supported through implementing the Center for Applied Special Technology (CAST) UDL guidelines (2018), which encourage teachers to consider the why, what, and how of instruction and provide multiple means of engagement, representation, and action and expression. Examples of these multiple means include providing options for individual choice, fostering collaboration, offering ways of customizing the display of information, activating background knowledge, guiding appropriate goal setting, and varying the methods for student response.

Students come to the classroom with different motivations, and providing multiple means of engagement allows a teacher to activate those motivations and generate interest in learning. Some students may respond well to collaborative work, while others prefer to work independently on a technical project. By giving students choices in how they learn the material and how they present that learning, teachers are more likely to engage every learner and motivate them to pursue further learning and exploration independently.

As illustrated in the vignette below, teachers might implement UDL strategies by allowing students to choose how to demonstrate their learning by selecting an assignment from a choice board or "menu" or negotiating a different assignment with the teacher.

As Mr. Miller plans his upcoming reading unit, he searches through his science curriculum and selects texts and vocabulary to support cross-curricular learning. He chooses several texts that relate to identifying the beneficial and harmful properties of the sun and builds learning objectives around these texts. He wants his students to personalize their learning, so he creates an activity menu that includes three options for an "appetizer," three options for a "main course," and three options for "dessert." The class will read a selected text together using an oral cloze reading strategy. The teacher reads the text aloud, pausing at key words. When the teacher pauses, the students chorally read the next word, and then the teacher continues reading. After the cloze reading, the students complete their menu cards by selecting one item from each category to build a "meal." Mr. Miller has selected specific vocabulary words and designated them within the text.

After whole-group reading, Tatiana selects the "divide vocabulary words into syllables" option for her appetizer, the "write a sentence and draw a picture showing an important part" option for her main course, and the "tell your friend what you learned" option for her dessert. She partners with Jamaal, who also chose "tell your friend what you learned" for dessert, and then the two share with the whole group. Daniel approaches Mr. Miller and asks if he can choose "make a rap that shows your learning" for his main course, an option from a previous week that was not included on the current menu, and Mr. Miller happily obliges. Other pairs and small groups share what they learned from their menu options, some of which were collaborative while others were independent.

Multi-Tiered System of Supports

Multi-tiered system of supports (MTSS) is a framework for supporting all students in meeting grade-level benchmarks and expectations. MTSS is often depicted by a triangle or pyramid with three tiers: Tier 1 consists of core instruction that every student receives and ideally meets the needs of approximately 80% of students; Tier 2 includes supplemental supports and interventions that around 15% of students may require, and Tier 3 involves the most intensive interventions, necessary for around 5% of students to be successful meeting grade-level benchmarks and expectations (Carta & Young, 2019). Teachers like Mr. Miller and Ms. Johnson use a universal screener to identify students who require additional interventions to achieve grade-level expectations. The teacher or a specific interventionist provides these interventions seamlessly within the general education classroom.

At the elementary level, schedules are often built with intervention and enrichment blocks in mind, and data is utilized to sort students into appropriate groupings based on their academic strengths and weaknesses (Fuchs & Fuchs, 2007). Teaching using centers or rotations is a customary practice that allows a core teacher to tailor instruction to groups of students based on individual needs determined by diagnostic and progress-monitoring data. Additional supports like paraprofessionals or teaching teams are often employed to provide the appropriate interventions or enrichments to every student in the class within the intervention block. MTSS teams meet regularly to review progress monitoring data, ensuring that each student receives the appropriate level of support throughout the school year (Fuchs & Fuchs, 2007). The data-driven nature of MTSS allows for fluidity and constant evaluation of student needs. Although a student may require Tier 2 or Tier 3 interventions for a time, quick progress may reduce or eliminate the need for intensive intervention. Students are not tracked into a specific tier, regardless of their level of need at any given time, and "it is imperative that students have the ability to freely move through tiered instruction based on their progress monitoring data" (Bouck & Cosby, 2019, p. 40).

INSTRUCTIONAL METHODS FOR CORE READING INSTRUCTION

As previously mentioned, the reading or literacy block in elementary classrooms is a dedicated block of time, often consisting of 90 to 120 minutes of daily instruction. During this time, we suggest teachers consider the block through the lens of an interactive literacy framework that considers students' needs (e.g., student characteristics, reading profiles), the context of instruction (e.g., grouping), and the target text for instruction (e.g., genre, skills to be learned). In the interactive literacy framework, the teacher plans explicit, data- and standards-based lessons that include applicable word work (e.g., phonological awareness, phonics, vocabulary), reading (e.g., comprehension, fluency), and writing.

The reading block is an appropriate time to integrate large-group, small-group, and independent work. Many teachers divide their students into groups and provide each group with small-group instruction every day or every other day. Ideally, the group most in need of support receives more teacher time than the other groups. This aim can be achieved by considering group size: students who need the most instructional support should have the fewest students in their small group. While the teacher works with a small group, other students can engage in interactive activities at learning centers, participate in computer-assisted instruction, or read with a partner. The teacher should carefully plan how to monitor these activities, group students, and guide learning based on classroom data.

Next, we address essential components of literacy instruction. We begin each component with a vignette describing a teacher delivering the component. Next, we describe additional information about each component.

General Knowledge

Mr. Miller has selected Christina Katerina and The Box *by Patricia Lee Gauch (1971), illustrated by Doris Burn, for a read-aloud. He chose this book because it is a wonderful story demonstrating the fun and adventure of using one's imagination with even the simplest items. Before he begins reading the story aloud, he assesses and activates his students' prior knowledge by asking open-ended questions. He starts with questions such as "What are some ways that children play pretend or make-believe?" and "When is a time that you remember playing pretend? What did you pretend was happening?" He then moves to more text-specific questions, such as, "What are different uses for boxes, especially when playing pretend?" After his questions, Mr. Miller determines that his class does not require additional information to understand the text, and he moves on to reading it aloud.*

Readers require a certain threshold of background or prior knowledge of the content to understand a given text (Hirsch, 2003). In fact, higher levels of background knowledge enable both skilled and low-skilled readers to comprehend text better because it can help them compensate for unknown words or unclear text structures (Smith et al., 2021). Students benefit from background knowledge instruction that is provided in an explicit and sequential manner (Connor et al., 2017; Kim et al., 2021). This instruction can be planned by the teacher or included in a "knowledge-rich" curriculum, if available (Hirsch, 2019). Knowledge-rich curricula provide instruction in reading and writing skills while also explicitly building students' vocabulary and understanding of literature, social studies, and science. Including domain-specific knowledge has the added benefit of additional content instruction opportunities at grade levels that do not focus heavily on science and social studies.

Background knowledge can be quickly assessed using direct questioning methods, such as the concept questions in the *Qualitative Reading Inventory 7* (Leslie & Caldwell, 2021). For example, if a teacher who lives in a warm climate were to select *A Snowy Day* by Ezra Keats (1996) as a text to use in her classroom, the teacher may ask questions such as "What can children do when there is snow outside?" and "How should one dress for cold, snowy weather?" The answers the students provide to this type of question will guide the teacher in determining the need to pre-teach vocabulary words such as *snowsuit* and *snow angels* or provide general background information on snow, snow days, and snow day activities. Depending on the students' understanding and prior experiences, this pre-teaching and scaffolding may be necessary because a lack of knowledge would directly impact their comprehension of the story (Smith et al., 2021).

Linguistic and Writing System Knowledge

Mr. Miller now begins his read-aloud of Christina Katerina and The Box. *As he reads, Mr. Miller provides descriptive language while reading and explaining the story, for example, stating, "Look how Christina and her mom are both delighted to see the 'grand and new' delivery. However, Christina's mom is thinking about the refrigerator inside the box, while Christina is only thinking about the box itself." He also asks open-ended questions such as "What do you think Christina will do with a box that large? What might she make out of it?" He then repeats a child's response and expands upon it or asks additional follow-up questions to add more language to the dialogue (e.g., "Yes, Christina could make a fort out of the box! If you had a fort, what would you name it?"). By being an active listener and following up on the child's comments, Mr. Miller has additional opportunities to engage the students in a richer conversation, further developing language.*

Oral language development has been identified as an area that is correlated to success in reading (National Early Literacy Panel, 2008). Oral language can be receptive or expressive; receptive language consists of the words that students hear and read, while expressive language consists of the words that students speak and write. All language consists of various systems that support word knowledge and text comprehension (Moats, 2020). The language systems that support word knowledge include phonology, which refers to speech sounds; morphology, which refers to the meaning of word parts; lexical semantics, which refers to word meanings and connections; and orthography, which refers to mapping speech sounds. Sentence and text comprehension are supported by pragmatics or social rules of language use, sentential semantics or sentence meaning, and syntax or rules for word order. When students read, write, listen, or speak, they use the language systems.

One way for teachers to support language development throughout elementary grades is through purposeful, high-quality conversations (Birsh & Carreker, 2018). Shared reading can support rich conversations (Beauchat et al., 2011). Shared reading, also called a read-aloud, is any instance when a text is read aloud with pauses during the reading for the reader and listener to discuss ideas and questions related to the text. These conversations might include discussing the story and pictures or making connections to prior experiences. Shared reading can be done at all grade levels with all types of texts, including storybooks, chapter books, informative texts, and poetry. Examples of texts that are popular for shared reading include *James and the Giant Peach* by Roald Dahl (1967); *The Street Beneath My Feet (Look Closer)* by Charlotte Gullain (2017), illustrated by Yuval Zommer; and *I've Lost My Hippopotamus* by Jack Prelutsky (2012), illustrated by Jackie Urbanovic. Planning for shared reading can be guided by a shared reading innovation configuration developed by Beauchat and colleagues (2011).

Phonological Awareness

Mr. Miller spends fifteen minutes with his students in whole-group phonemic awareness instruction. He starts by taking them through a sequence of phoneme manipulation activities, specifically focused on isolating the beginning phoneme in simple consonant-vowel-consonant (CVC) words. After writing the word "dog" on the whiteboard, he asks, "What is the first sound in the word 'dog'?" to a chorus of "/d/!" Next, he writes the word "pin" on the whiteboard and asks the students, "What's the ending sound in pin?" "/n/!" He then assesses their ability to isolate a middle phoneme. After writing the word "ap" on the whiteboard, he asks, "What sound comes in the middle of the word 'lap'?" "/a/!" As the class replies, Mr. Miller is careful to watch for responses from individual students. He notes when a student struggles with a skill so that he can remediate the skill immediately with another example. He sometimes asks for responses from only a select group of students to gauge understanding. "Wonderful! Now, just my red group—what sound is the same in big, bun, and ball?" "/b/!" Mr. Miller continues working on the different skills until he has ended with phoneme deletion.

Phonological awareness is the ability to identify and manipulate the spoken parts of language. There are four levels of phonological awareness, beginning with word knowledge, continuing to syllable knowledge, progressing to more complex onset-rime knowledge, and ending with the most complex level: phonemic knowledge or awareness. However, earlier-level skills continue to develop as children progress (Anthony & Francis, 2005). Phonemic awareness (PA) is the ability to identify and manipulate the individual sounds or *phonemes* that comprise spoken language. A phoneme is the smallest sound portion that differentiates words. For example, the word "cat" comprises three individual sounds or phonemes: /c/, /a/, and /t/. These phonemes can also be manipulated. For example, take the word "pan," made up of phonemes /p/, /a/, and /n/. If the phoneme /m/ were substituted for the phoneme /p/, the word would no longer be "pan," but "man," which completely changes the word's meaning.

PA is a crucial skill to develop in beginning readers because it is one of the best predictors of a child's future reading ability. Although PA is an aural skill, PA instruction should include phonics work with graphemes (i.e., letters or groups of letters) and be explicit and systematic. It should consist of the following components (Ehri et al., 2001):

> **Phoneme isolation**. Recognizing individual sounds in words. For example, "What is the first sound in the word 'toy'?" (/t/), "What is the middle sound in the word 'lip'?" (/i/), or "What is the ending sound in fan?" (/n/).
> **Phoneme identification**. Recognizing the sound shared by a set of words. For example, "What sound is the same in pay, pin, and pull?" (/p/).
> **Phoneme categorization**. Recognizing the sound that does not match in a sequence of words. For example, "Tell me which word does not belong: can, car, bit." (bit).
> **Phoneme blending**. Combining a sequence of spoken sounds into a word. For example, "What word does /n/ /a/ /p/ make?" (nap).
> **Phoneme segmentation**. Breaking a word into its individual phonemes by counting or tapping out sounds. For example, "How many phonemes are in the word 'bike'?" (3: /b/ /ie/ /k/).
> **Phoneme addition**. Adding a phoneme to an existing word to make a new word. For example, "What does pin become if you add /s/ to the beginning?" (spin).
> **Phoneme deletion**. Recognizing the remaining word when a specific phoneme is removed. For example, "What is spill without /s/?" (pill).
> **Phoneme substitution**. Changing one phoneme in a word to another to make a new word. For example, "What is fin if you change /i/ to /u/?" (fun).

Another common feature of phonological awareness instruction is onset-rime manipulation. An onset is the consonant or consonant blend that precedes the vowel in a word, and the rime is the vowel and following consonants—for example, p-ush or ch-eck. When teaching students word families, such as the /at/ family (bat, cat, fat, hat, mat, etc.), what is being taught is onset and rime identification and manipulation. Instructing students in onsets and rimes helps them recognize common chunks within words and can lead to stronger decoding skills as reading progresses. Once students understand that words with the same rime will always have the same ending sounds (meaning they will rhyme), they can begin decoding words with that spelling pattern more fluently.

Phonics

For a quick phonics lesson, Mr. Miller decides to work with small groups at a center. The students who are not working with him play phonics computer games, build words with letter cards to match picture cues with a partner on the floor, or sort word cards into groups with shared beginning, ending, or vowel sounds. The students rotate through the different activities every ten minutes, and Mr. Miller varies the activities from day to day. Today, Mr. Miller gives each student in his small group a laminated paper with a row of five connected boxes he will use for an Elkonin box activity. Each student also has a dry-erase marker and a piece of felt for erasing. Mr. Miller reminds the students to write one sound in each box. He says,

"Write the word 'flip' in your Elkonin boxes." The students use four boxes to write *"f-l-i-p."* Mr. Miller quickly praises their attention to each sound and has them erase. Then, he asks them to write class. Sienna writes two of the letter *"s"* in the fourth box. Mr. Miller asks her why, and she correctly explains, *"They only make one sound."* Other students who wrote one letter s in each of two boxes correct their work, and the lesson continues. When Mr. Miller asks the students to write tile, he is excited to see that a couple of them know to put the final *"e"* in the box with the *"l"* and to make it smaller. Mr. Miller invites Joel to explain his answer, and Joel reminds the group that the *"e"* is there so that we will say the name of the letter *"I,"* but it does not have a sound in this word.

While phonemic awareness is centered on the sounds in words, phonics relates to how letters or groups of letters represent those sounds. These relationships are referred to as letter-sound correspondence. Phonemic awareness instruction should continue alongside phonics instruction, but instead of the instructional focus being on the sound, it is on the grapheme or letters or groups of letters. There are 44 sounds or phonemes in the English language, and they are represented by 26 letters or combinations of these letters called digraphs (e.g., th, -ng), trigraphs (e.g., -ght, -dge), and quadrigraphs (e.g., eigh, -ngue). Students should be taught phonics explicitly with plenty of practice in decoding and spelling. Phonics should also be taught systematically, with more commonly used letter-sound correspondences taught earlier and more complex and rarer letter-sound correspondences taught after a student has a broader foundation on which to build. For example, most phonics programs teach that "a" represents the sound /a/ (short a), "m" represents the sound /m/, and "s" represents the sound /s/ long before complicating matters with "c" representing the sound /s/ or "eigh" representing the sound /ae/ (long a as in eight). It is essential to model the usage of correct terms for students. Letters do not say sounds; rather, a grapheme is the letter or group of letters that represents a phoneme or sound. Students should be taught how to sound out or decode words and how to spell or encode those words in the same lesson. Pairing this learning makes students stronger spellers and strengthens their decoding skills.

To provide phonics instruction effectively, teachers need a deep understanding of the material (Moats, 2009). Teachers should be skilled in correctly pronouncing the sounds represented by letters and letter combinations to model these for students. For example, when saying the sound represented by the letter *b*, teachers must be sure not to say /buh/ (i.e., add a *schwa* sound at the end of the consonant) but rather pop their lips open quickly and then clip the sound off. In practice, this might sound more like a short /i/ sound after the consonant, but teachers should work toward decreasing the presence of any vowel sound when pronouncing a consonant sound. The point here is that correct pronunciation facilitates blending sounds together to make words.

Teachers should be familiar with how the English language works. Although many people perceive English as unpredictable, 31 rules make the language more predictable and partially explain the pronunciation and spelling of 98% of English words (Eide, 2012). Many of these rules illuminate how words are broken into syllables. A syllable is a part of a word with precisely one vowel sound, though it may have several vowel letters. Vowels are the sounds we make by opening our mouths and pushing air through, while consonants are sounds formed by blocking air with some part of our mouths. Vowels are represented by the letters "a," "e," "i," "o," and "u," as well as the letter "y" in some cases, either alone or with another vowel letter. The letter "w" can also work with another vowel letter to make a vowel sound, such as /ow/. Additionally, the letter "r" after a vowel can modify the vowel sound, creating an r-controlled or r-influenced vowel (e.g. worker, hurt, learn). The letter "l" can also modify the sound of the letter "a" when placed after it (e.g., ball).

Once students have learned the basics of which sounds are typically represented by which letters or letter combinations and have practiced decoding and spelling single-syllable words, they are ready to move on to multi-syllable words. This process is easier when teachers explicitly explain how letters and sounds can combine to form syllables. There are six syllable types and recognizing them can help readers predict what sounds letters will represent, how to spell syllables and words, and how to flex the pronunciation of word parts, or morphemes, when suffixes are added to the end of them. For example, when we add the suffix "ence" to the word "infer," we get the word "inference." The /er/ sound must be flexed or adjusted to make the pronunciation sound like a real word.

Explicit phonics instruction is critical throughout elementary school, though it should take different forms as students progress through the grade levels and build their individual skills. By the end of the primary grades, teachers often stop providing daily instruction in phonics and transition to teaching word parts and how they are formed and read within the context of vocabulary instruction (e.g., morphemic decoding) or as they are encountered in reading.

To make an abstract concept, such as phonics, more accessible for students in a classroom guided by UDL principles, teachers should integrate oral language, visuals, hands-on activities, paired or group practice, and call-and-response activities. A quick pace will allow all students to experience numerous practice opportunities, and students will benefit from spaced practice with frequent review to master phonics. Elkonin boxes, as illustrated in the vignette above, can be used for phonics, with each box representing one sound and students writing the letters that represent those sounds in the boxes. Manipulatives may include letter tiles, flipbooks, and word wheels. Students will also benefit from word walls organized by sound or word part.

Fluency

To help his students practice fluent reading during whole-group instruction, Mr. Miller engages them in choral reading. Together, all students read aloud from a text, encouraging disfluent readers to match their fluent peers' pace and prosody. At other times, Mr. Miller models fluent reading of a text, then asks his students to read the same text independently using their whisper phones (devices that allow students to read text aloud quietly and hear their own voices amplified in one ear). Mr. Miller guides his students through repeated readings of the same text as many as four times, increasing both fluency and comprehension.

Mr. Miller loves having his students perform in readers' theater exercises because they are an engaging way to include even his most reluctant oral readers. He routinely searches for dialogue-heavy texts with multiple parts for students to act out. Using small groups as necessary for the number of parts, Mr. Miller assigns each student a character to read for. The students then practice their parts by reading aloud multiple times within their group until each student can fluently read their lines. Mr. Miller floats from group to group, correcting errors and suggesting more emotive text readings. The groups then have the chance to perform their texts for the rest of the class.

Fluency is reading text accurately, automatically, and with prosody or proper expression. When students can quickly and accurately identify words, they have greater cognitive resources to focus on meaning, leading to higher levels of comprehension (Stevens et al., 2017; Therrien, 2004). Unfortunately, little time is devoted to fluency instruction in many elementary classrooms (Didion & Toste, 2022), and some students do not receive sufficient fluency instruction, necessitating a higher level of support or intervention. However, fluency instruction can be incorporated seamlessly into the reading block through modeled fluent reading, wide reading, repeated reading, choral reading, and readers' theater.

Sustained silent reading (SSR) has been a common practice in many elementary classrooms, but research has shown that SSR is not the most effective way to build students' fluency (Esteves & Whitten, 2011). If a student does not read fluently aloud, there is no guarantee they will read fluently silently either. Additionally, SSR does not call for student accountability, making it a difficult practice to monitor with fidelity. Therefore, either modeled fluent reading or scaffolded silent reading (ScSR) are favorable to SSR to improve disfluent reading (Reutzel et al., 2008).

Unlike traditional SSR, where students are encouraged to read anything that interests them regardless of genre or level (Reutzel et al., 2008), ScSR requires students to read widely from several genres. During independent reading time, the teacher circulates throughout the room, pausing to hold mini-conferences with students for a minute or so. For example, a student might be asked to read a portion of selected text aloud, while the teacher listens for appropriate accuracy, rate, and prosody. If the student is reading disfluently, the teacher might model fluent reading. Like repeated reading, wide reading is a technique shown to improve students' fluency (Ardoin et al., 2016). By exposing students to a wide selection of texts and incorporating accountability and instructional measures through mini-conferences, ScSR can have a far more significant impact on students' fluency than traditional SSR (Reutzel et al., 2008).

When paired with printed text, audiobooks are an excellent tool for developing fluent reading skills and providing a model of fluent reading for students (Esteves & Whitten, 2011). Audiobooks can be selected to ensure that every student is engaging with an appropriately challenging text. There are numerous online resources for free audiobooks, many of which display the book pages and text through the platform.

Vocabulary

Before beginning a read-aloud, Mr. Miller goes through the book to determine whether any words in the story are Tier 2 words requiring pre-teaching. He selects three words—"suddenly," "consequence," and "predict"—and carefully evaluates the word lists included with the language arts curriculum and the words students will encounter when reading their weekly language arts lessons and content-area texts. He notes words he wants to teach explicitly and plans which instructional strategy he will use to deliver that instruction. For this lesson, Mr. Miller elects to use Anita Archer's vocabulary protocol (Archer & Hughes, 2011). He prepares a short slideshow for the class and decides which words to teach each day. He begins with the word "suddenly." Showing the word on the slide, Mr. Miller says, "The word is suddenly. What word?" When Mr. Miller cups his hand behind his ear, the class replies in unison, "suddenly." Mr. Miller says, "That's right: suddenly. Suddenly means quickly when not expected. What does suddenly mean?" Again, he cups his hand to his ear, and the class repeats, "Quickly when not expected." Mr. Miller shows a few pictures of sudden actions and gives a few oral examples, such as "When a snake suddenly appeared on my desk, I jumped so high I hit my head on the ceiling," and "Suddenly, I felt sick even though I had barely eaten." Then Mr. Miller invites the students to share with their seat partners an example of something they would do suddenly. He walks around to listen and invites a few students to share particularly precise examples with the class. Then, Mr. Miller asks, "If I slowly stand up and stretch before going outside, would you say I suddenly stood up?" The students reply, "No!" He then asks if they would suddenly stop their bicycle if they came upon a friend lying hurt on the sidewalk. After the students reply that they would, he asks, "If your grandma is cooking soup, would it suddenly be finished?" After students respond, he repeats this process for the next word.

Understanding the words and phrases we read is critical for reading comprehension, so teachers should be strategic about teaching words and strategies and giving students plenty of time to read independently to increase their exposure to challenging vocabulary. Additionally, students must understand figures of speech, be aware of nuances of word meaning, and consider multiple meanings of a word when encountering words in context (Deacon et al., 2017). Vocabulary instruction, especially in the content areas, often overlaps with teaching concepts since words are best learned in connection with other words.

Beck and her colleagues (2002) think of words in three tiers. Tier 1 words are everyday words that most students already know. For Mr. Miller's students, the words "circle," "box," and "phone" are likely Tier 1 words. Teachers typically do not teach these words explicitly, though they should be conscious of individual students, such as multilingual learners, who may need them explained. Tier 2 words are those words that appear in multiple academic contexts and are worthy of explicit instruction. For example, Mr. Miller may teach the words "environment," "citizen," and "opinion" as explicit Tier 2 words because they are useful across content areas and contexts. Tier 3 words are specialized words within a content area. They can be explained when encountered to protect instructional time. Mr. Miller tells students what the words "carnivorous," "icebox," and "torpedoed" mean because students can understand the passages they are reading with a quick explanation of these words, as these words are less likely to be encountered in their grade-appropriate reading and conversations.

Tier 2 words can be taught in several ways. Students may benefit from word study to consider the meaning of roots and how prefixes change the meaning of words, while suffixes change the tense, number, or part of speech. Ideally, students should work with new words over several days in several different ways—the more multisensory and engaging, the better. For example, students can create Frayer models by drawing a grid of four boxes with the word in the center in an oval or smaller box. Teachers can assign or give options for filling the other boxes with a student-friendly definition, the word in a sentence, a drawing, a synonym, an antonym, or a clarification about the word. Students may arrange word cards along a continuum of meaning organized by intensity. Generally, students enjoy acting out words, especially for their classmates to guess, or using them in creative writing, which is an often-neglected activity.

As illustrated in the vignette above, Archer (Archer & Hughes, 2011) developed an explicit vocabulary instruction protocol that teachers can utilize for words they most want students to remember. Protocols such as this do not have to take much time, and they are particularly effective because every student is included in every step.

In addition to teaching students the meaning of words, it is equally important to teach them strategies for figuring out the meaning of words. The two most common approaches are using morphology (i.e., breaking down words to look for familiar parts) and finding context clues. Morphemes are the smallest individual meaningful parts of a word. These can include root words, prefixes, suffixes, possessive endings, and comparative endings. If students can identify various morphemes in a word, they can apply that knowledge to determine the meaning. For example, if a student comes across the word "export" and knows the prefix "ex" means out of or away and the root word "port" means to carry, they could determine that the word "export" means something like carry away. Context clues are tools in the text that support students' ability to determine the meaning of unknown words. These tools include images, examples, comparisons, contrasts, synonyms, and even definitions. Students need a lot of direct instruction to internalize these processes. Even in upper elementary, teachers should model these skills and provide guided practice opportunities rather than simply assigning practice activities or reminding students to use the strategies.

Comprehension

Mr. Miller provides some comprehension instruction to his class as a whole group. Today, he is reviewing story grammar, which refers to the parts of a story, just as grammar is about parts of speech. Mr. Miller begins by reminding his students of the story map they had completed the day before after reading a fairy tale together. While asking questions such as "What do we call the people the story is about?" and "How do we organize the events of the story on our story map?" He distributes a large story map to each pair of students. He finishes reviewing with terms such as "problem," "solution," and "conclusion." He also gives some students smaller pieces of paper with the story elements typed on them, so students can sort the elements and glue them in place. He tells the students, "Work with your partner to complete a story map for The Paper Crane *(Bang, 1987), which we read earlier today. You may also spend up to seven minutes drawing the setting. Be sure to include details from the story about the time and place." The students organize a list of characters and place events from the story on a graphic showing the problem building, the problem being solved, and the story's conclusion. While students are working, Mr. Miller walks around the room and checks in with the pairs of students. He reminds a few students of the details included on the story map from yesterday, which is still on display. He asks others to tell him what they know about the characters. He follows up their answers by asking them how they learn. As the pairs of students complete their story maps, Mr. Miller invites them to use the story map to tell the other pair of students at their table about the story. The listeners can then add details from their story maps. After that, Mr. Miller deepens the discussion of story grammar by asking students how the characters changed throughout the story and why they think the author put certain events in the order she chose.*

The purpose of reading is comprehension. Beginning readers encounter many decodable texts that build decoding skills and reading fluency, but these texts often provide little substance to develop comprehension and build background knowledge. They should also be reading and listening to a mixture of children's literature and grade-appropriate informational text to build background knowledge and vocabulary. While reading comprehension instruction should grow in sophistication as students progress in school, reading comprehension strategies can be introduced through read-alouds in the primary grades. Teachers can model strategies, such as text structure and questioning the author, during read-alouds using think-alouds (e.g., I wonder if the rabbit will get in trouble for getting into the farmer's vegetables?).

Teachers must teach students how authors structure texts for different genres to support comprehension. This instruction and practice develop general knowledge about texts (see discussion of the reading systems framework above), which supports reading comprehension. As illustrated in the vignette above, authors structure narratives using story grammar, which includes story elements (e.g., characters, problem, solution). Although basic story elements are consistent across narratives (e.g., characters, setting, plot, resolution), other elements can vary by genre. For example, fairy tales feature wondrous or magical elements that improve the characters' lives (e.g., fairy godmother). Folk tales include conflicts resolved through courage, kindness, and intelligence by heroic characters (e.g., Paul Bunyan). For expository texts, authors signify what students need to understand through text structures (e.g., description, sequence, compare/contrast, cause/effect). Text structures use specific language to point readers to those structures (e.g., alike or different signify the compare/contrast structure). In a book about dolphins, an author might first describe the characteristics of dolphins (e.g., mammals, live birth) and then compare and contrast dolphins with fish (e.g., different systems for breathing).

Teachers can teach reading comprehension through various other strategies, including self-questioning, identifying main ideas or themes, and monitoring comprehension. Self-questioning is having students read and pause frequently to ask comprehension questions (McKeown et al., 2009). This method encourages students to read metacognitively, frequently checking their own comprehension and considering key ideas and shifts in a text. Students may question new characters, connections the author notes, meanings of words or phrases, purposes for the author's choices, or text structure.

ScSR was addressed previously as a means for building fluency. It can also provide an opportunity for teachers to support students with comprehension. During mini-conferences, the teacher and student discuss the text, which is a good way for teachers to check for understanding and ensure that students read at the appropriate level for their skills. These mini-conferences are also a great time to check on comprehension strategy integration. The ScSR approach encourages students to read widely by selecting a range of books on varied topics and from different genres. Teachers might prompt students to use a genre wheel, coloring a section after reading a book from each genre during each quarter of school (Reutzel et al., 2008). This practice can expose students to multiple text structures to support comprehension.

Finding and Evaluating Evidence-based Literacy Materials

To support students in generalizing reading comprehension strategies, teachers may find it helpful to supplement the instruction provided by most language arts curricula with online reading passages with question sets provided by their district or available online. ReadWorks (n.d.) for students in kindergarten and above and CommonLit (2014–2023) for upper elementary and older students are examples of web resources with passages that will build background knowledge and can be used to supplement the minimal time most elementary teachers can devote to science and social studies.

Many schools and districts adopt reading programs for teachers to use during Tier 1 instruction. There are many literacy programs on the market. Schools purchase one or more of these programs for teachers to use with their students (e.g., a core reading program and a program to teach phonics). Teachers need to explore the extent and quality of the evidence of effectiveness for programs they are expected to use. The What Works Clearing House (WWC; n.d.) is one place teachers can examine the available evidence on programs. The WWC gathers evidence on the research design and effectiveness of programs and strategies for instruction and intervention, including many for literacy. Evidence on the strength of the research design suggests how strongly the research design supports researchers' findings about the program or intervention, while the effectiveness suggests how well the program or intervention improves targeted outcomes for students. Teachers should pay attention to both aspects. If studies are not well designed, the findings might not be trustworthy. On the other hand, if the studies are well designed and implemented, teachers can look at the effectiveness of programs or interventions. Just because there are well-designed studies does not always mean the program is effective (i.e., demonstrates significant progress in one or more components of reading). Evaluation reports contain helpful information, including what kinds of students were included in studies and which literacy components were assessed. The WWC also provides practice guides on a wide range of topics. It includes webinars and other helpful information for teachers to support their instructional decisions. Teachers are encouraged to explore the WWC often, as the site is constantly updated.

CONCLUSION

Having considered the legal, theoretical, and research foundations for how we teach reading, we see the importance of selecting evidence-based strategies and paying close attention to what research tells us about how students can learn most effectively. Teachers are fortunate to have access to research on best practices. Using assessment data to drive instruction is critical for helping students make the most growth possible in our limited time. This process requires data analysis and using the data to guide grouping and instructional decisions about what to teach, when, and to what depth. We know that high-quality core reading instruction in Tier 1 addresses general knowledge, including how authors structure texts, alongside oral language, phonological awareness, phonics, fluency, vocabulary, and comprehension. By differentiating instruction and using the principles of UDL, we can design instruction that will support the development of knowledge and skills for reading, including students who might still require additional support through Tier 2 or 3. The next chapter will explain how to intensify reading instruction through intervention for students who need additional support.

REFERENCES

Anthony, J. L., & Francis, D. J. (2005). Development of phonological awareness. *Current Directions in Psychological Science, 14*(5), 255–259. https://doi.org/10.1111/j.0963-7214.2005.00376.x

Archer, A. L., & Hughes, C. A. (2011). *Explicit instruction: Effective and efficient teaching.* Guilford Press.

Ardoin, S. P., Binder, K. S., Foster, T. E., & Zawoyski, A. M. (2016). Repeated versus wide reading: A randomized control design study examining the impact of fluency interventions on underlying reading behavior. *Journal of School Psychology, 59,* 13–38. https://doi.org/10.1016/j.jsp.2016.09.002

Bang, M. (1987). *The paper crane.* Reading Rainbow.

Beauchat, K. A., Blamey, K. L., & Walpole, S. (2011). Building preschool children's language and literacy one storybook at a time. *The Reading Teacher, 63*(1), 26–39. https://doi.org/10.1598/RT.63.1.3

Beck, I. L., Kucan, L., & McKeown, M. G. (2002). *Bringing words to life: Robust vocabulary instruction.* Guilford Press.

Birsh, J. R., & Carreker, S. (2018). *Multisensory teaching of basic language skills*, Vol. 4. Brookes Publishing.

Bouck, E. C., & Cosby, M. D. (2019). Response to intervention in high school mathematics: One school's implementation. *Preventing School Failure, 63*(1), 32–42. https://doi.org/10.1080/1045988X.2018.1469463

Carta, J. J., & Young, R. M. (2019). *Multi-tiered systems of support for young children: Driving change in early education.* Brookes Publishing.

Center for Applied Special Technology (CAST). (2018). Universal Design for Learning Guidelines version 2.2. http://udlguidelines.cast.org

CommonLit. (2014–2023). https://www.commonlit.org/en

Connor, C. M., Dombek, J., Crowe, E. C., Spencer, M., Tighe, E. L., Coffinger, S., Zargar, E., Wood, T., & Petscher, Y. (2017). Acquiring science and social studies knowledge in kindergarten through fourth grade: Conceptualization, design, implementation, and efficacy testing of content-area literacy instruction (CALI). *Journal of Educational Psychology, 109*(3), 301–320. https://doi.org/10.1037/edu0000128

Dahl, R. (1967). *James and the giant peach.* Alfred A. Knopf.

Deacon, S. H., Tong, X., & Francis, K. (2017). The relationship of morphological analysis and morphological decoding to reading comprehension. *Journal of Research in Reading, 40*(1), 1–16. https://doi.org/10.1111/1467-9817.12056

Didion, L., & Toste, J. R. (2022). Data mountain: Self-monitoring, goal setting, and positive attributions to enhance the oral reading fluency of elementary students with or at risk for reading disabilities. *Journal of Learning Disabilities, 55*(5), 375–392. https://doi.org/10.1177/00222194211043482

Dunn, K. E., Airola, D. T., Lo, & W.-J., Garrison M. (2013). Becoming data-driven: The influence of teachers' sense of efficacy on concerns related to data-driven decision making. *The Journal of Experimental Education, 81*(2), 222–241. https://doi.org/10.1080/00220973.2012.699899

EdGate. (2023). United States Standards. https://edgate.com/standards/us-state-map

Ehri, L. C., Nunes, S. R., Willows, D. M., Schuster, B. V., Yaghoub-Zadeh, Z., & Shanahan, T. (2001). Phonemic awareness instruction helps children learn to read: Evidence from the national reading panel's meta-analysis. *Reading Research Quarterly, 36*(3), 250–287. https://doi.org/10.1598/RRQ.36.3.2

Eide, D. (2012). *Uncovering the logic of English: A common-sense approach to reading, spelling, and literacy*. Logic of English.

Elementary and Secondary Education Act of 1965, Pub. L. No. 89–10, 79 Stat. (1965). https://www.govinfo.gov/content/pkg/STATUTE-79/pdf/STATUTE-79-Pg27.pdf

Esteves, K. J., & Whitten, E. (2011). Assisted reading with digital audiobooks for students with reading disabilities. *Reading Horizons, 51*(1), 21.

Every Student Succeeds Act, 20 U.S.C. § 6301 (2015). https://www.congress.gov/bill/114th-congress/senate-bill/1177

Foorman, B., Beyler, N., Borradaile, K., Coyne, M., Denton, C. A., Dimino, J., Furgeson, J., Hayes, L.,Henke, J., Justice, L., Keating, B., Lewis, W., Sattar, S., Streke, A., Wagner, R., & Wissel, S. (2016). Foundational skills to support reading for understanding in kindergarten through 3rd grade (NCEE 2016-4008). Washington, DC: National Center for Education Evaluation and Regional Assistance (NCEE), Institute of Education Sciences, US Department of Education. Retrieved from the NCEE https://ies.ed.gov/ncee/WWC/Docs/PracticeGuide/wwc_foundationalreading_040717.pdf

Fuchs, L. S., & Fuchs, D. (2007). A model for implementing responsiveness to intervention. *Teaching Exceptional Children, 39*(5), 14–20. https://doi.org/10.1177/004005990703900503

Gauch, P. L. (1971). *Christina Katerina and the box*. Coward, McCann, & Geoghegan, Inc.

Gentry, R., & Ouellette, G. (2019). *How the science of reading informs teaching*. Stenhouse.

Goldberg, M., & Goldenberg, C. (2022). Lessons learned? Reading wars, Reading First, and a way forward. *The Reading Teacher, 75*(5), 621–630. https://doi.org/10.1002/trtr.2079

Gough, P. B., & Tunmer, W. E. (1986). Decoding, reading, and reading disability. PRO-ED. https://doi.org/10.1177/074193258600700104

Gullain, C. (2017). *The street beneath my feet (look closer)*. words & pictures.

Guthrie, J. T., Wigfield, A., Barbosa, P., Perencevich, K. C., Taboada, A., Davis, M. H., Scafiddi, N. T., & Tonks, S. (2004). Increasing reading comprehension and engagement through concept-oriented reading instruction. *Journal of Educational Psychology, 96*(3), 403–423. https://doi.org/10.1037/0022-0663.96.3.403

Hernandez, D. J. (2011). *Double jeopardy: How third-grade reading skills and poverty influence high school graduation*. (Report). Annie E. Casey Foundation. https://www.aecf.org/resources/double-jeopardy

Hirsch, E. D. (2003). Reading comprehension requires knowledge—of words and the world: Scientific insights into the fourth-grade slump and the nation's stagnant comprehension scores. *American Educator, 27*(1), 10–31.

Hirsch, E. D. (2019). *Why knowledge matters: Rescuing our children from failed educational theories*. Harvard Education Press.

Hughes, C. A., Morris, J. A., Therrien, W. J., & Benson, S. K. (2017). Explicit instruction: Historical and contemporary contexts. *Learning Disabilities Research & Practice, 32*, 140–148. https://doi.org/10.1111/ldrp.12142

Keats, E. J. (1996) *The snowy day*. Picture Puffin Books.

Kim, J. S., Burkhauser, M. A., Mesite, L. M., Asher, C. A., Relyea, J. E., Fitzgerald, J., & Elmore, J. (2021). Improving reading comprehension, science domain knowledge, and reading engagement through a first-grade content literacy intervention. *Journal of Educational Psychology, 113*(1), 3–26. https://doi.org/10.1037/edu0000465

Leslie, L., & Caldwell, J. S. (2021). *Qualitative Reading Inventory* (7th ed.). Pearson.

McKeown, M. G., Beck, I. L., & Blake, R. G. K. (2009). Rethinking reading comprehension instruction: A comparison of instruction for strategies and content approaches. *Reading Research Quarterly, 44*(3), 218–253. https://doi.org/10.1598/RRQ.44.3.1

Moats, L. (2009). Knowledge foundations for teaching reading and spelling. *Reading & Writing, 22*(4), 379–399. https://doi.org/10.1007/s11145-009-9162-1

Moats, L. C. (2020). *Speech to print: Language essentials for teachers* (3rd ed.). Brookes Publishing.

National Early Literacy Panel. (2008). *Developing early literacy: Report of the National Early Literacy Panel*. Washington, DC: National Institute for Literacy. https://lincs.ed.gov/publications/pdf/NELPReport09.pdf

National Reading Panel. (2000). *Report of the National Reading Panel: Teaching children to read*. National Reading Panel. https://www.nichd.nih.gov/publications/pubs/nrp/report

No Child Left Behind (NCLB) Act of 2001, Pub. L. No. 107–110, § 101, Stat. 1425 (2002). https://www.congress.gov/bill/107th-congress/house-bill/1

Perfetti, C., & Stafura, J. (2014). Word knowledge in a theory of reading comprehension. *Scientific Studies of Reading, 18*(1), 22–37. https://doi.org/10.1080/10888438.2013.827687

Prelutsky, J. (2012). *I've lost my hippopotamus*. Greenwillow Books.

Preston, T. (2022). A look back: A chronicle of Kappan's coverage of the reading wars. *Phi Delta Kappan, 103*(8), 5–7. https://doi.org/10.1177/00317217221100000

Rasinski, T. V. (2017). Readers who struggle: Why many struggle and a modest proposal for improving their reading. *The Reading Teacher, 70*(5), 519–524. https://doi.org/10.1002/trtr.1533

ReadWorks. (n.d.). https://www.readworks.org/

Reutzel, D. R., Fawson, P. C., & Smith, J. A. (2008). Reconsidering silent sustained reading: An exploratory study of scaffolded silent reading. *The Journal of Educational Research, 102*(1), 37–50. https://doi.org/10.3200/JOER.102.1.37-50

Scarborough, H. (2001). Connecting early language and literacy to later reading (dis)abilities: Evidence, theory and practice. In S. Newman & D. Dickinson (Eds.), *Handbook of early literacyrResearch* (pp. 97–110). Guilford Press.

Shanahan, T. (2020, March 7). Why following the simple view may not be such a good idea. *Shanahan on literacy*. https://www.shanahanonliteracy.com/blog/why-following-the-simple-view-may-not-be-such-a-good-idea

Smith, R., Snow, P., Serry, T., & Hammond, L. (2021). The role of background knowledge in reading comprehension: A critical review. *Reading Psychology*, *42*(3), 214–240. https://doi.org/10.1080/02702711.2021.1888348

Stevens, E. A., Walker, M. A., & Vaughn, S. (2017). The effects of reading fluency interventions on the reading fluency and reading comprehension performance of elementary students with learning disabilities: A synthesis of the research from 2001 to 2014. *Journal of Learning Disabilities*, *50*(5), 576–590. https://doi.org/10.1177/0022219416638028

Therrien, W. J. (2004). Fluency and comprehension gains as a result of repeated reading: A meta-analysis. *Remedial and Special Education*, *25*(4), 252–261. https://doi.org/10.1177/07419325040250040801

Tomlinson, C. A., & Imbeau, M. B. (2013). *Leading and managing a differentiated classroom* (2nd ed.). ASCD.

Torgerson, C., Brooks, G., Gascoine, L., & Higgins, S. (2019). Phonics: Reading policy and the evidence of effectiveness from a systematic 'tertiary' review. *Research Papers in Education*, *34*(2), 208–238. https://doi.org/10.1080/02671522.2017.1420816

Uccelli, P., Galloway, E. P., Barr, C. D., Meneses, A., & Dobbs, C. L. (2015). Beyond vocabulary: Exploring cross-disciplinary academic-language proficiency and its association with reading comprehension. *Reading Research Quarterly*, *50*(3), 337–356. https://doi.org/10.1002/rrq.104

What Works Clearinghouse. (n.d.). https://ies.ed.gov/ncee/wwc/

3

Reading Intervention for Elementary Students

Pamela Williamson, Andrea K. W. Smith, Jodi Arroyo Nagel, and Hanna Moore

LEARNING HOW TO READ independently is perhaps the most important work of elementary students. A variety of factors can influence students' reading trajectories, such as oral language development, exposure to early literacy events, and overall health and well-being. The purpose of this chapter is to describe reading intervention for students who need more support than excellent Tier 1 reading instruction to learn how to read. Early intervention in reading is critical, as children who do not learn to read are at increased risk for a wide range of poor life outcomes (e.g., college and career readiness, health) (e.g., Dogan et al., 2015; Nachshon & Horowitz-Kraus, 2019).

In this chapter, we will begin by examining the theoretical foundations of reading intervention and the research that guides this work, followed by intervention research. We will then examine how assessment guides interventions using a multi-tiered system of supports (MTSS) model. We will also discuss high-leverage practices (HLPs), intervention dimensions, and reliable sources of information about evidence-based practices to support reading. We will explore the areas in which students may benefit from intervention, including oral language, phonological awareness, phonics, fluency, vocabulary, and comprehension. This chapter will help you consider answers to the following guiding questions:

1. What are the theories that inform reading intervention delivery for elementary students?
2. What should guide instructional decision-making for elementary students receiving reading intervention?
3. What are some effective, evidence-based, reading intervention methods?
4. How can student data be used to intensify and individualize reading intervention?

BRIDGING FROM ELEMENTARY READING INSTRUCTION TO ELEMENTARY READING INTERVENTION

When students in elementary classrooms receive effective, evidence-based instruction in reading, we would expect about 80% of them to succeed in meeting expectations. When that percentage is smaller for a given school, grade level, or class, we should re-evaluate the instruction, curriculum, and environment to see if changes can be made to support more students in reaching expectations (Wright, 2010). As we implement those changes and continuously seek to improve, we may notice a few students who continue to struggle despite consistently receiving high-quality, evidence-based instruction at Tier 1 with appropriate differentiation. For these students, we want to provide additional interventions. These interventions typically take the form of extra instruction, whether provided by the classroom teacher or an interventionist who works across classrooms and grade levels. The interventions should be evidence-based, carefully monitored, and delivered with fidelity.

These interventions are typically considered Tier 2 when provided to a small group a few times a week or Tier 3 when provided individually several times a week, though there are certainly variations on this pattern (Pullen & Kennedy, 2018). Students who receive intervention at Tier 2 should still take part in Tier 1, whole-class instruction. Students who receive Tier 3 may benefit from additional Tier 2 intervention and should also participate in Tier 1 instruction. Interventions are intended to support students in Tier 1 success, fill in academic gaps, and build independence through strategy instruction. Remembering that interventions provide instruction in learning strategies rather than just accommodations is critical. For example, moving a student to a different seat or allowing him to listen to a recording of his science textbook may be helpful but is not considered an intervention for building skills or considering whether the student may have a learning disability. Interventionists and teachers will want to consider the Tier 2 and possibly Tier 3 interventions that will most directly impact student achievement. These may fall anywhere in the literacy model and often take the form of extra instruction in phonics, phonemic awareness, fluency, vocabulary, or comprehension. In the next chapter, we will more deeply examine how teachers can support students who need additional interventions to become successful readers.

THEORIES AND FOUNDATIONAL RESEARCH

Theoretical models that describe what is important when learning to read, including how reading processes (e.g., decoding, meaning retrieval) interact to result in skilled reading and comprehension, are helpful to teachers. They support teachers' instructional decisions regarding which evidence-based interventions might address students' reading challenges. Building upon earlier theoretical models of reading (e.g., simple view of reading [SVR]), Perfetti and Stafura (2017) proposed the reading systems framework (RSF). RSF incorporates top-down and bottom-up processes within three domains of knowledge, including linguistic, orthographic, and general knowledge of the world and text forms (e.g., genre, story grammar, text structure). Reading processes (i.e., decoding, word identification, meaning retrieval, sentence parsing, inferencing, and comprehension monitoring) use one or more of these domains of knowledge. For example, most young children know that an /s/ or /z/

on the end of a word means more than one and know that receiving cookies might be more exciting than getting a cookie. This represents their linguistic knowledge of the sound (phonology) and meaning (morphology). On the other hand, they are unlikely to know how to spell either word conventionally (orthography).

When it comes to comprehension, the RSF draws upon research in reading comprehension (Perfetti & Stafura, 2017). It signals to teachers that skilled reading requires children to make a wide range of inferences during reading, including text-based inferences, such as who or what a pronoun refers to (e.g., she and Lucy are the same person). Other inferences require children to draw upon their background knowledge to make sense of a text (e.g., chocolate is a kind of candy). The RSF also highlights the importance of developing children's knowledge of genres, story grammar, and text structures (e.g., "Once upon a time" signals the beginning of a fairy tale, which is a kind of narrative story; "because" in an expository text, signals a cause-and-effect text structure). Thus, the RSF helps teachers think deeply about why some students are challenged by aspects of reading. It explains the relationships between language, print, and background knowledge. It distinctly emphasizes the importance of teaching content and reading forms (e.g., genre, text structure) to build students' background knowledge.

Intervention Research

Connor and her colleagues (2014) synthesized the contributions of research conducted on behalf of the Institute of Education Sciences Research Centers, an important producer of evidence-based information. They found that providing extensive opportunities for preschool children to hear complex oral language reduces the risk for language disabilities, and fluency interventions that include repeated reading, wide reading, and lots of opportunities to practice improve both fluency and comprehension. They also concluded that basic cognitive (e.g., working memory, inferential reasoning) and linguistic processes (e.g., oral language skills, vocabulary) can be improved through intervention before reading challenges become entrenched reading problems.

For students who do not develop reading skills as expected, additional intervention is needed. Connor and colleagues (2014) concluded that when interventions are differentiated at the component-skills level based upon students' needs (e.g., phonemic awareness, comprehension), interventions are effective at improving students' reading development. For example, increasing the intensity of intervention in phonemic awareness and phonics rather than a global reading intervention in kindergarten and first grade can prevent reading difficulties for many students.

For upper-level elementary students, multicomponent reading interventions are more effective than those that address only one skill (e.g., word reading or comprehension, but not both) (e.g., Ahmed, et al., 2022; Donegan & Wanzek, 2021). There is also emerging evidence that providing instruction in very small groups may be warranted for students who need comprehension support (Ahmed et al., 2022). Finally, Berkeley and Larsen (2018) reviewed reading comprehension intervention research that embedded aspects of self-regulation as part of the intervention. They concluded that there were large effects immediately after instruction and that strategies that included self-regulation may have long lasting impacts on students' performance. They recommend that teachers include self-regulation as part of comprehension instruction (e.g., think aloud to illustrate the cognitive moves necessary to make sense of the text), explicitly teaching the steps of the strategy, explain why strategies are helpful, and when students should deploy them.

Multi-Tiered System of Supports

Student needs vary and interventions are planned in response to individual needs; however, this does not mean that all struggling learners need individual instruction. Instead, educators can meet student needs through a tiered approach to instruction and intervention, which is often referred to as multi-tiered system of supports (MTSS) (Pullen & Kennedy, 2018). It is important to note that all students should receive excellent Tier 1 core reading instruction, as the other tiers should supplement, not supplant, Tier 1 reading instruction. Tier 1 instruction is typically comprehensive literacy instruction delivered in a general education classroom. Tier 1 instruction addresses reading standards (e.g., national, state), and it might also include small group or individual instruction identified through assessment.

Typically, students who need consistent additional support to achieve grade-level success receive Tier 2 intervention. Unlike the breadth of Tier 1 instruction, Tier 2 instruction is typically focused on target skills. Tier 2 interventions might be provided by general or special education teachers. In co-taught settings, special education teachers might deliver Tier 2 instruction, whereas in classrooms that are not co-taught, general education teachers might deliver Tier 2 instruction. For Tier 2, students are typically organized in small groups based upon the similarity of their needs. The focus is to create independence with targeted skills. Targets are often developed from benchmark data and formative classroom data (e.g., phonics performance below benchmark). At Tier 2, progress monitoring might include dynamic assessment where the skill is assessed, instruction occurs, and the student is retested. Teachers need to understand if the intervention is improving the skill or skills, so adjustments can be made to support students' learning. For example, a phonics assessment might be used pre- and post-instruction and compared to norms to see if the student mastered the content taught. If the supplemental instruction catches the student up to their classmates, the student no longer receives Tier 2 support. If the support does not seem to be helping the student close learning gaps, a determination about how to change the intervention should be made. For example, teachers can increase the intensity of the intervention by reducing the number of students in the group or increasing the number of sessions per week. Either option increases the amount of time the student has intervention. Alternatively, the intervention might be changed altogether to a different evidence-based method.

Tier 3 involves individualized support and is provided to students who do not respond adequately to Tier 2 intervention. Some schools, districts, or states include special education in Tier 3, while others may consider it Tier 4, or an additional service, to supplement tiered instruction (Fuchs et al., 2017). More akin to Tier 1 instruction, Tier 3 instruction is more comprehensive and addresses literacy development more broadly. This supports connections among the components of literacy (e.g., make explicit connections between aural/oral language, reading, and writing). Tier 3 instruction might include specialized reading programs designed for intensive intervention.

To individualize instruction, formal (e.g., standardized assessment of phonics knowledge) and informal diagnostic assessments (e.g., informal reading inventories) are used to identify instructional targets (e.g., knowledge of text forms, fluency). Once again, progress monitoring is critical to determine if the intervention is effective at improving skills and improving students' independent reading abilities (i.e., improves comprehension). At Tier 3, progress monitoring occurs at the students' performance level or one level above. For example, if a fourth-grade student was reading at a second-grade level, progress monitoring assessments should be conducted at either the second- or third-grade level to determine if the student is making progress. Progress monitoring goals are individually developed for each student (e.g., partitioned to get to grade level). The idea is that interventions should accelerate the student toward on-grade-level performance over a reasonable period of time.

Further, progress monitoring plans might assess multiple components depending upon the student's needs and grade level. When possible, embedded measures that are included in instruction are preferred, as there is no loss of instructional time to monitor progress. For example, teachers collect students' performance on phonics knowledge (e.g., number of correct sounds identified out of ten) during instruction. There are circumstances when using other measures is also a sound decision (e.g., retest with screener or benchmark). In summary, MTSS supports delivery of reading instruction based upon standards and students' needs.

High-Leverage Practices

Most students with disabilities are taught in the general education classroom for much or all of the day (Williamson et al., 2020). As such, general and special educators must collaborate and use HLPs to help students with disabilities and their classmates learn (McLeskey et al., 2019). HLPs were developed to capture the essential knowledge of special education. Some HLPs summarize evidence-based practices (e.g., assessment, social/emotional/behavioral, and instructional), while others emphasize the importance of collaboration with other professionals and families to ensure sound instructional practices (e.g., learning goals, scaffolding, explicit instruction, flexible grouping, and generalization of strategies) are developed inclusively with all constituencies. Collaboration is essential to intervention, as alignment and transfer, or generalization, are critical features of any intervention. This emphasizes the importance of professionals and families working together to support students' learning that encourages congruence and mitigates fragmentation.

Intervention Dimensions

In addition to evidence-based instructional principles (e.g., explicit instruction), Fuchs and his colleagues (Fuchs et al., 2017) propose seven intervention dimensions that are critical for intervention planning. The first dimension, *strength*, refers to the measured effect size of the intervention when used with other struggling learners. The effect size guides the teacher about the amount of improvement she might expect when students participate in an intervention or program. *Dosage* is the number of opportunities for each student to respond and receive corrective feedback. Educators can ensure that each student engages in multiple learning opportunities during each session by providing interventions in small groups or one-on-one and maintaining a brisk pace. *Alignment* describes the match between the intervention and student needs, as evidenced by focusing on skills aligned to grade-level standards and not wasting time on previously mastered skills (e.g., alignment with Tier 1 instruction). *Attention to transfer* helps students generalize learning by teaching them to independently use the skills in other situations and recognize how skills connect. *Comprehensiveness* measures the number of principles of explicit instruction addressed in the intervention. Explicit instruction requires teachers to use straightforward language, model thinking rather than asking students to guess, check and build background knowledge, gradually remove support, provide practice opportunities, and include strategically planned review activities. Academic interventions are more successful when teachers provide *behavioral support* to minimize disruption and equip students to regulate their learning and organize their thinking. *Individualization* can be ensured by monitoring progress to adjust the intervention, so it works well for each student.

Evidence-Based Intervention and Assessment

Mr. Miller, a first-grade teacher, works closely with Ms. Johnson, a special education teacher. Together, they analyze summative assessments from the previous year to organize their students into learning groups at the beginning of the year. Rather than looking at the summary score, they focus on looking at details of students' performances using the component scores provided for their state's standardized, year-end reading assessment (i.e., scores for each area assessed instead of just the overall score). They plan to meet regularly to analyze progress monitoring data from school-wide and classroom assessments and supplement this information with data from computer-assisted instruction. This data-mining process helps them select students who need reteaching on a specific skill and those who need small-group or individual intervention several times a week. Their plan includes flexible grouping or assigning children to groups for a variety of instructional purposes based upon a variety of student factors, including evidence of reading performance.

As illustrated in the above vignette, assessment and instruction are part of a comprehensive approach to\ literacy intervention. As many as 40% of children enter kindergarten more than one year behind their peers in foundational language skills critical to early reading success (Wilkowski & Freeley, 2012). Without intervention, gaps widen. Therefore, it is imperative to "provide targeted instruction of essential emergent reading skills as soon as possible to those children who are likely to experience difficulty learning to read" (Wilkowski & Freeley, 2012, p. 1). Interventions should be *explicit* (clear, direct, and with frequent checks for understanding) and *systematic* (logically sequenced, building upon prior knowledge, proceeding in manageable steps, and scaffolded) and should include corrective feedback and behavior-specific praise (e.g., Archer & Hughes, 2011). Effective interventions are data-driven and individualized to student needs and are delivered with increasing frequency until data shows consistent progress.

Tiers 2 and 3 reading interventions may be delivered in small groups or individually. They should be designed to facilitate students' success in Tier 1 instruction (e.g., aligned, generalized to general education curriculum). As with all reading instruction, interventions should be evidence-based. Although evidence- and research-based practice and practices have long been emphasized in education, the term *the science of reading* has captured a lot of attention. Simply stated, the science of reading is the accumulation of information about what works to teach reading from well-designed research studies. In table 3.1, we provide a list of reputable websites that are tightly connected to the science of reading. Teachers and interventionists are encouraged to explore information listed on these websites regularly to consider how well they might work for students in their setting.

It is critical for teachers and interventionists to remain abreast of additions and changes to evidence- and research-based practices for reading instruction, as what is known continues to evolve as new research is conducted and older research is synthesized across studies, which can sometimes impact earlier research conclusions. Three of the websites listed (i.e., ESSA, National Center on Intensive Intervention [NCII], What Works Clearinghouse [WWC]) offer teachers information about the quality of the research that was conducted and information about effect size, or the how much improvement in outcomes teachers might expect from the intervention or reading program (i.e., strength). In addition, the NCII offers assessment evaluation. Reliability and validity information is on the website and, in some cases, how well

Table 3.1. Sources to Find Evidence-Based Reading Interventions

Source	Description
Evidence for ESSA, Johns Hopkins University https://www.evidenceforessa.org/programs/reading/	Identifies key program features (e.g., effectiveness, groups studied, communities studied). It also identifies programs cost (e.g., professional development, technology needed). Program ratings are easy to identify.
High-Leverage Practices for Students with Disabilities https://highleveragepractices.org/welcome-our-new-series-high-leverage-practices	This is a repository of videos provides examples of high-leverage practices implemented in classrooms. They demonstrate changes in intensity of intervention.
What Works Clearinghouse, Institutes of Educational Science https://ies.ed.gov/ncee/wwc/FWW	Contains program evaluations that summarize what is known about programs and interventions. Information includes effect sizes, groups studied, and communities studied. Published practice guides developed by well-established researchers who summarize research for areas of interest (e.g., foundational skills to support reading for understanding in kindergarten through third grade). Video models of practice are included on this site for a variety of evidence-based practices.
University of Florida Literacy Institute (UFLI) https://ufli.education.ufl.edu/foundations/	Evidence-based foundations of reading materials, including an evidence-based scope and sequence, instructional materials (e.g., slide deck for instructional routines), video models of implementation.

assessments predict later reading performance and whether assessments were examined for bias. The WWC provides practice guides on a variety of topics alongside useful videos to illustrate how to implement a variety of interventions. The HLP website includes videos to support the implementation of HLPs, including assessment and instruction practices.

The University of Florida Literacy Institute (UFLI) has developed a website for their UFLI Foundations program. It is an excellent source of evidence-based materials for teachers to support the foundations of reading. Foundations of reading are mostly code focused (Lane & Contesse, 2022). UFLI suggests the following eight-step instructional routine: (a) phonemic awareness, (b) visual drill, (c) auditory drill, (d) blending drill, (e) new concept, (f) word work, (g) irregular words, and (h) connected text. This routine includes a warm-up of previously taught concepts, explicit instruction of new content, and opportunities to apply what was learned through reading decodable connected texts and writing sentences. The UFLI website includes useful instructional materials, such as slide decks to support phonics instruction, decodable texts aligned with their recommended scope and sequence, as well as video models of teachers teaching foundational skills to children.

Oral Language

According to the American Speech-Language-Hearing Association (n.d.), by the age of five, children should be able to follow basic directions, speak in grammatically correct sentences, tell short stories, understand and use location (e.g., behind) and time (e.g., tomorrow) words, and use at least one irregular plural word (e.g., feet). However, approximately 3% of children ages three to 17 have a language disorder (Black et al., 2015). Thus, language interventions are often necessary, especially at young ages.

Dialogic reading is an effective interactive shared reading practice that supports young children's language skills (National Center for Education Evaluation and Regional Assistance, 2007; National Early Literacy Panel, 2008). It can be used for both Tier 2 and Tier 3 instruction. To implement dialogic reading, a teacher selects a book to read aloud and plans where to stop and ask questions to prompt a dialogue about the book. There are five question prompts that increase in order of higher-level thinking, illustrated by the acronym CROWD (completion, recall, open-ended, wh-, distancing). Distancing questions are decontextualized and are critical to language development (e.g., "Tell me about a time when you visited a park like Pete"). The teacher leads student thinking and discussion through an instructional routine represented by PEER (prompt, evaluate, expand, and repeat) to engage the student in a discussion. With PEER, the teacher prompts the student to say something about the book, evaluates the response, expands on the response, and repeats the prompt (National Center for Education Evaluation and Regional Assistance, 2007).

Dialogic reading can be used during small group instruction, with differentiated prompts based upon students' needs. For example, teachers can plan questions for each student based upon their language needs (e.g., prompt for color name for students earlier in their language development, expansion questions for students whose utterances are brief). If a teacher were reading, *Where the Wild Things Are* by Maurice Sendak (1963), the teacher might ask Edwin, an early language learner,

"What color is Max's shirt?" Next, the teacher provides feedback and elaboration saying, "Yes, that's right" (feedback). "Max is wearing a yellow, *striped* shirt" (elaboration). To Yara, the teacher might ask a distancing question, "Tell me about a time when you felt brave like Max." To intensify the instruction, the group size can be reduced, which provides more opportunities for each student to respond.

Language assessments can be formal or informal. They can include observation, language sampling, curriculum-based measures, and oral reading comprehension. Observations might include noticing the vocabulary children use in particular settings (e.g., knowledge of color words used during academic instruction; color words used with peers at centers). Additional assessments could include listening comprehension measures. All of these assessments are aimed at determining if early language development is on track.

Phonemic Awareness

After reviewing the universal screener diagnostic scores of the students on her caseload, Ms. Johnson finds that Nate, a first-grade student, scored especially low on his phonemic awareness skills. Nate has difficulty correctly blending and segmenting phonemes in consonant-vowel-consonant (CVC) words and cannot yet perform phoneme addition, deletion, or substitution. With systematic instruction in mind, Ms. Johnson designs a targeted intervention to address Nate's low scores in phoneme blending and segmentation first. She places him in an intervention group with two peers who also struggle with phoneme blending and segmenting. She plans to work with this small group for 20 minutes daily during the literacy intervention block.

To practice segmenting phonemes, Ms. Johnson gives the students in her small group letter cards. She passes each student a card with five empty squares and an arrow running left to right underneath. Then, she holds up a picture card of a ham with the word printed under the picture. "What is this picture?" she asks, to replies of "ham." Once she is sure every student comprehends the target word, "ham," she asks the students to say each sound in ham and slide one letter card into an empty box for each sound. The students and Ms. Johnson chorally break down "ham" into /h/ /a/ /m/, sliding their letter cards into boxes as they voice each phoneme. After everyone has moved the cards, she asks, "How many sounds are in the word 'ham'?" The students reply, "Three!" in unison.

To practice blending the phonemes, Ms. Johnson asks students to say each sound individually, then slide their fingers along the arrow to blend the sounds together into the word ham. Using their cards, the students say, "/h/ /a/ /m/, ham." Ms. Johnson repeats the segmenting and blending exercise with the words "cat," "hop," and "mat." After practicing as a group, she asks the students to segment and blend the target word without her. Then, she assesses each student as they perform the task individually, providing corrective feedback whenever necessary.

Multisensory approaches support Tier 2 and Tier 3 phonemic awareness practice. Multisensory approaches include one or more listening, speaking, reading, and tactile interactions with reading materials. Elkonin boxes, as demonstrated in the vignette above, is one practice where students use small manipulatives, such as

Table 3.2. Instructional Routine for Phonemic Awareness, Blending and Segmenting

Step	Teacher Says	Students Say	Assessment
1. Explain the task.	*We are going to segment a word into its sounds. This will help us learn to read.*		Look for attention.
2. Model the task.	*Listen. The word is* fish. *I'm going to stretch the word and count the sounds. / ffff / iiii / shshsh /* (Hold up one finger after each sound.) *The word* fish *has three sounds.* (Hold up one finger after each sound.) */ ffff / iiii / shshsh /*		Look for attention.
3. We do the task together.	*Say fish with me.* Fish. *Stretch the word with me and count the sounds. / ffff / iiii / shshsh /* (Hold up one finger after each sound).	Fish. (Hold up one finger after each sound). / ffff / iiii / shshsh /	Look to see if students are stretching the word and counting the sounds.
4. Individual practice.	*Working with your partner, say and stretch* fish.		Circulate and praise of model correction.

Source: Created based on the work of Archer and Hughes (2011).

counting discs, pom poms, metal washers, or connecting blocks, and move one manipulative for each phoneme they hear in a word. When practical and feasible, it is better to use letters to practice phonemic awareness activities (e.g., include picture cards with printed words and correct letter cards to spell words) (Hohn & Ehri, 1983; National Reading Panel [NRP], 2000). There are 26 letters than make 44 sounds in English. Graphemes represent the sound, which means some graphemes have more than one letter (e.g., ch-, -igh). At Tier 2, activities are aligned to Tier 1 instruction, and might include reteaching and practice. At Tier 3, these activities should increase in intensity and be part of more comprehensive lessons (i.e., include other reading components). In table 3.2, we present an instructional routine that includes what the teacher will do, what the student will do, and an assessment of how it's going. Notice that the routine includes components of explicit instruction (e.g., teacher modeling) (Archer & Hughes, 2011).

Phonics

Mr. Miller administers weekly progress monitoring for phonics using curriculum-based assessments that came with his classroom phonics program. When more than 20% of his class struggles with a skill, he reteaches the skill and provides additional multisensory practice. However, when only a few students struggle with a skill, he reteaches and provides additional practice in a small group. He carefully monitors progress to check for growth among the participating students. Because the interventions Mr. Miller offers are evidence-based, he can expect most of these students to catch up with their classmates with just a little extra push a few minutes a day.

Since the rest of the class has grasped decoding and blending, Ms. Johnson provides extra practice for a small group of students using Elkonin boxes to help students sound out individual letters and blend them to make words. The teachers integrate spelling into every phonics lesson, which supports reading and helps the students better understand the role of the letters in guiding sound production. They lead the activities in a fun, game-like fashion, with students engaging with letter cards, magnetic letters, and small whiteboards.

As Mr. Miller continues to monitor progress for the small group and the whole class, he notices that one student consistently struggles with most of the skills and does not seem to master them with the additional small group instruction. Mr. Miller consults with Ms. Johnson, the special education teacher, about this student. They work with the school MTSS team to identify different phonics interventions that can be delivered individually to this student.

Phonics instruction is typically guided by a scope and sequence that includes guidance on which skills and sounds should be introduced to students and in what order (e.g., UFLI scope and sequence; Lane & Contesse, 2022). The scope and sequence will show the order in which to introduce letter sounds, vowel rules or expectations, and more complicated concepts, such as letter patterns and silent letters. Phonics instruction should be explicit and multisensory. It may include using letter blocks or cards, word family booklets, and similar manipulatives that feature letters. Phonics intervention should include decoding (sounding out) and encoding (spelling) practice to solidify skills and promote generalization. Phonics intervention should focus on the specific skills students have not mastered and be based on an evidence-based scope and sequence. For Tier 2, progress monitoring would likely include pre- and post-assessments of an informal phonics assessment.

Below, we share an example of what small-group, Tier 2 intervention might look like. Providing feedback is an essential feature of phonics instruction.

Ms. Miller is working with Ms. Jackson, who teaches third grade. Ms. Jackson teaches word parts and spelling rules to her students, but they spend more time on vocabulary and comprehension because most of her students can decode. However, Jonathan, Robert, Javier, and Shaneese still struggle with determining the sounds that letters represent. Ms. Miller decides to provide explicit phonics instruction for these four students to help them learn to recognize letter patterns in words. She uses analogy phonics instruction where students learn words based on their similarity to other words (National Reading Panel, 2000). Today, the students are working on the "ell" word family. Ms. Johnson shows the students the word "sell" written on her whiteboard. She invites Shaneese to read the word. Once Shaneese reads the word correctly, Ms. Johnson writes the words "bell," "tell," "well," and "smell" on the board, and the students read them together. She has Jonathan circle the sound pattern on her whiteboard. The students discuss the sound of the word part "ell."

Next, Ms. Johnson integrates spelling activities having the students spell words she provides, including "spell," "well," and "shell." When Robert spells the word "shell" as "chell," Ms. Johnson praises him for getting the "ell" rime correct. She then asks him what other words he knows that start with the sound "ch" Robert responds with the word "chip." When prompted for more words, he adds the words "chill" and "chin." Ms. Johnson asks him to write these words on his board and note the beginning sound. She then asks him to read the word aloud while she points to the word "chell." Robert reads the nonsense word correctly as "chell," and Ms. Johnson encourages him to write the word "shell" again. This time, Robert spells it correctly. She asks him about other words that start with the sound "sh," and he comes up with the words "she" and "shake." While Ms. Johnson is taking advantage of this teachable moment to help Robert connect words with similar sounds and spelling patterns, she has the other students list words that end with the sound "ell." This extra spelling practice supports both decoding (reading) and encoding (spelling). Ms. Johnson has the three students who have written words that end with "ell" share their answers, so Robert also benefits. She then has them partner up to find words with the "ell" pattern in a pre-selected passage. Once the students have circled the words with the "ell" pattern, they read them to their partners. One of Ms. Johnson's priorities in this small group is to give each student as many practice opportunities as possible since she has only ten minutes with the students. Using a combination of choral reading, partner work, and writing on small whiteboards, Ms. Johnson can provide enough practice that the students remember the sound pattern when she reviews it in future lessons and, more importantly, when it comes up in class reading.

Fluency

Reading fluently with automaticity has a well-established connection to reading comprehension for students in grades 1 to 3, but less so for students in intermediate grades (Reschly et al., 2009). This is due to the importance of word-reading skills in earlier grades and the importance of background knowledge and language related to comprehension in later grades (Vellutino et al., 2007). Automaticity refers to a student's ability to effortlessly recognize words without decoding individual sounds and blending the phonemes to make meaning of the word. If a student is decoding words instead of automatically reading them, thinking is divided between the tasks of decoding and comprehending the decoded text (Stevens et al., 2017; Therrien, 2004). Elementary students who consistently score below expectations for their grade level on oral reading fluency (ORF) assessments should be considered for additional, comprehensive tiered interventions that include increasing accuracy, improving prosody (i.e., reading with proper expression), and increasing rate, as measured by the number of words correct per minute (WCPM) (Kovaleski et al., 2013).

To conduct an ORF assessment, the teacher provides the student with a section of connected text. The teacher has the same text where she will record any errors, such as mispronunciations, self-corrections, or missed or inserted words. The teacher times the student reading the text for one minute. At the end of the minute, the number of words read correctly is calculated, subtracting one word for each error made. The final word count is the student's WCPM score. Hasbrouck and Tindal (2006) provide a chart of evidence-based ORF fluency benchmarks, which is available online. It includes normed benchmarks for grades 1 through 8 and average weekly improvement students at various percentiles. This is a useful tool for teachers to establish progress monitoring goals. For students in grades 1 through 3, the ORF should be administered on three passages and averaged. For students above grade 3, conducting the ORF on only one passage is sufficient (Baker et al., 2015).

Ms. Johnson also works with a second-grade teacher, Ms. Williams. Ms. Williams notes that one of her students, Jasmine, has scored between 38 and 42 words per minute on her last three ORF assessments, placing Jasmine in the bottom quartile. Jasmine reads connected text in a monotonous voice and often stumbles over words, making her phrasing fragmented and inconsistent. After consulting with Ms. Williams and reviewing the data, Ms. Johnson agrees that Jasmine should begin fluency interventions three times weekly for 15 minutes each session.

Repeated reading as a technique for increasing fluency and comprehension is well supported by research and is appropriate for Tier 2 (combined with choral reading) and Tier 3 intervention (Esteves & Whitten, 2011; Stevens et al., 2017; Therrien, 2004). Teachers should give students immediate corrective feedback on their oral reading, supplying words that a student pauses on for three seconds or more and correcting any mistakes. Once the student has completed the passage, the teacher should model any sections where the student struggled with unknown words or failed to read with appropriate prosody, then ask the student to reread the passage. This process can be repeated as many as three times for a total of four readings by the student. Fluency gained from repeated reading of one passage transfers to reading of new material (Homan et al., 1993), allowing the student to improve their fluency on the repeated reading passage and future passages.

Ms. Johnson begins by having Jasmine read different selections of connected text about moon phases, a topic she knows Ms. Williams is covering in science class, until she has determined a text level where Jasmine can experience success. Once Ms. Johnson identifies an appropriate text, she asks Jasmine to read the selection aloud with her. Together, Ms. Johnson and Jasmine read the passage with Ms. Johnson modeling appropriate rate, emphasis, and expression. Next, Ms. Johnson asks Jasmine to read the text aloud independently. When Jasmine makes an error or pauses on a word for at least three seconds, Ms. Johnson immediately corrects her or supplies the unknown word and has Jasmine reread the sentence. After Jasmine's first independent reading, Ms. Johnson models any sections where Jasmine read without expression or with incorrect emphasis and then asks Jasmine to reread the passage.

Vocabulary

Vocabulary is part of language comprehension, which includes semantics, morphology, and syntax. In a review of the literature for language intervention, Silverman and her colleagues (2020) found that interventions that integrated vocabulary instruction (i.e., vocabulary and morphology; syntax and vocabulary) showed positive effects on reading comprehension. Vocabulary intervention should include specific words and word-learning strategies that include modeling, practice, and opportunities for generalization. Selecting which words to explicitly teach is an important instructional decision. Absent research evidence on which words to teach, Beck and her colleagues (2002) developed the three tiers of vocabulary approach. Tier 1 words are everyday words, and for students with extensive support needs, might be appropriate for intervention (e.g., Geist et al., 2021). Tier 3 words are content specific words, which are frequently taught during content area instruction (e.g., science class). Tier 2 words are those words used by mature literacy learners. Tier 2 words tend to be useful words that may not be taught during content instruction. Generally, the number of words targeted for explicit instruction should consider students' overall reading levels with lower-level readers being exposed to fewer words during an instructional segment.

Graphic organizers, such as the Frayer model, are useful for explicitly teaching words (e.g., Dazzeo & Rao, 2020; Westby, 2024). Frayer model graphic organizers include student-friendly definitions, characteristics of words, examples and nonexamples. On the other hand, explicitly teaching morphology to students in fourth grade and above is a strategic approach to understanding many different words through the study of the meaning of word parts, such as affixes (prefixes and suffixes), base words (basic words that have their own meaning), and roots (word parts, often from Greek or Latin, that carry meaning) (e.g., Claravall, 2016).

Comprehension

Reading comprehension is the goal of reading. For children with disabilities, Berkeley and Larsen (2018) found large effects for comprehension strategy instruction (e.g., text structure), which included self-regulation components immediately after they were taught, and, more importantly, they found evidence that the effects were maintained. This suggests that students internalized and changed their approaches to making sense of texts. The aspects of self-regulation recommended by Berkeley and Larson included, teacher think-alouds to demonstrate how readers make the cognitive moves necessary to implement the strategy (e.g., I see the word *because*, and I know authors of expository text use that word to signal that something is a cause, caused another thing, or is an effect. Let me see if I can find the cause and the effect in this section of the text. I know I might need to reread this section to find the effect first).

For students with disabilities, teaching a small package of comprehension strategies where students are taught to enact the strategies independently is critical (e.g., Berkeley & Larsen, 2018; Gersten et al., 2001). Teaching students to preview texts before reading activates background knowledge to support reading comprehension. For narrative texts, prereading strategies include a picture walk and reading the covers of chapter books to make predictions about what will be read. For expository text, previewing text features, such as headings, pictures and captions, and other parts of the text that are not the main body of the text, can support background knowledge activation. Comprehension is also supported when students read the summary at the end of the text first. This establishes what they should learn during reading.

During-reading strategies include identifying the main idea of expository texts or themes of narrative texts. Explicitly teaching students how to develop summaries or question the text supports comprehension. Many students with disabilities have executive functioning differences (e.g., Zelazo et al., 2016) that might make self-regulation more challenging (e.g., Lyons & Zelazo, 2011). Given the importance of background knowledge to reading comprehension, and the inclusion of text forms as part of relevant background knowledge for reading (e.g., Perfetti & Stafura, 2017), teaching text structures and story grammar with embedded elements of self-regulation during intervention is a logical choice. The assessment to determine if a story grammar or text structure intervention is needed is retelling.

Story grammar or narrative interventions can be used with elementary students (e.g., Boulineau et al., 2004; Faggella-Luby et al., 2007; Spencer & Petersen, 2020; Williamson et al., 2015). Story grammar interventions include explicit teaching of story grammar elements (i.e., character, problem, setting, actions, solution). Story grammar can be systematically taught (e.g., who doing what?; beginning, middle, end of a story) using explicit instruction. In the vignette below, Ms. Jackson explicitly teaches a small package of strategies, including text preview, story grammar, and summary writing to support her students' reading comprehension.

Owen is an autistic student in Ms. Jackson's second-grade classroom. Although he reads words on grade level, his comprehension for narratives is at the preprimer level. On a retelling assessment, Owen recalls only the setting of the story. Ms. Jackson concludes that a story grammar intervention might support his reading development. After pairing Owen with another student with a similar reading profile (i.e., good at grade-level word recognition, poor comprehension), Ms. Jackson begins her lesson.

"Today we are going to read Pete the Cat Goes Camping *by James Dean. Before we start reading, let's take a look at the pictures. Looking at and thinking about the pictures helps us put our mind on what we will be reading. When we read, the goal is to understand, or comprehend the story." As they view each page, Ms. Jackson draws the students' attention to the story grammar elements (characters, setting, problem, solution) by asking questions. Since the class has read other* Pete the Cat *books, she asks, "Who is this a picture of?" Owen replies, "Pete." To which she replies, "That's right, it is Pete. Pete is the main character of our story. What is Pete doing?"*

After they quickly preview the book, Ms. Jackson says, "Today, we are going to use a strategy to help us understand or comprehend the book." She holds up a whiteboard with a story grammar map on it. "Our strategy is called story grammar. Story grammar has four parts: the characters or who is in the story; the setting or where and when the story takes place; the problem or what happens to the characters in the story; and, finally, the resolution or how the story ends. Every time an author writes a story, they include all four of these story grammar elements. During reading, identifying these elements in the story helps us comprehend the story." During reading, Ms. Jackson pauses as each element is encountered. Together, Ms. Jackson and her two students decide what to write in each blank. After reading, Ms. Jackson prompts her students to retell the story using the story grammar elements. She plans to do progress monitoring on each students' ability to retell the story. She also plans to gradually release her students to completing their own story grammar graphic organizers during read-alouds. Next, she will have students read stories independently and complete story grammar maps. Eventually, she will transition students to writing their retellings to summarize what happened in the story.

Expository text structure strategies can be used with elementary students of all ages (e.g., Breit-Smith et al., 2017; Carnahan et al., 2016; Williams, 2018). Text structures are used by authors of expository pieces to organize the text. Unlike the routine structure of story grammar, authors can use structures in any number of different ways. Text structures found in elementary texts include description, compare and contrast, sequence, cause and effect, and problem and solution. Each structure has associated signal words (e.g., *first* signals a sequence; *unlike* signals compare and contrast). They also have associated graphic organizers (e.g., a Venn diagram for compare and contrast). For students who have reading levels at second grade and lower, explicitly teaching one text structure at a time is recommended. For students reading at higher levels, more than one structure can be taught at a time. Teachers can make explicit that graphic organizers support our brains in making sense of the text organized by these structures. In addition, teachers should begin strategy instruction with the end in mind. The University of Kansas Center for Research on Learning has created a series of Content Enhancement Routines to support reading comprehension and other aspects of learning for students with and without disabilities in upper elementary and beyond. For example, the Order Routine supports teachers and students in choosing the graphic organizer that best fits the text structure and then using it to enhance comprehension and support studying. Once students have internalized the routine and learned to generalize, they can use the graphic organizers on their own as would be expected of learners reading on or above grade level (Scanion et al., 1996).

Ms. Jackson wants to provide an intervention to support Yara's reading comprehension of her science text because Yara's retellings consistently do not include all the main ideas and at least one detail from the assessment passages. She is in fourth grade, but her instructional reading comprehension level for science texts is at a first-grade level.

Because Yara is reading below a second-grade level and needs a text structure intervention, Ms. Jackson is beginning with a first-grade level passage with one text structure—compare and contrast. Ms. Jackson selected this structure to start with after surveying the science text Yara will be using for class. The author frequently uses this text structure, so this increases the likelihood this will be a helpful structure for Yara to know.

Before delivering the intervention, Ms. Jackson prepares materials for Yara, including a list of key words that signal the compare and contrast text structure (e.g., like *and* different*), a Venn diagram to visually represent how Yara's brain should be organizing the information, and, finally, a model passage that uses the signal words written at her current first-grade reading level. This allows Yara's cognitive energy to be dedicated to learning the strategy rather than on comprehending the text. Ms. Jackson plans to use explicit instruction with scaffolding during the* *lesson (e.g., I do, we do, you do) to support Yara's acquisition of this strategy, and she has developed a progress monitoring data collection sheet to track Yara's performance that is embedded into her instruction (i.e., retelling rubric).*

Once Yara understands how to use the strategy, Ms. Jackson plans to give her a grade-level section of her textbook that contains the compare and contrast text structure to see if she can transfer her use of this strategy to a more challenging text that she comprehends. Ms. Jackson will scaffold this transition as necessary to help Yara learn to use the strategy with her textbook. She also plans to remind Yara's science teacher to prompt Yara to use this strategy when students are asked to read during class.

CONCLUSION

As we have seen, intervention is additional support for struggling students. However, it does not just take whatever form is easiest for the teacher to implement. Instead, students are identified through assessment as needing intervention with specific skills. Then, an evidence-based plan is selected to address one or more specific needs, and a plan is created to implement the intervention with fidelity for a set period, often six to 12 weeks. Student progress is frequently monitored, and the intervention is adjusted if a student does not make adequate progress.

Intervention can be provided in any of the literacy skills a student may not have mastered at grade level, but it is always planned to help the student succeed with Tier 1 instruction along with peers. Typically, the team looks for deficits that may lead to additional challenges and considers which foundational skills impact comprehension. For example, a student struggling with phonics needs to have that area of weakness addressed first if interventions in comprehension are to lead to success with understanding grade-level texts. Interventions may target oral language, phonemic awareness, phonics, fluency, vocabulary, or comprehension. However, they usually target specific areas within a category, such as blending phonemes within phonemic awareness or identifying the main idea within comprehension. The more targeted the intervention and the better aligned the instruction and progress monitoring, the easier it is to check if an intervention is successful so students can find success with Tier 1 instruction alone. Therefore, interventions should address specific areas that keep students from meeting expectations in Tier 1 and teach students strategies they can eventually apply independently. When interventions have questionable results, we intensify them, perhaps by having someone with more expertise deliver them or by increasing the frequency. When interventions are ineffective, the team may try an entirely different intervention. If a student does not make progress with Tier 2 and 3 interventions, or if the interventions are not adequate to meet a student's needs despite being provided with fidelity for an adequate amount of time per week over several weeks, the student may be considered for special education eligibility, typically with the intervention data and thorough evaluation results considered together.

When students struggle with Tier 1 instruction, our first responsibility is to check if the instruction is effective for most students and to provide small-group and other support within that Tier 1 instruction. However, when that is not adequate, Tier 2 and Tier 3 interventions are needed, and a team can work together to ensure they are as effective as possible in supporting students toward success in Tier 1.

REFERENCES

Ahmed, Y., Miciak, J., Taylor, W. P., & Francis, D. J. (2022). Structure altering effects of a multicomponent reading intervention: An application of the direct and inferential mediation (DIME) model of reading comprehension in upper elementary grades. *Journal of Learning Disabilities*, 55(1), 58–78. https://www.ncbi.nlm.nih.gov/pmc/articles/PMC8425275/

American Speech-Language-Hearing Association. (n.d.). Communication milestones: Four to five years. https://www.asha.org/public/developmental-milestones/communication-milestones-4-to-5-years/

Archer, A. L. & Hughes, C. A. (2011). *Explicit instruction: Effective and efficient teaching*. The Guildford Press.

Baker D. L., Biancarosa G., Park B. J., Bousselot T., Smith J. L., Baker S. K., Kame'enui, E. J., Alonzo. J., & Tindal G. (2015). Validity of CBM measures of oral reading fluency and reading comprehension on high-stakes reading assessments in grades 7 and 8. *Reading and Writing*, 28(1), 57–104. https://doi.org/10.1007/s11145-014-9505-4

Beck, I. L. McKeown, M., & Kucan, L. (2002). Choosing words to teach. In I. L. Beck, M. G. McKeown, & L. Lucan. *Bringing Words to life: Robust vocabulary instruction* (pp. 15–30). Guilford Press.

Berkeley, S., & Larsen, A. (2018). Fostering self-regulation of students with learning disabilities: Insights from 30 years of reading comprehension intervention research. *Learning Disabilities Research & Practice*, 33(2), 75–86. https://doi.org/10.1111/ldrp.12165

Black, L. I., Vahratian, A., & Hoffman, H. J. (2015, June). Communication disorders and use of intervention services among children aged three–17 years: United States, 2012. (NCHS data brief, no. 205). National Center for Health Statistics. https://www.cdc.gov/nchs/products/databriefs/db205.htm#children_age

Boulineau, T., Fore, C., Hagan-Burke, S., & Burke, M. D. (2004). Use of story-mapping to increase the story-grammar text comprehension of elementary students with learning disabilities. *Learning Disability Quarterly*, 27(2), 105–121. https://doi.org/10.2307/1593645

Breit-Smith, A., Busch, J. D., & Guo, Y. (2017). Interactive book reading with expository science texts in preschool special education classrooms. *Teaching Exceptional Children*, 49(3). https://doi.org/10.1177/004005991668

Carnahan, C., Williamson, P., Swoboda, C., Birri, N., & Snyder. K. (2016). Increasing science text comprehension through expository text instruction. *Focus on Autism*, 31(3), 208–220. https://doi.org/10.1177/1088357615610539

Claravall, E. B. (2016). Integrating morphological knowledge in literacy instruction: Framework and principle to guide special education teachers. *Teaching Exceptional Children*, 48(4), 195–203. https://doi.org/10.1177/0040059915623526

Connor, C. M., Alberto, P. A., Compton, D. L., & O'Connor, R. E. (2014). Improving reading outcomes for students with or at risk for reading disabilities: A synthesis of the contributions from the Institute of Education Sciences Research Centers (NCSER 2014–3000). National Center for Special Education Research, Institute of Education Sciences, US Department of Education. https://ies.ed.gov/ncser/pubs/20143000/

Dazzeo, R., & Rao, K. (2020). Digital Frayer model: Supporting vocabulary acquisition with technology and UDL. *Teaching Exceptional Children*, 53(1), 34–42. https://doi.org/10.1177/0040059920911951

Dean, J. (2018). *Pete the cat goes camping*. Harper Collins.

Dogan, E., Ogut, B., & Kim, Y. Y. (2015). Early childhood reading skills and proficiency in NAEP eighth-grade reading assessment. *Applied Measurement in Education*, 28(3), 187–201. https://doi.org/10.1080/08957347.2015.1042157

Donegan, R. E., & Wanzek, J. (2021). Effects of reading interventions implemented for upper elementary struggling readers: A look at recent research. *Reading and Writing*, 34, 1943–1977. https://doi.org/10.1007/s11145-021-10123-y

Esteves, K. J., & Whitten, E. (2011). Assisted reading with digital audiobooks for students with reading disabilities. *Reading Horizons*, 51(1), 21.

Faggella-Luby, M., Schumaker, J. S., & Deshler, D. D. (2007). Embedded learning strategy instruction: Story-structure pedagogy in heterogeneous secondary literature classes. *Learning Disability Quarterly*, 30(2), 131–147. https://doi.org/10.2307/30035547

Fuchs, L. S., Fuchs, D., & Malone, A. S. (2017). The taxonomy of intervention intensity. *Teaching Exceptional Children*, 50(1), 35–43. https://doi.org/10.1177/0040059917703962

Geist, L., Erickson, K., Greer, C., & Hatch, P. (2021). Initial evaluation of the Project Core implementation model. *Assistive Technology Outcomes and Benefits*, 15, 29–47. https://www.atia.org/wp-content/uploads/2021/03/V15_Geist_etal.pdf

Gersten, R., Fuchs, L. S., Williams, J. P., & Baker, S. (2001). Teaching reading comprehension strategies to students with learning disabilities: A review of research. *Review of Educational Research*, 71(2), 279–320. https://doi.org/10.3102/00346543071002279

Hasbrouck, J., & Tindal, G. A. (2006). Oral reading fluency norms: A valuable assessment tool for reading teachers. *The Reading Teacher*, 59, 636–644. https://doi.org/10.1598/RT.59.7.3

Hohn, W. E., & Ehri, L.C. (1983). Do alphabet letters help prereaders acquire phonemic segmentation skills? *Journal of Educational Psychology*, 75(5), 752–756.

Homan, S. P., Klesius, J. P., & Hite, C. (1993). Effects of repeated readings and nonrepetitive strategies on students' fluency and comprehension. *The Journal of Educational Research*, 87(2), 94–99. https://doi.org/10.1080/00220671.1993.9941172

Kovaleski, J. F., VanDerHeyden A. M., & Shapiro, E. S. (2013). *The RTI approach to evaluating learning disabilities*. Guilford Press.

Lane, H., & Contesse, V. (2022). *UFLI foundations: An explicit and systematic phonics program*. Ventris Learning.

Lyons, K. E., & Zelazo, P. D. (2011). Monitoring, metacognition, and executive function: Elucidating the role of self-reflection in the development of self-regulation. In J. B. Benson (Ed.), *Advances in child development and behavior* (Vol. 40, pp. 379–412). https://doi.org/10.1016/B978-0-12-386491-8.00010-4

McKeown, M. G., Beck, I. L., & Blake, R. G. K. (2009). Rethinking reading comprehension instruction: A comparison of instruction for strategies and content approaches. *Reading Research Quarterly*, 44(3), 218–253. https://doi.org/10.1598/RRQ.44.3.1

McLeskey, J., Billingsley, B., Brownell, M. T., Maheady, L., & Lewis, T. J. (2019). What are high-leverage practices for special education teachers and why are they important? *Remedial and Special Education*, *40*(6), 331–337. https://doi.org/10.1177/0741932518773477

Nachshon, O., & Horowitz-Kraus, T. (2019). Cognitive and emotional challenges in children with reading difficulties. *ACTA Paediatrica: Nurturing the Child*, *108*(6), 1110–1114.
https://doi.org/10.1111/apa.14672

National Center for Education Evaluation and Regional Assistance. (2007). What Works Clearinghouse (WWC). US Department of Education Institute of Education Sciences. https://ies.ed.gov/ncee/wwc/FWW

National Center on Intensive Intervention. (n.d.). Academic intervention tools chart. American Institutes for Research. https://charts.intensiveintervention.org/aintervention

National Early Literacy Panel. (2008). *Developing early literacy: Report of the National Early Literacy Panel*. National Institute for Literacy. https://lincs.ed.gov/publications/pdf/NELPReport09.pdf

National Reading Panel (NRF). (2000). *Report of the National Reading Panel: Teaching children to read*. National Reading Panel. https://www.nichd.nih.gov/publications/pubs/nrp/report

Perfetti, C., & Stafura, J. (2017). Word knowledge in a theory of reading comprehension. *Scientific Studies of Reading*, *18*, 22–37. https://doi.org/10.1080/10888438.2013.827687

Pullen, P. C., & Kennedy, M. J. (Eds.). (2018). *Handbook of response to intervention and multi-tiered systems of support*. Routledge.

Reschly A. L., Busch T. W., Betts J., Deno S. L., & Long, J. D. (2009). Curriculum-based measurement oral reading as an indicator of reading achievement: A meta-analysis of the correlational evidence. *Journal of School Psychology*, *47*, 427–469. https://doi.org/10.1016/j.jsp.2009.07.001

Scanion, D., Deshler, D. D., & Shumaker, J. B. (1996). Can a strategy be taught and learned in secondary inclusive classrooms? *Learning Disabilities Research and Practice*, *11*(1), 41–57.

Sendak, M. (1963). *Where the wild things are*. Harper & Row Publishers.

Silverman, R. D., Johnson, E., Keane, K., & Khanna, S. (2020). Beyond decoding: A meta-analysis of the effects of language comprehension interventions on K–5 students' language and literacy outcomes. *Reading Research Quarterly*, *55*(S1), S207–S233. https://doi.org/10.1002/rrq.346

Spencer, T. D., & Petersen, D. B. (2020). Narrative intervention: Principles to practice. *Language, Speech, and Hearing Services in Schools*, *51*(4), 1081–1096. https://doi.org/10.1044/2020_LSHSS-20-00015

Stevens, E. A., Walker, M. A., & Vaughn, S. (2017). The effects of reading fluency interventions on the reading fluency and reading comprehension performance of elementary students with learning disabilities: A synthesis of the research from 2001 to 2014. *Journal of Learning Disabilities*, *50*(5), 576–590. https://doi.org/10.1177/0022219416638028

Therrien, W. J. (2004). Fluency and comprehension gains as a result of repeated reading: A meta-analysis. *Remedial and Special Education*, *25*(4), 252–261. https://doi.org/10.1177/07419325040250040801

Vellutino, F. R., Tunmer, W. E., Jaccard, J. J., & Chen, R. (2007). Components of reading ability: Multivariate evidence for a convergent skills model of reading development. *Scientific Studies of Reading*, *11*(1), 3–32. https://doi.org/10.1080/10888430709336632

Westby, C. (2024). Frayer model for vocabulary development. *Word of Mouth*, *35*(3), 13–14. https://doi.org/10.1177/10483950231211841d

Wilkowski, T., & Freeley, M. E. (2012). An evaluation of a pilot early intervention phonemic awareness program. *Insights on Learning Disabilities*, *9*(2), 1.

Williams, J. P. (2018). Text structure instruction: The research is moving forward. *Reading and Writing*, *31*, 1923–1935. https://doi.org/10.10007/s11145-018-9909-7

Williamson, P., Carnahan, C., Birri, N., & Swoboda, C. (2015). Using character event maps to build comprehension of narrative stories for learners with ASD. *Journal of Special Education*, *49*(1), 28–38. https:/doi.org/10.1177/0022466914521301

Williamson, P., Hoppey, D., McLeskey, J., Bergmann, E., & Townsend, H. (2020). Trends in LRE placement rates over the last 25 years. *Journal of Special Education*, *53*(4), 236–244. https://eric.ed.gov/?id=EJ1238263

Wright, J. (2010). *The RIOT/ICEL matrix: Organizing data to answer questions about student academic performance and behavior*. Intervention Central. https://www.interventioncentral.org/sites/default/files/rti_riot_icel_data_collection.pdf

Zelazo, P. D., Blair, C. B., & Willoughby, M. T. (2016). Executive function: Implications for education (NCER 2017–2000). National Center for Education Research, Institute of Education Sciences, US Department of Education. https://ies.ed.gov/ncer/pubs/20172000/

4

Core Mathematics Instruction

Corey Peltier, Garret Hall, and Casey Hord

CURRENT DATA ON STUDENTS' MATHEMATICS ACHIEVEMENT

Since 1990, the US Department of Education has provided funding to administer the National Assessment of Education Progress (NAEP). This assessment aims to sample US students' performance across academic domains and provide information on academic achievement at the individual state level and the nation at large. From 2007 to 2019, the mathematics performance of fourth- and eighth-grade students was relatively stagnant (US Department of Education, 2022). The most recent data cycle, 2022, showed dramatic decreases in student performance with COVID-19 and the interruptions to student learning being a strong contributing factor. In fourth grade, 25% of students scored below the NAEP basic cut score and 39% of students scored in the NAEP basic category indicating that 64% of students were not performing at NAEP proficiency. In eighth grade, 38% of students scored below the NAEP basic cut score and 35% of students scored in the NAEP basic category indicating that 73% of students were not performing at NAEP proficiency. A central theme evident at both grade levels is difference in performance of the 90th percentile and 10th percentile is the largest it has ever been. At the risk of sounding like an alarmist, these data suggest we have a dire need to center our conversation on how core instruction in mathematics can be enhanced to support all students' mathematical development.

Individuals must use their mathematics knowledge to participate in many daily activities, such as cooking, adhering to medical advice, and engaging in personal health (Methe et al., 2011). Individuals' economic well-being is impacted by their mathematical knowledge by opening pathways to careers that provide higher salaries, their ability to file taxes, and their capability to make financially savvy decisions related to loans and investments (Dowker, 2005). Furthermore, to engage as an activity citizen, mathematics knowledge is needed to interpret polling data and evaluate the impacts of policies (Crowe, 2010). Thus, building student proficiency in mathematics is not just an endeavor to support student success within school, it also has huge ramifications on the quality of lives individuals can experience.

How do we ensure students leave school with the opportunity to choose postsecondary education or careers that require proficiency in mathematics? A firm foundation must be built at the elementary-grade span. We see early numeracy skills evaluated at kindergarten predict students' fifth-grade mathematics achievement (ten Braak et al., 2022). Similarly, we see students' knowledge of fractions and division at fifth grade predict students' high school mathematics achievement (Siegler et al., 2012). We must ensure our core instruction in mathematics targets pivotal skills, develops student mastery in these skills, and identifies and intervenes with students who are not mastering these skills. The failure of our core instruction to achieve these three outcomes will have detrimental outcomes for students. After reading this chapter, readers will be able to:

1. Identify educational policies and initiatives impacting mathematics instruction.
2. Describe the key competencies of mathematics education in elementary school.
3. Identify and describe the components of high-quality core mathematics instruction.

Educational Policies and Initiatives Impacting Mathematics Instruction

Several policies and initiatives have impacted the way schools view and approach mathematics instruction. The National Council of Teachers of Mathematics (NCTM) is the world's largest professional organization and has released various policy documents for mathematics educators. In the *Agenda for Action* (1980), the NCTM provided several recommendations with a central tenant around the need to reposition problem solving as a focus of mathematics. Building proficiency in procedures and concepts is integral but not an end goal, students must have the opportunity to apply this knowledge through rich problem-solving tasks. In 2000, NCTM released the *Principles and Standards for School Mathematics*, which outlined guiding principles for what high-quality equitable mathematics instruction should be comprised. Furthermore, the document included guidance on the mathematics content and processes that should be the central focus of preschool- through twelfth-grade mathematics education.

This document was influential in the creation of the Common Core State Standards for Mathematics (CCSS-M), which the NCTM openly endorsed in 2013. The CCSS-M were sponsored by the National Governors Association and Council of Chief State School Officers (2010) and aimed to develop a consistent set of standards in English language arts and mathematics that students should learn by the conclusion of each grade. The Standards for Mathematical Practice describe processes students should engage in when doing mathematics and mirror many of the recommendations provided by the NCTM in the *Principles and Standards for School Mathematics*. At the elementary grades, the CCSS-M organizes key learning targets into domains: counting and cardinality (kindergarten only); operations and algebraic thinking (kindergarten through fifth), number and operations in base ten (kindergarten through fifth), number and operations—fractions (third through fifth), measurement and data (kindergarten through fifth), and geometry (kindergarten through fifth).

Two other pivotal documents that have informed mathematics instruction are *Adding It Up* released by the National Research Council (2001) and *The Final Report of the National Mathematics Advisory Panel* (2008). Both reports have similar goals, they convene panels of experts across fields to synthesize research evidence that can inform mathematics education. *Adding It Up* was funded through a US Department of Education grant to the National Research Council and was written by a panel of 16 individuals from diverse fields that aimed at synthesizing research on pre-kindergarten through eighth-grade math learning. *The Final Report of the National Mathematics Advisory Panel* was created through an executive order that placed the US Secretary of Education in charge of appointing members and overseeing the panel.

Both documents provide guidance on content selection and teaching practices. First, they identify a need to better align learning targets across grade spans with a focus on ensuring there is a clear goal to support success in algebra. This may result in less emphasis and in some cases removing specific concepts to allow for more in-depth coverage and ensure student mastery of the most pivotal core pieces of knowledge students need. Second, both documents emphasize the need to reconsider mathematics proficiency as an amalgamation of processes and points of knowledge. The NRC (2001) has provided a visual, coined the "math rope," that emphasizes that true proficiency is intertwined between multiple strands (we describe this below in more detail; see figure 4.1 for a modified math rope diagram). The National Mathematics Advisory Panel (NMAP, 2008) report references the math rope as well. Third, both documents emphasize the importance of matching instructional tactics to the context teachers are working within. They identify the need to leverage off students' prior knowledge of preskills and scaffold the learning of the new skill through carefully selected, or constructed, tasks, clear explanations, and purposeful prompts and questions that support student reasoning and verbalization of mathematics. The NMAP was critical of the debates occurring at that time around "teacher-centered" versus "student-centered" instruction and proposed that the current research evidence suggested that students need a healthy diet of both types of instructional environments to achieve mathematical proficiency. The panel did identify that students who have experienced mathematical difficulty and students identified with a mathematics learning disability benefit from frequent explicit instruction. Last, the NMAP emphasized the overall poor quality of mathematics textbooks being used at that time and highlighted a need to condense textbooks to focus on the pivotal skills and remove unnecessary content not supporting that goal and ensure all content and descriptions of mathematics is accurate.

Two pieces of legislation that have had an impact on mathematics education are the Every Student Succeeds Act (ESSA; 2015) and the Individuals with Disabilities Education Improvement Act (IDEIA; 2004). ESSA was the reauthorization of No Child Left Behind and is a piece of legislation that governs K–12 public education. IDEIA (2004) is the reauthorization of IDEA (1997) and is a piece of legislation that governs education for students with disabilities. Both pieces of legislation explicitly reference that schools, and thus educators, must use research-based practices. Although there is lots of conversation and controversy around how to identify what

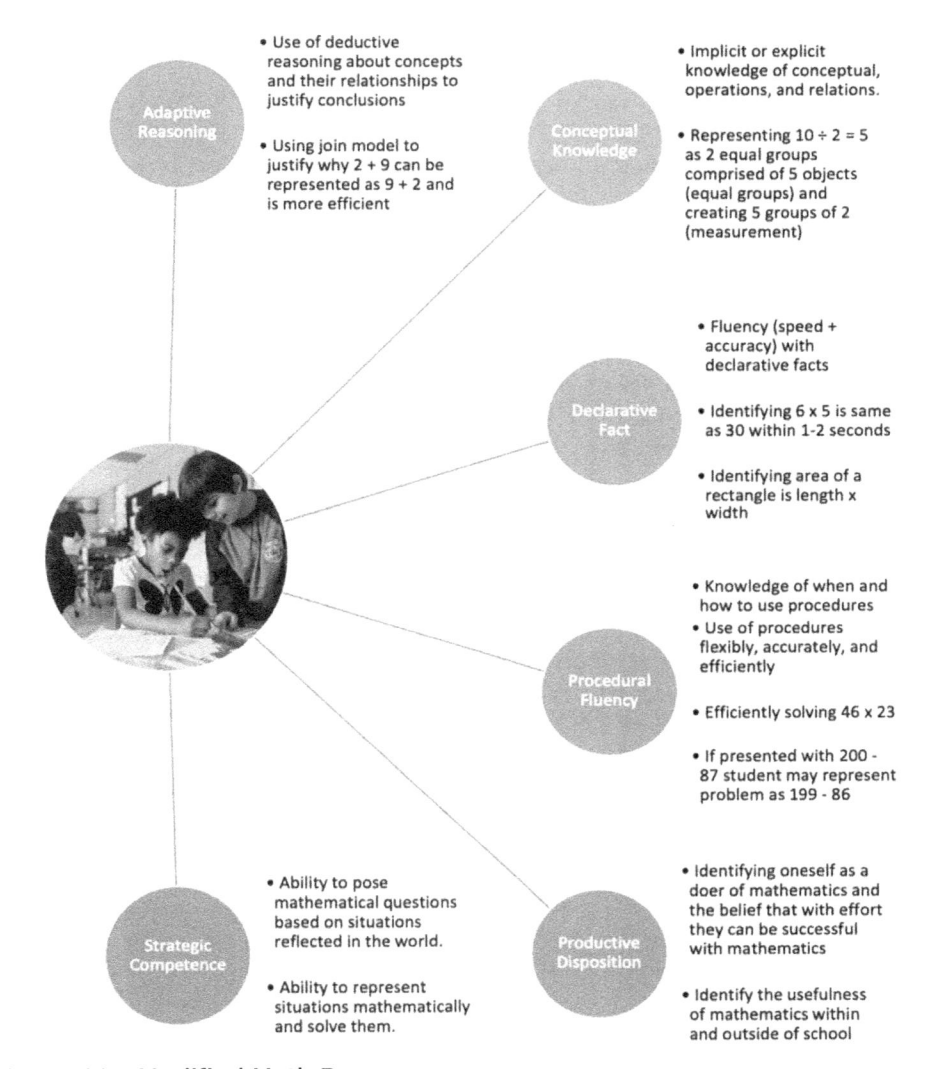

Figure 4.1. Modified Math Rope
Source: Strands of the National Research Council (2001) "math rope."

Adaptive Reasoning
- Use of deductive reasoning about concepts and their relationships to justify conclusions
- Using join model to justify why 2 + 9 can be represented as 9 + 2 and is more efficient

Conceptual Knowledge
- Implicit or explicit knowledge of conceptual, operations, and relations.
- Representing 10 ÷ 2 = 5 as 2 equal groups comprised of 5 objects (equal groups) and creating 5 groups of 2 (measurement)

Declarative Fact
- Fluency (speed + accuracy) with declarative facts
- Identifying 6 x 5 is same as 30 within 1-2 seconds
- Identifying area of a rectangle is length x width

Procedural Fluency
- Knowledge of when and how to use procedures
- Use of procedures flexibly, accurately, and efficiently
- Efficiently solving 46 x 23
- If presented with 200 - 87 student may represent problem as 199 - 86

Strategic Competence
- Ability to pose mathematical questions based on situations reflected in the world.
- Ability to represent situations mathematically and solve them.

Productive Disposition
- Identifying oneself as a doer of mathematics and the belief that with effort they can be successful with mathematics
- Identify the usefulness of mathematics within and outside of school

is or is not considered a "research-based" practice, it is important to note legislation is attempting to guide educators to consult scientific evidence to inform their practice. This is, in essence, the goal of this chapter.

Setting the Stage for Success: Key Competencies in Elementary School

Algebra competence has often been, and continues to be, a benchmark for student math success (e.g., NMAP, 2008). Setting students up to be successful in algebra (and beyond) begins early in elementary schooling. NMAP's 2008 report on the essentials of mathematics instruction across grade levels provides several key competencies to build in elementary core instruction:

1. Fluency with whole numbers (addition and subtraction by grade 3; multiplication and division by grade 5).
2. Understanding representations of rational numbers by grade 4 (e.g., placing them on a number line).
3. Fluency with addition and subtraction of rational numbers by grade 5.
4. Understanding of area and perimeter of triangles and quadrilaterals (with at least one set of parallel sides).

Two features of these competencies are important to highlight. First, they underscore the critical role of whole number understanding, with the gradual introduction of rational number arithmetic in late elementary. Performing arithmetic with rational numbers necessarily requires fluency with whole numbers (e.g., multiplying to find a common denominator), though some students tend to inappropriately apply procedures and concepts from whole number operations to rational number operations (the whole number bias). Second, conceptual understanding and procedural fluency with rational number operations is a necessity for more complex operations in algebra and geometry. Algebra has often been referred to as a "gatekeeper" to success, and Booth and Newton (2012) extend this metaphor to say that fractions (and rational number operations more generally) may act as the "gatekeeper's doorman." If rational numbers set the stage for algebra success, whole number competence gets a person to the gate in the first place.

The trajectory toward algebra is set in elementary core instruction when students acquire the essential conceptual competencies and procedural fluencies to conduct more complex, multistep problems. The NRC (2001) provides a visualization of the interconnected nature of conceptual and procedural knowledge with their "math rope" visual. In this rope, five strands are intertwined to facilitate development of math competence: adaptive reasoning, conceptual knowledge, procedural fluency, productive disposition, and strategic competence.

- **Adaptive reasoning** is coined "the glue that hold everything together" in the NRC (2001) report (p. 129). It refers to a student's ability to use deductive reasoning to justify conclusions made about mathematical situations by drawing upon facts, procedures, concepts, and solution methods.
- **Conceptual knowledge** is knowledge of concepts, operations, and relations between them. An important point is this knowledge may be implicit or explicit. For example, a student may be presented 2 + 9 and start with the greater addend, 9, and count up 2 to find the sum. This may suggest the student has an implicit knowledge of the commutative property of addition even if they are not currently able to explicitly justify this with language. It is often common for students to develop implicit knowledge of a concept before being able to explicitly demonstrate this knowledge through words.
- **Procedural fluency** is knowledge of procedures and when to apply them along with the skill to perform procedures accurately, efficiently, and flexibly. An easier aspect of procedural fluency to observe is the "fluency" piece. Students who have strong procedural fluency will have high accuracy (e.g., 95% to 100%) with appropriate speed (i.e., solve the problem efficiently given the complexity of the procedural task). A more difficult aspect to observe, yet

equally important if we aim to evaluate the depth of a student's procedural knowledge is flexibility (Star, 2005). One way to consider flexibility is students can select or order their use of specific procedures to maximize their efficiency given the goal of the problem.
- **Productive disposition** is the sum of affective attributes students internalize about their relation to mathematics and their perception of the usefulness of mathematics. If we consider attribution theory, supporting students in identifying their effort in learning mathematics is what contributes to their success, this will be instrumental to supporting their lifelong relation to mathematics in a positive way. This pivots off the idea that "we are all math people"—it just requires effort. The second aspect is to ensure our learning environments support students in identifying how mathematics is useful and worthwhile not only in school but also outside of school in their everyday lives.
- **Strategic competence** can be thought of as two strands: problem formation and problem solving. Problem formation is the ability to evaluate situations and pose mathematical questions or problems that could be investigated. Problem solving is the ability to represent a situation mathematically, devise a plan, carry out that plan, and check the reasonableness of their solution or conclusion.

In our view, one element that gets lost in the rope but is broken out in the NMAP (2008) report is the role of declarative facts in student proficiency. The NRC (2001) report included declarative facts within procedural fluency whereas the National Mathematics Advisory Panel (NMAP, 2008) separated out declarative facts. A declarative fact is any discrete piece of information. Most often when the term *fact* is used, we think of addition and subtraction facts (i.e., sums to 18) and multiplication and division facts (i.e., factors of 9). These are examples of declarative facts that must be known automatically to be able to be able to engage in deep procedural knowledge and support conceptual knowledge building. However, declarative facts are broader than just *math facts*; a student identifying the symbol 5 represents the spoken word "five" is also an example of a declarative fact. Building deep conceptual knowledge is essentially a student's ability to construct an organized schema of declarative facts—thus declarative facts are essential in this process. To engage in procedural fluency, students must use declarative facts.

To summarize, math competence is most likely to develop when students can flexibly apply problem-solving strategies, understand the concepts underlying the operations, fluently apply the basic procedures to execute essential operations, and develop a positive affect toward math. Although there is no debate as to procedures and concepts both being highly consequential to developing math competence, there has been debate about which is the most effective to develop first (Rittle-Johnson et al., 2015). As the math rope idea underscores, the reality of developing conceptual understanding and procedural fluency is likely a complex dynamic, and they are best viewed as mutually beneficial. High-quality core instruction in elementary school should leverage this mutuality of concepts and procedures to provide students with a foundation for generalizing whole and rational number knowledge to (pre)algebraic thinking and operations.

Components of High-Quality Core Mathematics Instruction

It is an enormous undertaking to consider writing a chapter that will include everything that could potentially be included during high-quality core mathematics instruction. We opted to highlight specific instructional recommendations that are low effort and high impact that educators can implement within their own context. However, given that we will undoubtedly leave out discussions of other useful practices, we also include free, open-source resources at the end of the chapter that educators can consult to learn more.

Manipulatives

One HLP that educators can implement to support student *acquisition* of new mathematical concepts are manipulatives. Manipulatives are defined as any physical object that educators may incorporate into the mathematics learning environment to support knowledge building. These objects may be advertised as such and purchased, such as base ten blocks, fraction tiles, or algebra tiles, but a manipulative could also be objects found and used during learning such as rocks or paper. Research has demonstrated manipulatives have been effective at supporting students' mathematical learning across various domains such as place value concepts, arithmetic, fractions, geometry, and algebra (Carbonneau et al., 2013). Furthermore, manipulatives have the potential to ensure equitable outcomes are achieved from mathematics instruction as research shows manipulatives are effective for students with disabilities as well (Peltier et al., 2020).

How can manipulatives support mathematical development? This is the critical aspect for educators to wrestle with, as they aim to incorporate manipulatives into their instruction. Manipulatives are in essence just an object; thus, they do not have the capacity to teach a child the concept. Furthermore, if manipulatives detract students' attention from the relevant features of the concept, then they will inhibit learning (Willingham, 2017). This highlights two critical factors for educators to consider: (a) What guidance should the teacher provide to the students for their use of the manipulatives? and (b) What characteristics of manipulatives should a teacher consider when selecting one to use?

The best theory for why manipulatives appear to be effective for student learning is they serve as an analogy for an abstract concept. For example, if a student is using base ten blocks to model the process of regrouping, the exchange of ten one cubes for a ten stick serves as an analogy for the regrouping process students apply when using an algorithm for addition and subtraction of multi-digit numbers. Similarly, using fraction tiles to create equivalent fractions serves as an analogy for the process of creating a new fraction that represents the same equal portions of a whole. Anything that may impede a student's ability to see the manipulative is serving as an analogy for the abstract concept may hinder learning. Below is a vignette that highlights an example of my own teaching experience where I did just that.

Mr. Peltier is attempting to support students' ability to represent division from a partitive and measurement perspective. Each student is given a different division problem with the maximum factors of 9. For the partitive model, students represent the dividend with counting discs and create the number of equal groups the divisor represents and share the dividend equally among groups. Students then share with a peer how the quotient matches their model. For the measurement model, students represent the dividend with counting discs and then create groups the size of the divisor until the entire dividend is gone. The students then share with a peer how the quotient matches their model (see figure 4.2). Henry has seemed disengaged with the task, so Mr. Peltier opts to pique his interest by allowing him to use a bunch of erasers that have pictures of minions. Henry loves minions; he has a backpack with minions and often wears shirts with minions on them. Mr. Peltier thinks this is the hook needed to help Henry engage with the task and learn the concept.

The vignette above is a true story! Why was my attempt at engagement misguided and not lead to conceptual or procedural knowledge building? In this experience, the pictures of minions became the core feature Henry focused on and detracted from his focus on how the dividend can be grouped in different ways to represent the two core division models we were focusing on.

The next area to consider is how to guide students in their use of manipulatives to support acquisition of knowledge. As we will reiterate again, a manipulative is just an object and cannot teach the concept. Educators' goal for the manipulative is to help serve as an analogy of the abstract concept. Thus, educators modeling the use of the manipulative and explicitly highlighting to students how it ties into the abstract concept or notation is critical. One framework to think about this from is the concrete-representational-abstract (CRA) instructional framework (Bouck et al., 2018), referred to as the concrete-pictorial-abstract framework in Singapore Math Inc. In this framework, educators introduce concepts through concrete or pictorial representations and provide the explicit connection to the abstract concept. Students

$$10 \div 2 = 5$$

How can we interpret the quotient in the partitive model?

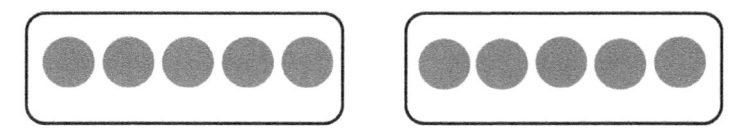

How can we interpret the quotient in the measurement model?

Figure 4.2. Parative and Measurement Model of Division
Source: Created by Corey Peltier.

then engage with the concept through concrete manipulatives and/or pictorial representations with a goal of connecting these to the abstract concept or notation. The manipulatives and/or pictorial representations are faded out as students build the conceptual and procedural knowledge of the abstract concept. This does differ from a related approach known as the concrete-abstract-instructional *sequence*. In the sequence approach, students must move from concrete to pictures to abstract in that order by demonstrating proficiency at each level, and the teacher will only model the skill within each level. Recent work has shown that both approaches work, yet the CRA framework yielded the same effects in roughly half the amount of instructional time—thus highlighting its efficiency (Morano et al., 2020). This is likely due to the analogy of the manipulative representing an abstract concept being crystal clear from the beginning of the unit because the abstract is consistently shown alongside the manipulative and pictorial models. This would also align with work from Rittle-Johnson and colleagues (2015) that focuses on building conceptual and procedural knowledge simultaneously, which leads to more effective outcomes, rather than prioritizing one over the other when designing an instructional unit.

Worked Examples

In the eloquent words of Michael Pershan, "Some of the dullest teaching on the planet comes courtesy of worked example abusers" (2021, p. 19). We want to start with the warning up front: worked examples can be extremely effective but the implementation can make or break their utility. Worked examples are completed problems that are presented to students to learn from. They have been studied extensively and shown to positively enhance learning, particularly when they are used during the acquisition of new knowledge for the student (Atkinson et al., 2000). For worked examples to be effective we will discuss three key elements to consider: (a) the design of effective worked examples, (b) the use of scaffolding in the presentation of worked examples, and (c) the use and reinforcement of a worked example routine.

When designing worked examples there are several factors to consider. First, a problem or item must be selected to guide the example around. The item should align to the desired content and be generalizable to highlight the overarching concept and procedure you aim for students to grasp. If we consider the vignette above, the target skill was teaching the two different ways to represent division: partitive model and measurement model. A poor worked example would be to use the problem 16 ÷ 4 = 4 for this skill—both pictures would look the same thus making it difficult for students to connect the different interpretations we want them to draw from the worked example. It is often useful to identify one common misconception you may see students make for a specific concept and design a worked example around this idea. A second element in designing the worked example is to be a minimalist. Embed as little "extra stuff" as possible so all students' attention can be focused on studying the critical attributes you want them to focus on. For example, a common error seen in worked examples is the creator will include a description in words of each step of the worked example. If we consider cognitive load theory, it suggests that our working memory is finite and can only processes a certain amount of information at a time. When the same exact information is presented in two ways—in this scenario, the worked example paired with written description—we run the risk of the redundancy effect (see Lovell, 2020, for a useful resource). If brief labels or short phrases are needed for students to access the worked example, ensure these are embedded within the worked example versus off to the side. If the words or phrases are presented separate from the worked example, this can lead to students' attention being split and may reduce learning (see Lovell, 2020). Last, if a lengthier description is necessary for the worked example, this will be best provided by the teacher verbally, so the students focus is solely on the worked example.

A second consideration is how to transition a student from studying a worked example to problem solving. For tasks that include an applied procedure, this can be accomplished by considering forward or backward chaining. In applying backward chaining, the teacher will construct a series of worked examples that repeatedly leave another step in the problem for the student to complete. For example, the first problem would have steps 1 to 5 completed and the student is tasked with completing the last step, 6. In the next problem, steps 1 to 4 are completed and the student is tasked with completing steps 5 and 6. This is repeated until the student is left to complete steps 1 through 6 independently (see figure 4.3 for an example). In forward chaining, the teacher will construct a series of worked examples in the exact opposite order. For example, the first problem would have steps 2 to 6 completed, and the student is tasked with completing the first step, 1. In the next problem, steps 2 to 6 are completed, and the student is tasked with completing steps 1 and 2. This is repeated until the student is left to complete steps 1 through

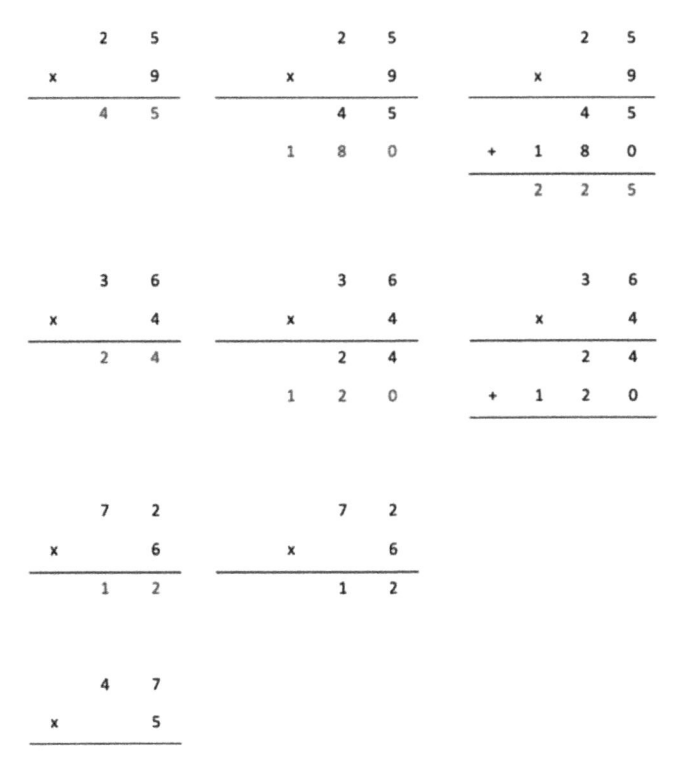

Figure 4.3. Backward Chaining with Worked Examples
Source: Created by Corey Peltier.

6 independently. Both approaches scaffold the multistep task for the student and provides repeated practice; however, the distribution of practice is not equivalent. In backward chaining, the student would have more practice opportunities solving the later steps in the procedure, and in forward chaining the student would have more practice opportunities solving the initial steps in the procedure. The application of either approach would depend on the context of the learning situation and the educator's assessment of where more practice opportunities would be more beneficial. See figure 4.3 for an exemplar.

An alternative to chaining procedures is to opt for interleaving, sometimes referred to as alternation. In an interleaving context, the educator would plan out a series of carefully selected problems. The first problem would be a worked example that the student studies, and the second problem would be a similar item for the student to solve. The third problem would be another worked example for the student to study, and the fourth problem would be a similar item for the student to solve. This quick alternation of worked examples and problem-solving items reinforces the problem-solving process and can allow educators to carefully sequence worked examples highlighting common misconceptions or errors that occur for the concept.

As you might remember from the beginning of this section, we mentioned that worked examples are excellent for initial acquisition, but their usefulness wears off and detracts from learning as students build proficiency with the knowledge being learned. This leads to a final application of worked examples, studying incorrect examples. The ability to evaluate, reason mathematically, and articulate incorrect mathematical thinking is clearly aligned with the strands from the NRC (2001) math rope. Educators can develop incorrect worked examples that include common errors or misconceptions they have observed so that students can build proficiency in detecting and verbalizing why the examples are incorrect.

The third consideration is how to build routines to ensure students study the worked example. One useful strategy is to chunk the presentation of steps of the worked example. For example, present only step 1 of the worked example and ask students to study what occurred. This is an excellent opportunity to provide pointed prompts of what to study along with highlighting specific mathematical vocabulary. Slowly, the educator will repeat this process until the entire worked example is visible to students. To ensure all students have an opportunity to verbalize their mathematical thinking, it can be beneficial to have students pair off and explain their thinking to a partner (see vignette below).

Mr. Peltier is a fifth-grade general education teacher, and he co-teaches math with Ms. Fern who is the special education teacher. To build students' self-explanations of their mathematical thinking and to promote the use of mathematical vocabulary, they start off the year using turn and talks with their students. The first several weeks they observe (a) partners talking about the football game the previous night, (b) partners silently staring at one another, and (c) partners rushing to share their thoughts with a peer but little evidence that active listening is occurring. To make the practice more effective, Ms. Fern suggests the following adjustments: (1) both teachers model a successful turn-and-talk, (2) post stems students can use to start their explanation, (3) provide key vocabulary students should consider using in their explanation, and (4) engage in better active supervision to reinforce groups that engage in productive dialogue. Last, when it is time for a whole class debrief, both teachers will intermix asking students what they have shared but also explicitly asking peers to share what their partner has shared to promote active listening.

Either following the partner discussion, or during, it is a helpful scaffold to provide specific prompts or questions that direct students' attention to the critical aspects of the worked example that align to the concept. Teachers can scaffold this task further by providing stems that students can complete that scaffold their self-explanation process (Rittle-Johnson et al., 2017).

Word-Problem Solving

Word-problem solving is embedded throughout the elementary grade span. Students are first tasked with solving additive word problems (addition and subtraction) up to sums of 10 (kindergarten), then sums to 20 (first grade), then sums to 100 (second grade), then with fractions (fourth grade). Similarly, students are tasked with solving multiplicative word problems (multiplication and division) within 100 (third and fourth grade) and with fractions (fourth and fifth grade). Thus, proficiency with word-problem solving is an essential skill for students to develop.

When students are struggling with something that is new and/or difficult for them, they may struggle with thinking about, remembering, and combining more than one piece of information (Barrouillet et al., 2007). Word problems often present situations for students where they must contend with a few significant challenges all at the same time. First, students need to read the text, which may be difficult for students with word-level reading difficulties; and students must comprehend the section of text relying on knowledge of language, which may be difficult for some students. Second, students must remember pieces of information from the problem to represent this mathematically. Third, to represent the situation mathematically, students must rely on their knowledge of specific math concepts that may still be developing. Fourth, students then must devise and apply a procedure plan relying heavily upon procedural and conceptual knowledge of mathematical concepts.

In these situations, education researchers have found ways to help students offload information (e.g., show their work on scratch paper; see Dunn & Risko, 2015) in strategic ways to help them remember important information, organize their thinking process, and see the structure of the problem in ways that help them solve the problem and understand the mathematical relationships in the context of that work problem (for review, see Lein et al., 2020; Myers et al., 2023).

Constructivism, as a theory of learning, suggests that students must construct their own knowledge by orienting new information with their prior experiences and knowledge (Bereiter, 1994). In this vein, students' success with word problems depends on their ability to develop their own schemas that apply to generalized situations correctly. This may be accomplished through trial and error and making adjustments (von Glasersfeld, 1995), through instructional experiences guided by an educator or peer, or through a combination of both.

In some cases, researchers have emphasized that "good" problem solvers tend to see abstract structures (or schemas) when solving word problems, while struggling learners may see surface-level features of the problem but not see the relationships between problem elements (e.g., Schoenfeld & Herrmann, 1982). While some models of instruction take a more indirect approach to supporting students' development of rich schemas, schema instruction is a more direct approach that is focused on explicitly teaching schemas and supporting students in internalizing a problem-solving process (see Powell & Fuchs, 2018).

For many years, researchers have used a variety of diagramming strategies for additive (addition and subtraction) and multiplicative (multiplication and division) story problems. For example, Jitendra and Hoff (1996) studied diagramming strategies based on schema frameworks (Marshall, 1995). These authors studied how schema-based instruction could support students with a mathematics learning disability to become successful in solving word problems. In this study, and many others over the past two decades or more, students with disabilities have demonstrated success with elementary school–level word problems using schema instruction (e.g., Myers et al., 2023). In other cases, the principles have been similar, but the diagrams may be more abstract to apply for more problem types (e.g., Xin, 2008) or structured using table-like structures to separate parts of problems into sub-steps (e.g., van Garderen, 2007).

Table 4.1. Open-Source Resources to Support Mathematics Instruction

What's Inside	How to Access
Full intervention curriculum focused on building declarative fact fluency.	https://brianponcy.wixsite.com/mind
Online course that consists of eight modules on how to build intensive intervention in mathematics.	https://intensiveintervention.org/training/course-content/intensive-intervention-mathematics
The National Center on Intensive Intervention evaluates intervention research and provides their findings on the evidence supporting their use.	https://intensiveintervention.org/tools-charts/overview
The National Center on Intensive Intervention evaluates the psychometric evidence for screeners and progress-monitoring measures in mathematics.	https://intensiveintervention.org/tools-charts/overview
Full intervention curriculum focused on building student proficiency in additive word problem-solving.	https://www.piratemathequationquest.com/
Project Stair's YouTube channel that includes brief videos demonstrating various ways to introduce mathematical concepts.	https://www.youtube.com/channel/UCE2puwDtUSNXFONIOhmYmvA
Curated lists of worked examples educators have used with students.	Pershan: https://mathwithexamples.wordpress.com/ Math by Example: https://www.serpinstitute.org/math-by-example Algebra by Example: https://www.serpinstitute.org/algebra-by-example

Although there are differences across approaches, a general guideline for integrating instruction on word problems should include three parts. First, students must learn how to "attack" a word problem. I am sure some educators reading this have encountered a situation where they have observed a student pulling out numbers, selecting an operation, and engaging in a computation procedure without reading the piece of text in front of them. It is critical to support students' understanding that successful word-problem solving requires (a) reading, analyzing, and understanding the problem; (b) representing the problem mathematically to devise a plan; (c) carrying out the plan; and (d) evaluating the reasonableness of the solution or conclusions drawn. Educators have found success designing a mnemonic and providing strategy instruction that consists of their own modeling of the strategy paired with teaching students how to self-monitor their own use of the strategy. Second, teachers provide a clear and concise definition for each problem type (i.e., for additive problems total, change, and difference) and a plethora of examples and non-examples aligned to each problem type. Third, teachers begin providing practice opportunities for students to solve word problems that fit one of the target structures. As students build proficiency, teachers introduce problems fitting the next target structure. Once both structures are proficient, teachers will use the interleaving practice so that students learn to discriminate between the two structures. Last, teachers introduce the last structure followed by more interleaving. For more materials on schema instruction and a free curriculum, please see table 4.1.

Blocked, Interleaving, and Distributed Practice

Student practice is influenced by the structure of the task. Teachers must systematically select items to practice and consider the order of the items for students to practice. This decision-making can impact the benefits of practice and support retention.

- **Blocked practice** consists of students solving multiple items consecutively that are highly structured and similar. For example, the following item sequence would be considered blocked practice of +1: (a) 7 + 1, (b) 8 + 1, (c) 4 + 1, (d) 5 + 1, (e) 6 + 1. Blocked practice is beneficial. First, because the task is controlled and following instruction student success rates will be high, thus students will have a high likelihood of encountering reinforcement from learning. Second, if errors are present, the educator has a clear goal on what needs to be retaught because the practice consisted of one highly structured task of a discrete skill. The drawback to blocked practice is that there will be little transfer to related skills and limited opportunity to engage in deeper conceptual knowledge building because it is one controlled, discrete task.
- **Interleaving practice** consists of students solving items that represent more than one skill (Rohrer et al., 2015). For example, the following item sequence would be considered interleaving practice of +1 and -1: (a) 8 + 1, (b) 6 − 1, (c) 4 − 1, (d) 5 + 1, (e) 9 − 1, (f) 7 + 1. Interleaving practice requires students to stop, analyze the problem, and discriminate between the two or three related skills to select the appropriate procedure. The skills to interleave should be related in some way to maximize the benefits students receive from having to stop, analyze, and discriminate between the two skills to select the appropriate procedure.

- **Distributed practice** consists of breaking up practice time across time. This time can be within day; for example, Schutte et al. (2015) found that multiple short practice sessions on declarative facts throughout the day led to more learning than one practice session of the same time frame. Another useful practice approach is to provide time between when a skill is initially learned until it is practiced again, thus providing space (Willingham, 2002). This spacing of practice across time enhanced retention of knowledge and can support students in drawing connections from new knowledge to previously learned knowledge—particularly if it is paired with interleaving practice.

Assessment within Core Mathematics Instruction

Universal screening is an important feature of rigorous core services that are responsive and preventative. Screening at key benchmarks in the year (e.g., fall, winter, and spring) provides critical information about the distribution of skills within and between classrooms, within and between grade levels, and at the school level. Within the context of a multi-tiered system of supports (MTSS), screening helps identify all students' performance relative to grade-level content, thereby providing an indicator of students who may be at risk of not meeting grade-level expectations by the end of the year. Following screening, these students can be identified for additional follow-up with more targeted measures (i.e., multiple-gated screening; Walker et al., 2014) or immediately routed for more intensive intervention services, depending on the structure of the school's MTSS (e.g., Tiers 2 or 3). Universal screening can also be helpful to core instruction teachers to better understand the relative distribution of skills within their classrooms, providing insight into the need and nature of core instruction differentiation. For example, if universal screening revealed that 40% of a teacher's class performed below expectations (when the normative percentage is 20%), this would indicate that several students in the class may need additional intervention, and this would also indicate that differentiation to meet the needs of all students may be more intensive and differ in nature from a classroom with fewer students performing below expectations within the same school. Although informal formative assessment techniques perform similar functions (e.g., informal data collected by the teacher, locally developed unit tests), school-wide universal screening offers a standardized, responsive, and preventative method for identifying needs relative to both national and local normative patterns (Hall et al., 2022). These different normative comparisons offer several different benchmarks against which data-based decisions can be made, which would promote replicable and equitable intervention-need identification (as compared to solely qualitative and/or anecdotal information, though this information should be considered along with quantitative screening data).

However, screening on its own does not lead to better core instruction. In fact, screening can be a significant waste of time and resources unless it is tied closely to instructional goals and well aligned with key grade-level competencies. Some research suggests that new universal screening data, in light of having prior-year state test scores (as schools would have in grades 4 to 9), may not always be cost-effective (Paly et al., 2022). Collecting data for the sake of having data—not for the purpose of improving and refining instruction—is time that could otherwise be spent on providing more high-quality core instruction. This means that the uses of universal screening data should be determined prior to data collection, including a plan for using the data at macro- (e.g., grade level, school level) and micro-levels (classroom level, individual student level), a system for collecting and managing the data to make it useable, and a clear plan for what happens after students' needs have been determined (requiring well-defined entry and exit criteria for Tier 2+ interventions).

A common issue with MTSS that has gained more attention in recent years is the coordination of core instruction with Tier 2–plus intervention, though most of this work has focused on reading MTSS (Fien et al., 2021; Wanzek et al., 2018). The basic idea of tiered intervention is that any interventions occurring at Tiers 2 or above should supplement and reinforce what occurs at the tiers below and vice-versa. Tier 2 intervention that is not supported by a strong core instruction foundation will likely fail to provide the student with the necessary skills; the Tier 2 intervention may in turn simply compensate for what a student could be receiving in core, which results in net-zero remediation of the original need through Tier 2. This student may appear as "non-responsive" to Tier 2 intervention, and they may be recommended for Tier 3 or other intensive supports. This is not an issue with only Tier 2 instruction; rather, the foundational support and "inoculation" mechanism (Mellard et al., 2010) of core instruction could be inadequate. Universal screening can help identify individual student need and describe the local distributions and patterns of performance to help inform data-based instructional decisions. However, the efficiency and preventative mechanisms of universal screening and the subsequent interventions students receive rely on the foundation of core instruction.

CONCLUSION

Research provides useful information to guide our approach to building high-quality learning environments in mathematics. However, the research base in mathematics is still growing in both breadth and depth; thus, we do not have guidance to draw upon for all the instructional decisions teachers make. For example, what is the exact order in which to introduce addition and subtraction facts? Are their certain mathematical skills that may differentially benefit from a larger focus on conceptual or procedural instruction?

A similar issue is there is no practice that is universally effective. A practice's effectiveness is bounded by the learning context, which involves students' prior learning history, mathematical content being taught, and the teachers' implementation. This is where educators must act as scientific practitioners. They are embedded within the learning community they have created and observe their students' mathematical learning day in and day out. Teachers use their clinical expertise to select the most appropriate practice that is likely to lead to student achievement. Through observation and data collection, teachers can evaluate the effectiveness of their instruction, and this data can inform future decision-making.

Core Instruction to Intervention

Core math instruction provides the essential foundation for building supportive tiered intervention. Typically, about 75 to 80% of students will benefit from high-quality (and well-differentiated) core (Tier 1) instruction on its own. For schools that have the traditional three-tiered MTSS, another 15 to 20% will likely need Tier 2 support, and the remaining approximate 5% may need Tier 3 support. These percentages are not objective figures but have been points of reference in the MTSS literature for years (e.g., Mellard et al., 2010) as a way to balance the strain on the implementation of MTSS and to differentiate intervention need/intensity, consistent with MTSS's public health foundations (Schulte, 2015). Catching a cold does not necessitate an emergency room visit for most people; likewise, struggling with some grade-level expectations does not require the most intensive intervention available. At the same time, it is unreasonable to expect core instruction differentiation to meet every student's needs, though it should meet most.

High-quality tiered intervention in math boils down to similar elements as core instruction: building procedural fluency, connecting procedures and concepts, and promoting students' flexibility in problem solving (Codding et al., 2016). However, the intensity of instruction in each of these areas will depend on the tier. Tier 2 interventions are designed to be less intensive (possibly group-based) and administered a few times a week with regular progress monitoring (e.g., biweekly), and Tier 3 is typically individualized, daily intervention with frequent progress monitoring (e.g., one time per week; Hosp et al., 2016). The goal of tiered intervention is to reinforce the strong foundation of core instruction. Weaknesses in core instruction are likely to show up in students' intervention needs, and tiered intervention that only compensates for insufficient core instruction will not actually help struggling students improve their skills. The entire tiered system needs to be linked across tiers to ensure that the tiered interventions in an MTSS are coordinated with core content. This gets to the idea of "supporting" rather than "supplanting" core instruction with tiered interventions. If a student is struggling with fifth-grade arithmetic expectations (e.g., based on their screening scores), they may receive supplemental, Tier 2 intervention on calculation fluency. However, if those calculation skills are not also being reinforced in core instruction (e.g., through regular calculation skill practice), those skills the student gains in Tier 2 are likely to fade out once the intervention ends. At the same time, just because a student receives Tier 2 intervention does not mean they should not receive their regular, core instruction. The goal of tiered intervention is to *support* students' success in core not to *supplant* core with remedial intervention.

REFERENCES

Atkinson, R. K., Derry, S. J., Renkl, A., & Wortham, D. (2000). Learning from examples: Instructional principles from the worked examples research. *Review of Educational Research*, 70(2), 181–214. https://doi.org/10.3102/00346543070002181

Barrouillet, P., Bernardin, S., Portrat, S., Vergauwe, E., & Camos, V. (2007). Time and cognitive load in working memory. *Journal of Experimental Psychology: Learning, Memory, and Cognition*, 33(3), 570–585. https://psycnet.apa.org/doi/10.1037/0278-7393.33.3.570

Bereiter, C. (1994). Constructivism, socioculturalism, and Popper's world 3. *Educational Researcher*, 23(7), 21–23. https://doi.org/10.3102/0013189X023007021

References

Booth, J. L., & Newton, K. J. (2012). Fractions: Could they really be the gatekeeper's doorman? *Contemporary Educational Psychology*, *37*(4), 247–253. https://doi.org/10.1016/j.cedpsych.2012.07.001

Bouck, E. C., Satsangi, R., & Park, J. (2018). The concrete–representational–abstract approach for students with learning disabilities: An evidence-based practice synthesis. *Remedial and Special Education*, *39*(4), 211–228. https://doi.org/10.1177/0741932517721712

Carbonneau, K. J., Marley, S. C., & Selig, J. P. (2013). A meta-analysis of the efficacy of teaching mathematics with concrete manipulatives. *Journal of Educational Psychology*, *105*(2), 380–400. https://psycnet.apa.org/doi/10.1037/a0031084

Codding, R. S., Volpe, R. J., & Poncy, B. C. (2016). *Effective math interventions: A guide to improving whole-number knowledge*. Guilford Publications.

Crowe, A. R. (2010). "What's math got to do with it?": Numeracy and social studies education. *The Social Studies*, *101*(3), 105–110. https://doi.org/10.1080/00377990903493846

Dowker, A. (2005). Early identification and intervention for students with mathematics difficulties. *Journal of Learning Disabilities*, *38*(4), 324–332. https://doi.org/10.1177/00222194050380040801

Dunn, T. L., & Risko, E. F. (2015). Toward a metacognitive account of cognitive offloading. *Cognitive Science*, *40*(5), 1080–1127. https://doi.org/10.1111/cogs.12273

Every Student Succeeds Act, 20 U.S.C. § 6301 (2015).

Fien, H., Chard, D. J., & Baker, S. K. (2021). Can the evidence revolution and multi-tiered systems of support improve education equity and reading achievement? *Reading Research Quarterly*, *56*, S105–S118. https://doi.org/10.1002/rrq.391

Hall, G. J., Kaplan, D., & Albers, C. A. (2022). Capturing multiple sources of change on triannual math screeners in elementary school. *Learning Disabilities Research & Practice*, *37*(4), 262–279. https://doi.org/10.1111/ldrp.12296

Hosp, M. K., Hosp, J. L., & Howell, K. W. (2016). *The ABCs of CBM: A practical guide to curriculum-based measurement*. Guilford Publications.

Individuals with Disabilities Education Improvement Act, 20 U.S.C. § 1400 (2004).

Jitendra, A. K., & Hoff, K. (1996). The effects of schema-based instruction on the mathematical word-problem-solving performance of students with learning disabilities. *Journal of Learning Disabilities*, *29*(4), 422–431. https://doi.org/10.1177/002221949602900410

Lein, A. E., Jitendra, A. K., & Harwell, M. R. (2020). Effectiveness of mathematical word problem solving interventions for students with learning disabilities and/or mathematics difficulties: A meta-analysis. *Journal of Educational Psychology*, *112*(7), 1388–1408. https://psycnet.apa.org/doi/10.1037/edu0000453

Lovell, O. (2020). *Sweller's cognitive load theory in action*. John Catt Educational Ltd.

Marshall, S. P. (1995). *Schemas in problem solving*. Cambridge University Press.

Mellard, D., McKnight, M., & Jordan, J. (2010). RTI tier structures and instructional intensity. *Learning Disabilities Research & Practice*, *25*(4), 217–225. https://doi.org/10.1111/j.1540-5826.2010.00319.x

Methe, S. A., Hojnoski, R., Clarke, B., Owens, B. B., Lilley, P. K., Politylo, B. C., . . . & Marcotte, A. M. (2011). Innovations and future directions for early numeracy curriculum-based measurement: Commentary on the special series.

Assessment for Effective Intervention, 36(4), 200–209. https://doi.org/10.1177/1534508411414154

Morano, S., Flores, M. M., Hinton, V., & Meyer, J. (2020). A comparison of concrete-representational-abstract and concrete-representational-abstract-integrated fraction interventions for students with disabilities. *Exceptionality*, 28(2), 77–91. https://doi.org/10.1080/09362835.2020.1727328

Myers, J. A., Hughes, E. M., Witzel, B. S., Anderson, R. D., & Owens, J. (2023). A meta-analysis of mathematical interventions for increasing the word problem solving performance of upper elementary and secondary students with mathematics difficulties. *Journal of Research on Educational Effectiveness*, 16(1), 1–35. https://doi.org/10.1080/19345747.2022.2080131

National Council of Teachers of Mathematics (NCTM). (1980). *An agenda for action: Recommendations for school mathematics of the 1980s*. NCTM.

NCTM. (2000). *Principles and standards for school mathematics*. NCTM.

National Governors Association (NGA) Center for Best Practices & Council of Chief State School Officers (CCSSO). (2010). *Common Core state standards for mathematics*. NGA Center for Best Practices & CCSSO.

National Mathematics Advisory Panel. (2008). *Foundations for success: The final report of the national mathematics advisory panel*. US Department of Education.

National Research Council. (2001). *Adding it up: Helping children learn mathematics*. National Academies Press.

Paly, B. J., Klingbeil, D. A., Clemens, N. H., & Osman, D. J. (2022). A cost-effectiveness analysis of four approaches to universal screening for reading risk in upper elementary and middle school. *Journal of School Psychology*, 92, 246–264. https://doi.org/10.1016/j.jsp.2022.03.009

Peltier, C., Morin, K. L., Bouck, E. C., Lingo, M. E., Pulos, J. M., Scheffler, F. A., . . . & Deardorff, M. E. (2020). A meta-analysis of single-case research using mathematics manipulatives with students at risk or identified with a disability. *The Journal of Special Education*, 54(1), 3–15. https://doi.org/10.1177/0022466919844516

Pershan, M. (2021). *Teaching math with examples*. John Catt Educational Ltd.

Powell, S. R., & Fuchs, L. S. (2018). Effective word-problem instruction: Using schemas to facilitate mathematical reasoning. *Teaching Exceptional Children*, 51(1), 31–42. https://doi.org/10.1177/0040059918777250

Rittle-Johnson, B., Loehr, A. M., & Durkin, K. (2017). Promoting self-explanation to improve mathematics learning: A meta-analysis and instructional design principles. *ZDM*, 49, 599–611. https://doi.org/10.1007/s11858-017-0834-z

Rittle-Johnson, B., Schneider, M., & Star, J. R. (2015). Not a one-way street: Bidirectional relations between procedural and conceptual knowledge of mathematics. *Educational Psychology Review*, 27, 587–597. https://doi.org/10.1007/s10648-015-9302-x

Rohrer, D., Dedrick, R. F., & Stershic, S. (2015). Interleaved practice improves mathematics learning. *Journal of Educational Psychology*, 107(3), 900–908. https://psycnet.apa.org/doi/10.1037/edu0000001

Schoenfeld, A. H., & Herrmann, D. J. (1982). Problem perception and knowledge structure in expert and novice mathematical problem solvers. *Journal of Experimental Psychology: Learning, Memory, and Cognition*, 8(5), 484–494. https://psycnet.apa.org/doi/10.1037/0278-7393.8.5.484

Schulte, A. C. (2015). Prevention and response to intervention: Past, present, and future. In S. R. Jimerson, M. K. Burns, & A. VanDerHeyden (Eds.), *Handbook of response to intervention: The science and practice of multi-tiered systems of support* (pp. 59–71). Springer US.

Schutte, G. M., Duhon, G. J., Solomon, B. G., Poncy, B. C., Moore, K., & Story, B. (2015). A comparative analysis of massed vs. distributed practice on basic math fact fluency growth rates. *Journal of School Psychology, 53*(2), 149–159. https://doi.org/10.1016/j.jsp.2014.12.003

Siegler, R. S., Duncan, G. J., Davis-Kean, P. E., Duckworth, K., Claessens, A., Engel, M., . . . & Chen, M. (2012). Early predictors of high school mathematics achievement. *Psychological Science, 23*(7), 691–697. https://doi.org/10.1177/0956797612440101

Star, J. R. (2005). Reconceptualizing procedural knowledge. *Journal for Research in Mathematics Education, 36*(5), 404–411. http://www.jstor.org/stable/30034943

Ten Braak, D., Lenes, R., Purpura, D. J., Schmitt, S. A., & Størksen, I. (2022). Why do early mathematics skills predict later mathematics and reading achievement? The role of executive function. *Journal of Experimental Child Psychology, 214*, 105306. https://doi.org/10.1016/j.jecp.2021.105306

US Department of Education. Institute of Education Sciences, National Center for Education Statistics, & National Assessment of Educational Progress (NAEP). (2022). Mathematics Assessment.

Van Garderen, D. (2007). Teaching students with LD to use diagrams to solve mathematical word problems. *Journal of Learning Disabilities, 40*(6), 540–553. https://doi.org/10.1177/00222194070400060501

von Glasersfeld, E. (1995). A constructivist approach to reaching. In L. Steffe & J. Gale (Eds.), *Constructivism in education* (pp. 3–16). Lawrence Erlbaum Associates.

Walker, H. M., Small, J. W., Severson, H. H., Seeley, J. R., & Feil, E. G. (2014). Multiple-gating approaches in universal screening within school and community settings. In R. J. Kettler, T. A. Glover, C. A. Albers, & K. A. Feeney-Kettler (Eds.), *Universal screening in educational settings: Evidence-based decision making for schools* (pp. 47–75). American Psychological Association. https://doi.org/10.1037/14316-003

Wanzek, J., Stevens, E. A., Williams, K. J., Scammacca, N., Vaughn, S., & Sargent, K. (2018). Current evidence on the effects of intensive early reading interventions. *Journal of Learning Disabilities, 51*(6), 612–624. https://doi.org/10.1177/0022219418775110

Willingham, D. T. (2002). How we learn. Ask the cognitive scientist: Allocating student study time. "Massed" versus "distributed" practice. *American Educator, 26*(2), 37. https://eric.ed.gov/?id=EJ660277

Willingham, D. T. (2017). Ask the cognitive scientist: Do manipulatives help students learn? *American Educator, 41*(3), 25–30. https://www.aft.org/ae/fall2017/willingham

Xin, Y. P. (2008). The effect of schema-based instruction in solving mathematics word problems: An emphasis on prealgebraic conceptualization of multiplicative relations. *Journal for Research in Mathematics Education, 39*(5), 526–551. https://doi.org/10.5951/jresematheduc.39.5.0526

5

Quality Mathematics Intervention for Elementary Students

Corey Peltier and Scott Dueker

DEFINING THE CONTENT AREA

Debates over the "how" and "what" to teach in mathematics have been reoccurring throughout the history of education (Schoenfeld, 2004). A deep dive into the history of this tension is beyond the scope of this chapter, but a critical element that is germane to the current conversation on math intervention is the "mile wide, inch deep" versus "mile deep, inch wide" debate. Mathematics is a rich field to study, with many nooks and crannies to investigate. Yet, each nook and cranny that is investigated requires the allocation of instructional time—which is finite based on our school schedules. This leads to an inevitable decision; educators designing curricular content must prioritize domains of mathematics that have the highest level of social valid from a utility standpoint for students. Luckily, a lot of research can inform this work for educators.

Congress commissioned the director of the National Institute of Child Health and Human Development and the secretary of education to convene a national panel to synthesize the available research on how to support students' reading development. The National Reading Panel (National Institute of Child Health and Human Development [NICHD], 2000) produced a report that has had a major impact on reading instruction and is frequently discussed to this day. What gets far less attention is that an executive order commissioned a national panel with the same goal but with a focus on children's' mathematics learning. The National Mathematics Advisory Panel (2008) released a report with specific guidance on how to promote mathematics proficiency.

A major finding was the structure and ordering of mathematical concepts can support or hinder students' development. At this time, "spiraling" was a common approach used as part of standard development, which in turn dictated curriculum development. Topics would be introduced without a goal for students to develop mastery during this initial presentation because the topic would be reintroduced again at a later point in time. In the report, the committee emphasizes that this should be avoided—topics should be mastered so that subsequent skills can build off this knowledge base. This has major implications for how we view mathematics intervention. Taking the approach of "they will get it next time around" inhibits mathematical learning. Furthermore, another piece of insight from the committee's evaluation is that claims such as "the student is not developmentally ready for this content" are not supported by research. The success of children learning a new skill is contingent on their knowledge of the preskills, not their age.

Another finding was that curriculum and standards need to be condensed to focus on fewer topics. The rationale for this is to ensure that students have more time to engage with fewer concepts to build deeper conceptual and procedural knowledge. The committee emphasizes the need to select pivotal points of knowledge that underly the foundations of algebra. Specifically, the need for students to build procedural fluency and conceptual knowledge of whole numbers, fractions, and specific aspects of geometry and measurement that correlate with success in algebra. This has major implications for mathematics intervention; we must use intervention time to bolster student proficiency in these core domains to set students up for success.

A third finding was that students' prior knowledge of mathematical concepts impacts their development of future knowledge. Specifically, the knowledge of mathematics that children enter kindergarten with has a strong relation to their learning rates throughout elementary, middle, and high school (e.g., Watts et al., 2014). What does this mean for mathematics intervention? Schools must have clear, structured screening procedures in place to identify students that require instructional support to build these foundational skills. The earlier students receive supplemental mathematics intervention the more benefits they will receive from their core instruction. Building preskills provides the requisite knowledge to access the grade level content. The other benefit to system-wide screening is schools can then be attuned to respond to these students if additional support is needed at later time points due to fade-out effects (see Bailey et al., 2016).

A fourth finding was the identification of useful instructional approaches and learning activities educators can use to promote learning. First, computational fluency with whole numbers is necessary for students to build proficiency with fractions. To achieve fluency, students must be automatic with declarative facts; students must have sufficient practice opportunities with standard algorithms; and students must have deep conceptual knowledge of core concepts such as the commutative, distributive, and associative property. For mathematics intervention, this guides decisions about screening, content to include in intervention, and the need to include sufficient, quality instructional practice opportunities. Second, overwhelming evidence supports the use of explicit instruction with students who have mathematical difficulties. Mathematics interventions are typically used to support students that are experiencing mathematics difficulty with grade-level content, thus interventions grounded in explicit instruction will likely be useful. Third, teachers' use of formative assessment data has been beneficial to indicate what content needs to be taught and how to adjust instruction to ensure students' rate of learning is appropriate. Mathematics interventions will benefit from having a robust framework to monitor students across time and gauge students' acquisition of new knowledge during instruction.

Last, building proficiency in mathematics is related to children's motivations, goals, and beliefs about learning mathematics. Learning environments must be created that explicitly show students that mathematics is useful and their effort in learning mathematics is what contributes to their learning. Motivation is a complex construct, but we see some evidence that suggests academic achievement and motivation exist in a bidirectional relation (Liu & Hou, 2018; Vu et al., 2022), which implies that more motivation leads to more success, but *also* that success will enhance motivation. Not all, but many students who will receive mathematics intervention have experienced a learning history that has shaped their perceptions of mathematics and their relation to the subject in a negative light. Thus, mathematics interventions must include components that are responsive to students' perceptions of math, beliefs of themselves as mathematicians, and motivation. Furthermore, designing interventions that affect student achievement will have a positive impact on their motivation—a useful by-product of good instruction. After reading this chapter, you will be able to:

1. Describe theories that inform mathematics intervention for elementary students.
2. Identify key factors that contribute to difficulties in mathematics for students in elementary school.
3. Describe key intervention methods that support learners of elementary mathematics.

Theories Informing Mathematics Intervention for Elementary Students

Within the field of reading intervention, there are a host of theoretical models that have been proposed for what contributes to reading comprehension, some of the popular ones include the (a) simple view of reading (SVR) (Gough & Tunmer, 1986), (b) the componential model of reading (Joshi & Aaron, 2000), and (c) the active view of reading (Duke & Cartwright, 2021). In mathematics, more of the conversation has centered around the time and place of teacher explanation of mathematical concepts.

In some models of instruction, the teacher's role is to design mathematical tasks that have multiple points of entry to ensure that, regardless of students' current mathematical knowledge, they can engage with the task. The teacher's role is to scaffold students' engagement with the task by providing pointed questions or prompts to support student thinking from their prior knowledge and to direct their attention to the critical aspects of the task, which is designed to encompass a new piece of mathematical knowledge. This experience is oftentimes followed by the teacher engaging in explanation, with input from students, to ensure all students gained the knowledge that was intended from the activity. In alternative models, the teacher's role is to have students engage in retrieval practice of previously learned skills that are the essential preskills for the new content. Then, the teacher engages in a back-and-forth dialogue with students to clearly and concisely explain, and/or model, the core attributes of the new skill. This is often followed by time for students to begin engaging in mathematical problem solving of tasks aligned to the new skill; the teacher's role is to provide scaffolded support to ensure accuracy rates are high and errors are minimized. Last, students are provided opportunities to problem solve independently to support acquisition and ensure prompts and supports are faded. The National Mathematics Advisory Panel (2008) emphasizes that students' entire mathematics experience should not be solely situated within one of these instructional models but rather be engaging in strategic usage of each based on students' current knowledge and the goals of the learning environment. Given this chapter is focused on mathematics intervention, we will focus more of our discussion around the later model as this has been found to be a necessary practice as part of mathematics intervention at the elementary age ranges (Fuchs et al., 2021).

In the search for a theoretical framework that may provide a consensus on what mathematics proficiency consists of, the National Research Council's (2001) math rope may be fruitful (see figure 5.1). The five strands included in the rope are (1) adaptive reasoning, (2) conceptual knowledge, (3) procedural knowledge, (4) productive disposition, and (5) strategic competence. The committee makes it explicitly clear that the strands are interwoven; thus, the development of all strands synchronously is what will promote mathematical proficiency. Thus, setting a goal of "teaching" adaptive reasoning around the commutative property of addition is not the right goal. The goal is to provide instruction and to design learning environments that will ensure that students can engage with each element of the strand and have the opportunity to receive feedback on their engagement with the mathematics.

Factors that Contribute to Mathematics Difficulty

Before discussing student-level factors that research suggest correlate with mathematics difficulty, we feel it is prudent to present an ethos to guide instruction. The initial coaches and trainers on the principles of *precision teaching* emphasized that "the child is always right" (Lindsley, 1990). This simple, yet impactful underlying principle emphasizes that student-level responding is consistently a product of the

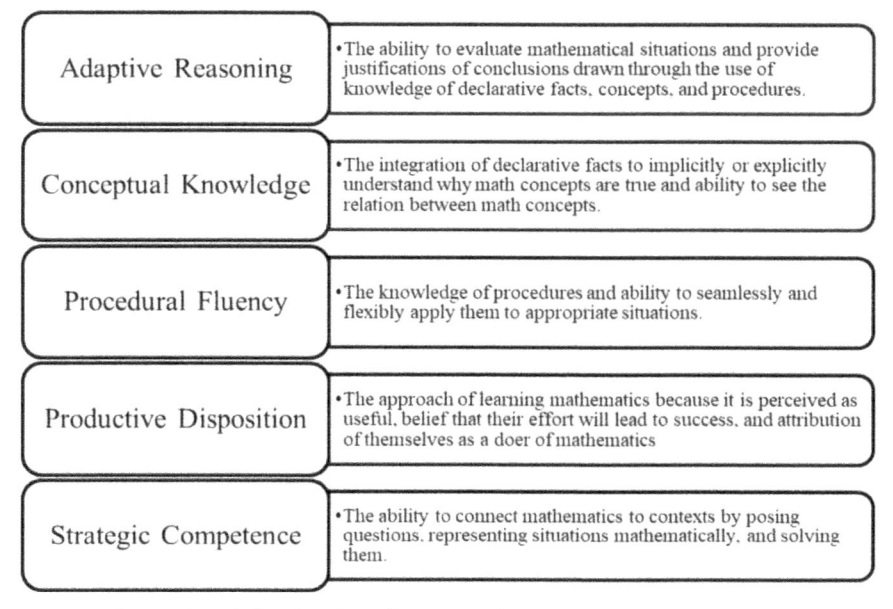

Adaptive Reasoning	• The ability to evaluate mathematical situations and provide justifications of conclusions drawn through the use of knowledge of declarative facts, concepts, and procedures.
Conceptual Knowledge	• The integration of declarative facts to implicitly or explicitly understand why math concepts are true and ability to see the relation between math concepts.
Procedural Fluency	• The knowledge of procedures and ability to seamlessly and flexibly apply them to appropriate situations.
Productive Disposition	• The approach of learning mathematics because it is perceived as useful, belief that their effort will lead to success, and attribution of themselves as a doer of mathematics
Strategic Competence	• The ability to connect mathematics to contexts by posing questions, representing situations mathematically, and solving them.

Figure 5.1. Strands of the National Research Council (2001) Math Rope
Source: Strands of the National Research Council (2001) math rope.

quality of the instructional environment—hence, variables are under the control of the educator. This mindset shifts our attention away from "What student-level factors are impacting their learning?" to "What variables do I need to adjust to ensure adequately learning is achieved for this student?" However, understanding about student-level factors that contribute to mathematics difficulty can enhance our ability to engage in better screening for risk status as well as to design intervention programs that are responsive to these factors.

Before discussing mathematics difficulty, it may be helpful to draw parallels to reading difficulty, given that this area has more awareness in the field and society. The term *dyslexia* has an operation definition; it is a specific learning disability in basic reading skills that leads to behavioral topographies that can be observed by difficulties in text-reading fluency, reading comprehension, spelling, and written expression. In mathematics we have a parallel term, *dyscalculia*. Although competing definitions can be found, we will use a definition that aligns with Von Aster and Shalev (2007); dyscalculia is a specific learning disability in mathematics that impacts a child's ability to learn and engage with number sense, memorization of arithmetic facts, fluent computation, and solving word problems.

The prevalence of students experiencing mathematics difficulty or identified with dyscalculia is difficult to estimate because researchers have used different cut scores for identifying students with the label and have used different instruments to evaluate student mathematical knowledge. L. Yang and colleagues (2022) have provided a recent review of 56 studies that estimates the prevalence of dyscalculia in students ranging from six to 13 years old; their mean estimate is 7.10% (95% confidence interval = 6.27% to 7.97%) of students. Given the operational definition of dyscalculia, this is an underestimate of children who would benefit from supplemental mathematics intervention. Cut scores for dyscalculia, or a mathematics disability, are often set at the 20th percentile rank, yet more children than this may require supplemental instruction to meet grade-level expectations. Furthermore, to be identified with a strictly mathematics-related disability, researchers apply exclusionary factors such as cognitive scores, ruling out co-occurring disabilities (e.g., autism) and ruling out children's native language. Students that may qualify under a different disability category, such as intellectual disability or autism, or who are emergent multilinguals, may require supplemental instruction to meet grade-level expectations. Thus, the actual prevalence of students who may need supplemental mathematics intervention is likely higher than 7%—indicating that we must have high-quality mathematics intervention frameworks in place in schools.

One factor that educators should be aware of is the relation between reading difficulty and mathematics difficulty. Joyner and Wagner (2020) have evaluated 36 studies that compare student reading and mathematics achievement, and they reported that students identified with dyscalculia were more than two times more likely (weighted odds ratio = 2.12, 95% confidence interval = 1.76 to 2.55) to also be identified with dyslexia. This has major implications on two fronts for teachers. As part of a school's MTSS, it is critical to ensure that screening occurs across both reading and mathematics, and a student identified with a reading risk should be monitored a little closer for the increased likelihood of also displaying a mathematics risk. Second, from an intervention standpoint, knowing students with a mathematics difficulty are at an increased risk of reading difficulty may impact instructional practice. A focus on bolstering vocabulary and language building is critical and when engaging in word-problem solving, or other denser language-dependent tasks, educators must ensure that students can access the text to allow them to engage in mathematics.

These shared risk factors have been investigated through research. Phonological awareness, rapid automatized naming, and phonological memory all correlate with reading development but also predict mathematics achievement, with the stronger prediction to fundamental mathematics skills, like declarative fact proficiency and computational tasks (X. Yang et al., 2022). We also see that vocabulary knowledge and oral language comprehension play a role in mathematics achievement, but these have stronger prediction to higher-level mathematics tasks, with one example being word-problem solving (Peng et al., 2020). Across these measures, we see students with math difficulty score lower than students with average levels of mathematics achievement, and students with both reading and mathematics achievement score lower than students with just math or reading difficulty.

A final cognitive factor that is worth mentioning is working memory. Students with math difficulties displayed lower numerical working memory performance compared to students with average levels of mathematics achievement (Peng et al., 2016). This is noteworthy as we think about intervention design. This may indicate that students with mathematics difficulties will be even more sensitive to instructional learning environments that do not consider extraneous cognitive load because their working memory performance with numbers is weaker compared to typically developing students.

Key Intervention Methods for Elementary Mathematics

The National Center for Education Evaluation and Regional Assistance at the Institute of Education Sciences convened a multidisciplinary team of experts to evaluate research that can inform mathematics intervention at the elementary grades (Fuchs et al., 2021). The team recommended six instructional practices educators should consider including in a mathematics intervention framework (see table 5.1). We will focus this section on systematic instruction, mathematical language, and assessment procedures that are beneficial to intensive intervention frameworks. Interested readers are encouraged to access the free practice guide on intensive intervention that fully explains all six recommendations (see Fuchs et al., 2021).

Provide Systematic Instruction and Mathematics Vocabulary

The first recommendation is to ensure the instruction is systematic both within a lesson and across a unit of study. The sequence of instruction is one foundational element. Ideally, the scope and sequence for the core mathematics program is built logically—meaning, skills build upon one another in a logical fashion. Educators can consult a vertical alignment document that will demonstrate how one skill develops across time and use it to backward-map how previous grade-level standards serve as the preskills for the current standard. Interested educators may consider the coherence map provided by Achieve the Core, although it is aligned to the Common Core State Standards, which some states have not adopted (https://achievethecore.org/page/1118/coherence-map). One clear example of this would be learning how to apply concepts of addition. First, students will master sums to 18. Then, students will master two-digit by two-digit addition problems without regrouping. As we

Table 5.1. Six Core Features of Mathematics Intervention

Feature	Evidence	Description	Keys to Implementation
Systematic Instruction	32 studies met WWC 11 studies met WWC with reservations	Systematic instruction includes building off students' prior knowledge through sequenced topics that are chunked incrementally across time to achieve a goal.	• Review prior knowledge and integrate prior knowledge with new knowledge. • For conceptual knowledge building, use numbers or computational demands students are fluent with so they can allocate working memory toward new concepts. • Order the presentation of new math topics in an incremental and logical way. • Use verbal and visual supports to scaffold students toward. • Provide immediate feedback on students' math thinking in a supportive manner.
Mathematical Language	12 studies met WWC Four studies met WWC with reservations	The use of clear, concise, and accurate math language during instruction and the support of students' development in their application of this as well.	• Frequently teach mathematical vocabulary and link this vocabulary to mathematical concepts and procedures. • Teachers use clear, concise, and accurate language when communicating mathematical ideas. Repeating language frequently during instructional time will enhance student exposures. • Provide opportunities for students to communicate their mathematical thinking through verbal and written explanations. Provide feedback to support student's use of accurate mathematical vocabulary.
Representations	19 studies met WWC Nine Studies met WWC with reservations	The use of representations such as manipulatives or pictorial representations, to build conceptual and procedural knowledge.	• Use manipulatives and pictorial representations that can effectively serve as a representation for the abstract concept or procedure being taught. • Explicitly connect the representation to the abstract concept or procedure being taught. • Ensure students have the opportunity to use the representations when engaging with mathematical tasks. • Revisit the representations at later time points so students can deepen their understanding of the abstract concepts and procedures.

Number Lines	11 studies met WWC Three studies met WWC with reservations	Teachers incorporate number lines as a specific type of representation when learning concepts and procedures.	• Design learning opportunities to represent whole numbers, fractions, and decimals on number lines, displayed both vertically and horizontally. • Design learning opportunities to compare numbers on number lines and determine their relative magnitude on number lines. • Use number lines during learning opportunities to build students' conceptual and procedural knowledge of concepts underlying operations.
Word Problems	15 studies met WWC Three studies met WWC with reservations	Teachers allocate instructional time to solving word problems with a focus on building conceptual and procedural knowledge and the application of mathematical ideas.	• Teach students to identify word problem types by focusing on the underlying structure of the situation. • Teach students solution methods for each type of word problem structure. • Teach students to identify relevant information to solve word problems by varying features of the word problem. • Provide instruction on vocabulary and language relevant to each type of word problem structure.
Timed Activities	21 studies met WWC Six studies met WWC with reservations	Teachers use timed practice activities on math concepts in which students have adequate understanding but need to enhance their fluency in. Teachers should ensure feedback and goal setting are included when using this practice.	• Select math content that is known but in need of fluency building. • Design learning activities to use timed practice and ensure clear expectations are set before their use. • Ensure students have a strategy to use to answer each item. • Use self-monitoring, self-evaluation, and self-graphing to reinforce learning and boost motivation. • Provide immediate feedback following practice and have students correct errors.

Note: WWC = What Works Clearinghouse Group Design Standards (Version 4.0).

can see, the mastery of sums to 18 is an essential preskill to this new skill, also with the new focus on the place value system. Then, students will master two-digit by two-digit addition problems with regrouping. It is evident that sums to 18 and two-digit by two-digit knowledge is necessary for this new skill, with composing and decomposing within our base ten system as the new bit of knowledge being learned. Sequencing of math concepts in this logical order is extremely beneficial because (1) it ensures that preskills are mastered by students to find success in the new learning, and (2) it allows for deeper conceptual and procedural knowledge building because the connection between related concepts is made more explicit.

Have you ever been in a situation where students have forgotten a concept that you know for a fact you had taught them and that they did show knowledge of at a previous point in time? This is a natural outcome of forgetting, and we all do it with all sorts of knowledge! When it comes to mathematics, this can inhibit student access to not only core instruction but also intervention because that prior knowledge is necessary to access future learning. One way to ameliorate the likelihood of forgetting to occur is to systematically space out retrieval practice opportunities. For example, an educator is beginning to start a unit on adding and subtracting fractions with unlike denominators. The educator knows that two core skills that were previously taught are essential to this skill: (a) adding fractions with like denominators and (b) finding equivalent fractions. By carefully spacing out brief opportunities at the beginning of intervention sessions to practice these skills before the unit on adding and subtracting fractions with unlike denominators, students are strengthening their knowledge of these skills, reducing the likelihood that they will be forgotten from their long-term memory, and are ultimately better able to connect how these preskills relate to the new knowledge of adding and subtracting fractions with unlike denominators. These brief review periods at the beginning of intervention sessions can be in the form of blocked practice (i.e., all the same skill) or interleaving practice (i.e., alteration between two related skills), but the core goal is that pivotal skills are being practiced at a time that is spaced out from when they were initially taught and will be useful preskills for a skill that will be taught in the near future.

Two foundational elements for instruction to be systematic within a lesson are the scaffolds provided during initial learning and the feedback students receive as they engage in mathematical thinking. A critical element to emphasize is the influential role language plays in students' mathematical development (Peng et al., 2020). An extremely beneficial activity for educators to engage in is identifying the core mathematical vocabulary that is introduced at each grade span. Educators can engage in cross-level meetings to ensure vocabulary usage and definitions are cohesive across teachers working at each grade level; this consistency will ensure students can acquire and build proficiency in the accurate use of mathematical vocabulary (see Nelson et al., 2020). This will support interventionists that provide vocabulary instruction on terms at and below grade level; the terms and definitions will be consistent across environments the student will be learning in. Interventionists will also want to pre-teach vocabulary prior to a unit being taught in the core instruction environment as a scaffold to support student access to new concepts.

A second consideration is the ways visual and verbal supports can be systematically used during initial learning of new skills and withdrawn as students build proficiency to ensure students do not remain prompt dependent. There are a host of ways visual supports can be used, such as manipulatives or pictorial representations when included in the concrete-representational-abstract instructional framework (see chapter 4 for a deeper description), number lines, graphic organizers when aiming to build connections between related concepts, and mnemonics to cue strategy usage. Verbal prompts can be carefully designed questions or directions teachers may provide when students are engaging in mathematical thinking (see figure 5.2 for an example). Related to the scaffolding of supports is the need for immediate, supportive feedback. Feedback is an integral aspect of how we learn about the world and the feedback can be explicit or implicit. For example, if I attempt to fix my audio on a video call and the audio begins working, that serves as a form of feedback that my action led to the correct outcome. If a child touches a stove that has just been used and gets burned, this is a form of feedback—albeit a painful one—that they made an incorrect decision. In learning academic content, the same is true; we need clear and concise feedback in order to reorient our knowledge of what is or is not correct. Oftentimes, feedback delivery is unambiguous for the educator.

1. Analyze This			2. Answer These	
+	3 2	4 3	A.	Why is the 3 in 23 placed below the 4 in 34?
		7	B.	What place value did they add first?
			C.	What is the value of the 5 in the sum?
+	3 2 5	4 3 7		
3. Analyze This			4. Answer These	
+	1 4 1	7 8 5	A.	Why is the 1 in 18 placed below the 4 in 47?
			B.	What place value did they add first?
			C.	Why did they put a 1 above the 4?
+	1 4 1 6	7 8 5	D.	What is the value of 6 in the sum?
			E.	Look back at problem 1. What extra step was required in problem 2? Why was this step required?
5. Try This				
+	5 3	1 7		
6. Try This				
+	3 4	8 9		

Figure 5.2. Worked Example Using Visual and Verbal Supports
Source: Created by Corey Peltier.

For example, declarative fact feedback is a relatively straightforward process. Consider this example,

>   TEACHER: Hi Johnny, let's practice naming our numbers today. I am going to show you a card and ask you to name the number you see. Can you do that?
>
>   STUDENT: Yes!
>
>   TEACHER: Excellent. (Teacher holds up a flashcard with "5" on it.)
>
>   STUDENT: Four.
>
>   TEACHER: Oh, nice try. (Teacher points at number.) This is five. What number is this?
>
>   STUDENT: Five.
>
>   TEACHER: Excellent work. (Teacher shows flashcard with "1" on it.) What number is this?
>
>   STUDENT: One.
>
>   TEACHER: Excellent work. (Teacher shows flashcard with "5" on it.) What number is this?
>
>   STUDENT: Five.
>
>   TEACHER: Great job, that is five.

This scenario shows a simple error correction procedure. When the error was made, notice that the teacher was kind but crystal clear that the response was incorrect. The teacher modeled the correct response and immediately provided the student the opportunity to correct their response, thus allowing for a correct response. Then, the teacher shifted to an item that is already known, 1, before going back to the item that was incorrect. This allows for another learning trial on the item that was initially incorrect.

When students are engaging in mathematical tasks that are chained skills, such as computational tasks, or applied problem solving, such as word-problem solving, merely providing feedback as correct versus incorrect is insufficient for student learning. Feedback must be specific to where the misconception or error occurred in the problem-solving process. This feedback may need to be more elaborate through a back-and-forth dialogue with the student to identify where the misconception lies and to provide an explanation and/or demonstration of the concept. It is important though to follow up this explanation with another chance for the student to engage in a similar task to correctly apply this knowledge.

Data-Informed Screening

To support students who would benefit from additional mathematics instruction, schools must have system-wide processes in place to identify the correct students. This is the role of universal screening. The role of screening is to address the following question, "Which students may be at risk for not meeting important end-of-year goals?" Typically, it is advised to screen all students three to four times during the year (e.g., fall, winter, spring; or at the beginning of each quarter). One seemingly less obvious bit of advice that sometimes gets overlooked: do not screen right after a long break from school. For example, do not screen the first week of school or the first week back from winter break. Poorly timed screening may result in students being identified as at risk when they are not.

Two features of a screener that schools must consider are the sensitivity and specificity. For screening, sensitivity provides information on how accurate the screener functions to identify students at risk who are truly at risk for not meeting important end-of-year goals. Did the screener identify all the students at risk who are truly at risk for not meeting end-of-year goals? For screening, specificity provides information on how accurate the screener functions in the identification of students that are not at risk. Did the screener identify all students not at risk who are truly not at risk? Screeners that have poor sensitivity will lead to schools missing out on identifying children who require supplemental math instruction to meet end-of-year goals. Screeners that have poor specificity will lead to schools over-identifying children in need of supplemental math instruction, which in turn can detract from the benefits of intervention for the children who do need supplemental instruction. See figure 5.3 for a visual that outlines these properties of screeners.

For preschool through first-grade students, four measures have been investigated extensively for screening type decisions and provide substantial evidence that they can be useful (Nelson et al., 2023). The first measure is oral counting and consists of a teacher telling a student to start at 1 and count as high as they can. The teacher scores how many correct counting sequences a student can say within one minute. The second measure is number identification. The teacher presents a sheet that will randomly display numbers, usually 0 through 20, and the student is asked to point and say the name of each number. The teacher scores how many correct numbers the student identifies in a minute. The third measure is missing number. The teacher presents a sheet with a bunch of items, such as (a) 5, __, 7; (b) __, 8, 9; and (c) 11, 12, __, and the student is asked to say what number would complete the number sequence. Usually, the sheet is restricted to numbers 0 to 20 and includes number sequences of three, although some sheets may include a sequence of four numbers. The teacher scores how many correct missing numbers the student can provide in one minute. The fourth measure is quantity discrimination. The teacher presents a sheet that presents a bunch of items, such as (a) 12, 8; (b) 7, 14; and (c) 5, 2, and the student is asked to identify the greater quantity. Usually, the sheet is restricted to numbers 0 to 20. The teacher scores how many correct responses the student can provide in one minute.

For students in the second through fifth grades, the two most researched types of screeners include computation-based, curriculum-based measures and concepts and application-based, curriculum-based measures (Nelson et al., 2023). Concepts and application curriculum-based measures are created by sampling items that reflect the core aspects of mathematics that are taught at that grade level. Students are instructed to do their best math and given a time frame to complete the assessment, usually around six minutes depending on the grade level and directions from the publisher of the instrument. Teachers score how many correct responses the student provides. Math computation curriculum-based measures have more nuance in their application (Christ et al., 2008; Nelson et al., 2023). One route that educators may take is to create a measure that isolates a specific skill, for example, sums to

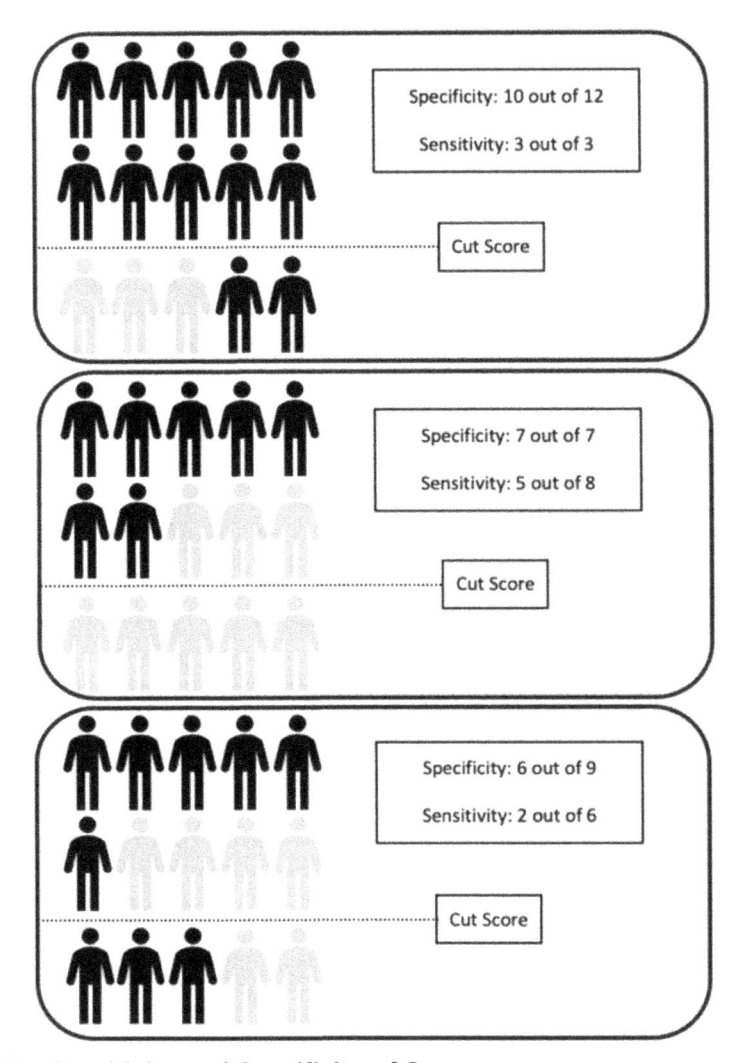

Figure 5.3. Sensitivity and Specificity of Screeners
Source: Created by Corey Peltier.

18 or two-digit by two-digit addition without regrouping. Another route educators may take is to build a multiskill measure, for example, sums to 18 and subtraction with a maximum minuend of 18 or two-digit by two-digit addition and subtraction without regrouping. In both examples provided, there are two skills included, but the curriculum-based measure could include more, such as two-digit by two-digit addition and subtraction with and without regrouping (four skills). Regardless of the structure, educators will score the number of correct digits provided per minute. For example, if the item is 23 + 34 and a student provides 47, this is scored as two correct digits, whereas a student providing 46 would score one correct digit. What will be altered is the time limit educators provide for students to answer items. For single-skill measures, two-minutes is likely long enough to get a sufficient sample

of student performance for decision-making, whereas multiskill or more complex computational tasks (e.g., multidigit multiplication or division) may require longer time frames (e.g., four minutes or more).

One additional factor for educators to consider as part of their screening procedures is the disposition students bring to the screening task. If students attempt the task without their full effort or attention, scores will provide inaccurate estimates of their knowledge and may potentially lead to over-identifying students in need of supplemental math instruction who do not need it, thus poor sensitivity. One potential way to ameliorate these concerns is through a "can't do/won't do" assessment (VanDerHeyden & Witt, 2008). In a can't do/won't do framework, the educator will start by sharing the student's prior score on the screening measure and tell them that if they beat their previous score, they can access a backup reinforcer. It is important to select backup reinforcers the student wants access to so that their effort when completing the screening measure will be high. The goal is to identify if the student's low math performance was a product of a skill need—meaning, they do not have the current knowledge to perform the skill—or a performance need—meaning, they did not perform to their maximum potential on the first screening. Thus, if the student's score on the second screening is close to their initial score, then we assume it is reflective of their true knowledge and they have a skill-based need and would benefit from intervention. However, if the student's score on the second screening is much higher, then we assume the initial screening data were not a true reflection of the student's knowledge but rather a reflection of low motivation. This would indicate that educators must consider how to enhance motivation for the student when engaging with mathematics and particularly when collecting data via assessments. The benefit of the can't do/won't do framework is that it is simple to use and can help ensure that we are correctly identifying students in need of skill building via supplemental math instruction versus not.

Data-Informed Progress Monitoring

A second assessment activity that schools must engage in is determining if the supplemental instruction is providing benefits from the students receiving it. This is the role of using a system-wide progress-monitoring framework. The role of progress monitoring is to address the following question, "Is this student making adequate progress to meet important end-of-year goals?" Typically, all students receiving supplemental math instruction (e.g., Tiers 2 and 3) will be progress monitored, although if resources are available, it is beneficial to progress monitor students who scored right above the cut score and are only receiving core instruction. The frequency of collecting progress-monitoring data will be dependent on the instrument used; however, we caution educators that more frequent data collection protects against waiting too long to adjust ineffective interventions and, theoretically, each progress-monitoring measure also serves as a form of retrieval practice for the students. One element that can be overlooked but impacts the usefulness of progress-monitoring data is the context in which they are collected. Educators who attempt to standardize, or maintain the consistency of, as many environmental factors as possible while collecting progress-monitoring data will reduce the amount of error in the data. For example, by fluctuating the time that data is collected (e.g., morning, after lunch), the person administering the curriculum-based measure (e.g., interventionist, paraeducator), or the setting in which students complete the measure (e.g., one-on-one in a separate room versus a small group in back of a general education classroom), educators may be allowing student data to be altered and to reflect changes in variables rather than the students' actual knowledge.

When progress monitoring, schools must consider how receptive the measurement tool is to pick up learning in a short amount of time. Because data are being frequently collected across time, the evaluation of progress monitoring data is centered around evaluating a student's trend and whether this will allow a student to meet the end-of-year goal that is set. The challenge that arises is when expected growth on a curriculum-based measure is small on a week-to-week basis because it requires weeks of data collection before an accurate trend can be established to allow for decision-making.

For preschool through first-grade students, the same four measures of oral counting, number identification, quantity discrimination, and missing number were investigated most frequently (Nelson et al., 2023). Oral counting and number identification had larger slope estimates compared to missing number and quantity discrimination, which would suggest these measures may be more sensitive to identifying student learning in short time spans.

For second- through fifth-grade students, Nelson and colleagues (2023) identified that no studies included in their review evaluated the trend of concepts and application curriculum-based measures. However, a prior review conducted by Foegen and colleagues (2007) found three studies that evaluated slope estimates for concepts and application curriculum-based measures, with week-to-week slope estimates ranging from 0.12 to 0.38 new problems solved correctly. For computation-based, curriculum-based measures the slope estimates were larger, which suggests these measures may provide more precision in identifying student growth in short time frames. For measures that focused on the four operations, average week-to-week slope estimates were 2.55 digits correct per minute. However, it is worth noting that Solomon and colleagues (2020) evaluated student-growth rates when receiving intervention, which may be useful as part of tiered intervention decision-making. The authors estimated that the growth rate on addition/subtraction was 2.21 new correct digits per minute for each 15 minutes of intervention received. For multiplication/division, the authors estimated a growth rate of 4.63 new digits correct per minute for each 15 minutes of intervention received. However, these estimates varied based on how many new facts students were learning (i.e., smaller set size led to larger growth) and student initial performance (i.e., higher initial performance led to more growth). One important finding from Nelson and colleagues (2023) was that scoring digits correct per minute led to a more sensitive evaluation of student growth compared to only scoring problems correct.

When deciding on a progress-monitoring approach for computation-based, curriculum-based measures, educators must decide on the framework they aim to use. One approach is to use an instrument that samples all of the computation-based items students are expected to learn that year. This creates a multiskill probe sheet and provides an overall estimate of student performance across all computation-based skills and can track progress throughout the entire year. The limitation here is educators will likely need to provide a longer time frame for students to complete the probe sheet to gather a larger sample of student performance, and educators will lose information on student performance in individual skills. For example, identifying whether a student is building fluency in multiplication facts will be lost because the score gathered from the instrument tool represents performance across a multitude of skills. The other option educators can take is to focus on single-skill progress monitoring through a mastery measurement approach (VanDerHeyden et al., 2022). In this approach, educators will select a curriculum-based measurement tool that isolates an individual skill. The educator will progress monitor this skill until the mastery criteria is met and then jump to the next skill. See figure 5.4

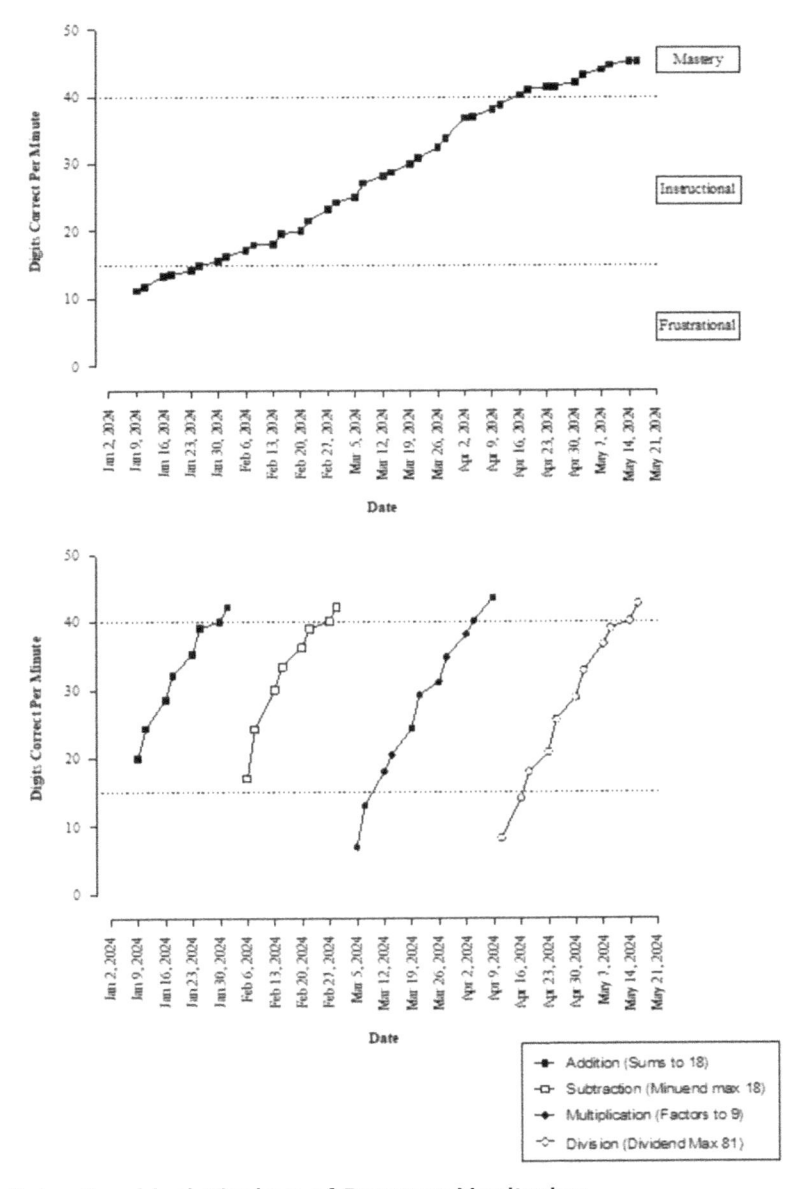

Figure 5.4. Graphical Displays of Progress Monitoring
Source: Created by Corey Peltier.

for examples of both approaches. We do caution educators that these two frameworks do not have to compete. Educators may opt to use the single-skill framework as their primary mode of progress monitoring but systematically use the multiskill curriculum-based measurement tool with longer time lags (i.e., once every two weeks) to see if the growth is observed on the more generalizable measurement tool that comprises all computation skills for that grade span. The major goal is if the observed student slope is not adequate to meet the mastery criteria by the end of the year, then educators must adjust the intervention—for example, enhancing practice trials, reducing set size, and embedding additional motivation components—and evaluate whether these adjustments support student learning rates.

CONCLUSION

There must be a sense of urgency around mathematics intervention. Table 5.2 includes information on additional resources for such intervention. Children's early mathematics knowledge influences their learning rates during core instruction. Thus, early intervention to build foundational skills allows the core instruction to become more fruitful for students. As part of mathematics intervention frameworks,

Table 5.2. Additional Resources for Mathematics Intervention

What's Inside	How to Access
The What Works Clearinghouse conducts syntheses of research to provide practice guides for educators to use to inform various aspects of education. There are several practice guides focused on teaching math to specific age groups and with specific mathematical concepts (e.g., algebra, fractions).	https://ies.ed.gov/ncee/wwc/practiceguides
Online course that consists of eight modules on how to build intensive intervention in mathematics.	https://intensiveintervention.org/training/course-content/intensive-intervention-mathematics
The National Center on Intensive Intervention evaluates intervention research and psychometric evidence for screeners and progress-monitoring measures in mathematics.	https://intensiveintervention.org/tools-charts/overview
Infographics, podcast recordings, and other materials to support educators' knowledge of research evidence around mathematics instruction.	https://www.thescienceofmath.com/
Full intervention curriculum focused on building student proficiency in additive word problem-solving.	https://www.piratemathequationquest.com/
Full assessment and intervention materials to build fluency in math facts and computation.	https://brianponcy.wixsite.com/mind/copy-of-mind-facts-on-fire
If you enjoyed this chapter, I (Corey Peltier) have a free substacks blog with other writings on more specific aspects of math instruction and intervention.	https://coreypeltier.substack.com/

assessment and instruction both need to be implemented well. Poor screening can lead to the wrong students receiving intervention, and poor progress monitoring makes it impossible to identify whether interventions are supporting students' learning. Conversely, excellent screening and progress monitoring is a waste of time if high-quality supplemental math instruction is not provided. Amanda VanDerHeyden has used the metaphor that continually weighing a pig will not increase its weight; continually assessing students will not enhance learning devoid of high-quality intervention.

REFERENCES

Bailey, D. H., Nguyen, T., Jenkins, J. M., Domina, T., Clements, D. H., & Sarama, J. S. (2016). Fadeout in an early mathematics intervention: Constraining content or preexisting differences? *Developmental Psychology*, 52(9), 1457–1469. https://doi.org/10.1037/dev0000188

Christ, T. J., Scullin, S., Tolbize, A., & Jiban, C. L. (2008). Implications of recent research: Curriculum-based measurement of math computation. *Assessment for Effective Intervention*, 33(4), 198–205. https://doi.org/10.1177/1534508407313480

Duke, N. K., & Cartwright, K. B. (2021). The science of reading progresses: Communicating advances beyond the simple view of reading. *Reading Research Quarterly*, 56, S25–S44. https://doi.org/10.1002/rrq.411

Foegen, A., Jiban, C., & Deno, S. (2007). Progress monitoring measures in mathematics: A review of the literature. *The Journal of Special Education*, 41(2), 121–139. https://doi.org/10.1177/00224669070410020101

Fuchs, L. S., Newman-Gonchar, R., Schumacher, R., Dougherty, B., Bucka, N., Karp, K. S., Woodward, J., Clarke, B., Jordan, N. C., Gersten, R., Jayanthi, M., Keating, B., & Morgan, S. (2021). *Assisting students struggling with mathematics: Intervention in the elementary grades* (WWC 2021006). National Center for Education Evaluation and Regional Assistance (NCEE), Institute of Education Sciences, US Department of Education. https://ies.ed.gov/ncee/WWC/PracticeGuide/26

Gough, P. B., & Tunmer, W. E. (1986). Decoding, reading, and reading disability. *Remedial and Special Education*, 7(1), 6–10. https://doi.org/10.1177/074193258600700104

Joshi, R. M., & Aaron, P. G. (2000). The component model of reading: Simple view of reading made a little more complex. *Reading Psychology*, 21(2), 85–97. https://psycnet.apa.org/doi/10.1080/02702710050084428

Joyner, R. E., & Wagner, R. K. (2020). Co-occurrence of reading disabilities and math disabilities: a meta-analysis. *Scientific Studies of Reading*, 24(1), 14–22. https://doi.org/10.1080/10888438.2019.1593420

Lindsley, O. R. (1990). Precision teaching: By teachers for children. *Teaching Exceptional Children*, 22(3), 10–15. https://doi.org/10.1177/004005999002200302

Liu, Y., & Hou, S. (2018). Potential reciprocal relationship between motivation and achievement: A longitudinal study. *School Psychology International*, 39(1), 38–55. https://doi.org/10.1177/0143034317710574

National Institute of Child Health and Human Development (NICHD). (2000). *Report of the National Reading Panel. Teaching children to read: An evidence-based assessment of the scientific research literature on reading and its implications for reading instruction: Reports of the subgroups* (NIH Publication No. 00-4754). https://www.nichd.nih.gov/sites/default/files/publications/pubs/nrp/Documents/report.pdf

National Mathematics Advisory Panel. (2008). *Foundations for success: The final report of the national mathematics advisory panel*. US Department of Education. https://files.eric.ed.gov/fulltext/ED500486.pdf

National Research Council. (2001). *Adding it up: Helping children learn mathematics*. J. Kilpatrick, J. Swafford, & B. Findell (Eds.). Mathematics Learning Study Committee, Center for Education, Division of Behavioral and Social Sciences and Education. National Academy Press. https://nap.nationalacademies.org/catalog/9822/adding-it-up-helping-children-learn-mathematics

Nelson, G., Hughes Pfannenstiel, K., & Zumeta Edmonds, R. (2020). Examining the alignment of mathematics instructional practices and mathematics vocabulary between core and intervention materials. *Learning Disabilities Research & Practice*, 35(1), 14–24. https://doi.org/10.1111/ldrp.12210

Nelson, G., Kiss, A. J., Codding, R. S., McKevett, N. M., Schmitt, J. F., Park, S., . . . & Hwang, J. (2023). Review of curriculum-based measurement in mathematics: An update and extension of the literature. *Journal of School Psychology*, 97, 1–42. https://doi.org/10.1016/j.jsp.2022.12.001

Peng, P., Lin, X., Ünal, Z. E., Lee, K., Namkung, J., Chow, J., & Sales, A. (2020). Examining the mutual relations between language and mathematics: A meta-analysis. *Psychological Bulletin*, 146(7), 595–634. https://psycnet.apa.org/doi/10.1037/bul0000231

Peng, P., Namkung, J., Barnes, M., & Sun, C. (2016). A meta-analysis of mathematics and working memory: Moderating effects of working memory domain, type of mathematics skill, and sample characteristics. *Journal of Educational Psychology*, 108(4), 455–473. https://psycnet.apa.org/doi/10.1037/edu0000079

Schoenfeld, A. H. (2004). The math wars. *Educational Policy*, 18(1), 253–286. https://doi.org/10.1177/0895904803260042

Solomon, B. G., Poncy, B. C., Battista, C., & Campaña, K. V. (2020). A review of common rates of improvement when implementing whole-number operation math interventions. *School Psychology*, 35(5), 353–362. https://psycnet.apa.org/doi/10.1037/spq0000360

VanDeryHeyden, A. M., & Witt, J. C. (2008). Best practices in can't do/won't do assessment. In A. Thomas & J. Grimes (Eds.), *Best practices in school psychology* (5th ed., pp. 131–140). National Association of School Psychologists. http://www.joewitt.org/Downloads/VanDerHeydenBP.pdf

VanDerHeyden, A. M., Burns, M., Peltier, C., & Codding, R. S. (2022). The science of math: The importance of mastery measures and the quest for the general outcome measure. *Communiqué*, 50(5), 28–30. https://eric.ed.gov/?id=EJ1322824

Von Aster, M. G., & Shalev, R. S. (2007). Number development and developmental dyscalculia. *Developmental Medicine & Child Neurology*, 49(11), 868–873. https://doi.org/10.1111/j.1469-8749.2007.00868.x

Vu, T., Magis-Weinberg, L., Jansen, B. R., van Atteveldt, N., Janssen, T. W., Lee, N. C., . . . & Meeter, M. (2022). Motivation-achievement cycles in learning: A literature review and research agenda. *Educational Psychology Review*, 34(1), 39–71. https://doi.org/10.1007/s10648-021-09616-7

Watts, T. W., Duncan, G. J., Siegler, R. S., & Davis-Kean, P. E. (2014). What's past is prologue: Relations between early mathematics knowledge and high school achievement. *Educational Researcher*, *43*(7), 352–360. https://doi.org/10.3102/0013189X14553660

Yang, L., Li, C., Li, X., Zhai, M., An, Q., Zhang, Y., . . . & Weng, X. (2022). Prevalence of developmental dyslexia in primary school children: A systematic review and meta-analysis. *Brain Sciences*, *12*(2), 240. https://doi.org/10.3390/brainsci12020240

Yang, X., Yan, M., Ruan, Y., Ku, S. Y. Y., Lo, J. C. M., Peng, P., & McBride, C. (2022). Relations among phonological processing skills and mathematics in children: A meta-analysis. *Journal of Educational Psychology*, *114*(2), 289–307. https://psycnet.apa.org/doi/10.1037/edu0000710

6

Quality Writing Instruction for Students in the Elementary Grades

Alyson A. Collins, Hope Rigby-Wills, and Stephen Ciullo

WRITING INSTRUCTION: LEARNING TO WRITE AND WRITING TO LEARN

Teaching students to write is one of the most essential roles that an elementary school teacher will play. By becoming a proficient writer, students can demonstrate their learning, engage with others through writing (e.g., chatting with friends on social media), or write to convey their emotions and opinions (Graham, 2019). Effective writing instruction in grades K–5 is necessary to build a solid foundation for future success in writing that will be critical throughout students' lives. For instance, writing remains a predominant method for assessing content learning across all subject matters in both K–12 classrooms as well as college-level settings (Graham & Hebert, 2010). Moreover, long-term life implications rest on the ability to craft coherent and thoughtful written products, such as critical decisions about college admission and scholarships that are often based on essays submitted as part of the application process (Early & DeCosta-Smith, 2011). Beyond traditional educational settings, employment decisions for hiring as well as future promotions may hinge on an employee's ability to write accurately and proficiently (Applebee & Langer, 2015). Ultimately, writing remains the primary method of communication for academic pursuits, advancement in the work force, and communication in daily life (e.g., text-messaging, email, social media). Therefore, it is important that all students receive quality writing instruction beginning in kindergarten.

Foundational Learning Theory: Writer(s)-Within-Community Model

The teaching strategies included in this chapter are consistent with a comprehensive theory about how students learn to write. This learning theory, the revised writer(s)-within-community (WWC) model (Graham, 2019), asserts that different writing communities (e.g., classrooms, groups of friends with common interests) continually shape what types of writing occur within a given community (e.g., classrooms). For instance, the writing activities within a book club about fictional scary stories would vary considerably from the writing activities observed in a fifth-grade class writing about a recent science experiment. Each writing community has different writers, interests, and goals that influence the writing activities and actions which occur.

The second key element of the WWC model is that the learner (i.e., the student) brings unique skills, aspirations, and experiences to each writing community. For instance, students possess a broad array of emotions, cognitive resources (e.g., beliefs, self-efficacy, working memory), and writing skills (e.g., conceptualization, ideation; Graham, 2019). Thus, teachers have the opportunity to foster a supportive writing community, while also providing quality writing instruction to support the development of individual students within each classroom. Although external and structural factors also shape the products created within a given writing community (e.g., state standards, school-adopted curriculum, technological resources), teachers still play a pivotal role in helping all students to become proficient writers (Graham, 2018). The "Big Ideas" and strategies described in this chapter will provide teachers with tools, techniques, and resources to support communities of writers in grades K–5.

Research, Policy, and Standards

Teaching writing to students in the elementary grades K–5 is a nuanced endeavor that is also shaped by three interrelated factors. In the forthcoming section of this chapter, we explore how research, educational policy relating to literacy instruction, and academic standards converge to define classroom writing instruction. First, we highlight key research that the Big Ideas and strategies included in this chapter are based on. Next, we share guidance provided by influential organizations focused on the advancement of literacy instruction, before concluding with a summary of relevant standards for written expression. By unpacking these three factors, we provide readers with a framework for incorporating evidence-based strategies, pedagogical principles, and grade-appropriate benchmarks into their classroom writing instruction.

Evidence-Based Writing Instruction. Currently, teacher preparation programs have access to reliable sources, which provide information on writing instruction grounded in high-quality research. Over the last two decades, systematic reviews of literature, including meta-analyses, have been conducted to determine effective writing interventions and instructional strategies for enhancing the writing achievement of students in grades K–5. In 2012, Graham and colleagues published a comprehensive meta-analysis that reviewed more than 100 school-based writing intervention studies implemented with elementary students. This literature review has helped teachers, preservice educational programs, and professional development providers identify which practices are most effective for helping students to become strong writers. In this review, Graham and colleagues reported that effective practices include: (a) teaching cognitive and metacognitive strategies, (b) teaching self-regulation techniques, (c) modeling text structure and essay planning (i.e., prewriting techniques), (d) setting specific writing goals, and (e) providing scaffolded supports, including peer assistance and teacher feedback. Three Big Ideas around theses effective instructional practices will be described in forthcoming sections of this chapter along with case study illustrations for how these practices can be implemented with elementary students in a classroom with a full range of diverse learners.

The instructional practices and teaching strategies presented in this chapter are also informed by writing studies on effective interventions for stiving writers, including students with learning disabilities. Incorporating findings from this research is important because today's classrooms are predominantly "inclusive," requiring educators to teach writing instruction to learners with varying needs (US Department of Education, 2015). A key source for this information is a meta-analysis of writing intervention for students with learning disabilities by Gillespie and Graham (2014). Similar to the previously referenced review of literature (Graham et al., 2012), authors reported that students with learning disabilities benefited from writing interventions that encompassed: (a) strategy instruction, including cognitive and meta-cognitive strategies; (b) self-regulation; (c) and setting specific goals for writing. Notably, several of the studies summarized in this review emphasize active student engagement, small group instruction, and constructive feedback from teachers on students' writing. In summary, the ideas, strategies, and concepts included in this chapter are grounded in empirical writing research that supports the use of the instructional practices.

Organizations and Policy. There are also several organizations who have considerable influence over classroom writing instruction. For instance, the Institute of Education Sciences (IES) is a research organization within the US Department of Education whose mission is to advance educational research and to inform classroom instruction. The What Works Clearinghouse practice guides are a valuable resource produced by IES. These practice guides, which cover numerous educational topics, summarize research evidence and provide practical instructional recommendations for educators. The practice guide focusing on elementary-level writing instruction, which was revised in 2018 (Graham, 2018), recommends that teachers prioritize writing instruction by: (a) writing across all subject areas (including social studies, mathematics, and science); (b) teaching a "process" approach to writing (e.g., planning, drafting, editing and revising, sharing writing); (c) teaching sentence construction and sentence-writing fluency; (d) promoting a community of writers; and (e) teaching genre-specific writing strategies with the gradual release of teacher support. The recommendations in this practice guide further shaped the three Big Ideas for best practices presented in this chapter.

Other organizations such as the International Literacy Association (ILA) and the National Council of Teachers of English (NCTE) also influence literacy instruction and policy. The ILA has published policy briefs and position statements about writing instruction that also emphasize writing across all subjects, using writing to enhance reading comprehension, using a process approach, and emphasizing to students that writing is a fun and meaningful endeavor (ILA, 2020). Further, the NCTE recommends that classroom writing should be "authentic" and personally meaningful to students and that writing should be a collaborative student activity (NCTE, 2022). Finally, organizations including the Center for Applied Special Technology (CAST) suggest that literacy instruction should include principles of universal design for learning (UDL) to ensure writing activities are accessible to all students (Hall et al., 2012). Strategies for making learning more accessible through UDL may include allowing students to represent their work in multiple ways, using innovative classroom technology, and allowing students to personalize their learning experiences. The strategies and suggestions included in this chapter represent principles of UDL given the importance of engaging all learners in a classroom of varying writing capabilities.

Relevant Standards. Finally, English language arts (ELA) standards in the United States for students in elementary school focus on developing students' written expression capabilities. Key examples include writing in different genres for specific purposes such as persuasive writing with supporting evidence (CCSS.ELA-Literacy.W.3.1), writing descriptive narrative stories (Florida Standards [LAFS: Write Narrative Texts to Develop Real or Imagined Experiences]), and drawing evidence from literary as well as informational texts to bolster writing quality (CCSS.ELA-Literacy.W.3.1.B). In summary, writing standards in all states are essential for teachers because they provide a developmentally appropriate framework for our expectations of student's development with written expression. Suggestions about how to assess student writing, another key aspect of standards and expectations, are included in the following section.

Chapter Objectives

After reading this chapter, readers will be able to accomplish the following objectives:

1. Summarize the three Big Ideas for best practices in general education writing instruction and explain their importance for supporting a diverse range of learners in grades K–5.
2. Identify at least one cognitive or meta-cognitive strategy for writing. Describe how you will introduce, model, and gradually build independence with this strategy.
3. Design a writing activity that utilizes UDL to facilitate skill development and address required curriculum components to encourage collaboration among students.
4. Explain how you would use flexible grouping during writing lessons to provide targeted practice opportunities that address individual learning goals and provide opportunities for students to receive feedback.
5. Establish classroom routines for giving and receiving feedback to facilitate dialogue and collaborations that promote growth in all writers within the classroom community.
6. Identify additional resources and next steps for extending learning of the three Big Ideas beyond this chapter.

BIG IDEAS FOR EFFECTIVE WRITING INTERVENTION FOR STUDENTS WITH DISABILITIES

The next part of this chapter includes specific strategies for writing instruction for students in grades K–5. We present three Big Ideas for effective writing instruction. Each Big Idea includes a definition of the concept as well as examples of classroom use. As described in the opening section of this chapter (see review of literature), this chapter's Big Ideas are influenced by a comprehensive theory of how students learn to write, as well as results from high-quality research studies. This chapter's Big Ideas were also shaped by the "high-leverage practice" series (McLeskey et al., 2017).

High-leverage practices are guidelines for effective classroom instruction that benefit all students within inclusive classrooms. HLPs are recommended for preservice teacher programs because they promote engaging instruction for a broad range of learners.

The forthcoming section of this chapter also includes a case study scenario of Mr. Anderson's third-grade classroom to illustrate implementation techniques for each of these Big Ideas. The case studies are designed to depict steps for utilizing the instructional practices with a full range of learners with varying writing abilities. Readers are also encouraged to utilize tables 6.1 and 6.2 for additional resources, examples, and suggestions for immediate classroom use.

- Big Idea 1: Teach cognitive and metacognitive strategies.
- Big Idea 2: Utilize principles of universal design for learning (UDL).
- Big Idea 3: Provide opportunities for feedback to promote collaboration among writers.

Big Idea 1: Teach Cognitive and Metacognitive Strategies

One effective instructional practice for teaching writing is teaching cognitive and metacognitive skills for writing, which were noted earlier in this chapter during the review of literature (Gillespie & Graham, 2014; Graham et al., 2012). The term *cognitive strategies* refers to mental operations, routines, or procedures used to carry out a task through conscious and controllable processes and activities (Dole et al., 2014; Gu, 2019; Pressley & Harris, 2009). Common cognitive strategies for writing take the form of structured tools that guide students in planning and organizing their written products as well as revising and editing those products to make progress toward end goals. *Meta-cognitive strategies* are specific procedures and operations for continuous monitoring and evaluating of written performance toward meeting specific writing goals and accomplishing certain tasks. In the writing process, metacognitive strategies are mental processes that assist students with procedures for monitoring and evaluating their writing as they move through the writing process (Harris et al., 2009). These types of strategies can also provide problem-solving strategies to guide decision-making in the writing process, which can be useful for students who need support with independent writing and resources to enhance cognitive control mechanisms. Students benefit from learning cognitive and metacognitive strategies and routines in the elementary grades because these strategies are used throughout our lives, such as while revising an essay in high school or carefully drafting a letter for a college application (Hayes, 2013).

Table 6.1 provides examples and resources of cognitive strategies that can be used to support students with different aspects of writing, including planning, drafting, and editing. These cognitive strategies are organized around different elements of writer's processes depicted in the WWC framework (Graham, 2018), including strategies to facilitate production processes that involve conceptualization of writing goals, application of transcription tasks such as editing or spelling, and reconceptualization of written products through revising strategies. In addition, table 6.1 includes examples of different metacognitive strategies to assist students in developing inner dialogue to monitor and evaluate their ongoing performance when writing (Gu, 2019; Harris et al., 2009). Although these strategies facilitate mental dialogue

Table 6.1. Cognitive and Metacognitive Strategies

Purpose	Strategy	Classroom Example	Resources
Planning	POW + TREE	Mr. Griffith teaches persuasive writing to fourth graders. He wants to build students' engagement in pre-writing or planning. He has previously taught students the POW (P = pick my idea, O = organize my notes, W = write and say more) mnemonic and his class uses it across content areas. In the current unit of study, students are expected to read a text, state an opinion based on a prompt, and support their opinion with examples. He selects the mnemonic TREE (T = topic sentence, R = reasons—three or more, E = explanation, E = ending). Mr. Griffith builds on what his class knows about POW and uses the six stages of SRSD with the corresponding graphic organizer to teach students to plan their essay.	SRSD online video: "Each Step of SRSD," https://srsdonline.org/each-step-of-srsd/ SRSD online video: "Writing to Learn Strategies to Empower Student Writing," https://www.youtube.com/watch?v=k7XSsVXofX0
Drafting	Self-statements	Ms. Ramirez notices that her third graders are comfortable using a graphic organizer to plan their writing, but they have difficulty with drafting from notes. She knows that self-talk is an integral component of SRSD and sets aside time during her next writing block to think aloud using self-statements as she models writing from plans or notes. In addition, she has the class brainstorm statements they can say to themselves during the writing process to build their self-efficacy. Students pick a few of the statements, such as "I know that I can use a question to write hook with my topic sentence." or "When I get stuck, it is okay to take a breath, read what I have so far, and then get back to work." Students write the self-statements in the front of their notebooks to have them available when writing.	IRIS Center Module: "Self-Instruction," https://iris.peabody.vanderbilt.edu/module/sr/cresource/q2/p05/ SRSD online video: "Self-Talk," https://www.youtube.com/watch?v=yMvrUqolkU8 "Personalize Students' Self-Talk Statements with SRSD," https://www.youtube.com/watch?v=URKHCeKxr58
Editing	CUPS + E	Mrs. Perelman has previously taught her fifth graders to use CUPS (C = capitalization, U = understanding, P = punctuation, and S = spelling) to edit their work. She recently noticed that while she has observed improvement in students editing, they need additional support with using descriptive language, vibrant examples, and elaborating on their ideas in their writing. She decides to introduce CUPS + E (E = extras). Mrs. Perelman prepares visuals of two cups of hot cocoa. The first cup only includes cocoa, but the second cup has cocoa topped with extras like whipped cream and sprinkles. She conducts a think-aloud about how hot cocoa by itself is good, but sometimes she likes to add the extras that make it special. Mrs. Perelman explains that when she reviews her writing using CUPS, she will now review for the E, extras she can add to make her writing special. Next, Mrs. Perelman takes out a paragraph the class collaboratively wrote, and they walk through the CUPS + E process together.	IRIS Center Module: "Mnemonics," https://iris.peabody.vanderbilt.edu/module/ss2/cresource/q1/p04/

Note: SRSD = self-regulated strategy development.

Table 6.2. Universal Design for Learning (UDL) Supports for Writing

UDL Principle	Examples	Resources
Provide Multiple Means of Engagement	Use writing prompts that connect to student experiences. Provide students with different choices for writing prompts, cognitive strategies, and tools. Allow students to choose to work independently, in pairs, or small groups. Provide students access to class charts and individually created self-statements. Set up writing stations and rotations that maximize peer-to-peer and teacher-to-student interactions.	CAST video: "Writing: UDL for Inclusive Literacy," https://www.youtube.com/watch?v=qc23rE-Nhrs CAST website: https://udlguidelines.cast.org/ CAST Tip Sheet: "UDL Tips for Designing an Engaging Environment," https://www.cast.org/products-services/resources/2016/udl-tips-designing-engaging-learning-environment
Provide Multiple Means of Representation	Pre-teach key vocabulary with definitions and symbols. Combine conducting think-aloud models with visual icons that represent the steps in the writing process. Model and support color coding of critical components of specific writing genres. Provide checklists for students to use when writing across content areas.	IRIS Center module: "Universal Design for Learning," https://iris.peabody.vanderbilt.edu/module/udl/ ASCD: "Lesson Planning with Universal Design for Learning," https://www.ascd.org/el/articles/lesson-planning-with-universal-design-for-learning
Provide Multiple Means of Action and Expression	Provide access to available technology such as word processors, spell checkers, or speech-to-text devices. Post previously introduced graphic organizers labeled for each type of writing. Display anchor charts or individual posters with sentence stems, transition words, and mnemonic devices. Provide exemplar essays with color coding or annotation.	CAST UDL Guidelines: "Provide Multiple Means of Action and Expression," https://udlguidelines.cast.org/action-expression Understood: "Universal Design for Learning (UDL): A Teacher's Guide," https://www.understood.org/en/articles/understanding-universal-design-for-learning?utm_source=google&utm_medium=cpc&utm_term=universal+design+for+learning&utm_campaign=EN_UDL_EJ2&gad_source=1&gclid=CjOKCQiAm4WsBhCiARIsAEJIEzVNS9zy_s-8wO1HZ5r1Qci3mCcaY1JjRSIyLIL72oZ3LyVzEX7x9UaArOhEALw_wcB&gclsrc=aw.ds

to assess and evaluate writing performance, there are instructional techniques (e.g., "think-alouds") and structured tools (e.g., graphic organizers to record self-statements) that can promote independent use of these internal procedures.

When teaching cognitive and metacognitive strategies for writing, it is important to develop both declarative and procedural knowledge for how to use the strategy (Gu, 2019; Pressley & Harris, 2009). Declarative knowledge is developed by discussing what the strategy is, how to engage in intentional use of the strategy, and the contexts in which a strategy may be useful. By contrast, development of procedural knowledge allows students to make use of the strategy and develop knowledge in how to implement a strategy when writing. The two knowledge sources complement each other to develop students' strategy application and execution.

Examples. Modeling using "think-alouds" to demonstrate how to use a strategy (rather than displaying the strategy and expecting students to know how to apply it) can facilitate development of both types of knowledge. When setting the stage to prepare for a think-aloud, teachers begin by explicitly stating the purpose of the demonstration before defining students' responsibilities and roles during the process. For example, telling students their primary role is to (a) watch the process and (b) make notes of the statements verbalized during the demonstration helps to provide students with a clear purpose as they observe the process of learning a new strategy. During a think-aloud, narrating the decision-making and planning processes can help students make connections to internal dialogue that successful writers use when engaging in the writing process. As such, think-alouds demonstrating the use of a strategy provide a space for teachers to show students authentic strategy application while also making self-regulation monitoring and evaluating strategies overt for students. For instance, modeling a compare-and-contrast chart for a classroom writing topic (like choosing a destination for an upcoming field trip) using a think-aloud as the teacher models planning and writing would provide an authentic opportunity to teach a new strategy. Modeling cognitive and metacognitive strategies also addresses a key principle of UDL because teachers can adjust how they model (and what they say and do) based on diverse learning needs in the classroom (Rose & Strangman, 2007). For example, a teacher may use different technological tools and adjust the "think-aloud" comments when modeling the aforementioned strategy (a compare-and-contrast chart) with an inclusive fifth-grade classroom that includes numerous striving writers and students who receive special educational services. Thus, adjusting strategies, tools, and approaches to both instruction as well as student representation (and application of strategies) is a principle of UDL that addresses the neurodiversity of most US classrooms (Rose & Strangman, 2007).

The following case study exemplifies how think-aloud models can be used to introduce and develop cognitive and metacognitive strategy use among students. Specifically, the general education teacher, Mr. Anderson, models for his students how to use cognitive and metacognitive strategies with empirical research evidence in facilitating higher writing performance in elementary students (Graham & Harris, 2018; Graham et al., 2020; Harris & Graham, 2018). The cognitive strategy depicted in the case study (POW + TREE) is often implemented as part of a larger multicomponent instructional framework, self-regulated strategy development (SRSD; see Harris et al., 2008, for example lesson plans and materials); however, this particular demonstration focuses on one component of SRSD in which teachers think aloud while modeling strategy use for students. In the scenario, Mr. Anderson makes his mental thought processes overt for students, and he demonstrates how he plans and prepares to write a persuasive essay. Through the modeling process, he builds declarative and procedural knowledge by showing students how to utilize the strategy and the metacognitive processes he engages in through direct application.

Mr. Anderson teaches the fourth-grade reading and writing block on his elementary campus. He prepares to begin teaching persuasive writing and has elected to teach the cognitive strategy POW (P = pick my idea; O = organize my notes; W = write and say more) + TREE (T = topic Sentence, R = reasons—3 or more, E = explain reasons, E = ending) to support his students in planning an essay. In a previous series of lessons, Mr. Anderson set the stage by building background knowledge around persuasive writing. His students read persuasive writing exemplars and color-coded TREE components in the essays. Mr. Anderson knows he needs to model using the POW + TREE strategy to ensure students understand how to utilize the strategy when planning and writing. Mr. Anderson prepares to think aloud as he uses the strategy to plan for writing.

Mr. Anderson begins by walking over to the whiteboard, where he has two pieces of chart paper. One piece has the writing prompt, and the other has the TREE graphic organizer. Mr. Anderson begins by telling his students that he will be acting as a student to show them how to use the POW + TREE strategy for planning a persuasive essay. He proceeds to read the prompt, "Some schools allow students to have three months off in the summer, while some attend year-round. Should students have to attend school during the summer? Write an essay persuading your principal why or why not students should attend school in the summer."

Mr. Anderson puts his hands on his hips, picks up a marker, and thinks aloud, "No way! Why would I want to go to school in the summer? Okay, hold on. Let me think about this. I know that this prompt is asking for me to persuade my principal why we should or should not go to school in the summer. If I am going to convince my principal or other adults (such as my parents) that kids should not have to go to school in summer, I need to back up the side I choose with some really good reasons."

Mr. Anderson walks over to the chart paper with the TREE graphic organizer. "I know that as a good writer, I can use a strategy to help me plan my essay. In this class, we always begin with POW. I know I need to pick *my idea,* organize *my notes, and then* write *and say more. Picking my idea is the easy part for this prompt. I do not think that kids should go to school in the summer. Now, I have to organize my notes. I can use TREE organizer, so I can jot down my topic sentence, my reasons, and how I want to end my essay. I also remember that when I use the graphic organizer, I don't need to write complete sentences. I can write just a few words as if I were texting these notes to a friend. Then, I can add more details as I write and say more when I write my essay."*

Mr. Anderson picks up the marker and pauses for a moment. Then he says, "The T in TREE stands for topic sentence. I'm not going to write out my entire topic sentence here. Instead, I am going to add some notes so that I remember what to write. I am going to write 'no school in summer.' Ok! This is a good start. Now that I picked a side, I need to think of all the reasons why students should not go to school in summer. I know! One reason we should not go to school in summer is because it gives us time off to spend time with our families. For the first R for reason *(which I know I need three for TREE), I will write 'spend time with families.' Alright, I am off to a good start. I get a little overwhelmed when I see I still have a lot to plan, but I can take a deep breath and remind myself that my TREE strategy will help me plan my essay. Okay! Next, I will write an explanation for my* reason . . ."

Mr. Anderson continues modeling the process of planning with TREE until all parts are planned on the graphic organizer. He continues verbalizing his thinking as he plans and modeling how the cognitive and metacognitive strategy can support him as he writes. In a subsequent lesson, he models how to take his notes and write complete sentences to complete his persuasive essay. At the end of each lesson, students discuss how Mr. Anderson used the POW + TREE strategy and how it helped him as a writer.

Big Idea 2: Utilize Principles of Universal Design for Learning (UDL)

A second important instructional practice for teaching a full range of learners is to utilize the principles of UDL. In nearly every classroom, there are a range of learners with levels of performance and varying needs. Utilizing a variety of means of engagement, presentation, and demonstration of mastery or action/expression through different formats (e.g., whole group, small groups, partners) helps to maximize engagement among students who may have different strengths as writers. Planning strategically in advance and anticipating the need to integrate different *materials* (e.g., modified graphic organizers with fewer genre elements; partially completed graphic organizers; text-to-speech devices) and *tasks* or *activities* (e.g., some students reviewing how to write a topic sentence in a small group while others are independently writing a short paragraph independently) outlines a path for meeting short- and longer-term writing goals. Although the pacing and lesson format may need to be adjusted due to student progress (e.g., students need a mini-lesson and additional practice on writing a concluding sentence in a paragraph) or unanticipated disruptions to the lesson progression (e.g., unanticipated snow day), a structured, yet strategic, instructional approach utilizing flexible groupings with scaffolded supports helps to provide writers with opportunities for success in their writing. In turn, advanced planning of groupings and supports, as well as how the supports will be faded to move toward independent writing, will further enhance students' self-efficacy and positive beliefs about their writing capabilities.

To align WWC framework outlined earlier in the chapter (Graham, 2018), flexible grouping also provides space for members of the classroom writing community to collaborate through different actions to produce different written products. Establishing a structure of flexible grouping when teaching students with varying ranges of abilities and skill levels provides opportunities for differentiated and individualized writing activities. By further embedding scaffolding supports, it fosters a classroom community of writers that work together to produce products that they otherwise may not be able to do independently (McLeskey et al., 2017). For example, a small group of students may collaboratively research and draft a brief report on three key elements of the US Constitution. Their actions may consist of collaborative efforts in reading, planning, and writing the report, including typing it on a computer and adding photographic examples to illustrate their key ideas. At different points in the writing process, different students may utilize different tools and materials depending on their strengths and capabilities. To extend this example, one student may need a screen reader to assist with accessing difficult text during the information-gathering phase in writing the report. Planning in advance for students to access a variety of tools and materials as students engage in different tasks will facilitate greater engagement and place students in a position where they will experience success in writing.

To support students in their writing, classrooms tend to have many scaffolded supports used daily. Classroom resources such as anchor charts and task checklists are effective scaffolded supports that students can consistently reference during small group and independent writing activities. These tangible supports can further be paired with activities that engage students through discussion, think-aloud demonstrations and modeling, and verbal rehearsal of writing tasks to facilitate dialogue around writing strategies that successful writers use. In today's classrooms, technology tools expand the types of UDL supports that can be made accessible to students. These technology supports may include drafting on the computer in a word processing program, using spelling and grammar applications, or using text-to-speech dictation devices to minimize students challenges with written transcriptions and maximize other strengths in ideation and translation (Graham, 2018). Table 6.2 displays examples for how to apply the principles of UDL to teaching writing. Table 6.2 also includes links to additional resources for further exploration of these principles.

To extend the cognitive and metacognitive strategies example previously described, using multiple means of engagement, representation, and action/expression provides a framework for transitioning students from teacher-led writing tasks to independently produced written products. To this end, supports may be gradually faded over multiple days of instruction to steadily move students toward independent writing. This next example illustrates how to utilize the UDL principles to provide students with multiple practice opportunities for using two revising and editing cognitive strategies. This lesson sequence is planned for simplicity purposes to span across a single instructional lesson, but the pacing may be spread across weeks and months depending on the complexity of the writing task and ongoing formative assessments to evaluate individual progress of students.

Mr. Anderson's students wrote their first persuasive paragraph, and they are now ready to engage in the revising and editing process. His class has been using the CUPS (C = capitalization; U = usage; P = punctuation; S = spelling) strategy for editing and the ARMS (A = add; R = remove; M = move; S = substitute) strategy for revising. Mr. Anderson also wants to conduct targeted instruction with two small groups of students. One group demonstrates difficulty taking their ideas from the graphic organizer and generating sentences, while the other group is ready to turn their single-paragraph response into a multi-paragraph essay. Therefore, Mr. Anderson has decided to set up two editing and two revising stations in his classroom. These stations will allow for him to create a total of five small groups, with four working collaboratively in small groups while the fifth meets with him at his teacher table.

Mr. Anderson prepares for the rotations by making sure all students have the CUPS and ARMS mnemonic chart in their interactive writing notebook to carry with them to each of the rotations. Mr. Anderson also displays a chart on the whiteboard labeled with the table numbers and group rotations to show each student what they will practice at each table. The stations are distributed across practice opportunities for editing, revising, or targeted instruction at the teacher table. Taped to each of the editing and revising tables is a checklist to guide collaborative peer writing. The checklists note everything from the expected voice level to examples of sentence stems for giving peer feedback.

Before the students move to station 1, Mr. Anderson reviews the routine for changing stations with the class. When he plays music (after about 15 to 20 minutes at a station), he reminds students it is time to clean up, stand up, push in chairs, and be ready to move to the next station.

Mr. Anderson begins with his first group of four students who have demonstrated difficulty transitioning from the graphic organizer to full sentences. He asks the four students to take out their TREE graphic organizers, and then hands them a copy of topic sentence stems and transition words. He pulls out his own graphic organizer and reminds the students that the notes are not complete sentences. Therefore, they need to work together as a group (with Mr. Anderson) to figure out a way to start the paragraph. He reads the notes from the T section of his graphic organizer, and then has the students read through the topic sentence notes. Together, they consider as a group how to write a topic sentence, with Mr. Anderson facilitating the discussion. Mr. Anderson prompts students with guiding questions, such as, "How can we take these few words and form a complete sentence? What do we need to tell our reader that we will be writing about in our persuasive essay? What is the side we took?" Mr. Anderson models for the small group by writing an example topic sentence. Then, Mr. Anderson has the students independently write their own topic sentence. As students share what they have written, he provides immediate affirmative and corrective feedback to individual students. Mr. Anderson and the students continue with this pattern (teacher models and then students write their own sentence) until all parts of the TREE notes have been transformed into complete sentences. The students check off each TREE part of the notes as each is added to their essay, and Mr. Anderson also guides students in using transition words to introduce new reasons in their essay. This small-group practice continues until it is time for the next group to rotate to Mr. Anderson's teacher table.

Additional Guidance for Integrating UDL Principles within Classroom Groups

A common pitfall when providing multiple means of engagement, representation, and action/expression is releasing the reigns of control too quickly and failing to provide sufficient practice opportunities before requiring students to complete a task independently. Across the continuum of students, each individual may need a varied number of practice opportunities, tools, and different instructional arrangements before embarking on independent application. In the preceding example with Mr. Anderson, the UDL supports remained available to all students as they moved toward completing a writing task independently. An important illustration in this is example is how Mr. Anderson used formative assessment techniques to evaluate which students were ready to shift from small groups toward independent performance and the time point at which those supports should be faded across students. As a contrasting non-example, had Mr. Anderson modeled the paragraph writing strategy and immediately asked students to apply the strategy in their writing completely independently (skipping the small-group practice), it is likely many students would have failed to apply the strategy successfully, consequently leaving both Mr. Anderson and his students frustrated with writing. Therefore, successful implementation of UDL principles hinges upon avoiding the assumptions that (a) a single demonstration will prepare students to write independently and (b) all students will benefit from the same tools and a one-size-fits-all approach to writing. Instead, embracing the perspective that all students have different needs in their present writing performance will provide steady progress toward long-term goals of independence.

Big Idea 3: Provide Opportunities for Feedback to Promote Collaboration Among Writers

A third Big Idea and best practice for developing a classroom community of writers is to provide students with opportunities to give and receive feedback from their teacher as well as their peers. To grow as writers, students need to learn their strengths in their writing while also receiving guidance with setting goals to facilitate writing growth. Empirical research suggests that both oral and written feedback can improve students' writing because it helps them learn to identify issues within their written communication (Graham et al., 2011; 2015). Moreover, prior research reports positive effects in the quality of students' writing when they receive opportunities to collaborate in revising writing products (Graham et al., 2012). However, students must be taught how to give valuable feedback through models and established classroom routines if a community of writers who collaborate and support each other when writing is to be established.

In most classrooms, it is common for teachers to provide feedback to students, and feedback from adults who may hold knowledge of more sophisticated writing approaches and techniques can have a positive effect on students writing (Graham et al., 2015). Holding one-to-one conferences or small-group discussions can enhance the effectiveness of teacher feedback because it expands the feedback beyond a one-way line of communication. For instance, if feedback is only provided in written form when papers are graded and returned to students, yet no discussions about the feedback are conducted, students may not fully understand how to take a different approach in future writing activities or may not even read the feedback. Instead, discussions and conversations around how students are growing as writers and specific goals they have set for future writing can promote active engagement and improve decision-making in the writing process.

When providing feedback to their peers, some students may similarly focus on mechanics and conventions, such as capitalization, punctuation, and spelling. Although these skills are necessary to convey a coherent message, only providing feedback on these writing components may stifle deeper collaborations around meaningful revisions to a written product, such as brainstorming more interesting ideas and developing more engaging sentence structure. One way to enhance teacher and peer feedback opportunities is to utilize cognitive strategies to help students develop routines for providing feedback. Cognitive strategies can provide a framework for how to give feedback to a peer and nudge students toward giving more conceptual feedback about a written product. For example, teaching students to sandwich positive aspects of a peer's writing (e.g., *You did a nice job of . . . ; I like the part where you . . .*) around thoughtful suggestions for improving a written product (e.g., *One idea to make your essay more interesting is . . . ; You might think about adding . . . in the part about . . .*) can help students engage in rich dialogue around their writing. Other activities such as establishing an "Author's Chair" where students share their written products and then the teacher facilitates a whole-class discussion around the shared piece of writing can help foster the routine of giving and receiving feedback while also highlighting students' work through a celebration of the written accomplishment (see the What Works Clearinghouse Educator's practice guide for *Teaching Elementary School Students to be Effective Writers* for more examples on how to encourage writing collaborations among students; Graham et al., 2012).

To illustrate how to facilitate teacher feedback and peer collaborations to promote a community of writers within a classroom, we continue our case study scenario of Mr. Anderson's classroom. In this scene, Mr. Anderson is utilizing peer-mediated activities to promote dialogue and discussions around students' writing. The goal in this context is to provide constructive feedback to enhance the written products students are producing with the classroom.

While Mr. Anderson is working with his small groups, the students at the peer-feedback tables begin the process of reading one another's work and sharing feedback. Students have about 15 to 20 minutes to share their writing and provide feedback to each other. At the editing rotation, students find a checklist taped to the table with the following items: (1) select who will receive feedback and take out your persuasive essay; (2) if you are giving feedback to a peer, open your interactive notebook to the CUPS (C = capitalization, U= understanding, P = punctuation, S = spelling) page; (3) if you are receiving feedback from a peer, read your persuasive essay to your partner in a level-two voice; (4) if you are giving feedback to a peer, select two sentence stems from the class poster and share positive feedback on the essay if you are giving feedback; (5) if you are giving feedback to a peer, select two sentence stems from the class poster and share no more than three recommendations for edits using the CUPS notes.

Marco and Aliyah begin to read the checklist together. Marco decides he will give feedback to Aliyah. He opens his notebook to the CUPS strategy sheet glued to the inside cover and he reviews each letter as a reminder of what to look for in Aliyah's essay. Each of the letters has a flap with examples of the CUPS components. For example, C for capitalization lists examples such as the first word of a sentence, names of people and places, months and days. After Marco reviews the CUPS strategy, he and Aliyah review the steps to determine what to do next. Marco listens to Aliyah reads her persuasive assay. After Aliyah is finished, Marco provides positive and constructive feedback to Aliyah.

While Marco and Aliyah work together, students in the revising rotation follow the same structure, except they use the ARMS (A = add more, R = remove, M = move, S = substitute) page of their interactive notebook. Students follow the same checklist when giving feedback using ARMS. At the station, students also share how the suggested changes will improve the student's writing (e.g., make it more specific, include more mature vocabulary, eliminate details that don't belong).

Using Formative Writing Assessments to Make Instructional Decisions and to Set Goals

With each of the Big Ideas and key instructional practices presented, formative ongoing writing assessments can be used to guide instructional decisions and to inform student writing goals. In this section, we present four key considerations and best practices for assessing students writing. These assessments practices are described with respect to how they relate to the three Big Ideas presented in this chapter. Further recommendations for best practices for assessing students' writing can be found in a Carnegie Corporation Report titled *Informing Writing: The Benefits of Formative Assessment* (Graham et al., 2011).

One key consideration when assessing students' writing is to assess students in the mode (i.e., paper/pencil or computer) they typically use to write and the one they have the most experience in writing. Some previous research suggests that if students are less familiar and less experienced with a particular writing mode, they will perform less well on the assessments (see Graham et al., 2011). Therefore, it is important to recognize that performance in one writing mode may not produce comparable student outcomes because the written products may be dependent upon students' proficiency with writing using a computer or through traditional paper/pencil methods. Alignment to individualized education program (IEP) goals or 504 accommodations are additional aspects to consider when selecting the most appropriate mode to assess students in writing. These considerations are particularly critical when preparing for high-stakes national and state assessments because if students are required to write using a particular mode (e.g., computer), yet most of their writing instruction has involved an alternative mode (e.g., paper/pencil), their scores on the assessment could be largely impacted by their lack of writing experience in a given mode. Accordingly, frequent and continuous practice in the mode that will be utilized on summative assessments will help to prepare students for success on those assessments and result in more accurate depictions of their writing capabilities.

A second recommended practice in the assessment of students' writing is to collect multiple samples of writing because a single assessment may not represent a writer's full capabilities. One reason multiple writing samples are needed is that research shows student performance in one genre (e.g., persuasive essays) is not always equivalent to another genre (e.g., narrative stories; Graham et al., 2016). Consequently, students need opportunities to produce different types of written products to fully demonstrate the breadth of their writing capabilities.

In addition to collecting multiple writing samples from students, writing assessments and products need to be collected across time. Research evidence suggests as many as eight to 14 writing samples may be needed to obtain a reliable estimate of students' essay composition quality, writing output (e.g., the number of words written), and vocabulary usage. Therefore, collecting writing samples across the school year helps to determine students' independent performance level. Ongoing assessments are also useful to determine if UDL practices are reaching all students and making the classroom curriculum accessible to all students. As such, a benefit of ongoing progress monitoring of students' writing is the formative assessments can inform flexible groupings and instructional adjustments necessary to scaffold students to the next level in their writing.

Finally, recognizing potential biases when scoring students' writing and utilizing techniques for minimizing biases can help to ensure assessment outcomes are not skewed. One easy method for minimizing biases is to randomly order students' papers each time you score (or grade) them (see Graham et al., 2011 for a discussion on the research evidence supporting this assessment practice). In a large class, it is common practice to alphabetize student assignments to simplify and ease entry of grades into the gradebook. However, scores can be skewed by the essays that precede a composition, with evidence to suggest essays receive lower scores if the previous essays are of higher quality. Mixing up the essays to read and scoring them in a random order for each assessment will help to minimize potential for skewed scores. Moreover, keeping in mind that students' writing may change across time and vary depending on the type of written product a student is asked to produce can further help to minimize preconceived assumptions about writing behaviors and skills.

CONCLUSION

In this chapter, three Big Ideas are presented to guide elementary teachers in effectively providing writing instruction to a full range of learners. Each is accompanied by a case study example to illustrate real-world approaches for implementing the instructional practices with students. Within these examples, it is important to remember that classroom writing communities are complex, with multiple facets that interact and contribute to how students develop as writers. Moreover, writers use multiple tools and strategies during the composing process, and it takes time for students to develop proficiency in using them independently. However, through modeling, application of UDL, and consistent opportunities for practice within a collaborative community of writers, all students can succeed at developing into successful writers.

Chapter Objectives Revisited

After reading through the three Big Ideas presented in this chapter, the overarching objective listed below can be completed independently or with a partner. It may be helpful to review the case studies provided within this chapter alongside each objective to visualize how specific activities may be successfully implemented with students. Tables 6.1 and 6.2 also offer additional examples and available resources to support instructional planning and implementation within a classroom that includes a full range of varying writing abilities. *A review of the chapter objectives:*

- Summarize the three Big Ideas for best practices in general education writing instruction and explain their importance for supporting a diverse range of learners in grades K–5.

- Identify at least one cognitive or metacognitive strategy for writing. Describe how you will introduce, model, and gradually build independence with this strategy.
- Design a writing activity that utilizes UDL to facilitate skill development and address required curriculum components to encourage collaboration among students
- Explain how you would use flexible grouping during writing lessons to provide targeted practice opportunities that address individual learning goals and provide opportunities for students to receive feedback.
- Establish classroom routines for giving and receiving feedback to facilitate dialogue and collaborations that promote growth in all writers within the classroom community.
- Identify additional resources and next steps for extending learning of the three Big Ideas beyond this chapter.

REFERENCES

Applebee, A. N., & Langer, J. A. (2015). *Writing instruction that works: Proven methods for middle and high school classrooms*. Teachers College Press.

Dole, J. A., Nokes, J. D., & Drits, D. (2014). Cognitive strategy instruction. In S. E. Israel & G. G. Duffy (Eds.), *Handbook of research on reading comprehension* (pp. 347–372). Routledge.

Early, J. S., & DeCosta-Smith, M. (2011). Making a case for college: A genre-based college admission essay intervention for underserved high school students. *Journal of Writing Research*, 2(3), 299–329.

Florida Department of Education. (2019). *Language arts Florida standards*. Tallahassee, FL.

Gillespie, A., & Graham, S. (2014). A meta-analysis of writing interventions for students with learning disabilities. *Exceptional Children*, 80(4), 454–473.

Graham, S. (2018). A revised writer (s)-within-community model of writing. *Educational Psychologist*, 53(4), 258–279.

Graham, S. (2019). Changing how writing is taught. *Review of Research in Education*, 43(1), 277–303.

Graham, S. (2023). Writer(s)-within-community model of writing as a lens for studying the teaching of writing. In R. Horowitz (Ed.), *The Routledge International handbook of research on writing* (pp. 337–350). Routledge.

Graham, S., & Harris, K. (2018). An examination of the design principles underlying a self-regulated strategy development study. *Journal of Writing Research*, 10(2), 139–187.

Graham, S., & Hebert, M. (2010). Writing to read: Evidence for how writing can improve reading: A report from Carnegie Corporation of New York.

Graham, S., Bañales, G., Ahumada, S., Muñoz, P., Alvarez, P., & Harris, K. R. (2020). Writing strategies interventions. In D. L. Dinsmore, L. K. Fryer, & M. M. Parkinson (Eds.), *Handbook of strategies and strategic processing* (pp. 141–158). Routledge.

Graham, S., Bollinger, A., Booth Olson, C., D'Aoust, C., MacArthur, C., McCutchen, D., & Olinghouse, N. (2012). *Teaching elementary school students to be effective writers: A practice guide* (NCEE 2012–4058). National Center for

Education Evaluation and Regional Assistance, Institute of Education Sciences, US Department of Education. http://ies.ed.gov/ncee/ wwc/publications_reviews.aspx#pubsearch

Graham, S., Harris, K., & Hebert, M. A. (2011). Informing writing: The benefits of formative assessment. A Carnegie Corporation Time to Act report. Washington, DC: Alliance for Excellent Education.

Graham, S., Harris, K. R., & Santangelo, T. (2015). Research-based writing practices and the Common Core. *The Elementary School Journal*, *115*(4), 498–522. https://doi.org/10.1086/681964

Graham, S., Hebert, M., Paige Sandbank, M., & Harris, K. R. (2016). Assessing the writing achievement of young struggling writers: Application of generalizability theory. *Learning Disability Quarterly*, *39*(2), 72–82. https://doi.org/10.1177/0731948714555019

Graham, S., McKeown, D., Kiuhara, S., & Harris, K. R. (2012). A meta-analysis of writing instruction for students in the elementary grades. *Journal of Educational Psychology*, *104*(4), 879–896. https://doi.org/10.1037/a0029185

Gu, P. Y. (2019). Approaches to learning strategy instruction. In A. U. Chamot & V. Harris (Eds.), *Learning strategy instruction in the language classroom: Issues and implementation* (pp. 22–37). Multilingual Matters.

Hall, T. E., Meyer, A., & Rose, D. H. (Eds.). (2012). *Universal design for learning in the classroom: Practical applications*. Guilford Press.

Harris, K. R., & Graham, S. (2018). Self-regulated strategy development: Theoretical bases, critical instructional elements, and future research. In R. Fidalgo, K. R. Harris, & M. Braaksma (Eds.), *Design principles for teaching effective writing: Theoretical and empirical grounded principles* (pp. 119–151). Brill.

Harris, K. R., Graham, S., Brindle, M., & Sandmel, K. (2009). Metacognition and children's writing. In D. J. Hacker, J. Dunlosky, & A. C. Graesser (Eds.), *Handbook of metacognition in education* (pp. 131–153). Routledge.

Harris, K. R., Graham, S., Mason, L. H., & Friedlander, B. (2008). Powerful writing strategies for all students. *Education Review*. https://edrev.asu.edu/index.php/ER/article/view/1013.

Hayes, J. R. (2013). A new framework for understanding cognition and affect in writing. In C. M. Levy & S. Ransdell (Eds.), *The science of writing: Theories, methods, individual differences, and applications* (pp. 1–27). Routledge.

International Literacy Association (ILA). (2020). *Teaching writing to improve reading skills: Research advisory*. Newark, DE.

McLeskey, J., Barringer, M-D., Billingsley, B., Brownell, M., Jackson, D., Kennedy, M., Lewis, T., Maheady, L., Rodriguez, J., Scheeler, M. C., Winn, J., & Ziegler, D. (2017). *High-leverage practices in special education*. Council for Exceptional Children & CEEDAR Center.

National Council for Teachers of English (NCTE). (2022). *Position statement on writing instruction in school*. https://ncte.org/statement/statement-on-writing-instruction-in-school/

National Governors Association (NGA) Center for Best Practices & Council of Chief State School Officers (CCSSO). (2010). *Common Core State Standards for English language arts and literacy in history/social studies, science, and technical subjects*. NGA Center for Best Practices & CCSSO.

Pressley, M., & Harris, K. R. (2009). Cognitive strategies instruction: From basic research to classroom instruction. *Journal of Education*, *189*(1–2), 77–94.

Rose, D. H., & Strangman, N. (2007). Universal design for learning: Meeting the challenge of individual learning differences through a neurocognitive perspective. *Universal Access in the Information Society*, *5*, 381–391.

US Department of Education (DOE). (2015). 37th Annual report to congress on the implementation of the Individuals with Disabilities Act, 2015. US DOE.

7

Quality Writing Intervention for Students with Disabilities in the Elementary Grades

Stephen Ciullo, Sagarika Kosaraju,
Alyson A. Collins, and John W. McKenna

THE ABILITY TO USE writing to effectively communicate has become more important than ever. Effective written expression is beneficial in the classroom, as well as for pursuing interests in other aspects of students' lives including socializing with friends online or on social media, researching hobbies, and advocating for social causes (Graham, 2018). Benefits of proficient writing also include reinforcing content and disciplinary concepts across subject areas, as well as enhancing reading comprehension by writing about textual content that students are reading or discussing in class (Graham & Hebert, 2011; Graham et al., 2020). In essence, research suggests that students benefit in a myriad of ways from receiving consistent and comprehensive writing instruction (Graham, 2018).

The foundation for effective written communication can be established in the elementary grades for all students, including students with disabilities (SWDs) and striving writers (i.e., students with emerging writing proficiency who do not receive special education services). Important writing competencies in grades K–5 include handwriting and keyboarding fluency, composing grammatically correct sentences, using a writing process approach (e.g., planning, drafting, revising, and publishing) to write across genres, and engaging with other students to discuss their writing, as well as peer revision. Elementary-level educators have a unique opportunity to equip students with these meaningful capabilities to enhance their ability to pursue complex writing tasks once they enter middle school such as argumentative writing from source text, synthesizing information, or composing scientific reports (Ciullo & Mason, 2017). In summary, students must acquire essential writing skills in grades K–5 to prepare for the numerous writing communities and purposes they will be engaged in throughout secondary school and during postsecondary education, employment, and real-world daily written communication (Graham, 2018).

Core Components of Writing in Grades K–5. Writing intervention for SWDs in grades K–5 should include key components that contribute to long-term writing proficiency (Walter et al., 2021). These component skills include (a) sentence structure and grammatical conventions of writing, (b) planning for writing and organization of text, (c) editing and revision as part of a writing process approach, and (d) genre-based specialized writing (e.g., informative writing, persuasive writing). Handwriting, typing fluency, and spelling are also emphasized in grades K–5. The examples included throughout this chapter for each "Big Idea" of effective instruction that will be presented integrate several of these aforementioned writing skills to elucidate how teachers use Big Ideas to help students to learn core components of writing and address grade-level standards using intervention that is supported by research.

Students with Disabilities. Students receiving special education services may encounter some specific challenges with writing. These writing challenges include sentence writing structure and fluency, difficulties with planning and organizing of essays, miscues with spelling or grammatical conventions, as well as a lower self-efficacy as writers compared to students who do not receive special education services (Berninger, 2009; Graham et al., 2017). Results from the National Assessment of Education Progress (NAEP) writing assessment have also consistently suggested that the majority of SWDs are not attaining a basic level of writing proficiency on this measure (National Center for Education Statistics [NCES], 2015).

Preparing teachers to provide effective writing instruction for SWDs and striving writers is a pivotal issue. In survey research studies, teachers have reported perceiving themselves as ill-prepared to provide evidence-based writing instruction, and that professional development in writing has not adequately met their instructional needs (Brindle et al., 2016; Troia & Graham, 2016). A recent survey with teacher dyads (pairs of general and special educators) reported that special as well as general educators both perceived their preparation to teach writing to SWDs as in need of improvement. However, the majority of teachers surveyed reported the belief that students' writing performance is malleable, suggesting that educators have confidence in all students to become better writers (Graham et al., 2023). Researchers, higher-education faculty members, and professional development providers have the opportunity to provide pre- and in-service teachers with effective strategies to reach all writers, including SWDs.

THREE BIG IDEAS FOR SPECIAL EDUCATION WRITING INTERVENTION: A PREVIEW

Examples of how to address core elements of elementary-level writing instruction are included in this chapter. *This chapter is organized through the presentation of three "Big Ideas," or high-leverage practices (HLPs), in special education, from the Council for Exceptional Children's (CEC) instructional toolkit.* The following three Big Ideas were chosen for their relevance to writing intervention for SWDs. The three Big Ideas/HLPs are defined in table 7.1 and described throughout the chapter. These Big Ideas are: (1) identify and prioritize long- and short-term learning goals (HLP 11), (2) provide explicit instruction (HLP 16), and (3) use flexible grouping (HLP 17). This chapter includes examples as well as a classroom case study to explain how each Big Idea can be implemented to incorporate evidence-based writing practices for SWDs in grades K–5. Table 7.1 includes a definition of each Big Idea/HLP, examples, and resources for extending learning.

Three Big Ideas for Special Education Writing Intervention: A Preview 109

Table 7.1. HLP, Definition, and Classroom Example

HLP	Definition	Classroom Example	Resources
Identify and prioritize long- and short-term learning goals	Teachers prioritize what is most important for students to learn by providing meaningful access to and success in general education and other contextually relevant curricula. Teachers use grade-level standards, assessment data and learning progressions, students' prior knowledge, and IEP goals and benchmarks to make decisions about what is most crucial to emphasize and about developing long- and short-term goals accordingly. They understand essential curriculum components, identify essential prerequisites and foundations, and assess student performance in relation to these components.	Ms. Malone is monitoring her students' progress in writing informational essays, a state-level standard, or long-term goal, for fourth graders. Based on formative data, Ms. Malone notices that Liya, a student with an IEP, is only including one idea instead of three to support her topic sentence. So, Liya's next short-term goal will be to include two more ideas after her topic sentence. To achieve this goal, Ms. Malone will work with Liya individually and model for her how to research facts or think of examples to support her topic sentence.	*High Leverage Practices in Special Education* (2017). pp. 134–139 Video: "HLP 11: Goal Setting," https://highleveragepractices.org/hlp-11-goal-setting HLP 11 leadership guide, https://exceptionalchildren.org/sites/default/files/2021-01/HLP%2011%20Admin%20Guide.pdf
Explicit Instruction	Teachers make content, skills, and concepts explicit by showing and telling students what to do or think while solving problems, enacting strategies, completing tasks, and classifying concepts. Teachers use explicit instruction when students are learning new material and complex concepts and skills. They strategically choose examples and non-examples and language to facilitate student understanding, anticipate common misconceptions, highlight essential content, and remove distracting information. They model and scaffold steps or processes needed to understand content and concepts, apply skills, and complete tasks successfully and independently.	Mr. Schneider is teaching first graders about how light travels when an object is placed in its path. Using explicit instruction, he demonstrates and conducts a think-aloud when showing the class how to use various objects, like a mirror or a small ball, in the path of the beam of light produced by a flashlight. Students record observations in their science journals. He shows examples and non-examples of ways to make notes, such as how light reflects a mirror but blocks the light with a ball. He gives students opportunities to practice with new objects. Finally, partners complete four more objects of their choosing to test the effects with the flashlight.	*High Leverage Practices in Special Education* (2017). pp. 157–160 Video: "HLP 16: Use Explicit Instruction," https://highleveragepractices.org/hlp-16-use-explicit-instruction HLP 16 leadership guide, https://exceptionalchildren.org/sites/default/files/2021-01/HLP%2016%20Admin%20Guide.pdf NCII, "What Every Teacher Needs to Know about Explicit Instruction," https://intensiveintervention.org/resource/What-Every-Educator-Needs-to-Know-About-Explicit-Instruction

(Continued)

Table 7.1. (Continued)

HLP	Definition	Classroom Example	Resources
Flexible Grouping	Teachers assign students to homogeneous and heterogeneous groups based on explicit learning goals to monitor peer interactions and provide positive and corrective feedback to support productive learning. Teachers use small learning groups to accommodate learning differences, promote in-depth academic-related interactions, and teach students to work collaboratively. They choose tasks that require collaboration, issue directives that promote productive and autonomous group interactions, and embed strategies that maximize learning opportunities and equalize participation. Teachers promote simultaneous interactions, use procedures to hold students accountable for collective and individual learning, and monitor and sustain group performance through proximity and positive feedback.	Mrs. Chang is a fifth-grade teacher assigning small-group social studies research projects. She places students in mixed-ability groups and has each group member take a responsibility on the project, such as the notetaker, communications leader, or presentation organizer. Each team member is required to research and prepare two slides for the group's presentation. Since Nathan has IEP goals targeting peer collaboration and writing an informational paragraph, the special education teacher, Ms. Davidson, provides guided support while Nathan meets with his group. She reduces her support throughout the semester as Nathan participates more independently.	*High Leverage Practices in Special Education* (2017), pp. 160-165 Video: "HLP 17: Use Flexible Groupings," https://highleveragepractices.org/hlp-17-use-flexible-grouping **HLP 17** leadership guide, https://exceptionalchildren.org/sites/default/files/2021-01/HLP%2017%20Admin%20Guide.pdf

Note: IEP = individualized education program.

Chapter Objectives

After reading this chapter, readers will be able to accomplish the following objectives:

1. Summarize the three Big Ideas (i.e., HLPs) for special education writing instruction and explain the importance of each Big Idea.
2. Write a measurable short-term objective (for an intervention lesson) as well as a long-term learning goal.
3. Plan an intervention mini activity using explicit instruction (e.g., modeling, practice opportunities) to address a writing skill in need of improvement.
4. Describe an example scenario for how to implement flexible grouping to address students' writing needs.
5. Identify additional resources and next steps for extending learning of the three Big Ideas that were included in this chapter.

Foundational Learning Theory Supporting Research, and Policy

The strategies and ideas presented in this chapter were influenced by theoretical and empirical research. First, Graham's (2019) writer(s)-within-community (WWC) framework contextualizes the overarching purpose of writing intervention. In the WWC framework, the "community" where writing occurs shapes the writing types, tasks, and the activities that writers engage in. For instance, a third-grade teacher has considerable influence over the writing activities conducted within her classroom writing community. Next, the skills and capabilities of the students coupled with available resources (e.g., technology, texts) also shape writing within a given community. Finally, the WWC model suggests that effective written expression is crucial for educational endeavors, socialization, and other facets of life; thus, writing must be consistently taught and advocated for (Graham, 2019; 2023). This chapter describes how teachers of SWDs can influence student outcomes within the classroom writing community.

Second, the ideas presented in this chapter were influenced by the instructional framework of explicit instruction, an approach with extensive theoretical and empirical research for SWDs (Hughes et al., 2017). Explicit instruction is an organized approach to teaching that involves providing clear learning objectives and explanations of new concepts, strategies or skills, teacher modeling and demonstration, and student practice with feedback to promote student independence (Hughes et al., 2017; Kauffman et al., 2011). The Council for Exceptional Children (CEC) published a guidebook of HLPs for teaching special education that pre- and in-service teacher preparation programs are encouraged to apply. Explicit instruction and other key principles of quality teaching are infused within these practice (see table 7.1; McLeskey et al., 2017). These ideas will be highlighted in this chapter due to their effectiveness for teaching SWDs.

Finally, the strategies presented in this chapter for each Big Idea are based on findings from systematic reviews of writing intervention research. For example, a meta-analysis by Gillespie and Graham (2014) that reviews writing interventions for students with learning disabilities has been a helpful source for identifying effective interventions. Further, intervention research for students with low-incidence disabilities, including intellectual disabilities, will be referenced (e.g., Rodgers & Loveall,

2023) because SWDs who receive writing intervention in inclusion or resource room settings possess a wide range of disability classifications. Thus, the ideas and suggestions presented in this chapter are grounded in relevant theory and research.

Policy and Standards. Effective writing intervention in the elementary grades can prepare students for the demands of writing across disciplines that occurs in middle school. The Common Core State Standards (CCSS), which were adopted by a majority of US states, are an example of how early writing skills are prioritized. For instance, by the end of fifth grade, students are expected to write opinion, informative, and narrative pieces with "clear and coherent writing in which the development and organization are appropriate to task, purpose, and audience" (ELA Standards: Writing, grade 5, 2021). These early standards are a foundation for advanced writing tasks presented in grades 6–12, where increased sophistication in language use and addressing disciplinary information are crucial. States without the CCSS, such as Texas and Virginia, have similar writing requirements within their standards. For instance, students in grades 6–8 in Texas must master the writing process, which spans from planning, to drafting, to revising an essay for added clarity (Texas Education Agency, 2019, p. 10). Ultimately, writing instruction and intervention for SWDs beginning in kindergarten is necessary to build a foundation for future writing success.

Several professional organizations have provided guidance on best practices to teach writing to striving writers and to SWDs. For instance, the Collaboration for Effective Educator Development, Accountability, and Reform (CEEDAR) Center recommends explicit and systematic instruction, setting specific writing goals, and assessing student progress. Further, the Institute of Education Sciences (IES) publishes practice guides that contain suggestions for effective educational programming across subject areas. Two IES practice guides focused on writing instruction (Graham, 2018; Graham et al., 2016) indicate that providing more time for students to write daily across all subjects is crucial in grades K–5 and grades 6–12. Thus, the practice guides urge school leaders to arrange teachers' schedules to allow for additional daily opportunities for students to write. Finally, evidence-based strategies taught to students should be used within a community of writers, which includes peer revision and support, sharing of written products, and allowing students to write about personally meaningful topics (e.g., social causes). Writing standards, policy, and professional recommendations clarify that writing is key to academic success: as educators, we must provide students with the resources to be successful.

A Note About Formative Writing Assessment

When implementing the three Big Ideas, practitioners should consider using formative assessment to guide their instructional decisions and facilitate continuous growth in students' writing. For SWDs, four methods of formative assessment can be particularly beneficial in enhancing students' writing and guiding instructional planning. In this section, we briefly describe the procedures for utilizing these formative assessment methods and the evidence to support them. Additional formative assessment recommendations can be accessed in a Carnegie Report titled *Informing Writing: The Benefits of Formative Assessment* (Graham et al., 2011).

First, research evidence suggests providing feedback to students about their writing is a simple method for continuously evaluating student writing progress (Graham et al., 2011; 2015). Although feedback from teachers and other adults can result in significant gains in writing progress, feedback from peers has also proven to be beneficial in improving writing quality (Graham et al., 2011). Opportunities for students to give and receive feedback can promote a community of writers in which all students are actively engaged in the writing process. Feedback can be provided orally or in written form, with both methods supported by empirical evidence in improving student writing (Graham et al., 2011). Feedback opportunities can be aligned with targeted short- and long-term goals, with teachers specifically focusing on writing development in those areas. For SWDs, positive, specific praise can promote good writing habits and reinforce the strategies they should engage in when writing.

Second, when using formative assessment with SWDs and striving writers, educators are encouraged to be cautious about how biases about the writers' identity may skew judgments about their writing (see Graham et al., 2011, for research on how knowledge of a student's disability may influence formative assessments). It is helpful to be mindful of the malleability of students' writing, recognizing that prior difficulties may not persist when students receive high-quality and effective writing instruction. Therefore, attempting to minimize preconceived assumptions about typical writing behaviors and skills ensures that students are provided safe spaces to take risks as writers and grow over the course of a school year.

A strategy that many teachers use is to collect multiple samples of students' writing and consistently progress-monitor students over time as part of their ongoing formative assessment. Prior research suggests teachers may need as many as eight to 14 writing samples to reliably evaluate writing output (e.g., the number of words written), vocabulary usage, and essay composition quality. As such, progress-monitoring writing development over a three- to four-month period allows teachers to gather a more comprehensive profile of who students are as writers.

Finally, teaching students to self-assess their own writing is a powerful method for facilitating growth in writers (Graham et al., 2011). When students learn to evaluate their own writing, they can determine their progress toward individual goals and identify misalignment in their ideation and planning versus the words that made it to the written page. Therefore, involving students in the formative assessment process and teaching them to utilize evaluation strategies promotes the development of successful and independent writers.

BIG IDEAS FOR EFFECTIVE WRITING INTERVENTION FOR STUDENTS WITH DISABILITIES

The next part of this chapter includes specific strategies for writing intervention with SWDs in grades K–5. To accomplish this aim, we present three Big Ideas for effective writing intervention. The following Big Ideas from CEC's HLP (McLeskey et al., 2017) toolkit will be presented along with a case study example, tips for classroom use, and resources for extended learning in tables 7.1 and 7.2. The following three Big Ideas are presented:

- Big Idea 1 (HLP 11): Identify and prioritize long- and short-term learning goals.
- Big Idea 2 (HLP 16): Explicit instruction.
- Big Idea 3 (HLP 17): Flexible grouping.

Table 7.2. Extend Your Learning

Writing Skills	Article Titles/Authors	Resources	Guiding Questions or Activities
Sentence Structure and Grammar	"The Effects of Supplemental Sentence-Level Instruction for Fourth-Grade Students Identified as Struggling Writers" (Furey et al., 2017)	Reading & Writing Quarterly	How could teachers integrate supplemental sentence-level instruction for lower- or upper-elementary students with the whole class, small groups, or with individual students?
	"Teaching Writing Through Content: Six Instructional Activities to Improve Students' Sentence-Level Writing Skills" (Chandler & Sayeki, 2021)	Teaching Exceptional Children	Teachers can create their own sample schedule to demonstrate how they will teach explicit sentence-level writing skills across content areas during the school day. This should be implemented each week.
	"Sentence-Writing Intervention for At-Risk Writers in Upper-Elementary Grades" (Smith et al., 2021)	Learning Disabilities: Research & Practice	Using the rubric provided by the authors, teachers can establish long- and short-term sentence-writing goals for students.
Planning/Text Organization	"Supporting the Writing Process with Technology for Students with Disabilities" (Evmenova & Regan, 2019)	Intervention in School and Clinic	When using a graphic organizer for planning writing, what are long- and short-term student goals to help students become independent writers?
	"A Computer-Based Graphic Organizer with Embedded Self-Regulated Learning Strategies to Support Student Writing" (Hughes, Regan, & Evmenova, 2019)	Intervention in School and Clinic	Teachers review the computer-based graphic organizers (CBGO) recommended in the article and create a lesson plan to teach students how to implement the CBGOs using explicit instruction and self-regulated strategies.
Editing and Revision Strategies	"Do Content-Revising Goals Change the Revising Behavior and Story Writing of Fourth-Grade Students At-Risk for Writing Difficulties?" (Graham et al. 2021)	Reading and Writing: An Interdisciplinary Journal	What are some long- and short-term goals that students can have for revising essays? How can teachers use flexible grouping to support students in revising their writing?
	"FIX: A Strategic Approach to Writing and Revision for Students with Learning Disabilities" (Sherman & De La Paz, 2015)	Teaching Exceptional Children	How can teachers confirm that students are correctly using revision strategies during small group instruction to promote eventual independence using the FIX strategy?
	"Steps for Success: Making Instructional Decisions for Students' Essay Writing" (Regan et al., 2021)	Teaching Exceptional Children	How can teachers make instructional decisions based on data to help students progress toward long- and short-term goals for essay writing? Practice by evaluating a student essay.
Genre-Based Specialization	"Teaching Spelling, Writing, and Reading for Writing: Powerful Evidence-Based Practice" (Harris & Graham, 2017)	Teaching Exceptional Children	Teachers begin by selecting one strategy from the article to model for students in a genre-based writing activity or assignment.
	"Writing Expository Essays from Social Studies Texts: A Self-Regulated Strategy Development Study" (Collins et al., 2021)	Reading and Writing: An Interdisciplinary Journal	How can teachers use partner feedback during the SRSD "Support It" stage to build independence with the TIDE strategy?

Big Idea 1: Identify and Prioritize Long- and Short-Term Learning Goals

Identifying, creating, and prioritizing learning goals is an essential element of writing intervention. For Big Idea 1 (HLP 11), teachers prioritize essential student writing needs that must be addressed with intervention. There are three useful principles to remember when applying this Big Idea. First, writing goals should be data driven and aligned with a specific need or standard. Second, teachers begin the goal development process by first identifying and creating the long-term goal. Next, teachers determine the necessary prerequisite skills that should be included within a short-term goal that will serve as a starting place for attaining the long-term goal (examples provided in the subsequent case study). Finally, all goals should be measurable and specific (Hedin & DeSpain, 2018) so that students, parents, and teachers understand what is expected and how the goal will be reached.

Examples. Several components must be included within student's long-term writing goals, as well as for individualized education plan (IEP) or intervention goals. Long-term goals contain: (a) the condition, (b) the learner(s), (c) the observable behavior or academic criterion for accomplishing the goal, and (d) the time frame (Hedin & DeSpain, 2018). Short-term goals or objectives are developed following the creation of the long-term goal to assist teachers with determining which prerequisite, or foundational skills, are prioritized to help students attain their long-term goal. An example of this for writing intervention is depicted in the following example.

Long-Term (IEP) Annual Goal Example for Sentence Writing
When providing writing prompts and when completing quarterly benchmark assessments, the student will independently demonstrate improved written sentence-writing ability by capitalizing the first letter of a sentence and utilizing correct punctuation. The student will achieve this goal with 75% accuracy across (three out of every four trials) by March 1.

Short-Term Intervention Goal Example for Sentence Writing
Given sentence prompts and/or visual aids (pictures), the student will independently compose a sentence with a subject and predicate in four out of five trials (80% of the time). The sentences will be evaluated based on their correct use of a subject and a predicate (e.g., Mike plays basketball on Fridays) and adherence to basic grammar rules (excluding capitalization and punctuation) in one month's time.

Case Study: Ms. Turner. *Ms. Turner is a special education teacher supporting students with individualized education plans (IEPs) in third grade. The majority of the students on her caseload have a learning disability (LD) in mathematics, reading, or writing. Ms. Turner has a new student named Amelia who requires an IEP goal in writing. The assessment data collected on Amelia, which includes formal results of achievement testing (i.e., nationally normed standardized assessments used for special education classification) formative assessment (e.g., classroom tests and work samples), and district-administered benchmark measures, indicate that Amelia* *currently writes at a first-grade level in the areas of sentence writing fluency and organization of ideas. Amelia's assessments further suggest that she can compose a grammatically correct sentence with a subject and predicate 80% of the time, but she requires intervention focused on organizing her ideas into a complete paragraph. Samples of her paragraphs from benchmark assessments indicate that her ideas are often lacking elaborations for key ideas and details.*

Mrs. Tuner and her colleagues use the aforementioned data to develop a writing goal for Amelia. The following one-year IEP goal is based on two factors: (a) Amelia's specific abilities and needs in writing, as revealed via assessment results; and (b) grade-level standards. Ms. Turner determines that it is feasible for Amelia to write a complete informational paragraph by the conclusion of the school year after receiving daily writing intervention. While it is possible that Amelia may be able to compose a multi-paragraph composition this school year (as specified in the third-grade standards), Ms. Turner concludes that a goal to compose one strong paragraph will address Amelia's needs, be rigorous enough to warrant intervention, and provide Amelia with a foundation for future success in writing. Ms. Turner wrote the following long-term goal for Amelia:

Long-Term Goal (IEP Goal in Writing for Amelia)

When engaging in classroom writing assignments and the third-grade benchmark writing assessment, the student will independently compose informational paragraphs with correct capitalization and punctuation. The paragraph will include a well-defined topic sentence, three supporting detail sentences, and a concluding sentence to the paragraph. The student will achieve this goal with 80% accuracy (four out of five trials) by May (one academic year).

Finally, Ms. Turner creates a short-term goal for Amelia that will influence her daily writing intervention and keep Amelia on pace for attaining her long-term writing goal. Ms. Turner decides that writing a compound sentence with correct capitalization and punctuation with a high degree of accuracy is attainable in the short term and supports with Amelia's long-term goal. The following short-term goal is created:

Short-Term Intervention Goal

When presented with teacher-provided writing prompts, the student will independently compose compound sentences with correct capitalization and punctuation in four out of five trials. The sentences will include two independent clauses joined by a coordinating conjunction (e.g., and, but, because, or). This goal will be attained by the end of the first marking period.

Ms. Turner now understands what Amelia needs to accomplish in writing this school year. Her next step is to use effective instructional practices (e.g., HLPs) and evidence-based writing interventions to assist Amelia with achieving her writing goals.

The following sections of this chapter provide examples of effective instruction, as well as resources.

Big Idea 2: Use Explicit Instruction

Explicit instruction (HLP 16) has historically been a highly effective teaching approach for improving the academic outcomes of SWDs (Hughes et al., 2019; Powell et al., 2021; Swanson, 1999). During explicit instruction, teachers introduce a new strategy, skill, or concept using a step-by-step approach that includes clear and informative tips for students. Explicit instruction is used across grade levels because teachers break strategies, skills, or concepts into bite-size, manageable steps, which is beneficial for learning new concepts. Importantly, explicit instruction is *not* a teaching approach consisting of extensive teacher lecture, lengthy rote skill practice, or an approach to teaching where students are passive learners. To the contrary, explicit instruction is a powerful teaching approach that allows educators to model, demonstrate, and explain something new in an easy-to-understand way so that students learn the strategy, engage in guided practice with a teacher or peer, and use the new strategy for independent learning and critical thinking (Martin & Evans, 2018).

Explicit instruction is depicted in the following example of teaching students the concept of "proper nouns" during writing. First, a teacher would provide a definition of proper nouns to students (i.e., the specific name of a place, person, organization, or thing written with a capital letter to begin the word). Next, the teacher lists examples of proper nouns such as names of students in the class, the school's name, and notable places such as the Smithsonian Museum of Natural History. The teacher then provides non-examples to increase understanding by offering a contrast. The teacher then reminds students that the lesson objective is to utilize proper nouns within a complete sentence (e.g., *We are visiting the Smithsonian Museum for a field trip in May*). The teacher assigns students to work with a partner to identify five proper nouns. Students turn and talk for several minutes and write their proper nouns on a tablet, computer, or whiteboard, before sharing with the class.

Explicit Instruction in Action: Example 1

Step 1. Setting the Stage. *Ms. Turner is teaching writing to students in the resource room in a small-group setting. She first points to the lesson objective and reads it aloud before her group of five students reads the objective in an echo reading fashion, "Today we will use the sentence combining strategy to write a longer sentence. Next, we will include one proper noun in our sentence." Ms. Turner explains that the purpose of today's lesson is to make their sentences more interesting for readers by making sentences longer, while using proper nouns to provide detail about the people or places they are writing about.*

Ms. Turner activates prior knowledge by reminding students of the activities about proper nouns they have been practicing. She shows examples of proper nouns, and non-examples, and asks students to describe why we use proper nouns in our writing. With this activity, Ms. Turner connects previous learning to today's lesson. Ms. Turner further activates prior knowledge by inviting students to share an example of an interesting story they have read about that contains extensive detail. Ms. Turner states, "for the next three minutes, talk to your shoulder partner about an article we have read before that has interesting details. What proper nouns were used in the article"? After three minutes, students share details from their discussion and Ms. Turner provides feedback, if necessary, to confirm that students comprehend this concept before using proper nouns during a sentence-writing strategy.

Step 2. Explicit Instruction: Modeling the Strategy. *The forthcoming step is crucial for building Ms. Turner's students' understanding and confidence. Here, she uses a "think-aloud" method to model the sentence-combining strategy. Thinking aloud while demonstrating a writing strategy is a common and highly effective approach to writing intervention for students with disabilities (e.g., Harris & Graham, 2017; Rodgers & Loveall, 2023). In the following example, Ms. Turner addresses the two objectives of today's lesson by modeling how to use the sentence combining strategy with a proper noun included in her sentence.*

Ms. Turner begins by displaying two sentences about Ruby Bridges, who the class read about last week during social studies. The two sentences state: "Ruby Bridges was courageous. Ruby Bridges was only six years old when she attended William Frantz Elementary School." Next, Ms. Turner thinks aloud as she writes (or types) to combine these two sentences into one longer sentence. She states, "These sentences make sense as separate sentences. But . . . my writing will be more interesting if I connect the sentences using the word because *to create one longer sentence." Ms. Turner then erases the period and writes the word* because *before rereading the whole sentence to confirm that it makes sense. The students then chorally read the new sentence together: "Ruby Bridges was courageous because she was only six years old when she attended William Frantz Elementary School." Finally, Ms. Turner asks the students to remind their partner which proper nouns were used in this activity.*

Step 3. Guided and Independent Practice. *Ms. Turner's students begin guided practice for the next few class sessions until they are ready for independent practice using the sentence combining strategy. Ms. Turner uses several options for guided practice during her writing intervention lessons to gradually increase her students' writing independence. One guided practice option is to provide students with clues, such as a bank of words (e.g., and, but, because) to use when merging two sentences into one longer sentence. A second option is to invite students to correct mistakes that the teacher has intentionally made, a technique that promotes active student engagement. For instance, Ms. Turner could invite students to describe why they believe she made a mistake and ask students to provide suggestions for improving the sentence. A variety of guided practice options, including having students practice the strategy with a with a partner (with immediate teacher feedback), promotes students' independence and confidence. Finally, students will practice this strategy independently using sentences that Ms. Turner highlights from the students' independent writing samples. After establishing independence, teachers still utilize recursive instruction when teaching writing to revisit (and to model and demonstrate again) the strategies, concepts, or skills that students need (Harris & Graham, 2017).*

Step 4. Confirming Student Learning and Selecting Next Steps. *After providing opportunities for independent practice (with ongoing feedback, as needed), Ms. Turner uses two types of formative assessment to determine if students have learned how to combine sentences and how to integrate proper nouns within those sentences. First, she assigns "exit tickets." This is a brief two- to-three-minute activity at the conclusion of a lesson where students are tasked with combining two sentences provided by Ms. Turner to gauge their understanding. Second, students* *will be completing different paragraph writing assignments over the next couple of weeks during which they will be required to use proper nouns and implement sentence-combining strategies while revising their essays. Immediate feedback and on-the-spot modeling are provided, as needed, to enable students to revise and enhance their sentences. Ms. Turner realizes that authentic writing (about students' experiences or interests) or writing about topics recently studied (e.g., a science concept) can strengthen student understanding and strategy proficiency (Graham & Sandmel, 2011).*

In the coming weeks, Ms. Turner repeats the process of explicit instruction that was previously described (e.g., introducing a new strategy, examples and non-examples, etc.) as she teaches new strategies. For instance, Ms. Turner may now focus on the long-term goal of paragraph writing, using a concept map graphic organizer to plan and organize the ideas that will be included in the paragraph (Collins et al., 2021). She may model the entire process (as previously described for proper nouns and sentence combining) as she shows students how to write brief notes while thinking aloud to model turning notes into complete sentences. Ms. Turner thinks aloud as she takes the words playground *and* fundraiser *from the concept map and demonstrates turning them into a complete sentence such as, "Ok. Now is the fun part! I take my notes that we wrote on the concept map and turn these notes into a full sentence. Let's see, I'm going to use my notes that say* playground *and* fundraiser *to create a sentence that says, "We can raise money for a new school playground by hosting a fundraiser on our campus!" Wow, I like this strategy because I can just use a few words as ideas that turn those words into sentences for my paragraph!*

Additional Considerations. Explicit instruction is a powerful way to teach students to learn writing strategies. It's important to remember that teachers need opportunities to practice modeling via explicit instruction to become comfortable with this instructional approach. You, the reader, are encouraged to utilize tables 7.1 and 7.2 to locate additional resources for learning to implement explicit instruction, while coupling these explicit instructional routines with research-based writing practices (also included in the tables). Students can establish a foundation for effective strategy use in writing by receiving explicit writing instruction.

Big Idea 3: Use Flexible Student Grouping

The final Big Idea presented in this chapter is the use of flexible grouping while providing evidence-based writing intervention. This HLP (17) recommends that teachers utilize several data sources and classroom observations to create flexible grouping arrangements for their students. Data sources used to make decisions about student grouping include formative assessments (as discussed earlier in the chapter), results of formal progress monitoring in writing, as well as consideration for factors including child's short- and/or long-term learning or behavioral goals (including IEP goals). Importantly, teachers are encouraged to implement heterogeneous as well as homogenous groups at different times. Student grouping decisions vary based on the writing strategy, skill, or concept taught, as well as considerations for promoting positive peer-to-peer interactions (McLeskey et al., 2017).

Examples and Non-Examples. One flexible grouping option is an "alternative teaching" co-teach model (Friend, 2015). Within alternative teaching, one teacher provides writing instruction to a larger group of students, while a second teacher provides small-group instruction in the same classroom for a specific activity, sometimes for just 20 to 30 minutes. For instance, a general educator could implement a whole-group writing lesson focusing on editing and revising strategies using the COPS mnemonic strategy (capitalization, organization, punctuation, and spelling; Ciullo & Mason 2017; Graham et al., 2012) for a persuasive essay with 15 students working on their laptops. Concurrently, the special educator provides explicit instruction (via modeling and thinking aloud while demonstrating) for five students who require support with writing a conclusion sentence to their paragraphs.

A non-example of flexible grouping would be consistently grouping the same students together without varying group membership. While students with IEPs all require targeted support based on IEP goals, it is unlikely that all students would benefit from being grouped together consistently because students learn concepts, strategies, or skills at a different pace. For instance, an educator who consistently uses alternative grouping to instruct the same five students with IEPs is not utilizing the Big Idea of flexible grouping.

Teaching Steps: Flexible Grouping for Writing Intervention. Educators can use the following steps to implement flexible grouping during writing intervention. After summarizing these three steps, we provide a case study example from Ms. Turner's class to depict flexible grouping within an inclusive third-grade classroom for an evidence-based writing intervention for SWDs: peer editing and revision (Cho & MacArthur, 2011; Stoddard & MacArthur, 1993; Wong et al., 1996).

Step 1. Teachers review writing data to inform their instructional grouping decisions. Teachers determine if there are specific writing skills (e.g., sentence construction, use of supporting details within informative essay writing) that several students in the classroom would benefit from additional practice with. Teachers may also use flexible grouping to provide enrichment to students who are more advanced in specific writing skills.

Step 2. Select a grouping strategy. Two common grouping options are (a) station teaching (Cook & Friend, 1995; Friend, 2015) characterized by a special education teacher and a general education teacher instructing separate small groups of students on different topics/activities, while the students in the class rotate to a different station every 15 to 20 minutes; and (b) a targeted small-group support, referred to as alternative teaching (introduced in the previous section of this chapter). Alternative teaching includes one teacher, potentially the special educator, providing small-group instruction for a specific amount of time, such as 20 minutes daily for one week, as students practice a writing skill, concept, or strategy.

Step 3. Intervention begins as the co-teachers monitor student progress in alignment with students' short- or long-term writing goals. Progress monitoring, observations of classroom writing performance based on lesson objectives, as well as ongoing planning with a co-teacher are proactive strategies to ensure that membership in student groups remains fluid. The following example of Ms. Turner and her third-grade co-teaching partner, Mr. Anderson, describes flexible grouping, with research-based writing strategies. Further, this section of the chapter concludes with suggestions for promoting active student engagement and positive social interactions.

Ms. Turner and Mr. Anderson Use Flexible Grouping. *Ms. Turner (special education teacher) and Mr. Anderson (third-grade general education inclusion) collaborate to address the vast range of writing needs that students in the classroom possess, including five students with IEPs. The teachers review formative assessment data and determine that most students in the class are ready to use an effective writing intervention strategy—peer editing and peer revision (Cho & MacArthur, 2011)—to improve their recently written essays. They also decide that six students (including several students with IEPs) would benefit from a review lesson focusing on writing a complete conclusion sentence to a paragraph. The teachers decide that Mr. Anderson will instruct the larger group of students with peer editing and revision while Ms. Turner will review conclusion sentences with a small alternative group of students.*

On Monday, Mr. Anderson teaches a whole-group lesson on peer editing and peer revision to help students improve the quality of their previously written essays. During this lesson, Mr. Anderson provides a checklist of what partners will provide feedback on when they trade essays with a partner. Using the COPS strategy (capitalization, organization, punctuation, and spelling), Mr. Anderson provides an example of how, today, the students will only focus on the first two parts of COPS with an editing partner: they will check capitalization of proper nouns (and beginning of sentences), and they will review organization and appearance by checking if paragraphs are indented and if proper spacing appears between words. Mr. Anderson realizes that writing strategies like COPS have multiple components for writers to check, so scaffold writing strategies by focusing on specific parts that are feasible to complete is helpful to young writers (Ciullo & Mason 2017).

Concurrently, Ms. Turner convenes a group of six students (i.e., an alternative teaching format) for an intervention lesson on writing a concluding sentence to paragraphs. First, Ms. Turner reminds students that they previously wrote paragraphs about the roles of different leadership positions in state and local government (e.g., mayor, governor, city council) and today they will review tips for writing an ending sentence. Ms. Turner leads the class in choral reading of the lesson objective, "Today we will write a complete concluding sentence to our paragraph." Ms. Turner also explains why this skill is important by stating, "A strong and complete ending sentence helps to wrap up our ideas and remind our readers of the topic that we just wrote about. Stopping writing without adding a detailed conclusion sentence is sort of like a movie stopping before the ending."

Ms. Turner then activates students' prior knowledge. First, she displays an example of a quality conclusion sentence to a previously written essay, before presenting a non-example of ending the essay with a less effective sentence. Ms. Turner proceeds to use explicit instruction to model (by thinking aloud and writing to demonstrate, as described in the previous section for Big Idea 2). After modeling, Ms. Turner initiates guided practice and then independent practice using the steps outlined in Big Idea 2 (explicit instruction). During guided practice, students work with a partner on using a sentence stem to conclude a previously written paragraph about the school's mascot. Next, students use a sentence stem to write a complete sentence to their own paragraph such as, "In conclusion, the governor of our state is elected for a four-year term."

As a reminder, flexible grouping arrangements are meant to be fluid. Although the aforementioned example suggest that students were placed in Ms. Turner's group for a week to review the skill of concluding sentences, two students who mastered the skill after two days of practice may no longer require this small-group support. Targeted intervention, progress monitoring, and communication between co-teachers can help flexible grouping during writing intervention to be more successful.

Tips for Promoting Positive Behavior Within Small Groups. Some students with learning and/or behavioral difficulties may experience writing tasks and instruction as aversive, resulting in escape-maintained challenging behavior (e.g., behaviors to avoid writing). To address this challenge, educators can implement a variety of strategies to promote academic engagement, positive student behavior, and prosocial peer interactions. These include providing reinforcement to students when they perform desired behaviors during writing intervention, ongoing preference assessment, and behavioral momentum instructional methods.

First, educators can provide reinforcement to students when they are observed performing on-task behaviors, putting forth effort when completing a writing task, using instructional feedback to correct errors, and encouraging peers (McKenna & Bettini, 2018). Reinforcement can be provided in the form of behavior-specific praise (Royer et al., 2019), such as stating the following when a student is observed fixing their work and continuing with guided practice: "Great job correcting that proper noun capitalization change and moving on to the next part of the COPS editing strategy, organization of text." By specifically stating aloud why the student is being praised, the statement becomes instructive to other students in the group (e.g., they are told why a student was praised), thus increasing the likelihood that other students will perform a similar behavior.

Educators can also provide reinforcement in the form of awarding points for desired behavior that can later be redeemed to obtain a tangible item or a privilege (Adamson et al., 2019). However, it is critical that educators perform a preference assessment to identify the tangible items and privileges that students experience as reinforcing (McKenna & Bettini, 2018). To do this, educators like Ms. Turner first create a list of rewards that they feel comfortable providing to students. Each item on the list can be paired with a simple Likert scale so that students can rate the degree to which they perceive the item as reinforcing. For example, the following scale could be used to rate each item: 0 = not at all, 1 = I like it, 2 = I like it a lot! Next, educators provide a space on the preference assessment sheet for students to list their own ideas for reinforcers. Next, educators explain the purpose of the preference assessment (e.g., "I want to find out what things you are motivated to earn by working hard and being positive during our writing group when we use the COPS editing strategy to improve our essays") and model for students how to complete it. Students then complete the preference assessment, and educators aggregate student responses to create a menu of reinforcers. When creating the menu, teachers ensure that each student has at least one thing listed that they are motivated to earn, which is critical for students who perform frequent and/or persistent challenging behavior.

Furthermore, educators should view preference assessment as an ongoing process, as student preferences change over time. Thus, educators can conduct a preference assessment approximately every three weeks to track changing student preferences.

Behavioral momentum can also be used to promote academic engagement. This behavioral strategy involves having students first complete tasks that they perceive to be as easy or of interest before moving on to other types of tasks that are progressively more difficult and/or less of a personal interest (Mace et al., 1988). For example, students could participate in an editing lesson that focuses on a topic of interest among group members and then participate in a lesson that is based on content that more closely aligns with curriculum standards. Explicit instruction, with its progression from teacher modeling to guided practice and independent practice, also incorporates behavioral momentum as the instructional sequence requires students to take on increasing levels of responsibility.

CLOSING THOUGHTS AND NEXT STEPS

In addition to completing the activities embedded within each chapter objective, we also conclude with two suggestions. First, remember that students' writing needs will vary extensively (i.e., from sentence-level writing to multi-paragraph genre-based writing). Thus, teachers utilize HLPs, such as the three Big Ideas presented in this chapter, as an instructional framework for teaching strategies that address those specific skills. For instance, the Big Idea of explicit instruction for modeling and demonstrating strategies can be used for foundational skills such as writing a complete sentence with a subject and predicate, or with a more complex skill such as writing a persuasive essay. Finally, we must continually remind ourselves that the ultimate purpose of writing intervention is to provide students with tools to effectively communicate their ideas, thoughts, and emotions not just for academic purposes but also to enrich their lives (Graham, 2019). Please use the following chapter objectives and the additional resources in tables 7.1 and 7.2 as you embark on the challenging but meaningful role of helping SWDs to become strong and confident writers.

Chapter Objectives Revisited

You should complete the activity included within each objective listed below independently or with a partner. Further, please reference the resources in tables 7.1 and 7.2 to boost your understanding as well as your instructional planning.

- Summarize the three Big Ideas (i.e., HLPs) for special education writing instruction and explain the importance of each Big Idea.
- Write a measurable short-term objective (for an intervention lesson) as well as a long-term learning goal.
- Plan an intervention mini activity using explicit instruction (e.g., modeling, practice opportunities) to address a writing skill in need of improvement.
- Describe an example scenario for how to implement flexible grouping to address students' writing needs.
- Identify additional resources and next steps for extending learning of the three Big Ideas that were included in this chapter.

REFERENCES

Adamson, R., McKenna, J., & Mitchell, B. (2019). Supporting all students: Creating a tiered continuum of behavior support at the classroom level to enhance school-wide multi-tiered systems of support. *Preventing School Failure*, 63(1), 62–67. https://doi.org/10.1080/1045988X.2018.1501654

Bailey, T., Kennedy, M. J., & Jackson, D. (2017). High leverage practice #11: Identify and prioritize long and short-term learning goals. https://highleveragepractices.org/hlp-11-goal-setting

Berninger, V. W. (2009). Highlights of programmatic, interdisciplinary research on writing. *Learning Disabilities Research & Practice*, 24(2), 69–80.

Brindle, M., Graham, S., Harris, K., & Hebert, M. (2016). Third and fourth grade teacher's classroom practices in writing: A national survey. *Reading and Writing*, 29(5), 929–954.

Chandler, B. W., & Sayeki, K. L. (2021). Teaching writing through content: Six instructional activities to improve students' sentence-level writing skills. *Teaching Exceptional Children*. http://dx.doi.org/10.1177/00400599211050087

Cho, K., & MacArthur, C. (2011). Learning by reviewing. *Journal of Educational Psychology*, 103(1), 73.

Ciullo, S., & Mason, L. (2017). Prioritizing elementary school writing instruction: Cultivating middle school readiness for students with learning disabilities. *Intervention in School and Clinic*, 52(5), 287–294.

Collaboration for Effective Educator Development, Accountability, and Reform (CEEDAR) Center. (2016). Write from the start: Evidence-based writing instruction (PowerPoint presentation). http://ceedar.education.ufl.edu/wp-content/uploads/2016/03/Writing-Anchor-Presentation.pptx

Collaboration for Effective Educator Development, Accountability, and Reform (CEEDAR) Center. (2023). CEEDAR Center: About us. Gainesville, FL. https://ceedar.education.ufl.edu/about-us/

Collins, A., Ciullo, S., Graham, S., Sigafoos, L., Guerra, S., David, M., & Judd, L. (2021). Writing expository essays from social studies texts: A self-regulated strategy development study. *Reading and Writing: An Interdisciplinary Journal*, 34, 1623–1651. https://doi.org/10.1007/s11145-021-10157-2

Cook L., & Friend, M. (1995). Co-teaching: Guidelines for creating effective practices. *Focus on Exceptional Children*, 28, 1–16.

Evmenova, A. S., & Regan, K., (2019). Supporting the writing process with technology for students with disabilities. *Intervention in School and Clinic*, 55(2), 78–85. http://dx.doi.org/10.1177/1053451219837636

Evmenova, A. S., Regan, K., & Hutchison, A. (2020). AT for writing technology-based graphic organizers with embedded supports. *TEACHING Exceptional Children*, 52(4), 266–269. http://dx.doi.org/10.1177/0040059920907571

Friend, M. (2015). Welcome to co-teaching 2.0. *Educational Leadership*, 73(4), 16–22.

Furey, W. M., Marcotte, A. M., Wells, C. S., & Hintze, J. M. (2017). The effects of supplemental sentence-level instruction for fourth-grade students identified as struggling writers. *Reading and Writing Quarterly: Overcoming Learning Disabilities*, 33(6), 563–578. http://dx.doi.org/10.1080/10573569.2017.1288591

Gillespie, A., & Graham, S. (2014). A meta-analysis of writing interventions for students with learning disabilities. *Exceptional Children*, *80*(4), 454–473.

Graham, S. (2018). A revised writer(s)-within-community model of writing. *Educational Psychologist*, *53*(4), 258–279.

Graham, S. (2019). changing how writing is taught. *Review of Research in Education*, *43*(1), 277–303. https://doi.org/10.3102/0091732X18821125

Graham, S. (2023). Writer(s)-Within-Community model of writing as a lens for studying the teaching of writing. In R. Horowitz (Ed.), *The Routledge international handbook of research on writing* (pp. 337–350). Routledge.

Graham, S., & Hebert, M. (2011). Writing to read: A meta-analysis of the impact of writing and writing instruction on reading. *Harvard Educational Review*, *81*(4), 710–744.

Graham, S., & Sandmel, K. (2011). The process writing approach: A meta-analysis. *The Journal of Educational Research*, *104*(6), 396–407.

Graham, S., Bollinger, A., Booth Olson, C., D'Aoust, C., MacArthur, C., McCutchen, D., & Olinghouse, N. (2012). Teaching elementary school students to be effective writers: A practice guide (NCEE 2012-4058). National Center for Education Evaluation and Regional Assistance, Institute of Education Sciences, US Department of Education. http://ies.ed.gov/ncee/wwc/publications_reviews.aspx#pubsearch

Graham, S., Bruch, J., Fitzgerald, J., Friedrich, L., Furgeson, J., Greene, K., Kim, J., Lyskawa, J., Olson, C. B., & Smither Wulsin, C. (2016). Teaching secondary students to write effectively (NCEE 2017-4002). National Center for Education Evaluation and Regional Assistance (NCEE), Institute of Education Sciences, US Department of Education. http://whatworks.ed.gov.

Graham, S., Collins, A. A., & Ciullo, S. (2023). Special and general education teachers' beliefs about writing and writing instruction. *Journal of Learning Disabilities*, *56*(3), 163–179.

Graham, S., Collins, A. A., & Rigby-Wills, H. (2017). Writing characteristics of students with learning disabilities and typically achieving peers: A meta-analysis. *Exceptional Children*, *83*(2), 199–218.

Graham, S., Harris, K., Adkins, M., & Camping, A. (2021). Do content revising goals change the revising behavior and story writing of fourth grade students at-risk for writing difficulties? *Reading and Writing: An Interdisciplinary Journal*, *34*, 1915–1941. https://doi.org/10.1007/s11145-021-10142-9

Graham, S., Harris, K., & Hebert, M. A. (2011). *Informing writing: The benefits of formative assessment*. A Carnegie Corporation Time to Act report. Alliance for Excellent Education.

Graham, S., Hebert, M., Sandbank, M. P., & Harris, K. R. (2016). Assessing the writing achievement of young struggling writers: Application of generalizability theory. *Learning Disability Quarterly*, *39*(2), 72–82. https://doi.org/10.1177/0731948714555019

Graham, S., Kiuhara, S. A., & MacKay, M. (2020). The effects of writing on learning in science, social studies, and mathematics: A meta-analysis. *Review of Educational Research*, *90*(2), 179–226.

Harris, K. R., & Graham, S. (2017). Self-regulated strategy development: Theoretical bases, critical instructional elements, and future research. In M. Braaksma, K.

R. Harris, & R. Fidalgo (Eds.), *Design principles for teaching effective writing* (pp. 119–151). Brill.

Hedin, L., & DeSpain, S. (2018). SMART or not? Writing specific, measurable IEP goals. *Teaching Exceptional Children*, *51*(2), 100–110.

Hughes, C. A., Morris, J. R., Therrien, W. J., & Benson, S. K. (2017). Explicit instruction: Historical and contemporary contexts. *Learning Disabilities Research & Practice*, *32*(3), 140–148. https://doi.org/10.1111/ldrp.12142

Hughes, M. D., Regan, K. S., & Evmenova, A. (2019). A computer-based graphic organizer with embedded self-regulated learning strategies to support student writing. *Intervention in School and Clinic*, *55*(1), 13–22. https://journals.sagepub.com/doi/10.1177/1053451219833026

Kauffman, J. M., Hallahan, D. P., & P. C. Pullen. (Eds.). (2011). *Handbook of special education*. Routledge.

Mace, F., Hock, M., Lalli, J., West, B., Belfiore, P., Pinter, E., & Brown, D. (1988). Behavioral momentum in the treatment of non-compliance. *Journal of Applied Behavior Analysis*, *21*(2), 123–141. https://doi.org/10.1901/jaba.1988.21-123

Martin, A. J., & Evans, P. (2018). Load reduction instruction: Exploring a framework that assesses explicit instruction through to independent learning. *Teaching and Teacher Education*, *73*, 203–214.

McKenna, J., & Bettini, E. (2018). Improving reading fluency skills for secondary students with emotional and behavioral disorders. *Beyond Behavior*, *27*(2), 74–81. https://doi.org/10.1177/1074295618779374

McLeskey, J., Barringer, M-D., Billingsley, B., Brownell, M., Jackson, D., Kennedy, M., Lewis, T., Maheady, L., Rodriguez, J., Scheeler, M. C., Winn, J., & Ziegler, D. (2017). *High-leverage practices in special education*. Council for Exceptional Children & CEEDAR Center.

National Center for Education Statistics (NCES). (2015). NAEP data explorer. Institute of Education Sciences.

National Center for Intensive Intervention & Council for Exceptional Children Division for Research. (n.d.). *To be clear: What every educator needs to know about explicit instruction*. https://intensiveintervention.org/resource/What-Every-Educator-Needs-to-Know-About-Explicit-Instruction

National Governors Association Center for Best Practices & Council of Chief State School Officers. (2010). *Common core states standards for English language arts*. NGA Center for Best Practices and CCSSO.

Olson, C.B., Woodworth, K., Arshan, N., Black, R., Chung, H.Q., D'Aoust, C., Dewar, T., Friedrich, L., Godfrey, L., Land, R., Matuchniak, T., Scarcella, R., & Stowell, L. (2020). The pathway to academic success: Scaling up a text-based analytical writing intervention for latinos and english learners in secondary school. *Journal of Educational Psychology*, *112*(4), 701–717.

Powell, S. R., Mason, E. N., Bos, S. E., Hirt, S., Ketterlin-Geller, L. R., & Lembke, E. S. (2021). A systematic review of mathematics interventions for middle-school students experiencing mathematics difficulty. *Learning Disabilities Research & Practice*, *36*(4), 295–329.

Regan, K., Evmenova, A., Hutchison, A., Day, J., Stephens, M., Verbiest, C., & Gafurov, B. (2021). Steps for success: Making instructional decisions for students' essay writing. *Teaching Exceptional Children*, *54*(3), 202–212. http://dx.doi.org/10.1177/00400599211001085

Rodgers, D. B., & Loveall, S. J. (2023). Writing interventions for students with intellectual and developmental disabilities: A meta-analysis. *Remedial and Special Education*, *44*(3), 239–252.

Royer, D., Lane, K., Dunlap, K., & Ennis, R. (2019). A systematic review of teacher-delivered behavior specific praise on K–12 student performance. *Remedial and Special Education*, *40*(2), 112–128. https://doi.org/10.1177/0741932517751054

Sherman, C. K., & De La Paz, S. (2015). FIX: A strategic approach to writing and revision for students with learning disabilities. *Teaching Exceptional Children*, *48*(2), 98–101. http://dx.doi.org/10.1177/0040059915605823

Smith, A., Allen, A. A., Panos, K. L., & Ciullo, S. (2021). Sentence writing intervention for at-risk writers in upper elementary grades. *Teaching Exceptional Children*, *36*(4). 367–379. http://dx.doi.org/10.1111/ldrp.12266

Stoddard, B., & MacArthur, C. A. (1993). A peer editor strategy: Guiding learning-disabled students in response and revision. *Research in the Teaching of English*, 76–103.

Swanson, H. L. (1999). Instructional components that predict treatment outcomes for students with learning disabilities: Support for a combined strategy and direct instruction model. *Learning Disabilities Research & Practice*, *14*(3), 129–140.

Texas Education Agency. (2019). *Chapter 110. Texas essential knowledge and skills for English language arts and reading: Subchapter B. middle school*. https://tea.texas.gov/about-tea/laws-and-rules/sboe-rules-tac/sboe-tac-currently-in-effect/ch110b.pdf

Troia, G. A., & Graham, S. (2016). Common core writing and language standards and aligned State assessments: A national survey of teacher beliefs and attitudes. *Reading and Writing*, *29*(9), 1719–1743. https://doi.org/10.1007/s11145-016-9650-z

Virginia Department of Education. (2017). *Writing skills progression by grade (PDF)*. https://www.doe.virginia.gov/teaching-learning-assessment/k-12-standards-instruction/english-reading-literacy/literacy

Walter, K., Dockrell, J., & Connelly, V. (2021). A sentence-combining intervention for struggling writers: response to intervention. *Reading and Writing*, *34*, 1825–1850.

Wong, B. Y., Butler, D. L., Ficzere, S. A., & Kuperis, S. (1996). Teaching low achievers and students with learning disabilities to plan, write, and revise opinion essays. *Journal of Learning Disabilities*, *29*(2), 197–212.

8

Modeling in Elementary Science

Kelly Feille and Stephanie Hathcock

"HIGH-QUALITY ELEMENTARY SCIENCE EDUCATION is essential for establishing a sound foundation of learning in later grades, instilling a wonder of and enthusiasm for science that lasts a lifetime, and in addressing the critical need for a well-informed citizenry and society" (NSTA Board of Directors, 2018). With the incorporation of the Next Generation Science Standards (NGSS) (NGSS Lead States, 2013e), the National Science Teaching Association (NSTA) has identified four key principles to guide elementary science teaching and learning:

1. The elementary educational environment plays a key role in student learning;
2. Elementary students have the capacity to engage in scientific and engineering practices as they develop conceptual understandings over time;
3. Elementary students can and should engage in science within the broader community of science;
4. There must be adequate time in every school day to engage elementary students in high-quality science instruction that actively involves them in the processes of science.

(NSTA Board of Directors, 2018)

In light of these guiding principles, it is the responsibility of elementary science educators to identify and incorporate educational experiences that engage students in authentic science learning by building on students' existing knowledge and experiences and promote science as a social endeavor that is based on empirical evidence (National Research Council, 2012).

Even, or especially, at the elementary level, helping students to formulate a foundational understanding of the nature of science is essential. In grades K–5, students can experience the major themes, or tenets, of the nature of science in a variety of ways (see table 8.1). The tenets of the nature of science inform and are associated with the Science and Engineering Practices (SEPs) and the Crosscutting Concepts featured in the NGSS (NGSS Lead States, 2013e). Through engaging in

Table 8.1. The Nature of Science in Elementary Grades

Nature of Science Tenets	Grades K-2	Grades 3-5
Scientific investigations use a variety of methods.	• Science investigations begin with a question. • Scientists use different ways to study the world.	• Science methods are determined by questions. • Science investigations use a variety of methods, tools, and techniques.
Scientific knowledge is based on empirical evidence.	• Scientists look for patterns and order when making observations about the world.	• Science findings are based on recognizing patterns. Scientists use tools and technologies to make accurate measurements and observations.
Scientific knowledge is open to revision in light of new evidence, science models, laws, mechanisms, and theories explain natural phenomena.	• Science knowledge can change when new information is found. • Scientists use drawings, sketches, and models as a way to communicate ideas. • Scientists search for cause-and-effect relationships to explain natural events.	• Science explanations can change based on new evidence. • Science theories are based on a body of evidence and many tests. • Science explanations describe the mechanisms for natural events.
Science is a way of knowing.	• Science knowledge helps us know about the world.	• Science is both a body of knowledge and processes that add new knowledge. • Science is a way of knowing that is used by many people
Scientific knowledge assumes an order and consistency in natural systems.	• Science assumes natural events happen today as they happened in the past. • Many events are repeated.	• Science assumes consistent patterns in natural systems. • Basic laws of nature are the same everywhere in the universe.
Science is a human endeavor.	• People have practiced science for a long time. • Men and women of diverse backgrounds are scientists and engineers.	• Men and women from all cultures and backgrounds choose careers as scientists and engineers. • Most scientists and engineers work in teams. • Science affects everyday life. • Creativity and imagination are important to science.
Science addresses questions about the natural and material world.	• Scientists study the natural and material world.	• Science findings are limited to what can be answered with empirical evidence.

Source: NGSS Lead States (2013d).

authentic practices of science (NGSS Lead States, 2013b) and epistemic engagement in interdisciplinary, cross-cutting themes (NGSS Lead States, 2013c), elementary students construct deep, conceptual understanding of the disciplinary core ideas of the subject (NGSS Lead States, 2013a).

One essential practice that supports student development of conceptual understanding is the development and use of models. Models in science can be two- or three-dimensional diagrams, replicas, analogies, or computer simulations (NGSS Lead States, 2013b) and identify relevant aspects, relationships, and interactions of scientific phenomena (J. K. Gilbert, 2013; Nelson & Davis, 2012). A scientific model is not a replica of an object or system (Böschl et al., 2023; S. W. Gilbert, 1999; NGSS Lead States, 2013b; Yenilmez Turkoglu & Oztekin, 2016) but rather a simplified, visual representation of the target system or phenomenon that displays interactions and processes explicitly in order to both support the development of student conceptual knowledge and as a tool for students to represent current understanding of often complex and abstract scientific concepts (Barrett-Zahn, 2020; Nelson & Davis, 2012; Zangori et al., 2015). A scientific model is always evolving and is unique to the lived experiences, background knowledge, and current understanding of the model creator (S. W. Gilbert, 1999). In the science classroom, students follow an iterative process to evaluate and refine scientific models using empirical evidence and real-world experiences (NGSS Lead States, 2013b).

Through the development and use of scientific models, elementary students engage with several tenets of the nature of science including the essential nature of empirical evidence, the tentative nature of scientific knowledge, science as a way of knowledge, and science as a human endeavor. Additionally, modeling as a practice supports student communication of complex topics and interactions and engages systems thinking as students conceptualize and explain complex systems including system parts and interactions (Barrett-Zahn, 2020; Zangori et al., 2015). The emphasis of this chapter on modeling in elementary science will support the development of an understanding of an important way to facilitate student knowledge construction of complex scientific ideas through authentic practices. After reading this chapter, you should be able to:

- Define scientific modeling and modeling instructional practice through the elementary grades.
- Understand and describe the relationship of the theoretical framework of modeling at the elementary grade level.
- Describe the progression of modeling practice for grades K–2 and 3–5.
- Identify and discuss instructional practices that support student development and use of scientific models at the elementary grades for all students.

THEORETICAL FOUNDATIONS OF SCIENTIFIC MODELING IN ELEMENTARY SCHOOL

Student use and construction of models in the elementary classroom can provide teachers with insight into student learning and understandings of complex scientific ideas (Nelson & Davis, 2012). Models support student visualization of the unseen or difficult to observe and can support students as they consider interactions of complex systems (Zangori et al., 2015). Additionally, the reiterative process of model use and construction in elementary science can help teachers and students explore how thinking and cognitive processes change throughout science instruction.

Model use and construction in elementary science is derived from classic theories of learning in science (see figure 8.1). Theories of classic conceptual change, drawing from Piaget and Thomas Kuhn, suggest that students come to learning environments with prior experiences and conceptual understandings. While students can learn from those experiences to build on to construct accurate understandings of science, frequently, prior conceptions are counter to scientific principles and exist as alternative or naïve conceptions of science that are resistant to change. Incorporating strategies such as mental models and analogies, teachers can support students through conceptual change by responding to and building on students' prior experiences and conceptions. Adding to this approach, Vygotsky includes the social environment as a contributing factor to students' construction of knowledge. Through interaction and communication with peers and teachers, learners negotiate through the construction of knowledge using linguistic and cultural tools to communicate understandings. See figure 8.1.

Model-based teaching and learning is also informed by theories related to multimodality in science instruction. Multimodality is the use of multiple modes (e.g., oral language, images, designed objects) to investigate ideas and communicate findings. "Coordinating modes is important because every mode has limitations; any single representation only partly reflects a phenomenon" (Fitzgerald et al., 2022, p. 28). Incorporating multiple modes through the use and construction of models helps support student conceptual understanding and challenge alternative or naïve conceptions.

Building from theories of science learning and multimodality, investigations into model use and construction have demonstrated that modeling supports sense-making in elementary science (Forbes et al., 2019; Fried et al., 2019; S. W. Gilbert, 1999; Zangori et al., 2015; Zangori & Forbes, 2015). When model-based instruction is used to engage students in complex scientific ideas, students have been

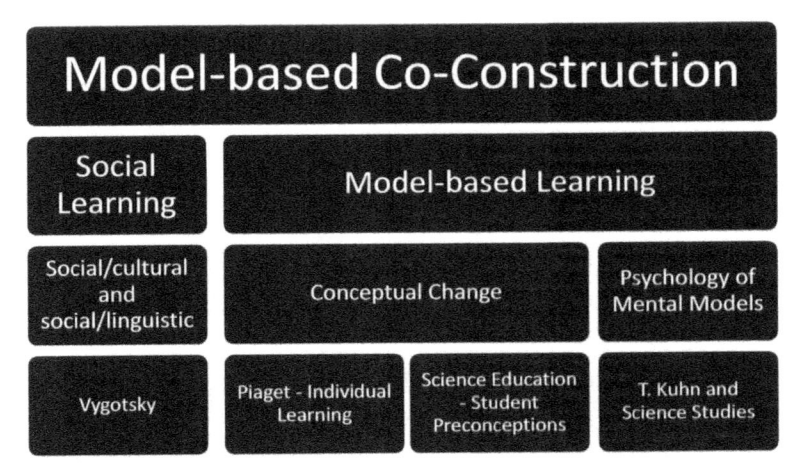

Figure 8.1. Theories of Learning in Science
Source: Adapted from J. K. Gilbert (2013, p. 25).

shown to communicate more sophisticated understandings of the phenomena under investigation (Forbes et al., 2019). Student representations of relationships and both visible and non-visible components of a system through modeling provide powerful explanatory tools that benefit both the learner and the teacher (Zangori & Forbes, 2015). Models allow for student conceptualizations to become visible and usable as a reasoning tool to construct a scientific explanation of a phenomenon. In turn, classrooms that engage in model-based instruction have demonstrated increases in student academic performance related to scientific content (Zangori et al., 2017).

Modeling and the Next Generation Science Standards

"Modeling can begin in the earliest grades, with students' models progressing from concrete 'pictures' and/or physical scale models to more abstract representations of relevant relationships" (National Research Council, 2012, p. 58). Practice 2 of the NGSS Science and Engineering Practices is "developing and using models." In science, models represent systems or parts of systems under investigation. Models should be refined and reevaluated through a reiterative process throughout a unit of investigation and used to test hypotheses and communicate scientific ideas. In engineering, models help to analyze a system and flaws or possible solutions to a problem. Models can be used to visualize a design and communicate features of a solution to an engineering problem.

The ways in which students engage with models grows in complexity throughout their academic career (see table 8.2). In the early grades of K–2, students' prior experiences of drawing and diagraming are built upon to help students compare

Table 8.2. Science and Engineering Practices: Developing and Using Models in Grades K–5

Grades K–2	Grades 3–5
Modeling in K–2 builds on prior experiences and progresses to include using and developing models (i.e., diagram, drawing, physical replica, diorama, dramatization, or storyboard) that represent concrete events or design solutions. • Distinguish between a model and the actual object, process, and/or events the model represents. • Compare models to identify common features and differences. • Develop and/or use a model to represent amounts, relationships, relative scales (bigger, smaller), and/or patterns in the natural and designed world(s). • Develop a simple model based on evidence to represent a proposed object or tool.	Modeling in 3–5 builds on K–2 experiences and progresses to building and revising simple models and using models to represent events and design solutions. • Identify limitations of models. • Collaboratively develop and/or revise a model based on evidence that shows the relationships among variables for frequent and regularly occurring events. • Develop a model using an analogy, example, or abstract representation to describe a scientific principle or design solution. • Develop and/or use models to describe and/or predict phenomena. • Develop a diagram or simple physical prototype to convey a proposed object, tool, or process. • Use a model to test cause-and-effect relationships or interactions concerning the functioning of a natural or designed system.

Source: NGSS Lead States (2013b).

models to actual objects or events, identify differences and similarities among models, use models to show amounts or relationships, and develop simple models to represent scientific ideas. In upper elementary, third through fifth grade, students are building on their earlier experiences with models toward more complex representations. In third through fifth grade, students should work to identify limitations of models and collaborate with others to develop and revise models based on collected or presented evidence. Models can be used to describe abstract scientific principles and predict scientific phenomenon. Additionally at the upper elementary grades, models can be used to demonstrate or test interactions between parts of a system and cause-and-effect relationships (NGSS Lead States, 2013b). See table 8.2.

Student Models as Assessment

Student use and construction of models can provide a powerful tool for teachers to gain insight into student learning and scientific conceptions. Models become most useful as an assessment tool when students engage in the reiterative process of model evaluation and revision throughout engagement with a scientific phenomenon. Student models can provide evidence of student sense-making and communication of scientific ideas. Additionally, student-constructed models can demonstrate how students understand and use scientific terminology and explain scientific mechanisms or processes. Evaluating student models requires the teacher to attend to scientific accuracy as well as whether student representations are consistent with scientific evidence (Nelson & Davis, 2012).

In addition to providing valuable insight for teachers, student use and construction of models allows for students to continuously assess their own understanding and engage in epistemic reasoning about scientific ideas. As students work to conceptualize scientific phenomena through the process of model construction and revision, they are invited to challenge their original conceptions and alter their thinking in light of new experiences and scientific evidence (S. W. Gilbert, 1999). Using models to express scientific ideas asks students to make their thinking visible and demonstrate complex or unseen parts and relationships of a system and/or scientific phenomenon. The collaborative nature of model critique and revision supports the social construction of deep understandings of scientific concepts called for in the "Framework for K–12 Science Education" (National Research Council, 2012).

CASE STUDIES OF MODELING IN ELEMENTARY SCIENCE

The case studies in this section illustrate two of the many ways modeling can be used in the science classroom. The first case study showcases modeling as the culminating problem-based challenge in a lower-elementary classroom. At the end point of the unit, students should be well equipped to create the models required to demonstrate their understanding of the topic, and as they create their models, they should continue to add to their understanding of the scientific phenomenon. The second case study takes a different approach, demonstrating how modeling can be used as an opening activity in an upper elementary classroom and revisited throughout a unit, building toward summative assessment. In this scenario, the model first serves as a baseline assessment, allowing students to show their understanding at the start of the unit. The models they create are then revised and updated throughout the unit as students add to their understanding of the topic and are finally used as evidence of student learning in a final explanatory model.

Case Study 1. K–2: 2-LS2-2 Ecosystems: Interactions, Energy, and Dynamics

Ms. Field is preparing to use the Next Generation Science Storyline, *Why Is Our Corn Changing?* (Farkash et al., 2019). In this open-source science educational resource, second-grade students can grapple with the anchoring phenomenon of wet harvest corn that has begun sprouting (see https://thewonderofscience.com/phenomenon/2018/7/9/corn-cob-sprouting-in-water). Throughout the storyline, second graders determine what happens to the corn as it changes, generating an explanation of what plants need to grow. This corresponds with the NGSS performance expectation 2-LS2-1: plan and conduct an investigation to determine if plants need sunlight and water to grow (NGSS Lead States, 2013e). 2-LS2-1 supports the interdependent relationships in ecosystems DCI (disciplinary core idea) that helps learners understand that plants depend on water and light to grow and uses cause-and-effect cross-cutting concepts by having learners observe that events have causes that generate observable patterns (NGSS Lead States, 2013e). As she begins planning the storyline unit for her classroom, Ms. Field realizes that an additional performance expectation can be bundled in with 2-LS2-1 to create a more robust and coherent storyline. She adds in 2-LS2-2: develop a simple model that mimics the function of an animal in dispersing seeds or pollinating plants (NGSS Lead States, 2013e). This addition challenges second graders to learn more about how animals help plants move from place to place via seed dispersal and pollination.

Ms. Field is now focusing her planning on how second graders might go about modeling pollination and seed dispersal as a culminating activity for the unit. She starts by considering the structures and functions of various animal parts that contribute to this important work. To ensure she has a deep conceptual understanding of the topic, she has been learning more about pollination by looking at slow-motion videos of bees landing on flowers as an example. She notes that as a bee lands on a flower, some of the pollen in that flower sticks to the hair on the bee (structure). When the bee goes to another flower, it transfers some of the pollen on its hair to the other flower (function). To examine seed dispersal, Ms. Field considers bur-type seeds that have hooks or teeth (structures) that cause them to attach to an animal's fur or a person's clothing, which allows them to be carried away from the plant to another location (function). She also reads about animals that eat seeds that do not break down in their digestive systems (structure), allowing the seeds to pass through and out of the body in the animal's feces and thus travel to a new location to sprout (function), but she decides to show and talk about it with students rather than include it as a possibility for the modeling portion. Because the performance expectation was specific to animals being involved in pollination or seed dispersal, Ms. Field does not include other forms of seed dispersal that she finds, such as wind or water. However, she knows that some students might be ready to learn more about other types of seed dispersal, so she gathers some materials in preparation for extension activities.

After considering some types of pollination and seed dispersal, Ms. Field creates a modeling scenario for her storyline unit that challenges second graders to work toward the performance expectation of developing a simple model that mimics the function of an animal in dispersing seeds or pollinating plants based on what they have learned (see figure 8.2 for modeling scenario). In their models, Ms. Field is ultimately looking for students to demonstrate and be able to explain their understanding of the structures of the animal and the functions those structures carry out. See figure 8.2.

Ms. Field considers two different model possibilities that students can choose to work toward. Students at the second-grade level need concrete experiences with modeling because their abstract thinking ability is not yet solidified. The concrete experience also provides a more thorough look at the processes that must take place. Because of this, students may start their ideas about modeling through drawings, but they should then create their models in three dimensions using physical elements in order to fully process the structure and function of the design. Ms. Field adds pictures and videos of flowers, bur-type seeds, bees, and dogs to help scaffold students as they consider the various structures of flowers, seeds, and animals and their functions. She also translates the words for each animal, flower, and seed for her emergent bilingual students and matches those to the pictures and videos she has collected. Last, Ms. Field collects some small bur-type seeds to show to students who are not familiar with them. They can touch the seeds and see how they cling to socks and fuzzy materials.

The first possible model type Ms. Field considers is creating a bee pollinator model using materials such as chenille sticks or pom-poms for bee hair, cheese, or drink-mix powder (or another type of powder) for pollen, and paper cut-outs of flowers with shallow cups in the middle to hold the powder. Students might begin their design planning by reviewing the pictures and videos of bees and flowers provided and then drawing how they think they will manipulate the chenille sticks to pick up the maximum amount of cheese or drink-mix powder. After their initial planning, students will gather their chenille sticks and/or pom-poms and create an initial design of their bee. This could take the form of wrapping the chenille stick around their finger, creating a chenille stick wand they can hold in their hand, and/

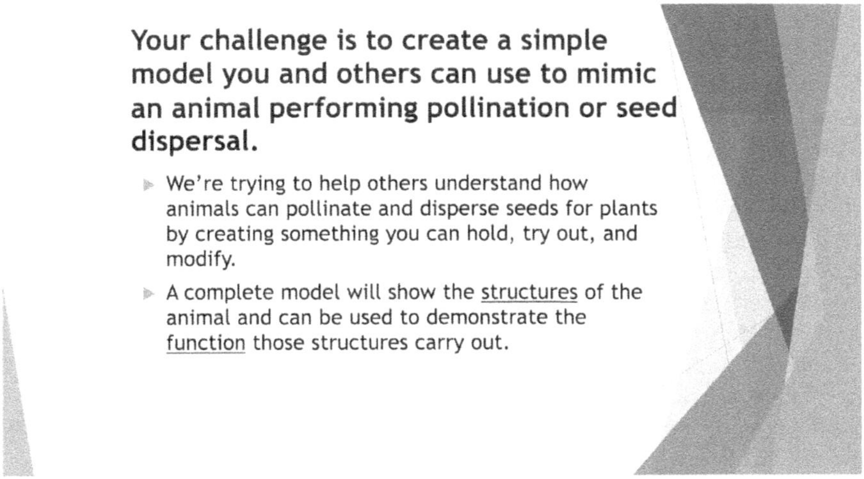

Your challenge is to create a simple model you and others can use to mimic an animal performing pollination or seed dispersal.

- We're trying to help others understand how animals can pollinate and disperse seeds for plants by creating something you can hold, try out, and modify.
- A complete model will show the structures of the animal and can be used to demonstrate the function those structures carry out.

Figure 8.2. Modeling Scenario

or adding a pom-pom to the chenille stick or another material such as a pencil or straw to simulate the bee.

The second model type would be to use hook-and-loop fasteners such as Velcro and a fuzzy type of material such as felt to model how the hooks in bur-type seeds work. Students would create a dog seed dispersal model using the fuzzy material as the dog fur and the Velcro as the bur-type seed. Students might start their design planning by reviewing pictures of dogs and bur-type seeds. They might also watch a video of dogs running around a yard to see how easy it would be for them to pick up the seeds in their fur. Next, students can draw their initial model before creating a physical model using materials provided. In addition to the fuzzy fabric, Ms. Field also has small play dogs that students can use as the base as well as materials to build their own dog figures. She has Velcro dots and strips as well as various sizes of beads that students can use to make the seeds in multiple ways.

Once students have created their initial designs, they can test their models to see how well they are able to pick up the pollen or seed. Testing their initial design is an important part of creating and modifying models in order to produce the best representation of the phenomenon. Students may then redesign their models to better meet their structure and function capabilities and then test the models again. Ms. Field builds in opportunities for students to share their models with others and identify common features as well as what makes their models unique. Students will also refer back to the pictures and videos to identify how their models are different from the real things, helping them to consider the limitations of models. To close the lesson, Ms. Field facilitates a discussion about what students have learned about pollination and seed dispersal from creating the models, what questions they still have about the topic, and includes an overarching discussion of how animals perform pollination and seed dispersal that moves plants to different areas.

Case Study 2. Grades 3–5: 5-PS1-1 Matter and Its Interactions

Mr. Scott and Ms. Nelson are co-planning the first lesson for their fifth-grade science unit on matter and its interactions. They have decided to begin the lesson by demonstrating a common phenomenon: sugar dissolving into hot water to create a solution. The focus of this lesson is the performance standard 5-PS1-1: develop a model to describe that matter is made of particles too small to be seen (NGSS Lead States, 2013e). 5-PS1-1 engages learners in the DCI of structure and properties of matter and includes the content that matter of any kind can be divided into smaller parts that are too small to be seen, but that the matter still exists, has mass, and takes up space using the cross-cutting concept of scale, proportion, and quantity (NGSS Lead States, 2013e). Mr. Scott and Ms. Nelson have decided to use before-during-after drawings (B-D-A, see figure 8.3) to model the solution creation (Keeley, 2015). For the lesson, they will heat water using a kettle, pour it into a glass container, and stir in sugar. As they stir the sugar, students will observe that it completely dissolves into the water, creating a sugar water solution, and use the B-D-A model template to explain the unseen processes at work during the physical change. See figure 8.3.

Students will be asked to work individually to create an initial model of the phenomenon. Mr. Scott and Ms. Nelson will guide their students so that they are sure to draw and label each ingredient, and in the case of the during and after drawings,

Before-During-After Drawings

For each box, draw a picture and label with words what you can see and what you think might be happening that you cannot see.

Before	During	After

Figure 8.3. B-D-A
Note: For each box, draw a picture and label with words what you can see and what you think might be happening that you cannot see.
Source: Adapted from Keeley (2015).

what they think is happening to the sugar and water inside the container. This will include (1) a drawing of the hot water and sugar before they are added together, (2) a drawing of what they think is happening as the sugar is being stirred into the hot water, and finally, (3) a drawing of what they think has happened after the sugar has dissolved into the hot water. Students will be asked to place particular focus on the second and third drawings as they try to determine what happened to the sugar and water as they combined, and the sugar appeared to disappear. Mr. Scott and Ms. Nelson also have an extension idea ready, in which they will transfer a small portion of the water into a petri dish and leave it to sit out long enough for it to evaporate and leave the sugar crystals behind so students can draw a second version of their after drawing. This extension would also contribute to helping students understand that mixing water and sugar does not produce a chemical (irreversible) change, which is one of the later topics in the unit.

Mr. Scott and Ms. Nelson anticipate that many students do not yet have an understanding that sugar crystals can break down further into molecules that are too small for them to be seen. Students at this age are beginning to grapple with abstract ideas such as this, and the teachers know that helping them begin to form this understanding is a key to the remainder of the unit. Because of this, they will focus their discussions on how the sugar seemed to disappear and what that might mean. After completing their B-D-A models, students will share in small groups, noting the similarities and differences between their models and trying to come to a group consensus on what they think is happening. During the small-group meetings, students are encouraged to record questions that they have related to their own and their peers' models. Next, Mr. Scott and Ms. Nelson will facilitate a whole group discussion, asking student small groups to share their ideas and questions related to what they have shown in their models. This will lead to students asking questions on a whole-group "driving questions board" that will be used in the next few lessons in the unit. A driving questions board is a place for students to ask, keep track of, organize, and revisit their questions. More information on driving questions boards can be found at https://www.openscied.org/driving-question-board/.

With students' initial models in place and a lot of questions to address, Mr. Scott and Ms. Nelson will then choose a driving question from the board that fits with where they need to go next to move their unit forward. As additional investigation or lessons are facilitated, students gather additional evidence they can use to explain what happens during the physical change of dissolving sugar into water. Students will come back to the B-D-A drawings *at least* one more time in groups to update their thinking by revising, removing, adding, or asking questions about their models. Students will then use a gallery walk or other peer-review process to provide constructive feedback to their peer groups as they work toward an explanatory model. After receiving feedback and questions related to their models, student groups make additional revisions. Groups make revisions to original models using a different color, a tool such as Jamboard (https://jamboard.google.com/) to place sticky notes on their models, or alternatively, they may create a new version of their models. Ultimately, the reiterative process can help both students and teachers see how their conceptions related to matter being made of particles too small to be seen have changed over the course of the unit.

As a summative assessment, Mr. Scott and Ms. Nelson will have students complete an individual final explanatory model that invites them to diagram and explain what happens before, during, and after mixing sugar and water. In addition to the labeled diagrams, students will write an explanation of the processes at work beneath each of the three pictures. Because of the reiterative process used throughout the unit and the engagement with peers as they construct and revise initial models, student final explanations will likely be more sophisticated and represent a deeper conceptual understanding of the physical change of dissolving.

CONCLUSION

Elementary science educators are tasked with identifying and incorporating educational experiences that engage students in authentic science learning. Science teaching and learning should build on students' existing knowledge and experiences and promote science as a social endeavor that is based on empirical evidence (National Research Council, 2012). To do so, teachers must help students to formulate a foundational understanding of the nature of science. One way that elementary science teachers can do this is through the development and use of scientific models. Modeling also helps students communicate their understanding of complex scientific ideas and interactions within systems (Barrett-Zahn, 2020; Zangori et al., 2015). Through student-constructed models, students show relationships and both visible and non-visible components of a system. These models provide powerful explanatory tools that allow students to explore their own thinking and make their thinking visible for teachers (Zangori & Forbes, 2015).

Models are a reasoning tool to help students construct a scientific explanation of a phenomenon. Student use and construction of models can provide a powerful tool for teachers to gain insight into student learning and scientific conceptions, particularly when teachers facilitate the reiterative process of model evaluation and revision throughout investigation of a scientific phenomenon. With appropriate scaffolds and support, students can build on their prior experiences with drawing and building to use models to construct sophisticated explanations of complex systems and scientific phenomena.

MODELING RESOURCES

Next generation science storyline, second grade, *Why is our corn changing?* https://www.nextgenstorylines.org/why-is-our-corn-changing

Before-during-after template—(represented in figure 8.3 of this chapter).

Driving question board. https://www.openscied.org/driving-question-board/

Jamboard. https://jamboard.google.com/

Wonder of science: Developing and using models. https://thewonderofscience.com/videos/2017/12/10/sep2-developing-and-using-models

Graphic organizers for scaffolds. https://thewonderofscience.com/graphics

REFERENCES

Barrett-Zahn, E. (2020). Mindful modeling. *Science and Children*, 57(7). https://www.nsta.org/science-and-children/science-and-children-march-2020/mindful-modeling

Böschl, F., Forbes, C., & Lange-Schubert, K. (2023). Investigating scientific modeling practices in US and German elementary science classrooms: A comparative, cross-national video study. *Science Education*, 107(2), 368–400. https://doi.org/10.1002/sce.21780

Farkash, L., Michael, N. J., Purdie-Dyer, R., Elliot, M., Fattaleh, K., McGill, T. A. W., Novak, M., & Voss, D. (2019). *Why is our corn changing?* Next Generation Science Storylines. https://www.nextgenstorylines.org/why-is-our-corn-changing

Fitzgerald, M., Bismack, A. S., Gotwals, A. W., Wright, T. S., & Washburn, E. K. (2022). Modeling, reading, and talking, Oh my! *Science and Children*, 59(6), 27–32.

Forbes, C. T., Cisterna, D., Bhattacharya, D., & Roy, R. (2019). Modeling elementary students' ideas about heredity: A comparison of curricular interventions. *The American Biology Teacher*, 81(9), 626–635. https://doi.org/10.1525/abt.2019.81.9.626

Fried, D. B., Tinio, P. P. L., Gubi, A., & Gaffney, J. P. (2019). Enhancing elementary science learning through organic chemistry modeling and visualization. *European Journal of Science and Mathematics Education*, 7(2), 73–82. https://doi.org/10.30935/scimath/9535

Gilbert, J. K. (2013). *Models and modeling in science education* (Vol. 53).

Gilbert, S. W. (1999). *The model as a vehicle for understanding the nature and processes of science.*

Keeley, P. (2015). *Science formative assessment* (Vol. 2): *Fifty more strategies for linking assessment, instruction, and learning.* Corwin.

National Research Council. (2012). *A framework for K–12 science education: Practices, crosscutting concepts, and core ideas.* National Academies Press.

Nelson, M. M., & Davis, E. A. (2012). Preservice elementary teachers' evaluations of elementary students' scientific models: An aspect of pedagogical content knowledge for scientific modeling. *International Journal of Science Education*, *34*(12), 1931–1959. https://doi.org/10.1080/09500693.2011.594103

Next Generation Science Standards (NGSS) Lead States (Ed.). (2013a). Appendix E: Disciplinary core idea progressions in the Next Generation Science Standards. In *Next Generation Science Standards: For states, by states* (pp. 374–381). National Academies Press.

NGSS Lead States (Ed.). (2013b). Appendix F: Science and engineering practices in the Next Generation Science Standards. In *Next Generation Science Standards: For states, by states* (pp. 382–412). National Academies Press.

NGSS Lead States (Ed.). (2013c). Appendix G: Crosscutting concepts in the Next Generation Science Standards. In *Next Generation Science Standards: For states, by states* (pp. 413–429). National Academies Press.

NGSS Lead States (Ed.). (2013d). Appendix H: Understanding the scientific enterprise: The nature of science in the Next Generation Science Standards. In *Next Generation Science Standards: For states, by states* (pp. 430–436). National Academies Press.

NGSS Lead States. (2013e). *Next generation science standards: For states, by states*. National Academies Press.

National Science Teaching Association (NSTA) Board of Directors. (2018). *NSTA position statement: Elementary school science*. https://www.nsta.org/nstas-official-positions/elementary-school-science

Yenilmez Turkoglu, A., & Oztekin, C. (2016). Science teacher candidates' perceptions about roles and nature of scientific models. *Research in Science & Technological Education*, *34*(2), 219–236. https://doi.org/10.1080/02635143.2015.1137893

Zangori, L., & Forbes, C. T. (2015). Exploring third-grade student model-based explanations about plant relationships within an ecosystem. *International Journal of Science Education*, *37*(18), 2942–2964. https://doi.org/10.1080/09500693.2015.1118772

Zangori, L., Forbes, C. T., & Schwarz, C. V. (2015). Exploring the effect of embedded scaffolding within curricular tasks on third-grade students' model-based explanations about hydrologic cycling. *Science & Education*, *24*(7–8), 957–981. https://doi.org/10.1007/s11191-015-9771-9

Zangori, L., Vo, T., Forbes, C. T., & Schwarz, C. V. (2017). Supporting third-grade students' model-based explanations about groundwater: A quasi-experimental study of a curricular intervention. *International Journal of Science Education*, *39*(11), 1421–1442. https://doi.org/10.1080/09500693.2017.1336683

9

Inclusive Instruction and Intervention in Elementary Science Education

Maria B. Peterson-Ahmad and Randa G. Keeley

ACROSS THE UNITED STATES, kindergarten through fifth-grade science instruction consists of core instructional categories including physical science, life science, and earth and space science and consists of looking at the world through observation, listening, and recording to gain understanding through thoughtful action. Scientists propose hypotheses and test ideas through the scientific method to gain further understanding or "theory." Because science instruction is not a step-by-step approach to discovery and can consistently embed cross-content instruction (e.g., reading, writing, mathematics), learning opportunities for students in kindergarten through fifth grade must garner experiences through high-impact strategies that support students with and without disabilities in an inclusive classroom environment. Instructional strategies that can support science acquisition include use of evidence-based practices, high-leverage practices (HLPs), co-teaching, and tiered supports that can increase student success, mitigate academic, social-emotional, or behavioral challenges, and support access to the general education science curriculum. When teachers focus on instructional activities that provide students with active engagement and opportunities to interact with the world around them, students are better able to access and effectively work their way through scientific inquiry by learning how to observe, question, research, hypothesize, test, analyze, and report conclusions.

Chapter Objectives

The following objectives outline the key areas of focus for developing scaffolded strategies and differentiated instruction plans to meet the diverse needs of students.

1. Examine how scaffolded strategies and interventions can support students' science and cross-content learning.
2. Explore planning mechanisms that incorporate differentiated instruction based on the individual needs of students.

These objectives will provide educators with the knowledge and tools to effective support diverse learnings in science and across various content areas through tailored instructional strategies.

EDUCATIONAL THEORY ALIGNED WITH SCIENCE INSTRUCTION

Science education lends itself to the behaviorist- and constructivist-based learning theories in that they allow students to make sense of what is being taught through interaction with the world around them and to have an increased understanding of the world around them through a negotiation of meaning, observing, and analyzing how variable changes affect outcomes. The constructivist philosophy focuses on "seeing the world" to include the nature of reality (i.e., mental representations of relations between categories and concepts), the nature of knowledge (i.e., individual construction of already known knowledge), the nature of human interaction (i.e., shared meaning of knowledge), and the nature of science (i.e., making meaning through activities) (Cakir, 2008). As students experience the world and reflect upon their learning experiences, they can build their representations and incorporate them into their preexisting schemas. Constructivist-based science instruction focuses on providing learning experiences that facilitate the construction of knowledge through engaging experiences in a social context as teachers and students work together to build knowledge. For teachers to foster these educational approaches for their students, they must understand students' science misconceptions, which can allow for monitoring of students' learning difficulties with a science curriculum (Cakir, 2008). To better understand potential student misconceptions, teachers can design instructional opportunities that promote conceptual change and development and utilize learning supports (e.g., analogies, concept maps, demonstrations, and activities) (Cakir, 2008). The behaviorist philosophy posits that learning occurs through learned interactions with the environment and can include classroom strategies such as scaffolded learning, communicating clear objectives, decomposing complex tasks into a series of steps, and feedback (Stewart, 2012) (see table 9.1).

As these theories are integrated in the classroom, they can be seamlessly accompanied by teaching modalities that support effective instructional practices for students who are at risk or who receive special education services (Kinder et al., 2005), through direct instruction (DI), explicit instruction (EI), or precision teaching.

Direct instruction. DI focuses on curriculum design and instructional delivery, which guides teachers in instructional organization (e.g., grouping and time, continuous assessment) and presentation techniques (e.g., student participation through response mechanisms, instruction pacing aimed at teaching mastery, error correction, and motivation) (Fuchs, 1996; Fuchs & Fuchs, 1995; Watkins & Slocum, 2004). DI uses student-specific learning objectives accompanied by breaking targeted skills into smaller components with step-by-step prompts, which are gradually faded as students begin to generalize skills (Rosenshine, 1986). These approaches have been documented as effective approaches for improving academic skills for students with disabilities.

Explicit Instruction. EI is a way of teaching where the teacher selects an important objective, specifies the learning outcome, designs instructional experiences, explains directly, models the skills being taught, and provides scaffolded

Table 9.1. Traditional versus Constructivist and Behaviorist Science Classroom Approaches

Traditional Classroom	Constructivist-Based Science Classroom	Behaviorist-Based Science Classroom
Curriculum emphasizes basic skills and individual parts of a whole concept.	Curriculum starts with the whole concept and expands learning into individual parts.	Students are provided with continuous opportunities to practice skills toward the target competency.
Fixed curriculum.	Curriculum impacted by student questions and interests.	Target competencies are defined for students.
Textbooks and workbooks used as primary materials.	Manipulatives and primary sources of materials are used.	
Repeated information.	Interactive learning that is scaffolded.	
Teachers directly present information to students.	Teachers engage in a working dialogue with students as they construct their own knowledge.	Clear instructions are provided to students. Students are acknowledged when a competency is achieved.
Assessment is conducted through testing and correct answers.	Assessment is inclusive of the entire scientific learning process in addition to tests.	Frequent measurements and feedback are provided to students to inform them on their progress.
Individual student work.	Students work in groups.	

practice to help students achieve mastery (Kearns & Whaley, 2019). EI can support student learning across academic, social, and behavioral tasks in all grade levels and content areas (Hughes et al., 2022) and is described in great detail later in this chapter.

Precision Teaching. Precision teaching encompasses a multisensory approach to create an engaging learning experience. Precision teaching can enhance science content instructional strategies and can be combined with any curricular approach (Lindsley, 1992) as it facilitates carefully designed tasks through a systematic approach in progress monitoring to adapt instruction and support student growth and development (McDowell & Keenan, 2001). Through step-by-step procedures that include baseline student assessment, intervention sessions, observations of student performance, and continuous progress monitoring, teachers can monitor student performance and adjust teaching methodologies based on the individualized needs of students (Marchand-Martella et al., 2004).

POLICIES SUPPORTING INCLUSIVE PRACTICES IN K-5 CLASSROOMS

The Education for All Handicapped Children Act of 1975 (PL 94-142) laid the foundation by defining "special education" as specially designed instruction provided at no cost to meet the unique needs of children with disabilities. This legislation marked a pivotal moment in advocating for inclusive education for students receiving special education services. Following PL 94-142, the No Child Left Behind (NCLB) Act was enacted, emphasizing accountability and standards-based education. Although NCLB didn't directly address special education, it played a significant role in shaping educational policies and practices that impacted students with disabilities. In 2004, the Individuals with Disabilities Education Act (IDEA) was reauthorized as IDEA 2004 (PL 108-446), reinforcing the principles of PL 94-142 and expanding on its provisions. IDEA 2004 mandated that children with disabilities receive a free and appropriate public education (FAPE), including free special education services tailored to their individual needs. This legislation solidified the importance of individualized education programs (IEPs) to guide the educational journey of each student with a disability. Furthermore, IDEA 2004 emphasized the necessity for schools to offer a continuum of placement options for students with disabilities, ensuring that their educational environments support their diverse needs. Among these options, inclusive education within the general education classroom emerged as a key component. Inclusive education involves educating all students together and providing access to the curriculum while fostering participation in the classroom community (Odom et al., 2011; Vandercook et al., 2018–2019; Yell et al., 2020). This approach aligns with the inclusive principles championed by PL 94-142 and reflects a commitment to supporting the educational rights and opportunities of students with disabilities. Transitioning to 2015, the Every Student Succeeds Act (ESSA) (PL 114-95) replaced NCLB, shifting the focus toward closing achievement gaps and raising academic standards. While ESSA did not specifically address special education, its emphasis on flexibility in funding and implementation indirectly supported the goals of inclusive education by providing schools with the resources and autonomy to meet the diverse needs of all students, including those with disabilities (Nagro et al., 2022).

Although specific protections are put into place for students with disabilities by IDEA (2004), educators are also required to comply with ESSA that requires states to maintain challenging academic standards that are aligned to states' public college and technical college and career readiness standards. IDEA (2004) requires that students identified as having a disability, or disabilities, and who qualify for special education services be provided with an individualized education program (IEP). Within the IEP, accommodations and modifications are set forth that determine what individual students need academically and behaviorally and provides individual students with access to the general education curriculum (Barrio et al., 2022). Specific to inclusive science instruction, accommodations and modifications assist by identifying academic goals and objectives that guide instructional planning and intervention strategies to best support learning. Together, general education teachers and the special education teachers can work together to ensure that content and specially designed instruction is planned to meet the individualized needs of students within the inclusive classroom environment.

IDEA 2004 also requires that states establish and maintain qualifications to ensure that personnel are appropriately and adequately prepared and trained and have the content knowledge and skills needed to serve children with disabilities with specially designed instruction by adapting, (as appropriate) to the needs of eligible children through the content, methodology, and delivery of instruction. This ensures access to the general curriculum so that children can meet the educational standards under specific state jurisdictions (34 C.F.R. §300.39[b][3]).

MULTI-TIERED SYSTEM OF SUPPORTS (MTSS) TO SUPPORT INCLUSIVE INSTRUCTION

The MTSS framework embraces the "whole child" approach and integrates data and instruction to maximize students' academic and social-emotional achievement through a strengths- and evidence-based perspective (Center on Multi-Tiered System of Supports, 2023) through the creation of a school system where students are valued, supported, and engaged in learning that focuses on excellence and equity for students (Sailor et al., 2021). MTSS encompasses prevention, enrichment, and intervention strategies to support the whole child through parent engagement, school/community collaboration, curriculum design, professional development, and the creation of postsecondary goals. This integrated approach provides increased access to high-quality, differentiated classroom curriculum, systemic/sustainable continuous improvement processes, integrated data systems, and positive behavioral supports (California Department of Education, n.d.) based on the unique needs of each student. Universal screening, data-based decision-making, continuous progress monitoring, a focus on successful student outcomes, and the utilization of a continuum of evidence-based interventions are the critical tenets of the MTSS process, and research has documented the positive effects across school settings (e.g., Billingsley & Bettini, 2019; CEEDAR, 2023; Lane et al., 2016; Sailor & McCart, 2014; Satter et al., 2019). See figure 9.1 for more.

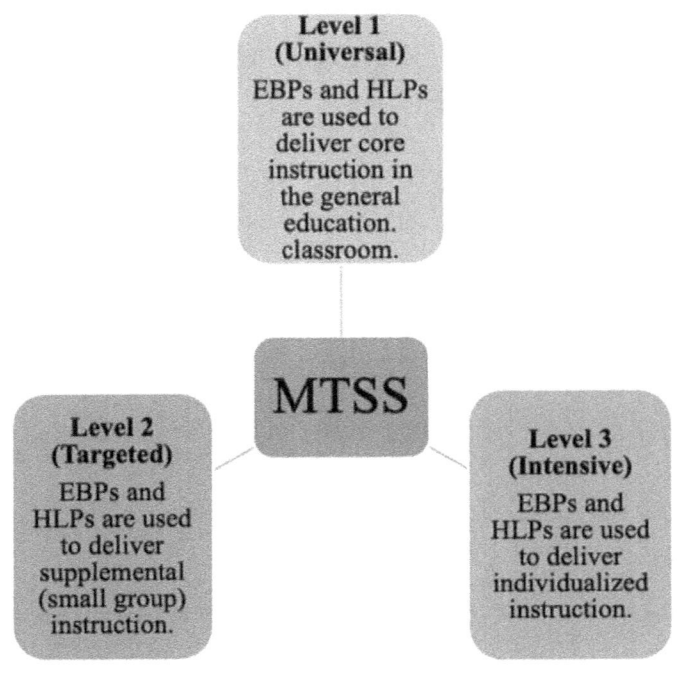

Figure 9.1. Relationship Among MTSS, EBPs, and HLPs.

Source: Adapted from High Leverage Practices and Evidence-Based Practices: A Promising Pair (McCray, et al., 2017)

The core of MTSS is data-based decision-making that involves the collection of data, the continuous monitoring of student performance, and the design and implementation of strategies and levels of support needed for each student (National Center on Intensive Intervention, n.d.). The MTSS framework begins in the general education classroom and includes three levels of core programming. In Tier 1, teachers use universal instructional strategies that support academic and social-emotional growth in the general education context using evidence-based core curriculum and positive behavioral management strategies. In Tier 1 instruction, teachers support science instruction by using the systematic district-adopted science curriculum and teaching sequence/pacing guide. Teachers can support this level of instruction by activating students' knowledge of previously learned science concepts and by engaging students in instructional practices that use clear directives, active learning through demonstration, and examples/non-examples of science content and provide opportunities for students to review and assess their understanding of the science lesson material. Tier 1 should support most students (i.e., approx. 80%); however, some students may need additional support through supplemental interventions provided in Tier 2. Students in Tier 2 are typically in small groups (approx. 15%) that have not responded to Tier 1 instruction and are provided with supplemental small-group, targeted instruction. In Tier 2 instruction, additional time and intensity of science content instruction takes place based on areas of strategic need identified in Tier 1 instruction (i.e., through student work samples or content assessments). In Tier 2, the teacher consistently monitors student progress so that adjustments to instruction can be made. Tier 3 provides intensive and frequent interventions that support students (approx. 5%) who have persistent academic or social-emotional needs and who have not made progress in Tier 2 instruction. Tier 3 interventions are

Table 9.2. Steps in the MTSS Screening and Progress-Monitoring Process

Steps	Descriptions
Step 1. Design the screening process.	School teams design a process for screening that is directly aligned to desired outcomes. This process should have a clear process for identifying the target population that is inclusive of a schedule, implementation procedures, and a data-analysis approach.
Step 2. Select screening tools.	As schools select screening tools for academic and behavioral screeners, the needs, context, priorities, and technical adequacy of the measures need to be considered.
Step 3. Train school staff.	Ongoing professional learning for staff should focus on understanding the purpose of the screening and acquiring the skills needed to administer screens with fidelity.
Step 4. Collect data and monitor for fidelity of implementation.	Schools plan how to ensure the fidelity of screening implementation so that errors in scoring and data entry are minimal.
Step 5. Analyze the screening data.	Schools screen data to note trends and identify areas of effectiveness as well as areas of additional need for schoolwide goals or for individual, tiered student instruction and/or supports.

Source: Adapted from the Center on Multi-Tiered System of Supports (2023).

increasingly individualized and indicate strengths and weaknesses to better inform which evidence-based practices should be used or adapted. For example, students receiving Tier 3 science instruction may receive instruction from a reading specialist or special education teacher who uses intervention strategies outside of the core science curriculum. If students do not progress at Tier 3, they may be eligible for referral to special education evaluation (CEEDAR, 2023).

MTSS Screening. The universal screening process in the MTSS framework allows for a systematic process in identifying students who may be at risk in their learning or social-emotional development. When screening, it is vital that valid and reliable measures are selected, and that fidelity of implementation is maintained. Screening measures should also be attentive to the cultural and linguistic needs of students and recognize what students already do well and what they need to make increased progress. The five steps of the MTSS screening process are shown below in table 9.2.

Progress Monitoring. Progress monitoring is used to assess students' performance and identify the extent to which they have been responding to instruction and interventions. When progress monitoring, teachers must be sure to use assessment measures that are valid and reliable and are implemented with fidelity. Formative and summative assessments can be used as part of the progress-monitoring data-gathering process. Formative assessment has a positive impact on student achievement and is a powerful mechanism that utilizes a systematic process that continuously gathers data to provide feedback during students' learning process and can be used as a guide for future instruction (Deno, 1985; Fuchs et al., 1989; Thorndike & Thorndike-Christ, 2010). It can be informal and occur during a typical cycle of instruction while teachers check for student understanding, or it can be formal by using a standardized and validated instrument that occurs on a specific schedule (Fuchs & Deno, 1991; Vanderheyden & Solomon, 2023). Formative assessment occurs frequently, moment by moment, daily, or weekly and can occur before, during, or after a lesson (e.g., curriculum-based measurement), informal teacher questioning, quizzes, or exit tickets. Formative assessment provides continuous feedback about performance and informs and guides instruction and generate questions that purposefully activate students' thinking. Summative assessment evaluates student learning at the end of an instruction unit or grading period and typically measures specific standards or benchmarks. Summative assessments can provide information about student learning over time and can include assessments such as final projects or exams.

Data-Based Decision-Making. During the screening and progress-monitoring process within the MTSS framework, continuous decisions are made about instructional strategies (i.e., intensity or potential identification of a student with a disability) and movement of a student within the three tiers. For example, after a teacher evaluates a student's rate of growth or performance level within the classroom, they can use this information to make informed science instructional decisions that are differentiated to meet the unique needs of the students in their classroom. This could include small-group instruction, using leveled science readers so that students can access the science lesson content at their reading level, or using strategies to pre-teach and support science vocabulary (see section on "Literacy Strategies" below for additional information). MTSS teams should meet regularly to monitor implementation and focus on meetings that are data-driven to ensure appropriate decisions are made. Ongoing professional development should occur so that MTSS teams maintain effective strategies throughout the screening, progress-monitoring, and implementation phases. MTSS teams should use multiple data sources to make decisions about instruction, movement across the three tiers, modifying intensity of the interventions, and potential disability identification in accordance with state law (Center on Multi-Tiered System of Supports, 2023).

Inclusive classrooms support students with a wide array of abilities and teachers must adapt curriculum and tasks so that all students make academic progress. Specially designed instruction (SDI) specifies the instruction that students with disabilities should receive. SDI can be created through instructional content changes, methods, or delivery so that it meets the individualized needs of the specific student. SDI should also provide students with disabilities opportunities to access the general science curriculum through their IEP goals (e.g., the student will demonstrate an understanding of grade-level science vocabulary) and objectives (e.g., by the end of the nine-week grading period, the student will use new science words in context with 85% accuracy in two out of three trials as evidenced by student work samples and teacher-recorded data) (Riccomini et al., 2017). Before systematically designed instruction can occur, teachers must look at the long- and short-term goals and identify the needs of their students based on grade-level standards, assessment data, student placement in the MTSS tier process, and students with an IEP. Once this is accomplished, teachers can then identify clear learning goals that include expectations for student learning, what will be taught and assessed, and how families will be communicated with regarding their child's progress (Konrad et al., 2022). These clear learning goals "provide teachers with direction, so they know where they are going" while "systematically sequenced instruction helps them get there" (Konrad et al., 2022, p. 176).

Specific interventions to support inclusive science instruction can be built into the classroom for at-risk students in Tier 2 or Tier 3 of the MTSS framework. For example, a teacher may work with a small group of students in Tier 2 to support science instruction. During this small-group instruction, the teacher focuses on strategic science vocabulary words from the whole-group lesson and models her thinking by reading the word and stopping to ask the students what they think the word means before having them practice this strategy on their own. In Tier 3, a teacher might work one-on-one with a student by segmenting a science reading passage into smaller pieces, modeling reading the passage out loud to the student, and then asking the student to summarize the text and vocabulary in their own words, with feedback from the teacher. Students that have already been identified as having a disability and qualifying for special education services will have specific accommodations and/or modifications that are required to be implemented by the teacher of record for the classroom.

INTERVENTIONS AND STRATEGIES TO SUPPORT INCLUSIVE SCIENCE INSTRUCTION

While evidence-based practices (EBPs) and HLPs should be incorporated in all levels of student support, some students may require more intensive interventions and support to access the general education curriculum throughout the MTSS process or as indicated in their IEP. Students who are at risk or have a disability experience academic challenges across content and subject areas and typically score significantly below their peers on standardized science assessments (Kaldenberg et al., 2011; National Center for Education Statistics [NCES], 2011). Typically, classroom instructional support focuses on reading, math, and writing as areas often measured through state standardized assessments; however, progress should be seen in all academic subject areas, including science (Scruggs et al., 2008). Given the unique and individualized needs of students who are at risk or who have a disability, specialized cross-content intervention and instruction must be utilized. Supporting elementary students in inclusive science classrooms with the provision of EBPs and HLPs can support science acquisition.

However, teachers should also consider specific EBPs and HLPs that can be embedded in instructional practices that anticipate greater learning needs from other students present in the classroom. Therefore, the consideration of EBPs and HLPs in combination with the required accommodations and/or modifications for students that receive special education services should be implemented into the general education classroom instruction.

Evidence-Based Practices and High-Leverage Practices

Inclusive classroom structures and practices rely on the use of EBPs and are mandated for use by educators to the greatest extent possible by IDEA (2004) and must match based on students' specific needs as it allows for the possibility of greater academic or behavioral outcomes. The Council for Exceptional Children (CEC) developed standards for EBPs to ensure their effectiveness and that they are supported by multiple, rigorous research studies that have been shown to have positive effects on improvement and outcomes for students (CEC, 2014; Cook et al., 2009; Cook & Odom, 2013). To determine that the use of EBPs have a magnitude of effect, efficacy of methodological research design and the number of studies conducted (Cook et al., 2009) are important factors, however, "EBPs cannot determine effectiveness until they are implemented" (Cook & Odom, 2013, p. 142). Each system has different standards for determining if a practice is considered evidence based. What Works Clearinghouse (WWC) is a commonly used organization for evaluating EBPs in the field of education. WWC uses a rating system that evaluates interventions tested through research and rates the evidence of effectiveness of the practice "without reservations" or "with reservations." A practice that has been evaluated by WWC as "without reservations" has been found effective, with a research design that has few to no flaws. Additionally, a practice that has been evaluated by WWC as "with reservations" indicates that the practice may be effective but should be implemented with caution due to some flaws in the research design.

In 2017, CEC and the Center for Effective Educator Development, Accountability, and Reform (CEEDAR) Center developed 22 recommended special education HLPs that encompass four main domains that include collaboration, assessment, social/emotional/behavioral, and instruction (McLeskey et al, 2017). HLPs encompass EBPs across each domain with broad cognitive and instructional strategies that support students across all grade levels and content areas (Klinger et al., 2016) that offer strategic skills and actions for implementation (Kennedy et al., 2020). For HLPs to be most effective, they must focus on instructional practice, occur in teaching with high frequency in any setting, be research based and known to impact student learning and engagement, and be broadly applicable in any content area or approach to teaching as they are fundamental to effective teaching when skillfully implemented (McLeskey et al., 2017).

To integrate EBPs and HLPs into the elementary inclusive science learning process, *direct instruction* (an EBP), where students are supported through a systematically sequenced learning process, can be used in tandem with *explicit instruction* (HLP 16) *and intensive instruction* (HLP 20). DI is where students attain mastery of concepts and general skills related to new content incrementally, with gradually reduced guidance (Adams & Engelmann, 1996). Explicit instruction is "a structured, systematic, and effective methodology" (Archer & Hughes, 2011, p. 1) and can support direct instruction by supporting students with the "appropriate levels of support, guidance, and scaffolds, as well as multiple opportunities to respond, followed by effective feedback" (Hughes et al., 2022, p. 235). Intensive instruction can support direct instruction and explicit instruction by increasing the dosage (i.e., decreasing the size of the intervention group and frequency of instructional lessons) and complexity (i.e., the number of explicit instruction elements present in the instructional program) (Riccomini et al., 2017).

Literacy Strategies

Science instruction is inextricably linked to both language development and learning to read (Perfetti & Stafura, 2014; Shanahan, 2016). Early language skills provide the foundation for advanced reading skills and children who have enhanced language and vocabulary skills are more successful in learning to read; this is becoming increasingly successful in cross-content subject areas (Massonnié et al., 2018; Suggate et al., 2018). Therefore, cross-content integration is a powerful practice for students to learn science content while developing skills needed for other subject areas, and literacy integration across subject areas has added potential for students to understand content at deeper levels (Eick, 2012).

Strategic interventions that provide students support in science content should be deeply rooted in disciplinary literacy. Disciplinary literacy focuses on the aspects of reading and writing specific to an academic area (e.g., science) with a focus on reading to learn and understand concepts by focusing on the unique characteristics of discipline-specific text (Fisher & Frey, 2015; Shanahan & Shanahan, 2014). In addition, there are similarities between literacy and science in that cognitive processes inherent in literacy are also significant to science, and when taught together, they can propel learning (Casteel & Isom, 1994). For example, the science skill and process of formulating a conclusion is equivalent to the reading skill of analyzing and interpreting information (Klentschy & Molina-De la Torre, 2004). Disciplinary literacy strategies provide teaching tools and techniques that educators can use to model content-specific demands so that students can become successful in reading, writing, speaking, and critically thinking in science-related content (Hughes, 2022).

Teaching Vocabulary. Knowing vocabulary is one of the tenets of increased reading comprehension that leads to enhanced functioning across the scientific inquiry learning process. "Combining the teaching of word recognition skills with vocabulary instruction and incorporating the meaning of vocabulary words with subject concepts, allows teachers to help students improve their reading ability and subject learning" (Palumbo et al., 2015, p. 110). Teachers can pre-teach students complex vocabulary from a lesson or activity to acquaint them with words that they will identify in context by providing concrete examples of their meaning—for example, using pictures or illustrations on a whiteboard. When doing this, teachers should also explain the meaning with a student-friendly definition, provide an example of how the word can be used, ask students to repeat the word, and engage the students in an activity to enhance mastery. Giving students the opportunity to learn about grapheme, phoneme, and morpheme patterns allows for transfer to other words (Moats, 2005–6), while restating the words helps students decode the graphic representations of phonemes and morphemes through oral practice (Rosenthal & Ehri, 2010). Vocabulary should also be posted in the classroom to reinforce learning and as a resource for students to refer to. This strategy increasingly supports students who are at risk, receiving special education services, or who are English language learners. These strategies assist students in generalizing concepts and transferring learned sound/symbol correspondences to unfamiliar words (Adams & Henry, 1997).

Previewing Nonfiction Text. Allowing students to preview the text prior to teaching a lesson or starting an activity allows for the activation of prior knowledge, recognition of specific features of the content, and identification of common features within nonfiction science text (e.g., headings, bolded words, picture captions, labeled diagrams). Students who struggle with reading and learn how to effectively navigate text-preview strategies will be able to "expand their understanding and direction to internalize instruction and better understand the importance of the text which will enable them to better navigate anything they choose to read more effectively" (Bluestein, 2010, p. 600). When students can familiarize and engage themselves with text content, it can build interest, generate questions, and construct meaning (Honig et al., 2000; Nagy & Scott, 2004; Ruddell, 2009). Before a teacher models a science reading selection with students, they can preview the material to build on prior knowledge and make predictions, allowing them to make connections through guided practice and explicit teacher questioning while simultaneously making connections to the text (Walton, 2006).

Graphic Organizers. Graphic organizers serve as visual aids designed to help students organize and comprehend concepts, text, and content so that it is easier to process and understand information and relationships across concepts (Boyle, 2000; Kim et al., 2004). Graphic organizers allow students to break apart key information into smaller pieces and can help students organize their thoughts in a visual way. They can also support students with notetaking and comprehension of different text structures (e.g., descriptive, cause and effect, problem and solution, classification) (Calvin & Gray, 2023; Dexter et al., 2011). Teachers must select graphic organizers that will best convey the information and relationships they wish their students to learn and explicitly model them to their students.

Inquiry-Based Learning

Inquiry-based learning is a teaching method in which students learn by actively engaging in real-world and personally meaningful projects and recognize that learning is a social activity while simultaneously activating their prior knowledge and recognizing their misconceptions (NRC 2000; 2001). This type of teaching and learning can be particularly effective for science-based content, as the underlying premise of science education and acquisition is through the process of inquiry. During inquiry-based learning, students work on a project over an extended period of time in a scaffolded approach, by engaging in solving a real-world problem or answering a complex question that allows students to develop deep content knowledge as well as critical thinking, collaboration, creativity, and communication skills. This type of strategy is particularly effective for students with disabilities as it allows students to move from basic knowledge to higher-level thinking and can improve overall science and other content-area achievement (McCarthy, 2005; Miller et al., 2015; Scruggs et al., 1993; Taylor et al., 2018).

Reciprocal Teaching. Reciprocal teaching is an instructional method that promotes group problem solving by using four strategies: summarizing, question generating, clarifying, and predicting (Alfassi et al., 2009). This strategy encourages students to think about their own thought process during reading and to become actively involved in monitoring their comprehension as they read and to ask questions during reading to help make text more comprehensible. Students learn the four strategies of reciprocal teaching through gradual release of responsibility that includes explicit modeling from the teacher, guided student practice, and then independent practice (Alfassi, 2004; Slater & Horstman, 2002). This strategy is intended to provide students with the opportunity to learn from peers. Research indicates that reciprocal teaching shows positive effects related to reading comprehension (Reichenberg, 2014) and social connectedness with peers (Alfassi et al., 2009; Lundberg & Reichenberg, 2013). Universal design for learning (UDL) can be incorporated with reciprocal teaching to provide reading comprehension instruction for students in inclusive classroom settings by integrating read-alouds or audio recordings of the text prior to group reading, reading text aloud with visual guides, or by incorporating graphic organizers (Coyne et al., 2017; Hovland, 2020; Wood et al., 2015).

Specific interventions to support inclusive science instruction can be implemented into the general education classroom to support all students, including those that require special education services. In addition to interventions, there are specific practices that can also be considered to provide a more inclusive learning environment for all students.

PRACTICES THAT SUPPORT INCLUSIVE SCIENCE INSTRUCTION

Universal Design for Learning

UDL is a framework for planning instruction that strategically considers students that may have difficulty with the learning process. UDL should be the starting point and the foundation of instructional design (Keeley, 2022). The instructional considerations within a UDL framework include: (1) multiple means of representation, (2) multiple means of action and expression, and (3) multiple means of engagement. Following the Center for Applied Special Technologies (CAST) (2018) guidelines, multiple means of engagement address the "why" of learning and ask educators to consider methods for recruiting the interest of students, sustaining their effort and persistence, and, finally, addressing self-regulation. Multiple means of representation include the "what" of learning and address student perception, language, and symbols, as well as comprehension. Overall, the purpose of UDL is to prepare students that are committed and motivated, resourceful, and knowledgeable, and strategic and goal-directed (CAST, 2018). Therefore, when preparing for instruction, teachers should consider different ways in which students with specific instructional needs may access the content, engage with instruction, and demonstrate their understanding of the content. The application of UDL to instructional design aids as a reminder to educators to allow students with disabilities opportunities to interact in different ways with content while building their background knowledge as well as to put scaffolded supports into place to support learning. Essentially, teachers are "minimizing barriers and maximizing accessibility" for all students (Rice-Doran, 2015, p. 3). Investment in designing instruction from a UDL perspective can positively impact students with disabilities, low-achieving students, and students that do not have specific learning needs (Baker et al., 2002; Montague & Applegate, 2000; Palincsar et al., 2001).

There are three overarching considerations related to instructional design and UDL (CAST, 2018). The first is representation, and this facet considers how students are accessing the instructional content. Another consideration is expression that incorporates different levels of support into assessment methods to identify students' acquisition of knowledge. Finally, educators should consider the methods used for engagement to ensure that students remain invested and involved in the learning process. Examples of each of these instructional considerations are included below.

Representation. The representation aspect of UDL involves the consideration of how students are accessing instructional materials in the classroom. For example, a strategy that educators could implement is the use of both auditory and visual representations of content to facilitate multiple opportunities for content acquisition. An additional instructional consideration would be to clarify important vocabulary that may be relevant to instruction as well as provide necessary background information and emphasize big ideas or patterns (CAST, 2018). Considerations regarding how content is represented in the classroom provides further reach as to how the information is accessed by all students; therefore, by building considerations for representation into instructional design, educators assist in reaching more students.

Expression. Instructional considerations related to how students act on or express understanding of content can also enhance student learning and performance. For example, offering students multiple means for communication of their understanding offers many opportunities to demonstrate understanding. Additionally, setting short-term goals that include plans and strategies for acquiring those goals can assist students in monitoring their progress over time. Consideration of instructional practices that accommodate students' means for expression of learning can help students develop methods for managing instructional information (CAST, 2018).

Engagement. Prior to delivery of instruction, educators should consider methods to explain the relevance of the topic to students, minimize any potential distractions, emphasize the importance of the learning goals, and reinforce the classroom expectations. During instruction, educators employ the strategy of focusing on means for how students can remain engaged in the lesson. These considerations could include choices in the learning modality, variation of the difficulty level, collaboration, and embedded self-assessment checkpoints. There should also be a mechanism for checking in with students that may reach frustration levels during instruction (CAST, 2018).

Co-Teaching

Both EBPs and HLPs, theoretically, can be more successfully implemented into classroom instruction when collaboration and partnerships for instruction are present. Schools must also inhabit a culture of inclusion, meaning that all school personnel must create a culture of support, acceptance, and value for all students, including those with disabilities (Rowe et al., 2023). It is difficult to discuss the matter of inclusive education and collaboration without considering the opportunity for co-teaching. Essentially, co-teaching is an instructional delivery option that allows a student that has been identified as having a disability and requires special education services to receive instruction in the general education classroom with the support of a general education teacher and a special education teacher (King-Sears et al., 2021). Co-teaching is an instructional model that can be considered for the inclusive classroom that would allow for more opportunities to embed EBPs and HLPs into teaching practices. The theory behind the benefits of a co-taught classroom suggests that students that receive special education services could be well supported by a special education teacher in a least restrictive environment (LRE) in which the student has access to the general education curriculum. There are five co-teaching models that are widely recognized and can be incorporated into the instructional delivery of the co-taught classroom, those models include: one teach/one assist, station teaching, parallel teaching, alternative teaching, and team teaching (Cook & Friend, 1995; Friend et al., 2010; Friend & Bursuck, 2012) (see figure 9.2). Studies have investigated the impact of the co-teaching models on the student experience and also achievement and found that benefits exist (King-Sears et al., 2021). Studies have also investigated the use of specific strategies embedded in the instructional practices within the co-taught classroom and found that selecting the appropriate model accompanied by evidence-based practices is beneficial to students (Keeley et al., 2020; Keeley et al., 2023). Each co-teaching model has a specific purpose and function and when embedded into instruction correctly will be beneficial to the students in the classroom (Conderman, 2011; Keeley, 2018; Keeley et al., 2017). The identified issues related to co-teaching include a lack of parity between co-teaching partners, inadequate planning time, lack of professional development opportunities, and an unclear division of responsibilities among co-teaching partners (Dieker, 2001; Friend, 2008; Pancsofar & Petroff, 2016; Scruggs et al., 2007). As a result of these challenges, co-teachers tend to rely on the one teach/one assist model too frequently and do not select a model based on what may complement instruction

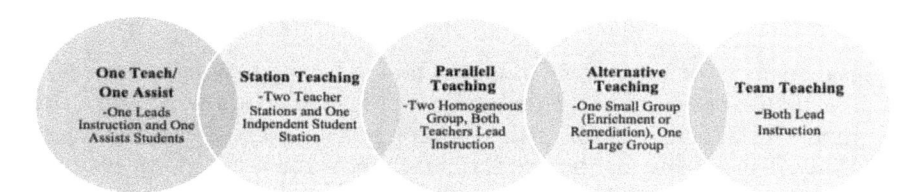

Figure 9.2. Five Co-Teaching Models and Abbreviated Structures
Source: Created by the authors.

but, rather, that requires the least amount of planning (Dieker, 2001; King-Sears & Strogilos, 2020; Pancsofar & Petroff, 2016; Solis et al., 2012).

The discussion of co-teaching efficacy is typically centralized around areas of expertise across co-teaching partners. For example, the general educator in a co-taught classroom is typically the content expert (e.g., science) in the classroom while the special education teacher is the instructional delivery specialist. On occasion, both the general educator and the special educator are content specialists; however, this is not always the case. Many times, the special education teacher is assigned as a co-teacher in multiple classrooms, and while one of those classrooms could include a content area in which they specialize, many times the special educator is placed in the classroom based on need and content expertise is not considered (Dieker & Murawski, 2003; Pancsofar & Petroff, 2016; Weiss & Lloyd, 2002). As a result, a decrease in efficacy with special education teachers can occur due to a lack of familiarity with the content in which they are asked to provide instructional support. To further complicate the issue, co-teachers do not receive enough professional development to support their growth as co-teaching partners and identify methods for mitigating negative factors that could impact their effectiveness as co-teachers (Pancsofar & Petroff, 2013).

Case Study 1

Mr. Skye is a third-grade general education teacher who oversees teaching English language arts reading (ELAR) and science content for his grade level. He is preparing for a follow-up meeting with the multi-tiered system of supports (MTSS) team about a particular student who has not been making adequate progress in science. After placement in Tier 2 for six weeks, Mr. Skye recognizes that this student struggles with reading comprehension. Mr. Skye has been assigned a special education co-teaching partner but isn't sure how to define either his or the special education teacher's role and responsibilities. Currently, the special education teacher spends time in his general education classroom to support specific students, but Mr. Skye wishes he knew more about how to make co-teaching function more cohesively.

At the start of the six weeks prior to starting the Tier 2 small-group interventions, Mr. Skye collected baseline data using the DIBELS Benchmark fluency materials, since all his students completed this assessment at the end of the first quarter to identify the progress in reading. Mr. Skye knew that the student scored at a mid-second grade reading fluency level, based on data from the previous end of quarter benchmark, so Mr. Skye used the second-grade mid-benchmark DIBELS fluency materials as a data-gathering starting point. Following the data collection, Mr. Skye was a bit disheartened to find that the student remained at the 2.5 fluency level; however, this aligned with what he had been noticing over the past six weeks and the progress-monitoring data that he had been collecting over that time period. Because it is nearing the winter break, Mr. Skye is becoming increasingly concerned.

During the six weeks of Tier 2 intervention for reading fluency, Mr. Skye has been working with the student three times per week for 30 minutes in a small-group setting of three students, right after the whole-group reading lesson takes place. Mr. Skye has been using repeated reading, which allows the reader to repeatedly rehearse the same reading passage aloud while receiving corrective feedback. Following the repeated reading, he selects a grade-level fluency activity from the Florida

Center for Reading Research materials. During the small-group intervention sessions, Mr. Skye follows Tier 2 teaching procedures and is providing fluency instruction with modeling, checking that the student is doing the activity correctly, having the student demonstrate what they are doing and repeat instructions, and provides corrective feedback as needed (IRIS Center, 2006).

In preparation for the MTSS meeting, Mr. Skye gathers student work samples from across subject areas and other data (i.e., quizzes or test scores) and anecdotal notes from his small-group meetings with the student to support his case and to foster discussion. For example, Mr. Skye notices that the student's reading fluency deficiencies are also continuing to impact learning in other content areas like science and wishes to address this.

Case Study Questions:

1. What questions might the MTSS team ask Mr. Skye about the student's data? What recommendations do you feel the MTSS team will make for the student in Mr. Skye's class and why? Provide a rationale to support your answer.
2. Did Mr. Skye utilize any specific EBPs or HLPs? Provide a rationale to support your answer.
3. How could the special education teacher support Mr. Skye during Tier 2 instruction? What questions could Mr. Skye ask the special education teacher?
4. What other recommendations or ideas would you suggest after reading this case study?

Case Study 2

Mr. Skye recently met with the MTSS team at his school to discuss student data and to gain advice on a particular student who had not been making adequate progress in Tier 2 interventions. Part of the recommendations that the MTSS team provided to him were to strategically identify additional teaching processes that may more explicitly teach cross-content. They suggested that he meet with his grade-level team to do more intentional planning so that all the teachers across the third-grade level are sure to understand the specific needs of students and utilize similar strategies to support those students during their teaching rotations. Prior to the grade-level weekly meeting, Mr. Skye gave each teacher a pre-planning form that the MTSS team recommended so that each teacher could come prepared to ensure that the weekly content area topics were covered, and that pertinent information was addressed, based on the individualized needs of specific students. When the third-grade level team meets for their weekly planning meeting, Mr. Skye brings the following planning template to the meeting to discuss the specific needs of the students in his ELAR and science content rotations. See the sample lesson plan, template 9.1, below.

PRE-PLANNING TEMPLATE
Week of December 1–7
Mr. Skye—Third-Grade ELAR/Science

Learning goal:

(ELAR) Students will recognize characteristics and structures of nonfiction, informational text, including features such as sections, tables, graphs, timelines, bullets, numbers, and bold and italicized font to support understanding.

(Science) students will make a claim about how to reduce the impact of a weather-related hazard by finding a solution to a problem by citing relevant evidence about how it meets the criteria and constraints of the problem.

Standards:
CCSS.ELA-LITERACY.RI.3.4
- Determine the meaning of general academic and domain-specific words and phrases in a text relevant to nonfiction science text.

CCSS.ELA-LITERACY.RI.3.5
- Use text features and search tools (e.g., key words, sidebars, hyperlinks) to locate information relevant to a given topic efficiently.

CCSS.ELA-LITERACY.RI.3.7
- Use information gained from illustrations (e.g., maps, photographs) and the words in a text to demonstrate understanding of the text (e.g., where, when, why, and how key events occur).

CCSS.ELA-LITERACY.RI.3.3
- Describe the relationship between a series of historical events, scientific ideas or concepts, or steps in technical procedures in a text, using language that pertains to time, sequence, and cause/effect.

NGSS 3
- ESS3 Earth and Human Activity

Short-term objectives:	Specific supports:
Students can identify nonfiction text structures. Students can accurately use nonfiction vocabulary to explain and describe a weather-related hazard.	• Pre-teach relevant vocabulary, preview text, use graphic organizers to reinforce concepts/content, student small-group work, reinforce content project-based learning activities

Day 1 (Monday):	Explicit instruction (I do):
(Recall) students will be able to recall three nonfiction science vocabulary words related to weather related hazards.	• State daily goals and expectations • Use clear and concise language (pre-select vocabulary from science basal section on weather-related disasters)—post on board. • Provide examples and non-examples of vocabulary words with images and reference to text features in science basal-post examples by words on board. • Ask students to recall newly learned science vocabulary in a fact or fiction science sentence game. • Monitor student learning and responses and correct throughout as needed.

Days 2/3 (Tuesday and Wednesday): (Identify) Students will identify and match nonfiction science vocabulary pertinent to weather-related hazards. (Illustrate) Students will create a weather-related hazard.	Guided practice (we do): • (Tues.) Review vocabulary from Monday. • (Tues.) Go over nonfiction text features from yesterday's reading passage. • (Tues.) Students will complete a nonfiction text feature worksheet. • (Tues.) Students will complete a cloze activity with a partner using vocabulary words from the science basal. • (Wed.) Students will create a weather-related hazard and input three relevant words and their meanings in context. Students will share their creations with the whole group.
Days 4/5 (Thursday and Friday): (Defend) Students will select, research, and read about a nonfiction weather-related hazard passage. (Write) Students will write a cause/effect to a weather-related hazard.	Independent practice (you do): Students will independently complete a Frayer model inclusive of relevant vocabulary from the week. • Students will use their created Frayer model to write a cause/effect to one weather-related hazard and include a minimum of three learned vocabulary words from the week.

Specific student needs/strategies:
Three students are receiving Tier 2 interventions for reading comprehension:
• Two of those students (Lily and Sid) are making slow but steady progress. One student (Taj) has not been making progress over the past six weeks.
  – Utilize small-group instruction to reteach and reinforce content lesson concepts.
  – Pre-teach relevant vocabulary, preview text, use graphic organizers to reinforce concepts/content, use student small groups (i.e., reciprocal teaching), and reinforce content with project-based learning activities.
  – Collect ongoing data through student work samples.	

Case Study Questions:

1. Does Mr. Skye use cross-content pre-planning strategies to guide his instruction? Explain why or why not.
2. What explicit teaching strategies does Mr. Skye use as part of his pre-planning ideas?
3. Do you feel that Mr. Skye has enough information to discuss with his third-grade level team so that they understand the individual needs of students? Why or why not?

Case Study Activity:

Using the pre-planning template that Mr. Skye created above, write a lesson plan for "Day 1" ensuring that you focus on explicit and cross-content instruction that embeds science and ELAR. See the sample lesson plan, template 9.2, below.

Practices that Support Inclusive Science Instruction

LESSON PLAN	
Third-Grade ELAR/Science	
Lesson objective with measurable criteria:	
Assessment tools and data collection procedures:	
What teacher does:	**What student does:** **Assessment:** **Contingencies:**
Before (Gaining student interest, activating prior background knowledge, pre-teaching):	
During (How will the student self-monitor?):	
After (How will the student comprehend their learning and integrate into existing knowledge?):	
Communication skill and planned supports:	
Plans for generalization or self-directed learning:	
Resources and materials:	
Strategies to support students who are at risk (i.e., below grade level) **or who have an IEP:**	
Strategies to support differentiated learning (i.e., above grade level, on grade level, below grade level, students who are English learners and/or culturally and linguistically diverse learners):	

Resources to Support Inclusive Science Instruction

There are several resources and professional organizations that can be utilized to support evidence-based, cross-content science instruction and teacher professional development in the elementary inclusive classroom, which are identified below, in table 9.3.

Table 9.3. Resources and Professional Organizations to Support Inclusive Science Elementary Classrooms

Resources	
Association for Science Teacher Education (ASTE)	https://theaste.org/
Co-Teaching Configurations	https://edu240coteaching.wordpress.com/what-does-co-teaching-look-like/
Co-Teaching Conversation Starters	https://beckettlhaight.com/2019/03/10/engaging-all-learners-through-push-in-support-2/
Explicit Instruction with Dr. Anita Archer	https://explicitinstruction.org/
High-Leverage Practices	https://highleveragepractices.org/
Iris Resources on Co-Teaching and Collaboration	https://iris.peabody.vanderbilt.edu/resources/iris-resource-locator/
National Science Teachers Association (NSTA)	https://www.nsta.org/
Next Generation Science Standards	https://www.nextgenscience.org/sites/default/files/AllTopic.pdf
Universal Design for Learning Guidelines	https://udlguidelines.cast.org/

Source: Compiled by the authors.

CONCLUSION

Scaffolded strategies and interventions can support elementary students' science and cross-content learning. Teachers must explore planning mechanisms that incorporate differentiated instruction based on the individual needs of students. This can be supported through an MTSS framework that utilizes evidence-based strategies, interventions, and practices in addition to collaboration between general and special education teachers (i.e., co-teaching).

Co-teaching is an essential practice within an inclusive classroom setting. While the specific roles of the general and special education teachers within the inclusive classroom may differ (i.e., general education teacher = content expert; special education teacher = instructional practice expert), when combined, they can be very effective in bridging content and best meet the needs of a diverse group of students. Developing trust between general and special education teachers is essential. This can be fostered by finding recurring, common planning times and through support from building administrators in arranging a schedule to make this happen.

General educators should carefully consider the instructional methods incorporated into general education classroom instruction and ensure that those practices can be considered evidence-based by making appropriate, data-based selections that correlate with students' specific needs. Additionally, general educators must remember that while EBPs and HLPs are designed to provide high-level instruction, they do not replace accommodations and/or modifications that are required for special education programming for students. However, when implementing both EBPs and HLPs in daily classroom instruction, teachers will have the opportunity to reach a wider breadth of students. Special education teachers must make sure that general education teachers understand how to provide the accommodations and/or modifications that are written in students' individualized education programs (IEP) and discuss strategies on how to support students in the inclusive classroom environment. Also, ideas for how to implement EBPs and HLPs across content areas should be shared with general education classroom teachers.

When general and special education teachers understand their roles and responsibilities, they will be better prepared to implement inclusive practices that can support at-risk students or students with disabilities. When general and special educators effectively plan and implement instructional practices that embed EBPs, HLPs, integrate UDL, and co-teaching, all students will have increased access to the curriculum and achievement toward academic and behavioral goals.

REFERENCES

Adams, G. & Engelmann, S. (1996). *Research on direct instruction: 25 years beyond DISTAR*. Educational Achievement Systems.

Adams, M., & Henry, M. (1997). Myths and realities about words and literacy. *School Psychology Review*, 26, 425–437.

Alfassi, M. (2004). Reading to learn: Effects of combined strategy instruction on high school students. *Journal of Educational Research*, 97(4), 171–184. https://doi.org/10.3200/JOER.97.4.171-185

References

Alfassi, M., Weiss, I., & Lifshitz, H. (2009). The efficacy of reciprocal teaching in fostering the reading literacy of students with ID. *European Journal of Special Needs Education*, 24(3), 291–305. https://doi.org/10.1080/08856250903016854

American Institutes for Research. (2023). Center on Multi-Tiered System of Supports. *Essential components of MTSS*. https://mtss4success.org/essential-components

Archer, A. L., & Hughes, C. A. (2011). *Explicit instruction: Effective and efficient teaching*. Guilford Publications.

Baker, S., Gersten, R., & Scanlon, D. (2002). Procedural facilitators and cognitive strategies: tools for unraveling the mysteries of comprehension and the writing process, and for providing meaningful access to the general curriculum. *Learning Disabilities Research & Practice*, 17, 65–77.

Barrio, B. L., Hott, B. L., & Randolph, K. M. (2022). Developing an individualized education program. In J. A. Rodriguez & W. W. Murawski (Eds.), *Special education law and policy: From foundation to application* (1st ed., Vol. 1, pp. 227–261). Plural.

Billingsley, B., & Bettini, E. (2019). Special education teacher attrition and retention: A review of the literature. *Review of Education Research*, 89(5), 697–744. https://doi.org/10.3102/0034654319862495

Bluestein, N. A. (2010). Unlocking text features for determining importance in expository text: A strategy for struggling readers. *Reading Teacher*, 63(7), 597–600.

Boyle, J. R. (2000). The effects of a Venn diagram strategy on the literal, inferential, and relational comprehension of students with mild disabilities. *Learning Disabilities*, 10(1), 86–98. https://doi.org/10.1016/B978-0-12-388409-1.00007-2

Cakir, M. (2008). Constructivist approaches to learning science and their implications for science pedagogy: A literature review. *International Journal of Environmental and Science Education*, 3(4), 193–206.

California Department of Education. (n.d.). Multi-tiered system of supports. https://www.cde.ca.gov/ci/cr/ri/

Calvin, K. L., & Gray, S. (2023). Improving expository text comprehension in adolescent Spanish-English bilingual learners with learning disabilities using a graphic organizer. *Learning Disability Quarterly*, 1–13. DOI: 10.1177/07319487231176780.

Casteel, C. P., & Isom, B. A. (1994). Reciprocal processes in science and literacy learning. *Reading Teacher*, 47(7), 538–545. https://eric.ed.gov/?id=EJ483184

Center for Applied Special Technologies (CAST). (2018). *Guideline 1: Provide options for perception*. UDL Guidelines. https://udlguidelines.cast.org/representation/perception

Collaboration for Effective Educator Development, Accountability, and Reform (CEEDAR). (2023). *MTSS: Multi-tiered system of supports*. https://ceedar.education.ufl.edu/mtssudldi-professional-development-module/mtss-chapter/

Conderman, G. (2011). Middle school co-teaching: Effective practices and student reflections. *Middle School Journal*, 42(4), 24–31.

Cook, B., Tankersley, M., & Landrum, T. (2009). Determining evidence-based practices in special education. *Exceptional Children*, 75, 365–383. DOI: 10.1177/001440290907500306.

Cook, B. G., & Odom, S. L. (2013). Evidence-based practices and implementation science in special education. *Exceptional Children, 79*, 135–144. https://doi.org/10.1177/001440291307900201

Cook, L., & Friend, M. (1995). Co-teaching: Guidelines for creating effective practices. *Focus on Exceptional Children, 28*(3),1–16. https://doi.org/10.17161/fec.v28i3.6852

Council for Exceptional Children (CEC). (2014). Council for exceptional children: Standards for evidence-based practices in special education. *Teaching Exceptional Children, 46*(6), 206. http://doi.org/10.1177/0022487120948046

Coyne, P., Evans, M., & Karger, J. (2017). Use of a UDL literacy environment by middle school students with intellectual and developmental disabilities. *Intellectual and Developmental Disabilities, 55*(1), 4–14. https://doi.org/10.1352/1934-9556-55.1.4

Deno, S. L. (1985). Curriculum-based measurement: The emerging alternative. *Exceptional Children, 52*(3), 219–232. https://doi.org/10.1177/001440298505200303

Dexter, D., Park, Y., & Hughes, C. (2011). A meta-analytic review of graphic organizers and science instruction for adolescents with learning disabilities: Implications for the intermediate and secondary science classroom. *Learning Disabilities Research & Practice, 26*(4), 204–213. https://doi.org/10.1111/j.1540-5826.2011.00341.x

Dieker, L. A. (2001). What are the characteristics of effective middle and high school co-taught teams for students with disabilities? *Preventing School Failure, 46*, 14–23. https://doi.org/10.1080/10459880109603339

Dieker, L. A., & Murawski, W. W. (2003). Coteaching at the secondary level: Unique issues, current trends, and suggestions for success. *The High School Journal, 86*(4), 1–13. https://doi.org/10.1353/hsj.2003.0007

Education for All Handicapped Children Act of 1975, Pub. L. 94-142, 89 Stat. 773, codified at 20 U.S.C. § 1400.

Eick, C. J. (2012). Use of the outdoor classroom and nature-study to support science and literacy learning: A narrative case study of a third-grade classroom. *Journal of Science Teacher Education, 23*, 789–803.

Fisher, D., & Frey, N. (2015). Teacher modeling using complex informational texts. *The Reading Teacher, 69*(1), 63–69.

Friend, M. (2008). Co-Teaching: A simple solution that isn't simple after all. *Journal of Curriculum and Instruction, 2*, DOI: 10.3776/joci.2008.v2n2p9-19.

Friend, M., & Bursuck, W. D. (2012). *Including students with special needs: A practical guide for classroom teachers* (6th ed.). Pearson.

Friend, M., Cook, L., Hurley-Chamberlain, D., & Shamberger, C. (2010). Co-teaching: An illustration of the complexity of collaboration in special education. *Journal of Educational and Psychological Consultation, 20*, 9–27.

Fuchs, D. (1996). Educational intervention and students with learning disabilities. *Learning Disabilities: A Multidisciplinary Journal, 7*, 63–67.

Fuchs, D., & Fuchs, L. S. (1995). What's "special" about special education? *Phi Delta Kappan, 76*, 522–530.

Fuchs, L. S., & Deno, S. L. (1991). Paradigmatic distinctions between instructionally relevant measurement models. *Exceptional Children, 57*(6), 488–500. https://doi.org/10.1177/001440299105700603

Fuchs, L. S., Fuchs, D., & Stecker, P. M. (1989). Effects of curriculum-based measurement on teachers' instructional planning. *Journal of Learning Disabilities*, *22*(1), 51–59. https://doi.org/10.1177/002221948902200110

Honig, B., Diamond, L., & Gutlohn, L. (2000). *Teaching reading: Sourcebook for kindergarten through eighth grade*. Arena.

Hovland, J. B. (2020). Inclusive comprehension strategy instruction: Reciprocal teaching and adolescents with intellectual disability. *Teaching Exceptional Children*, *52*(6), 404–413. DOI: 10.1177/0040059920914334.

Hughes, C. A., Riccomini, P. J., & Dexter, C. A. (2022). Use explicit instruction. In J. McLeskey, L. Maheady, B. Billingsley, M. T. Brownell, & T. J. Lewis (Eds.), *High-leverage practices for inclusive classrooms* (2nd ed., pp. 235–264). Routledge.

Hughes, T. G. (2022). Disciplinary literacy strategies to support transactions in elementary social studies. *Journal of Language & Literacy Education*, *18*(1), 1–11.

IRIS Center. (2006). *RTI (part 3): Reading instruction*. https://iris.peabody.vanderbilt.edu/module/rti03-reading/

Kaldenberg, E., Therrien, W., Watt, S., Gorsh, J., & Taylor, J. (2011). Three keys to success in science for students with learning disabilities. *Science Scope*, *35*, 36–39.

Kearns, D. M., & Whaley, V. M. (2019). Helping students with Dyslexia read long words: Using syllables and morphemes. *Teaching Exceptional Children*, *51*(3), 212–225. https://doi.org/10.1177/0040059918810010

Keeley, R. G. (2018). Using an alternating treatment design in a co-taught classroom to measure student on-task behavior. *Journal of the American Academy of Special Education Professionals (JAASEP)*, spring/summer, 31–43.

Keeley, R. G., (2022). High fidelity co-teaching through collaboration, varied co-teaching models, and differentiated teaching strategies. In M. Peterson-Ahmad & V. L. Luther (Eds.), *Collaborative approaches to recruiting, preparing, and retaining teachers in the field* (pp. 67–92). IGI Global.

Keeley, R. G., Alvarado-Alcantar, R., & Keeley, D.W. (2020, Fall). The development of AISSEND: An observation tool to assess inclusive practices. *Journal of the American Academy of Special Education Professionals (JAASEP)*, fall, 122–137.

Keeley, R. G., Alvarado-Alcantar, R., Peterson Ahmad, M. B., & Yeatts, P. (2023). Measuring the implementation of inclusive strategies in secondary classrooms using an observation rubric. *Special Education Research Policy and Practice Journal*, *7*, 122–134.

Keeley, R. G., Brown, M. R., & Knapp, D. (2017). Evaluating the student experience in the co-taught classroom. *International Journal of Special Education*, *32*(3), 520–537.

Kennedy, M. J., Cook, L., Cook, B., Brownell, M. T., & Holdheide, L. (2020). *Special video: Clarifying the relationship between HLPs and EBPs*. Council for Exceptional Children. https://highleveragepractices.org/clarifying-relationship-between-hlps-and-ebps

Kim, A., Vaughn, S., Wanzek, J., & Shangjin, W. (2004). Graphic organizers and their effects on the reading comprehension of students with LD: A synthesis of research. *Journal of Learning Disabilities*, *37*(2), 105–118. https://doi.org/10.1177/00222194040370020201

Kinder, D., Kubina, R., & Marchand-Martella, N. E. (2005). Special education and direct instruction: An effective combination. *Education Publications*, *26*(5), 1–36.

King-Sears, M. E., & Strogilos, V. (2020). An exploratory study of self-efficacy, school belongingness, and co-teaching perspectives from middle school students and teachers in a mathematics co-taught classroom. *International Journal of Inclusive Education*, 24(2), 162–180. https://doi.org/10.1080/13603116.2018.1453553

King-Sears, M., Stefanidis, A., Berkeley, S., & Strogilos, V. (2021). Does co-teaching improve academic achievement for students with disabilities? A meta-analysis. *Educational Research Review*, 34(1), 100405. https://doi.org/10.1016/j.edurev.2021.100405

Klentschy, M. P., & Molina-De La Torre, E. (2004). Students' science notebooks and the inquiry process. In E. W. Saul (Ed.), *Crossing borders in literacy and science instruction: Perspectives on theory and practice* (pp. 340–354). International Reading Association.

Klinger, J. K., Brownell, M. T., Mason, L. H., Sindelar, P. T., Benedict, A. E., Griffin, G. G., . . . Park, Y. (2016). Teaching students with special needs in the new millennium. In D. Gitomer & C. Bell (Eds.), *Handbook of research on teaching* (5th ed., pp. 639–717). American Educational Research Association.

Konrad, N., Hessler, T., Alber-Morgan, S. R., Graham-Day, K. J., Davenport, C. A., & Helton, M. (2022). Systematically design instruction toward a specific goal. In J. McLeskey, L. Maheady, B. Billingsley, M. T. Brownell, & T. J. Lewis (Eds.), *High-leverage practices for inclusive classrooms* (2nd ed., pp. 172–188). Routledge.

Lane, K., Oakes, W. P., Cantwell, E. D., & Royer, D. J. (2016). *Building and installing comprehensive, integrated, three-tiered (Ci3T) models of prevention: A practical guide to supporting school success*. https://books.apple.com/us/book/building-installingcomprehensive/id1171269209?mt=13

Lindsley, O. R. (1992). Precision teaching: Discoveries and effects. *Journal of Applied Behavior Analysis*, 25, 51–57.

Lundberg, I., & Reichenberg, M. (2013). Developing reading comprehension among students with mild intellectual disabilities: An intervention study. *Scandinavian Journal of Educational Research*, 57(1), 89–100. https://doi.org/10.1080/00313831.2011.623179

Marchand-Martella, N. E., Slocum, T. A., & Martella, R. C. (Eds.). (2004). *Introduction to direct instruction*. Allyn and Bacon.

Massonnié, J., Bianco, M., Lima, L., & Bressoux, P. (2018). Longitudinal predictors of reading comprehension in French at first grade: Unpacking the oral comprehension component of the simple view. *Learning and Instruction*, 60, 166–179. https://doi.org/10.1016/j.learninstruc.2018.01.005

McCarthy, C. B. (2005). Effects of thematic-based, hands-on science teaching versus a textbook approach for students with disabilities. *Journal of Research in Science Teaching*, 42(3), 245–263. https://doi.org/10.1177/1053451208321564

McCray, E. D., Kamman, M., & Brownell, M. T. (2017). *High-leverage practices and evidence-based practices: A promising pair*. https://ceedar.education.ufl.edu/wp-content/uploads/2017/12/HLPs-and-EBPs-A-Promising-Pair.pdf

McDowell, C., & Keenan, M. (2001). Developing fluency and endurance in a child diagnosed with attention deficit hyperactivity disorder. *Journal of Applied Behavior Analysis*, 34, 345–348.

McLeskey, J., Barringer, M.-D., Billingsly, B., Brownell, M., Jackson, D., Kennedy, M., . . . Ziegler, D. (2017). *High-leverage practices in special education.* Council for Exceptional Children & CEEDAR Center.

Miller, B., Doughty, T., & Krockover, G. (2015). Using science inquiry methods to promote self-determination and problem-solving skills for students with moderate intellectual disability. *Education and Training in Autism and Developmental Disabilities, 50*(3), 356–368.

Moats, L. (2005–6). How spelling supports reading. *American Educator, 29,* 12–22, 42–43. https://www.aft.org/ae/winter2005-2006/moats

Montague, M., & Applegate, B. (2000). Middle school students' perceptions, persistence, and performance in mathematical problem solving. *Learning Disability Quarterly, 23,* 215–226.

Nagro, S. A., Markelz, A. M., & Davis., R. E. (2022). Every Student Succeeds Act as it applies to special education. In J. A. Rodriguez & W. W. Murawski (Eds.), *Special education law and policy: From foundation to application* (1st ed., pp. 157–193). Plural.

Nagy, W. E., & Scott, J. A. (2004). Vocabulary processes. In R. B. Ruddell & N. J. Unrau (Eds.), *Theoretical models and processes of reading* (5th ed., pp. 574–593). International Reading Association.

National Center for Education Statistics (NCES). (2011). *National assessment of educational progress: Science assessment.* http://nces.ed.gov

National Center on Intensive Intervention. (n.d.). *Intensive intervention and MTSS.* https://intensiveintervention.org/special-topics/mtss

National Research Council. (2000). *Inquiry and the national science education standards: A guide for teaching and learning.* National Academy Press.

National Research Council. (2001). *Educating teachers of science, mathematics, and technology: New practices for the new millennium.* National Academy Press.

Odom, S. L., Buysse, V., & Soukakou, E. (2011). Inclusion of young children with disabilities: A quarter century of research perspectives. *Journal of Early Intervention, 33*(4), 344–356. https://doi.org/10.1177/1053815111430094

Palincsar, A. S., Magnusson, S. J., Collins, K. M., & Cutter, J. (2001). Making science accessible to all: Results of a design experiment in inclusive classrooms. *Learning Disability Quarterly, 24,* 15–32.

Palumbo, A., & Loiacono, V. (2009). Understanding the cause of intermediate and middle school comprehension problems. *International Journal of Special Education, 24*(1), 75–81.

Palumbo, A., Kramer-Vida, L., & Hunt, C. V. (2015). Teaching vocabulary and morphology in intermediate grades. *Preventing School Failure: Alternative Education for Children and Youth, 59*(2), 109–115. https://doi.org/10.1080/1045988x.2013.850649

Pancsofar, N., & Petroff, J. G. (2013). Professional development experiences in co-teaching. *Teacher Education and Special Education, 36*(2), 83–96.

Pancsofar, N., & Petroff, J. G. (2016). Teachers' experiences with co-teaching as a model for inclusive education. *International Journal of Inclusive Education, 20*(10), 1043–1053. https://doi.org/10.1080/13603116.2016.1145264

Perfetti, C., & Stafura, J. (2014). Word knowledge in a theory of reading comprehension. *Scientific Studies of Reading, 18,* 22–37. https://doi.org/10.1080/10888438.2013.827687

Reichenberg, M. (2014). The importance of structured text talks for students' reading comprehension: An intervention study in special schools. *Journal of Special Education and Rehabilitation*, 15(3/4), 77–94. https://www.proquest.com/scholarly-journals/importance-structured-text-talks-students-reading/docview/1615272605/se-2

Riccomini, P. J., Morano, S., & Hughes, C. A. (2017). Big ideas in special education: Specially designed instruction, high-leverage practices, explicit instruction, and intensive intervention. *Teaching Exceptional Children*, 50(1), 20–27. DOI:10.1177/0040059917724412.

Rice-Doran, P. (2015). Language accessibility in the classroom: How UDL can promote success for linguistically diverse learners. *Exceptionality Education International*, 25(3), 1–12. https://doi.org/10.5206/eei.v25i3.7728

Rosenshine, B. V. (1986). Synthesis of research on explicit teaching. *Educational Leadership*, 43(7), 60–69.

Rosenthal, J., & Ehri, L. (2010). Pronouncing new words aloud during the silent reading of text enhances fifth graders' memory for vocabulary words and their spellings. *Reading & Writing*, 24, 921–950.

Rowe, D., Blevins, M., Kittelman, A., & Walker, V. L. (2023). Supporting inclusive practices in the least restrictive environment. *Teaching Exceptional Children*, 55(3), 152–154. DOI: 10.1177/00599231156042.

Ruddell, R. B. (2009). *How to teach reading to elementary and middle school students: Practical ideas from highly effective teachers*. Pearson.

Sailor, W., & McCart, A. B. (2014). Stars in alignment. *Research & Practices for Persons with Severe Disabilities*, 39(1), 55–64. https://doi.org/10.1177/1540796914534622

Sailor, W., Skrtic, T. M., Cohn, M., & Olmstead, C. (2021). Preparing teacher educators for statewide scale-up of multi-tiered system of supports (MTSS). *Teacher Education and Special Education*, 44(1), 24–41. DOI: 10.11770888406420938035.

Satter, A., Meisenheimer, J., & Sailor, W. (2019). Equity and inclusivity in education. In M. J. Schuelka, C. J. Johnstone, G. Thomas, & A. J. Artiles (Eds.), *The SAGE handbook of inclusion and diversity in education* (pp. 133–144). Sage.

Scruggs, T. E., Mastropieri, M. A., & McDuffie, K. A. (2007). Coteaching in inclusive classrooms: A metasynthesis of qualitative research. *Exceptional Children*, 73(4), 392–416. https://doi.org/10.1177/001440290707300401

Scruggs, T., Mastropieri, M., Bakken, J., & Brigham, F. J. (1993). Reading versus doing: The relative effects of textbook-based and inquiry-oriented approaches to science learning in special education classrooms. *Journal of Special Education*, 27(1), 1–15. https://doi.org/10.1177/002246699302700101

Scruggs, T. E., Mastropieri, M. A., & Okolo, C. M. (2008). Science and social studies for students with disabilities. *Focus on Exceptional Children*, 41, 1–24.

Shanahan, C., & Shanahan, T. (2014). Does disciplinary literacy have a place in elementary school? *The Reading Teacher*, 67(8), 636–639.

Shanahan, T. (2016). Relations among oral language, reading, and writing development. In C. A. MacArthur, J. Fitzgerald, & S. Graham (Eds.), *Handbook of writing research* (pp. 171–186). Gilford.

Slater, W. H., & Horstman, F. R. (2002). Teaching reading and writing to struggling middle school and high school students: The case for reciprocal teaching. *Preventing School Failure*, 46(4), 163–166. https://doi.org/10.1080/10459880209604416

Solis, M., Vaughn, S., Swanson, E., & McCulley, L. (2012). Collaborative models of instruction: The empirical foundations of inclusion and coteaching. *Psychology in the Schools*, 49(5), 498510. https://doi.org/10.1002/pits.21606

Stewart, M. (2012). Understanding learning: Theories and critique. In L. Hunt & D. Chalmers. *University teaching in focus: A learning-centered approach*. Routledge.

Suggate, S., Schaughency, E., McAnally, H., & Reese, E. (2018). From infancy to adolescence: The longitudinal links between vocabulary, early literacy skills, oral narrative, and reading comprehension. *Cognitive Development*, 47, 82–95. https://doi.org/10.1016/j.cogdev.2018.04.005

Taylor, J. C., Tseng, C-M., Murillo, A., Therrien, W., & Hand, B. (2018). Using argument-based science inquiry to improve science achievement for students with disabilities in inclusive classrooms. *Journal of Science Education for Students with Disabilities*, 15(1), 27–39. http://doi.org/10.14448/jsesd.10.0001

Thorndike, R. M., & Thorndike-Christ, T. (2010). *Measurement and evaluation in psychology and education* (8th ed.). Pearson.

US Department of Education, Institute of Education Sciences, National Center for Education Evaluation and Regional Assistance, What Works Clearinghouse.

Vandercook, T., Kleinert, H., Jorgensen, C., Sabia, R., & Lazarus, S. (2018–19). The hope of lessons learned: Supporting the inclusion of students with the most significant cognitive disabilities into general education classrooms. *IMPACT*, 31(2). https://ici.umn.edu/products/impact/312/#Cover

Vanderheyden, A. M. & Solomon, B. G. (2023). Valid outcomes for screening and progress monitoring: Fluency is superior to accuracy in curriculum-based measurement. *School Psychology*, 38(3), 160–172. https://doi.org/10.1037/spq0000528

Walton, S. (2006). Three steps for better reading in science: Before, during, and after. *Science Scope*, 30(4), 32–37.

Watkins, C., & Slocum, T. (2004). The components of direct instruction. In N. E. Marchand-Martella, T. A. Slocum, & R. C. Martella (Eds.), *Introduction to direct instruction* (pp. 2865). Allyn & Bacon.

Weiss, M. P., & Lloyd, J. W. (2002). Congruence between roles and actions of secondary special educators in co-taught and special education settings. *The Journal of Special Education*, 36(2), 58–68. https://doi.org/10.1177/00224669020360020101

Wood, L., Browder, D. M., & Flynn, L. (2015). Teaching students with intellectual disability to use self-questioning strategy to comprehend social studies text for an inclusive setting. *Research and Practice for Persons with Severe Disabilities*, 40(4), 275–293. https://doi.org/10.1177/1540796915592155

Yell, M. L., Katsiyannis, A., Ennis, R. P., Losinski, M., & Batman, D. (2020). Making legally sound placement decisions. *Teaching Exceptional Children*, 52(5), 291–303. https://eric.ed.gov/?id=EJ1254027

10

Social Studies in the Elementary Grades

David A. Brunow

SOCIAL STUDIES

The study of social studies is paramount in today's schools because of its broad-reaching potential to teach students concrete and transferrable skills. On the surface, social studies expose students to different countries, our own government, and how countries around the world engage with each other. However, the National Council for the Social Studies (NCSS) categorizes social studies into social science and humanities that are used to promote better understanding of civics. Social studies maintain a broader purpose of assisting students in the formation of decision-making skills.

Today's world is complex. The global economy in which we live is fueled by an understanding of social studies. Having knowledge of the geography and the histories of other countries, as well as our own in the United States, provides important historical and cultural information. It fosters a more complete understanding of not only our own country and our democratic society, but also of other countries and their respective societies. Shared values and an understanding of history help students to form connections and share fundamental understanding of American history. By extension, social studies teaches students about other cultures and their values. This additional knowledge helps students to understand people from other cultures better, increases their understanding of diversity, and prepares them for the future.

Social studies also teaches problem-solving skills by examining various civics and cultural issues. Students also benefit in various other academic capacities, such as increased literacy through analysis of varied historical writings, increased mathematical and map-reading skills through geography, and increased critical-thinking skills through the discussion and analysis of numerous historical documents and concepts. As a whole, social studies embodies numerous characteristics and skills necessary for not only understanding history and civics but also teaches skills that reach beyond the classroom and into real life and real-world situations.

While there are numerous skills and benefits to studying social studies, in the following sections of this chapter, we will explore academic standards and assessment, and—using a case study—discuss best practices and interventions to assist all students in your classroom. After reading this chapter, you will be able to:

1. Identify central ideas relating to social studies.
2. Relate educational theory to best practices for teaching.
3. Discuss the role and interplay of academic standards and assessments.
4. Provide examples of best practices and interventions to meet the academic needs of all students.

Learning, whether social studies or another subject, is a complex process. While learning takes place in many environments and in differing contexts, at the end of the day, learning is guided by the one doing the learning (Fernando & Markiar, 2017). The learning process is not a passive activity. On the contrary, learning is an active process where the learner uses their previous knowledge, and their experiences and social interactions with others, to weave the new information in to create a new or augmented and expanded body of information. This new and expanded information may not only be a body of enhanced information but may also cause the learner to reevaluate and reconstruct their understanding of a concept given the new perspective that has been created (Bada & Olusegun, 2015; Hein, 1991). When considering the learning process, it is important to make sure that learners have access to not only direct exposure of the content through the learning environment but also through teaching—the act of transmitting knowledge to the learner—that is sensitive to how each learner gains knowledge. Learning involves numerous steps, including answering and formulating questions, and assessing what we know (Bada & Olusegun, 2015). As active participants and creators of our individual learning, this can inform numerous classroom practices.

CONSTRUCTIVISM

Constructivism is a psychological learning theory (Bada & Olugeson, 2015) based on the idea that learning results from the process through which learners build or construct knowledge based on what they already know. Learners combine new information with what they are learning to create new knowledge (Bada & Olusegun, 2015; Hein, 1991). Learners construct knowledge as they learn by incorporating meaning from personal experiences and, therefore, constructivism is directly applicable to the school classroom (Bada & Olusegun, 2015). Because constructivism allows students to create their own knowledge and to be active participants in their learning, constructivism has valuable benefits for teaching students to think critically and how to problem solve using real-world application (Bada & Olusegun, 2015; Fernando & Marikar, 2017; Tam, 2000). In this way, learning is derived from previous and new knowledge, the learners' social experiences in relation to the question to be answered or the problem to be solved. Learners learn through others by applying and refining their understanding as learning happens (Fernando & Marikar, 2017; Bada & Olusegun, 2015).

Constructivism in the Social Studies Classroom

Constructivism used in the classroom is transformative to student learning. In traditional classrooms, the teacher often gives students knowledge. However, in the constructivist classroom, the learning focus transfers from the teacher to the students to make the learning process more student-centered and active (Bada & Olusegun, 2015; Fernando & Marikar, 2017). While the teacher still possesses most of the knowledge, in the constructivist classroom, the teacher's role becomes one where knowledge is shared between the teacher and the students. The teacher assists the students in connecting prior knowledge and experiences, both socially and culturally, with new knowledge to form new meaning and learning (Bada & Olusegun, 2015; Fernando & Marikar, 2017; Tam, 2000). Honebein (1996) summarizes constructivist learning environments as (a) providing experience and knowledge to help students understand how they learn, (b) providing exposure and understanding of multiple perspectives to find alternate solutions to problems or questions, (c) providing realistic contexts for learning, (d) providing student-centered learning and ownership, (e) facilitating collaboration between students in a social manner, (f) using multiple modes of representation and technology, and (h) allowing reflection and processing of new knowledge learned (Bada & Olusegun, 2015).

Constructivism learning theory affords numerous benefits in teaching and learning for students. Active participation in the learning process and opportunities to refine and reexamine knowledge while enhancing and constructing meaning and knowledge is an important part of learning and provides numerous real-world skills and exposure to higher-level thinking skills students will need throughout their lives.

Socratic Seminar

One of the ways constructivism is used in the middle school social studies classroom is through Socratic seminars. The Socratic seminar is a teaching method wherein students prepare for the seminar by reading and analyzing the same predetermined text (Hunter, 2019). Students then formulate open-ended questions based on the text that are given to the teacher. On the day of the seminar, students sit in an inner circle and an outer circle. Those students in the inner circle actively participate in the discussion while those students in the outer circle silently observe and listen to the inner-circle discussion. In the second part of the seminar, students switch circles and roles in the seminar. The teacher will use a student-generated question to begin the discussion and, if necessary, distribute a question to any student who does not have one (Hunter, 2019). Students will then respond to the question and respond to each other, one at a time, to create a discussion and civil discourse to talk about the issue. By using this method, students have the opportunity to use open-ended questions as vehicles for discussion between their peers. Students are able to use and hone their critical-thinking skills as they analyze each other's responses through their discourse. The Socratic seminar, although sometimes flawed in the event that students cannot justify their claims (Hunter, 2019), offers students a chance to hear their peers' opinions and to understand differing perspectives while learning about a text.

Project-Based Learning

A second method used in middle school social studies classrooms is project-based learning (PBL). These projects, usually lasting multiple days are student-centered in nature, in contrast to traditional teacher-centered teaching methods (Turk & Berman, 2018). Because of the high variability of potential projects, creating a reproducible and standard definition is difficult (Larmer, 2018). However, Bradley-Levine and Mosier (2014) define PBL as:

> Projects requiring students to apply the knowledge and skills they learn are the focus of the curriculum rather than being added as a supplement at the end of traditional instruction. The entire PBL process is organized around an open-ended driving question that teachers use to connect content to current and relevant issues or problems. Through this process, students develop their own questions to drive learning, study concepts and information that answer those questions, and apply that knowledge to products they develop.

For many students, PBL is effective because it requires them to be active participants in the learning process. Additionally, students are able to pursue topics of interest, which encourages motivation to continue learning and developing critical thinking skills for adulthood.

SOCIAL STUDIES STANDARDS

In 1992, the National Council for the Social Studies (NCSS) defined social studies as:

> the integrated study of the social sciences and humanities to promote civic competence. Within the school program, social studies provides coordinated, systematic study drawing upon such disciplines as anthropology, archeology, economics, geography, history, law, religion, and sociology, as well as appropriate context from the humanities, mathematics, and natural sciences. The primary purpose of social studies is to help young people make informed and reasoned decisions for the public good as citizens of a culturally diverse, democratic society in an interdependent world. (NCSS, 1994; NCSS, 2023)

The NCSS last revised their standards in 2010 into 10 themes:

1. Students learn about Culture through the lives of other people.
2. Students learn about Time, Continuity, and Change through learning about the values and beliefs of historical figures in order to gain an understanding of how historical events shape modern society.
3. Students learn about People, Places, and Environment through refinement of their knowledge of world geography.
4. Students learn about Individual Development and Identity through discussions of factors that shape personal and individual identity.
5. Students learn about Individuals, Groups, and Institutions through increased knowledge of groups and institutions (e.g., civic, government, religious) and how these influence daily life.

6. Students learn about Power, Authority, and Governance through exploration of government's function and authority.
7. Students learn about Production, Distribution, and Consumption through exploring how people use goods and services in daily life.
8. Students learn about Science, Technology, and Society through exploring how these areas have evolved over time and how these areas influence modern life.
9. Students learn about Global Connections through exploring geography, culture, and technology.
10. Students learn about Civic Ideals and Practice through discussions on the importance of participating in civic duties and how to be part of a democracy.

(NCSS, 2023)

ASSESSMENT

Assessment is a pervasive topic in education. From state-mandated assessments to those in the classroom, assessments are a way to measure student learning. The more information we have on student learning, through assessments, the more teachers are able to pinpoint learning successes and learning gaps. In the classroom, assessments can be thought of as either formative or summative. Each of these assessment types provide different and pertinent information that informs the status of student learning.

Formative assessments and summative assessments provide opportunities for students and teachers alike, and each carry their own advantages. Formal assessments occur during the learning process while students are forming their knowledge. These assessments provide feedback for students and teachers so that students know how to make improvements to learning in real time. Likewise, teachers receive feedback on student understanding and can adjust their teaching to meet student need (Bhat & Bhat, 2019; DuFour et al., 2016).

Professional Learning Communities

As teachers, we want our students to be actively engaged in the learning process. We know that students learn best when content is relevant to their lives and experiences. When students see the value and relevance of concepts they are learning, they are more engaged in the learning process. The professional learning community (PLC) process affords students the opportunity to be actively engaged in their learning as well as the opportunity for teachers to provide a stimulating learning environment for students. The PLC process operates on the premise that all students can learn at high levels through an ongoing cycle of teacher collaboration and analysis of student work (DuFour et al., 2016). On its surface, PLCs aim to answer four questions:

- What do we want each student to learn?
- How will we know when each student has learned it?
- How will we respond when a student has trouble learning?
- How will we expend learning for students already proficient? (DuFour, 2004; DuFour et al., 2016).

When teachers use the PLC lens to inform their teaching practices, both students and teachers benefit (DuFour et al., 2016). The PLC process provides opportunity for active student engagement in the learning process while providing teachers the opportunity to collaborate, assess, and adjust their teaching strategies to create a healthy and viable learning environment for all students.

Common Formative Assessments

Formative assessments provide insight into content students already know, do not know, and the learning that is yet to come. When teachers create common formative assessments (CFAs), benefits to students and teachers are numerous (DuFour et al., 2016). Not only does the collaborative environment of writing CFAs make the process of assessment more streamlined but it also ensures that students are assessed on the same content regardless of the teacher. Additionally, teachers receive input on teaching strategies that may not be working well with students and the opportunity to collaborate with colleagues to make the necessary adjustments so that struggling students can learn more effectively (DuFour et al., 2016).

FEDERAL LEGISLATION

It is important to reference federal statutes that impact the education of students with exceptionalities (special education, students who are gifted and talented, and students who are English language learners).

Individuals with Disabilities Education Act

The Individuals with Disabilities Education Act (IDEA), written in 1978 and reauthorized in 2004, is federal legislation whose purpose is "to ensure that all children with disabilities have available to them a free appropriate public education that emphasizes special education and related services designed to meet their unique needs and prepare them for further education, employment, and independent living" (20 U.S.C § 1400 [d][1][a]). It defines special education as "specifically designed instruction, at no cost to parents, to meet the unique needs of a child with a disability" (20 U.S.C § 1401[29]). IDEA outlines six principles to guide the education of children with disabilities. Two principles (zero reject and non-discriminatory evaluation) guide identification and eligibility of special education services, two other principles (procedural due process and parent and student participation) guide parent safeguards and protections. The other two principles directly effect and guide teachers in public schools (free and appropriate public education and least restrictive environment), known by their respective acronyms, FAPE and LRE.

Free and Appropriate Public Education (FAPE)

This principle ensures that every student receives an education that is appropriate for them. Schools determine this through a team of individuals (the student's parents, general education teachers, special education teachers, school administrators) that create the student's individualized education program (IEP). In determining the meaning of *appropriate*, in 2017, the US Supreme Court updated its definition, changing the standard of appropriate from educational benefit to progress as determined by the student's individual and unique circumstances (Kern et al., 2019).

Least Restrictive Environment (LRE)

This principle is two-pronged. The first prong is that students with disabilities should be educated, to the extent possible, with their peers without disabilities. The second prong is that students with disabilities should only be removed from the general education setting (least restrictive) when learning—even with aids and services—cannot be achieved. LRE is determined on an individual basis and is part of the IEP for every student with a disability. However, the word *environment* may be misleading, as environment may not mean just a physical location (e.g., general education classroom). Environment, in this case, is an umbrella term for services that the student with disabilities may need to be successful in school (Turnbull et al., 2020a). LRE can be thought of as a continuum. Within LRE, the least restrictive setting is the general education classroom (or a co-taught setting with students with and without disabilities), where the student with disabilities is educated with their peers without disabilities. More restrictive settings include separate special education classrooms or schools, and residential schools or hospital settings. This continuum is needed to ensure that the varying needs of all students with disabilities are adequately and appropriately supported. In short, LRE is where a student with a disability learns best.

INTERVENTIONS AND ACCOMMODATIONS

In the classroom, there are numerous students with varying degrees of needed educational support. Students who have difficulties with reading and focusing, in addition to those learning English or those who are gifted, complicate the teaching and learning landscape in schools today. While each of these characteristics can create varying degrees of specific educational support, the challenges each of these presents are not insurmountable. It is important to distinguish between interventions and accommodations. Interventions are developed for all students and are often schoolwide. These interventions, like universal design for learning (UDL), are intended for all students to teach or to remedy a knowledge or a skill deficit. Accommodations, on the other hand, are implemented individually to students to grant access to the general education curriculum. Accommodations, in effect, mitigate the effects of a disability without changing the curriculum.

SCHOOLWIDE SUPPORTS AND INTERVENTIONS

Response to Intervention

As part of IDEA (2004), response to intervention (RTI), while now expanded to help address the academic needs of students in both the general education and special education settings (Kashima et al., 2009), was originally conceived as a framework to identify students with learning disabilities in reading (Johnson et al., 2006). RTI was in reaction to the discrepancy model—noting a discrepancy in actual student achievement when compared to expected student achievement—and was not sufficient to identify learning disabilities in reading and was seen as an alternative to the IQ-based discrepancy model (Hughes & Dexter, 2011). Using the discrepancy model, substantial amounts of time were lost during the identification process, creating a wait-to-fail scenario for students (Johnson et al., 2006). RTI, on the contrary, aims to provide more immediate intervention to students who need it in a timelier manner. As an intervention, the purpose of RTI is to combine all available resources in order to minimize the effect of negative learning outcomes and to strengthen the process of identifying students with learning needs and disabilities (NCRTI, 2010). RTI provides information about a student's current level of academic performance in comparison to peers at the same level, identifies academic interventions that are currently working, and those interventions that are not working, as well as the frequency and intensity of the academic interventions that will be necessary to help the student be academically supported and successful. The National Center of Response to Intervention (NCRTI) (2010) defines RTI as:

> integrat[ing] assessment and intervention within a multi-level prevention system to maximize student achievement and to reduce behavioral problems. With RTI, schools use data to identify students at risk for poor learning outcomes, monitor student progress, provide evidence-based interventions, and adjust the intensity and nature of these interventions depending on a student's responsiveness, and identify students with learning disabilities or other disabilities. (p. 2)

RTI consists of three tiers, or "levels" (NCRTI, 2010) and three basic components: (a) evidence-based instruction, (b) universal screening, and (c) progress monitoring of students (Hughes & Dexter, 2011; NCRTI, 2010).

Tier 1

Tier 1 interventions are designed to occur in the general education classroom as whole-class activities. Universal screening consists of brief and targeted assessments to determine whether students are working at grade level (IRIS Center, 2018). Additionally, these screenings assist in identifying potential learning challenges and disabilities. These screenings occur in this tier and are vital to identifying students in the general education classroom who may need additional support. This screening typically occurs three times per year for all students (Hughes & Dexter, 2011). Tier 1 is designed to meet most students in the general education setting—approximately 80% of students (IRIS Center, 2018).

Tier 2

Tier 2 interventions are designed to meet the needs of students—approximately 15% of students (IRIS Center, 2018)—who need additional academic support in addition to support they are already receiving in Tier 1. In this tier, interventions become more intensive. Students typically receive evidence-based instructions in small groups for approximately 15 weeks, three or four times per week, for 20 to 40 minutes (NCRTI, 2010).

Tier 3

Tier 3 interventions are designed to meet the needs of students—approximately 5% of students who need more intervention and academic support than students in Tier

2 (IRIS Center, 2018). In this tier, interventions often become more frequent and longer in length.

Throughout the RTI framework, student performance is assessed to evaluate whether the interventions in each tier meet the needs of students within the tiers. Additionally, this progress monitoring helps teachers to evaluate when students need to move from Tier 2 to Tier 3 or vice versa. The use of data—from universal screening and regular progress monitoring of students—helps to inform students, teachers, and RTI teams of student learning and assists teachers in meeting the academic needs of students.

Example of RTI Implementation

Julie is an eighth-grade student. At the beginning of the school year, Julie's teachers used evidence-based teaching with the entire eighth grade to help students gain the necessary grade-level knowledge in reading comprehension. Teachers engaged in explicit instruction involving comprehension strategies, vocabulary, and reading fluency. In October, Julie, along with the rest of her class, completed a benchmark exam. This benchmark exam was used as a universal screening tool to identify students who may need additional support. Julie's teachers were already concerned that Julie had difficulty with reading comprehension and reading fluency. While most students scored at grade level on the benchmark, Julie did not. After the benchmark test, Julie was, in fact, identified through this universal screener as having potential reading challenges. Despite the teachers' best efforts, Julie was still struggling with reading.

Recognizing that Julie needed additional academic support, she received small-group instruction on reading fluency, vocabulary, and comprehension using evidence-based targeted interventions designed to help her with reading. These interventions were in addition to the activities the rest of the eighth-grade class was completing. While these interventions were occurring, Julie's teachers monitored her progress through assessments and assignments, and they adjusted Julie's interventions, as needed, to help her as quickly as possible.

During this time, Julie made some progress, but there were still large gaps in her reading ability and skills. To assist, teachers gave Julie more intensive interventions, now five days per week instead of four, and one of the interventions involved one-on-one tutoring from the school's reading specialist. Teachers continued to review data to monitor Julie's academic progress. They continued to adjust interventions, as needed, to help Julie. As Julie started to make more progress, teachers were in communication with parents and school administrators to keep lines of communication open and to help Julie with reading comprehension and reading fluency.

Through the RTI framework exemplified above, we see that Julie's academic performance improved through the use of universal screening, evidence-based interventions, progress monitoring, and collaboration between all parties involved. This collaboration played a vital role in Julie's academic success.

Positive Behavior Interventions and Supports

Research for positive behavior interventions and supports (PBIS) dates back to the 1980s (Turnbull et al., 2020b). Since then, researchers have studied student behavior and realized that environment and student behavior can sometimes interact. Changing the environment can sometimes change student behavior. Because students come from varied backgrounds and homelife expectations, consistent values and expectations can help students' behavior in school. Additionally, consistent values and expectations can also guide teachers in how they should respond to student behavior. From these realizations, PBIS was born.

PBIS, like RTI, is separated into tiers, focusing on students needing Tier 2 and Tier 3 supports. These supports, unlike the academic supports available in RTI, focus on nonacademic areas—namely social and emotional—needs of students (Childs et al., 2015). According to Turnbull et al. (2020b), PBIS contains two main elements: (a) the PBIS framework must be implemented schoolwide so every student has access to the supports PBIS offers and (b) the PBIS framework must address the social and emotional needs of students in smaller more formal groups in Tier 2 and more individual supports for students in Tier 3.

Tier 1

In Tier 1 of the PBIS framework, like that of the RTI framework, the supports offered to students are available to all students. Because supports in this tier are meant for all students, these behavior reminders are often general and apply to various situations. For example, "be respectful," "be safe," and "be responsible" are common, and can be used to remind students of the schoolwide behavior expectations in common areas such as hallways. These expectations are taught and discussed with students often so that students truly become familiar with the expectations and the expectations become automatic for them. Like in RTI, teachers acknowledge positive behavior and monitor students' behavior to evaluate and identify who may need additional behavior support. A team of school professionals monitor student behavior and determine students who need additional support available in Tier 2.

Tier 2

Approximately 15 to 20% of students from Tier 1 will need more intensive social and emotional supports and, thus, will move to Tier 2 (Turnbull et al., 2020b). In this tier, students receive support to practice a skill they already possess, or to learn a new skill they do not yet have. A popular intervention in this tier is check in/check out (Turnbull et al., 2020b). With this intervention, for example, students have an identified adult in the building at school who they visit or check in with first thing in the morning. This visit can be brief. The adult will review the student's behavior goals while at school. Often, the student has a behavior tracker, either paper and pencil or digital, such as a Google Form, where teachers enter feedback on the student's behavior in class. At the end of the day, the student returns to the same identified adult they visited or checked in with in the morning, to check out with at the end of the day. During this check out, the adult and the student review the feedback the student received on the behavior tracker form from their teachers. If the student meets their behavior goals, they receive a predetermined reinforcer as an incentive to continue the positive behaviors (Turnbull et al., 2020b).

Tier 3

Just as in the RTI model, those students who need social and emotional support beyond what is offered in Tier 1 and in Tier 2 will move to Tier 3. Students in this tier often struggle academically and behaviorally and will need intensive supports to meet their academic and behavioral needs. Students in this tier may receive a functional behavior assessment (FBA) (Turnbull et al., 2020b). The purpose of an FBA is to determine the function of a given behavior. This helps teachers and students understand the reasons why a behavior or behaviors is/are occurring. This information, brought to light by the FBA, will give teachers insight into how to develop a plan for the student, known as a behavior intervention plan (BIP). The BIP gives detailed steps and strategies to teachers so that they know how to respond to the student behavior when it occurs. Continued data collection and data analysis will give teachers the information needed to support the student's behavior needs at school.

Example of Positive Behavior Interventions and Supports Implementation

Lucas is an eighth-grade student who struggles academically and behaviorally in the classroom. To assist and support Lucas, the school applied its PBIS framework to help Lucas with his behavior. Lucas has moved through Tier 1, including universal supports that are available to everyone, such as clear expectations, rules, and routines at school—such as visual reminders like posters for everyone at school. He has also moved through Tier 2 of the PBIS framework, including the Tier 2 interventions and supports—as well as check in/check out, a behavior tracking form, a token economy and reward system to reinforce positive behaviors, and the opportunity to take short breaks when needed. Even with all supports, Lucas is still struggling in his classes. Through the completion of an FBA, including talking to Lucas and his parents and reviewing Lucas's school discipline record, the reasons for Lucas's behavior were hypothesized and a behavior plan, including specific strategies and accommodations specific to Lucas, were put in place to promote positive behavior in the classroom and at school.

After the BIP was enacted in Tier 3, Lucas's teachers met regularly to discuss his progress. Lucas's parents were also part of the discussions about reinforcement strategies and challenges. They were consulted when making necessary adjustments to Lucas's behavior plan. Over time, Lucas's behavior improved as he gained skills to self-regulate and refocus in the classroom.

In this example, Lucas was able to learn the skills needed to adjust his behavior through supports given to him by his teachers. This was reinforced through collaboration with Lucas and his parents.

Multi-Tiered System of Supports (MTSS)

With the passage of the Every Student Succeeds Act (ESSEA) in 2015, a federal definition of MTSS was developed. Accordingly, MTSS is defined as "a comprehensive continuum of evidence-based, systemic practices to support a rapid response to students' needs with regular observation to facilitate data-based instructional decision making" (20 U.S.C. § 7801[33]). MTSS is a combination of the evidence-based research and practices of RTI and the social, emotional, and behavior supports of PBIS (Turnbull et al., 2020b). Although more comprehensive than RTI, in the MTSS framework, interventions are still in increasingly intensive tiers. However, instead of focusing solely on academic needs, MTSS incorporates PBIS, mental health, and restorative practices to address the entire individual and their needs to foster success for all students in educational environments.

Example of Multi-Tiered System of Supports Implementation

Amanda is an eighth-grade student who, in Tier 1, receives high-quality, evidence-based instruction in her general education classes. The curriculum is aligned with state standards and differentiated instruction is included to meet the needs of diverse learners in the classroom. Amanda, like the other students, is assessed with regular screenings to identify academic or behavioral concerns, and her progress is monitored and tracked. Based on the information and data collected, Amanda qualifies for additional academic support in writing and moves into Tier 2 of the MTSS framework. Here, she receives more targeted, small-group instruction with explicit and specific instruction in strategies to address writing. Her progress is regularly monitored through assessments and data analysis. This monitoring allows for the implementation of targeted supports as needed to help Amanda's writing skills. However, despite these interventions, Amanda continues to struggle. In Tier 3, more intensive interventions and supports, including one-on-one interventions, are utilized to meet Amanda's need. A collaborative team of school professionals and parents meet to discuss her academic needs and their concerns so adjustments to strategies and resources can be made to support her.

As Amanda moves through the MTSS tiers of support, she demonstrates improvement and gains confidence, not only in her writing but also in general. For Amanda, this improvement in writing and increased confidence has resulted in improved classroom behavior. She is more engaged and, through the MTSS supports she received, she now has a skill set that includes having learned strategies to enhance self-regulation, focus in the classroom, and engage in more positive interaction with her friends inside and outside of the classroom. This progress, due to the MTSS framework, led not only to improved academic performance but also to increasing Amanda's self-esteem and confidence. The MTSS framework had a positive impact on her social and emotional well-being and increased her feeling of belonging in the school community.

By combining the components of RTI with the social, emotional, and behavioral supports of PBIS, the comprehensive approach of the MTSS framework was able to support all of Amanda's academic and behavioral needs. The collaboration with not only school professionals but also with Amanda and her parents allowed the necessary supports and interventions to be put into place to make her academically and socially successful.

Universal Design for Learning

UDL is a framework, originally conceived in the 1980s by the Center for Applied Special Technologies (CAST) (Meyer et al., 2014) and draws from architectural design, education, technology, and brain research (CAST, 2018). The UDL framework is based on three principles:

- Provide multiple means of engagement.
- Provide multiple means of representation.
- Provide multiple means of action and expression.

(Meyer et al., 2014, p. 7)

As technology has advanced, these principles have been expanded and updated to include nine guidelines, each with multiple checkpoints with ideas for implementation in the classroom (Meyer et al., 2014). Additionally, UDL contains four main components: (a) goals for the learner, (b) instructional supports developed and adjusted through progress monitoring, (c) media to demonstrate and present concepts, and (d) assessment of the learner's skills (Ralabate, 2011).

A core tenant of UDL is to create expert learners who continually learn and gain knowledge of the content. The goal of becoming an expert learner is shared by teacher and student alike. Expert learners can self-monitor their individual learning, maintain their motivation to continue learning, and continue the learning process through continued interest in the content (Ralabate, 2011). Let us explore the principles of UDL further to develop a greater understanding of the framework. In all three principles, students access the content, build their knowledge, and internalize the knowledge on their journey to becoming expert learners (CAST, 2018).

Engagement

In this principle, students access content by choosing a topic that is relevant and interesting to them. When students find academic content interesting, they are more engaged in the learning process. As students continue to learn about content they are interested in, they continue to put forth effort in learning and begin to share knowledge as well as to seek feedback. As students continue to gather information, they stay motivated and can use personal coping skills and strategies to stay on task as well as to reflect and assess their knowledge and understanding. All these milestones lead to an expert learner who can share knowledge due to the effort and motivation they put forth due to their sustained engagement (CAST, 2018).

Representation

The goal of this principle is to create expert learners who have gained knowledge and were given the opportunity to represent that knowledge in various ways. To assist students, varying the way information is presented, visually and auditorily, will give students increased access to content. Illustrating and explaining content in multiple ways will assist students with building and gathering knowledge, especially when information is presented in different formats (CAST, 2018).

Action and Expression

The third principle of UDL aims to create expert learners who are interested and motivated to continue learning. To assist students in accessing content, multiple ways to respond and to use assistive technology is critical. As students build and expand their knowledge, the use of multimedia is vital as well as varying levels of teacher support and feedback as students build greater and deeper content knowledge (CAST, 2018).

Example

In the following example, we will learn about John, an eighth-grade student who struggles with reading comprehension. As we implement a UDL framework, we will discuss the teacher's role in assisting John in the learning process as he becomes engaged with the content through multiple modes of representation by the teacher and by John.

The class is reading a text on the supremacy clause in preparation for a Socratic seminar next week. John likes social studies, but his reading comprehension deficits cause him to struggle in class. Ms. Jones, his social studies teacher, wants to help John learn. To assist John, she develops flexible materials, such as an audio recording of the text and a couple of diagrams to help John access the material. Ms. Jones also makes sure John has access to the text in PDF and Google Docs so that he can take advantage of text-to-speech features on his MacBook if he wants. When Ms. Jones thinks about how she will present the information to John, she decides to include visual components, such as a graphic organizer and a concept map, to aid his understanding and comprehension of the text. For John, graphic organizers help him to understand what information is important to know. Ms. Jones knows this will keep John from becoming frustrated and overwhelmed as he reads the text. To help John stay focused, she offers him a choice of seating in her classroom: near her desk, or in the reading nook in the far corner of the classroom. Ms. Jones and John know that the reading nook is a quiet space where he can work undistracted, and he can even relax in a beanbag chair with an overhead lamp if he needs that flexibility. Additionally, Ms. Jones allows John to use assistive technology, such as speech-to-text and text-to-speech functions that are already built into the operating systems of his computer. These features allow John to interact with the text, including allowing him to annotate it, while giving him autonomy and independence in reading. To sustain John's interest, Ms. Jones also plans a hands-on activity that relates to their text on the supremacy clause as well as a group discussion of how the supremacy clause is relevant to John and the world today. This way, Ms. Jones can help John stay motivated in the learning process, but he will also have autonomy.

For John, these supports allow him to discuss his individual academic needs involving reading and reading comprehension so his reading challenges can be mitigated. He also can discuss the other accommodations and supports that are necessary to help him be successful. Because of this, John can be an active participant in not only the Socratic seminar but also in other class discussions. Because he has a grasp of the content, supported by the UDL framework, he can ask and answer questions, give his opinions, and contribute to small-group discussions and assignments with his peers. The option to use assistive technology also helps John to access text and improve and practice his reading skills. Other classroom accommodations that Ms. Jones provides, such as preferential seating, digital formats, and visual supports accounted for in the UDL framework, allow John to be actively engaged in the lesson content and classroom discussions. Finally, John can assess which strategies and supports work best for him so that he and Ms. Jones can make the necessary adjustments for future assignments. These adjustments will ensure that John is able to continue the learning process through setting new goals and continuing to be actively engaged in learning so he can enjoy continued academic growth.

From the example above, we learn that the UDL framework, as implemented for John, provided him academic supports for his learning challenges in reading. The flexible learning environment created by Ms. Jones allowed John to learn based on his individual and unique needs and preferences. John, too, collaborated in his own learning through active participation and collaboration with Ms. Jones so they could determine the most effective strategies, including the use of assistive technology, to support John's learning and increase his overall academic success.

CASE STUDY AND LESSON PLAN

Below is a description of a student, James, who has difficulty focusing. Following the description is a lesson plan that is typical of what would be presented on an average day in his eighth-grade social studies class. Following the lesson plan, we will discuss accommodations and interventions, utilizing UDL principals, that may assist James in his social studies endeavors.

James

James is a 13-year-old student in eighth grade. Although James likes school and being with his friends, he struggles with understanding his social studies assignments (encompassing assorted topics including history, geography, government, and cultures). Additionally, James has difficulty focusing on class. He often appears uninterested in class discussions and rarely participates in class activities. James usually exhibits impulsive or hyperactive behavior in class that disrupts himself and others around him. When James completes assignments, he often struggles with effective time management and fails to submit completed homework assignments in a timely manner.

Lesson Plan

Objective

Students will identify the structure and responsibilities of elected and appointed officials within the three branches of government, focusing on the legislative process, the role of Congress and the president, and the Supreme Court's power of judicial review.

Introduction

Ask students what they know about the three branches of government and engage in a brief discussion about the importance of each branch of government.

Lesson

Students will read the handouts for each branch of government and underline key facts and concepts. Engage the class in a discussion about each handout when they are finished with their annotations.

Activity

Divide students into small groups and ask them to create a poster or diagram illustrating the structure and responsibilities of the three branches of government and the Supreme Court's power of judicial review. Ask groups to present their posters when finished.

Summary

Review key points and answer questions.

Homework

Students will write a 300-word essay discussing a notable Supreme Court decision. They should explain the decision and analyze the impact on American society.

INTERVENTIONS AND STRATEGIES

While many different interventions may help James, there is no one-size-fits-all, cookie cutter approach to helping students achieve academic success. Often, what works for one student like James may not work for another student. However, some possible interventions and accommodations are discussed below:

Explicit Instruction

Effective teaching requires extensive and meticulous planning. When developing a lesson plan, teachers typically demonstrate, assist students, and ask students to try the task on their own. In many ways, explicit instruction does not deviate from this road map. However, explicit instruction does require additional organization and specific preparation. Explicit instruction is a way to organize teaching so that students benefit from the lesson content in real time (Smith et al., 2016). Using this method, the teacher demonstrates the task students are learning. This is done through specific explanation and uses multiple simple steps. The student then has an opportunity to practice the task or use the information to build confidence and to become familiar with the task or content. At this point, an integral part of explicit instruction is that the teacher gives immediate and specific feedback to the student so that the student can understand how to accurately complete the task and where gaps in knowledge still exist. Finally, the student should be given opportunity to practice the task or use the content independently to demonstrate knowledge learned as well as to ascertain where additional help and instruction from the teacher may be necessary. Using explicit instruction will help students to remain focused on learning (Martinussen, 2015; Raggi & Chronis, 2006).

Visual Representation

Classrooms in today's schools are diverse. English learners and students with disabilities can be found in most classrooms across the country (Regan et al., 2017). The varying academic needs of these diverse students can create a challenge for teachers who are striving to meet the academic needs of all students.

Graphic Organizers

For students who have difficulty with reading or comprehension—because of a disability or because of a language barrier—the use of graphic organizers can assist students with comprehension and content understanding (Praveen & Rajan, 2013). Although various types of graphic organizers exist (Gallavan & Kottler, 2007; Praveen & Rajan, 2013), they are pictorial representations—often using shapes and colors—to present large amounts of information in short periods of time. When students complete graphic organizers, they can interact with lesson content and build a summarized, organized, and shortened representation of the information to assist with comprehension and understanding (Lubin & Sewak, 2007). These graphic organizers may be used in a variety of ways depending on lesson content because they can be easily adapted to incorporate essential concepts (e.g., basic facts, thematic content, important dates, and people, etc.). In the social studies classroom, given the large amounts of information students may need to learn, graphic organizers can be an essential tool for teachers and students to manage large quantities of information (Gallavan & Kottler, 2007).

Visual Cues

In addition to graphic organizers, presenting information with graphical representation, such as a checklist of class tasks for the day and consistent daily completion of classroom tasks, can assist students in focusing on learning and completing tasks in the classroom (Reid, 1999). Students and adults alike appreciate knowing what to expect during the school day. Schools have daily routines, such as morning announcements and bell schedules, so that normalcy and routine can be created and followed. In classrooms, this is the same. Often, students will ask teachers what they are learning about today before the class or lesson begins. In this case, a list of class activities for the day can be helpful. Students, then, can see what they will do first, second, and so on during the lesson. This type of organization allows students to stay focused on the current task because they are better able to process when a task has been completed and what task will be next. Additionally, the use of visual prompts, such as timers and schedules, can assist students in transitioning from one classroom activity to another because students are able to visually see the amount of time left to complete an activity. Visual timers give students a chance to mentally prepare to transition to the next activity (Pierce et al., 2013).

Color Coding

Much of our world today is visual. Visual images abound on personal electronic devices, cellphones, television, and billboards. When specific colors are used for a certain item, it has the potential to aid students with organization and understanding. For example, using the same color of paper for instructional handouts and a different color for graphic organizers may help students to stay organized and to know the function of each item (I read blue sheets, but I write on yellow sheets). In another way, color itself can be used, especially in text, to draw attention to important information or different types of information (Maldonado-Otto & Ormsbee, 2019).

Chunking

Chunking, or dividing information into smaller, more digestible bites, has been shown to aid in student learning (Humphries & Clark, 2021). When information is presented in smaller pieces, students have an easier time deciphering, learning, and recalling it (Suppawittaya & Yasri, 2021). Large amounts of information can often overwhelm students. When content is given in smaller pieces, students can actively interact with the information (i.e., ask clarifying questions and process content) before augmenting and expanding their knowledge. Often, chunking tasks into smaller amounts of time will allow students to remain focused and engaged in tasks and on the learning process (Tucha et al., 2017).

Flexibility

Many students have difficulty focusing on tasks in the classroom. This inability or difficulty in focusing and time-on-task behavior can have negative effects on education. In information-heavy classes, such as social studies and science, the traditional one-way flow of information from teacher to student can be the norm. This traditional form of imparting knowledge—where students are responsible for large amounts of information at one time—can be challenging for students.

Temporal Adjustments

Other temporal adjustments may also assist students in the learning process. For example, giving students extended time to complete classroom tasks may not only assist them in completing the activity but also provide them the necessary time to process and understand the content. Allowing students to take measured and planned breaks while working may also help them refocus on the task. Often, after working for a period, students need a few minutes to stop a task to reset their mental capacity before returning and continuing the classroom task.

Example Lesson Plan for All Students

Using the lesson plan from earlier, we can make adjustments to meet the academic needs of all students using various interventions and accommodations. The example below illustrates how these adaptations can be implemented to assist and support the academic needs of students.

Objective

The objective for the lesson plan will remain the same. Students, even those needing additional academic supports, should learn grade-level content and concepts when possible.

Introduction

In our original lesson plan, it states to ask students what they know about the three branches of government. Using a visual support, such as a graphic organizer, may help students process information. For example, a simple chart expressing what students know and what they want to know (commonly known as a KWL chart) can assist students in understanding and organizing what information they already know about the question (Sinambela et al., 2015). This chart can then be used to guide the brief discussion about the importance of each branch of government as they use the want to learn (WL section of the KWL chart) to continue organizing their thoughts and ideas.

Lesson

In the original lesson plan, students are asked to read the handouts for each branch of government and underline key facts and concepts. For some students, this is an impossible task. Students with difficulty focusing, or with reading difficulties, will struggle with the task of reading large amounts of text. To assist, implementing opportunities to use assistive technology, such as text-to-speech, to meet their learning needs may be beneficial. For students who have difficulty reading, they are often reluctant to engage in reading. The use of text-to-speech or other assistive technologies such as digital versions of the handouts that allow them to adjust font size, color, and highlight on screen may best meet their learning needs and make the content more accessible to them. Additionally, graphic organizers and color coding can help students understand information by bringing the most important content to the forefront to increase their understanding and engagement. Using different modes of media, such as integrating short video explanations into the lesson or images that correspond to each branch of government may help students to stay focused and engaged in the lesson content. While the lesson has natural divisions in the handouts, one for each branch of government, further chunking of the information may be necessary to reach the learning needs of students.

Activity

In the original lesson plan, students were to divide into small groups to create a poster or diagram illustrating the structure and responsibilities of the three branches of government. For students with reading, focus, or language barriers, this activity as presented can be potentially limiting and exclusionary. To address academic needs, the implementation of multimedia formats may be helpful. Since the purpose of the activity in the lesson is to provide evidence of learning, this can be achieved in ways beyond a poster. Allowing students to create a short video, slideshow presentation, or a digital poster may increase student engagement and interest in the lesson. It is important to remember that these suggestions are not meant to replace the original idea of the poster. For many students, a poster will be sufficient to enhance their learning experience. However, the opportunity to add other media formats to show evidence of learning will meet the learning needs of all students. This is especially true for students who are English learners because they may need to use translation options as well as for students who may need further enrichment activities. The use of digital formats and resources can present additional academic supports and resources to enhance learning for all students.

Summary

The original lesson asks the teacher to review key points and answer questions. The addition of a graphic organizer with key points, or an activity with a partner to process, discuss, and share their findings, may help students better understand lesson content because they can learn from their peers. Additionally, the addition of a multimedia question system—whether digital, written, verbal, or video—will give all students the opportunity to ask questions during class.

Homework

The homework assignment in the original lesson plan was to write a 300-word essay. In much the same way as described in the activity section of this lesson plan, the addition of some or all those multimedia formats, as well as additional time for specific students for whom that is beneficial, would allow students to show evidence of learning in a way that best meets their academic needs.

For many students, the addition of interventions, strategies, and supports can enhance their interest and learning in the classroom. The opportunity to choose supports that each individual students may need to be successful will allow all students to learn and be included in the educational process.

CONCLUSION

In this chapter, we discussed social studies learning theory, academic standards, assessments, interventions, and accommodations. One limitation of this chapter is that it is difficult to predict the academic needs and supports for students. Without knowing each individual student, it is impossible to generalize or guarantee that any one intervention or support will positively impact every student. A second limitation is that this chapter, while representative of current research, is not exhaustive in any way. However, numerous generalizations in supports and accommodations, in various combinations, to support students can be made for different age levels, environments, and situations. Key points in this chapter illustrate how constructivism impacts learning in middle school social studies classrooms, especially when implemented with project-based learning and Socratic seminar techniques. Additionally, academic standards and assessments, if used and written collaboratively, have the potential to inform students and teachers on learning progress and sequence while making the academic content accessible to all students. For students with learning challenges, this is of utmost importance to ensure curriculum is accessible through schoolwide interventions as well as through individual accommodations to create and maintain the necessary supports for learning to occur.

For the general education teacher, there may be hesitation at the thought of implementing some of the instructional adaptations mentioned in this chapter. However, if teachers choose essential standards from the curriculum that every student must understand and learn, all students will benefit. The addition of specific accommodations or schoolwide interventions will help every student be successful, and the perspective students gain will be invaluable not only to them but to the entire class as well. Greater understanding of content will allow all students to be active participants in the learning process and to increase their capacity for working with and learning from their peers.

For the special education teacher, the educational adaptations discussed in this chapter are not new. However, the discussion presented in this chapter is a valuable reminder of the endless possibilities of educational support that is available to all students—not only students with learning challenges. Like the general education teacher, the special education teacher will gain valuable insight into pedagogical practices and supports that are effective in the general education setting for most students. These insights will inform teaching practices and enhance understanding of academic and behavioral supports for all students in the educational settings. A shared understanding of the unique roles of the general education and the special education teacher, through collaboration, can positively impact learning outcomes for all students regardless of the level of educational support they may need to be successful in the educational setting.

REFERENCES

Bada, S. O., & Olusegun, S. (2015). Constructivism learning theory: A paradigm for teaching and learning. *Journal of Research & Method in Education*, 5(6), 66–70.

Bhat, B. A., & Bhat, G. J. (2019). Formative and summative evaluation techniques for improvement of learning process. *European Journal of Business & Social Sciences*, 7(5), 776–785.

Bradley-Levine, J., & Mosier, G. (2014). *Literature review on project-based learning*. University of Indianapolis Center of Excellence in Leadership of Learning.

Center for Applied Special Technology (CAST) (2018). Universal Design for Learning guidelines version 2.2. http://udlguidelines.cast.org

Childs, K. E., Kincaid, D., George, H. P., & Gage, N. A. (2015). The relationship between school-wide implementation of positive behavior intervention and supports and student discipline outcomes. *Journal of Positive Behavior Interventions*, 18(2), 89–99.

DuFour, R. (2004). What is a "professional learning community"? *Educational Leadership*, 61(8), 6–11.

DuFour, R., DuFour, R., Eaker, R., Many, T., & Mattos, M. (2016). A guide to action for professional learning communities at work. In R. DuFour (Ed.), *Learning by Doing: A handbook for professional learning communities at work* (3rd ed., pp. 9–15). Solution Tree Press.

Every Student Succeeds Act of 2015, 20 U.S.C. § 7801 *et seq*. (2015).

Fernando, S. Y., & Marikar, F. M. (2017). Constructivist teaching/learning theory and participatory teaching methods. *Journal of Curriculum and Teaching*, 6(1), 110–122.

Gallavan, N. P., & Kottler, E. (2007). Eight types of graphic organizers for empowering social studies students and teachers. *The Social Studies*, 98(3), 117–128.

Hein, G. (1991). Constructivist learning theory [paper presentation]. Committee for Education and Cultural Action CECA (International Committee of Museum Educators) Conference 1991, Jerusalem, Israel. https://www.exploratorium.edu/education/ifi/constructivist-learning

Honebein, P. (1996). Seven goals for the design of constructivist learning environments. In B. G. Wilson (Ed.), *Constructivist learning environments: Case studies in instructional design* (pp. 11–24). Educational Technology Publications.

Hughes, C. A., & Dexter, D. D. (2011). Response to intervention: A research-based summary. *Theory Into Practice*, 50(1), 4–11.

Humphries, B., & Clark, D. (2021). An examination of student preference for traditional didactic or chunking teaching strategies in an online learning environment. *Research in Learning Technology*, 29. https://doi.org/10.25304/rlt.v29.2405

Hunter, J. (2019). *Thinking beyond the text: Examining teachers' dispositions of critical thinking in elementary social studies classrooms through the use of Socratic seminar* [Doctoral dissertation, Kennesaw State University]. Office of Collaborative Graduate Programs. https://digitalcommons.kennesaw.edu/teachleaddoc_etd/37

Individuals with Disabilities Education Act of 2004, 20 U.S.C. § 1400 *et seq.* (2010).

IRIS Center. (2018). *MTSS/RTI: Mathematics.* https://iris.peabody.vanderbilt.edu/module/rti-math

Johnson, E., Mellard, F. F., Fuchs, D., & McKnight, M. A. (2006). *Responsiveness to intervention: How to do it.* National Research Center on Learning Disabilities.

Kashima, Y., Schleich, B., & Spradlin, T. (2009). The core components of RTI: A closer look at leadership, parent involvement, and cultural responsivity. Special Report. Center for Evaluation and Education Policy, Indiana University.

Kern, L., George, H. P., Evanovich, L. L., & Martinez, S. (2019). Addressing the need for progress in special education: Understanding Endrew F. and the role of special educators. *Journal of the American Academy of Special Education Professionals*, spring–summer, 68–81

Larmer, J. (2018). Project-based learning in social studies. *Social Education*, 82(1). 20–23. https://www.socialstudies.org/system/files/publications/articles/se_820120.pdf

Lubin, J., & Sewak, M. (2007). Enhancing learning using graphic organizers: A Review of the literature. *LC Journal of Special Education*, 2(1), 5.

Maldonado-Otto, C., & Ormsbee, C. (2019). Color-coding affect on writing instruction for students with learning disabilities. *International Conference of Education, Research and Innovation* (pp. 11421–11432). ICERI2019 Proceedings. https://doi.org/10.21125/iceri.2019.2848

Martinussen, R. (2015). The overlap of ADHD, reading disorders, and language impairment. *Perspectives on Language and Literacy*, 41(1), 9–14.

Meyer, A., Rose, D., & Gordon, D. (2014). Re-envisioning education through UDL. In A. Meyer (Ed.), *Universal design for learning: Theory and practice* (pp. 1–20). Center for Applied Special Technology (CAST) Inc.

National Center of Response to Intervention (NCRTI). (2010). *Essential components of RTI: A closer look at response to intervention.* US Department of Education, Office of Special Education Programs.

National Council for the Social Studies (NCSS). (1994). *Expectations of excellence: Curriculum standards for social studies.* NCSS.

NCSS. (2023). *Executive summary.* Retrieved December 3, 2023, from https://www.socialstudies.org/standards/national-curriculum-standards-social-studies-executive-summary

Pierce, J. M., Spriggs, A. D., Gast, D. L., & Luscre, D. (2013). Effects of visual activity schedules on independent classroom transitions for students with autism. *International Journal of Disability, Development and Education*, 60(3), 253–269.

Praveen, S. D., & Rajan, P. (2013). Using graphic organizers to improve reading comprehension skills for the middle school ESL students. *English Language Teaching*, 6(2), 155–170.

Raggi, V. L., & Chronis, A. M. (2006). Interventions to address the academic impairment of children and adolescents with ADHD. *Clinical Child and Family Psychology Review*, 9, 85–111. https://doi.org/10.1007/s10567-006-0006-0

Ralabate, P. K. (2011). Universal design for learning: Meeting the needs of all students. *The ASHA Leader*, 16(10), 14–17.

Regan, K., Evmenova, A. S., Good, K., Legget, A., Ahn, S. Y., Gafurov, B., & Mastropieri, M. (2017). Persuasive writing with mobile-based graphic organizers in inclusive classrooms across the curriculum. *Journal of Special Education Technology*, *33*(1), 3–14. https://doi.org/10.1177/0162643417727292

Reid, R. (1999). Attention deficit hyperactivity disorder: Effective methods for the classroom. *Focus on Exceptional Children*, *32*(4), 1–20.

Sinambela, E., Manik, S., & Pangaribuan, R. E. (2015). Improving students' reading comprehension achievement by using KWL strategy. *English Linguistics Research*, *4*(3), 13–29.

Smith, J. L. M., Saez, L., & Doabler, C. T. (2016). Using explicit and systematic instruction to support working memory. *Teaching Exceptional Children*, *58*(6), 275–281. https://doi.org/10.1177/0040059916650633

Suppawittaya, P., & Yasri, P. (2021). The comparison of chunking methods to enhance the cognitive capacity of short-term memory to retain textual information among high school students. *International Journal of Research in STEM Education*, *3*(1), 27–35. https://doi.org/10.31098/ijrse.v3i1.502

Tam, M. (2000). Constructivism, instructional design, and technology: Implications for transforming distance learning. *Journal of Educational Technology & Society*, *3*(2), 50–60.

Tucha, L., Fuermaier, A. B., Koerts, J., Buggenthin, R., Aschenbrenner, S., Weisbrod, M., Thome, J., Lange, K., & Tucha, O. (2017). Sustained attention in adult ADHD: Time-on-task effects of various measures of attention. *Journal of Neural Transmission*, *124*, 39–53. https://pubmed.ncbi.nlm.nih.gov/26206605/

Turk, D. B., & Berman, S. B. (2018). Learning through doing: A project-based learning approach to the American civil rights movement. *Social Education*, *82*(1), 35–39.

Turnbull, A., Turnbull, R., Wehmeyer, M. A., & Shogren, K. A. (2020a). The purposes, people, and law of special education. In A. Turnbull (Ed.), *Exceptional lives: Practice, progress, and dignity in today's schools* (9th ed., pp. 1–33). Pearson.

Turnbull, A., Turnbull, R., Wehmeyer, M. A., & Shogren, K. A. (2020b). Schoolwide systems of support. In A. Turnbull (Ed.), *Exceptional lives: Practice, progress, and dignity in today's schools* (9th ed., pp. 130–158). Pearson.

11

Inclusive Social Studies Instruction

Caroline Fitchett and Jacquelyn Purser

WHAT IS SOCIAL STUDIES?

Defining social studies comprehensively has been an ongoing effort as social studies draws upon knowledge of several disciplines and can mean something different from individual to individual. For the purpose of this chapter, we will adhere to the definition most accepted by educators. The National Council for the Social Studies (NCSS) defines social studies as the "study of individuals, communities, systems, and their interactions across time and place that prepares students for local, national, and global civic life." Further, the study of social studies draws on many disciplines including anthropology, archeology, economics, geography, history, law, philosophy, political science, psychology, religion, and sociology. Through selective integration of these disciplines, the purpose of social studies instruction is to prepare learners for a lifelong practice of civil disclosure and civic engagement in their communities (NCSS, 2023). By examining the past, engaging in civic activities in the present, and learning how to plan for the future, teachers can not only shape their students but also have a hand in impacting the community at large.

Although all subjects suffer an occasional identity crisis, social studies, since its birth during the Progressive Era, has been in a perpetual state of division over the purposes, importance, strategies, and even the definition of the field (Vontz et al., 2007). What exactly is "social studies"? Is it history or is it civics? Does it include sociology and geography? In the twenty-first century, social studies are distinctive in the American public school curriculum because they are the courses in which civic values, norms, and behaviors are most directly addressed. Students learn how to be a good citizen and learn about government and politics, economics, and history. A majority of the social studies curriculum is consistent with a heavy emphasis placed on the Founding Era, the branches of government, and general US history. The choices about which material to include or exclude indicate what civic values and skills students need to learn to become a good citizen. These values can be and often are defined by the controlling political party within a state. By studying the revision process and the content of a state's social studies curriculum, it is possible to gain a better understanding of the potential influences that liberal and conservative ideologies have on student learning (Williams & Maloyed, 2013). Although the movement toward standards, assessment, and accountability has dominated the national discussion on public education for several decades, it has centered on math, science, and language arts. The content area of social studies is not included in the battery of tests prescribed by No Child Left Behind of 2001, and as of now, there is no independent social studies curriculum in the Common Core Curriculum standards that have been adopted by forty-five states (Williams & Maloyed, 2013).

A Case for Social Studies

Since the enactment of No Child Left Behind of 2001, which (among numerous other expectations) increased teacher accountability of student learning, student achievement on state exams has become increasingly important. Due to social studies topics being tested in less than 20 states, attention to social studies instruction decreased to allow for more instructional time allotted to tested subjects (i.e., English language arts, math). One study in 2008 found that instructional time for social studies decreased by 17 minutes while reading instructional time increased by 40 minutes (Center on Educational Policy, 2008). A recent national survey of elementary and middle school social studies teachers suggests that "most elementary teachers devote less than one hour per day to social studies in any form," and the majority "didn't perceive their schools as placing much importance on social studies in general or associated subjects" (Leming et al., 2006).

Competency in history, geography, civics, economics, and government can lead to students becoming active and involved in the democratic processes (Levy & Akiva, 2019). An excellent social studies education has also been shown to increase student's political interest through experiences that enable them to explore multiple sides of pollical issues and actively use their knowledge and increase students use of blogging or canvassing to communicate their perspectives (Levy et al., 2016).

While there are many topics that could be covered teaching social studies to elementary-aged students, this chapter attempts to highlight central ideas about planning instruction for young students and considerations for teaching students with mild intellectual disabilities. After reading this chapter, readers should be able to:

- Describe the differences and overlap of guiding social studies standards and frameworks.
- Explain why instruction in each content area is vital to producing civically competent graduates.
- Create a comprehensive and engaging social studies lesson using tools and examples from a case study at the end of this chapter.
- Describe considerations for developing social studies lessons for students with mild intellectual disabilities to access the general curriculum.

Guiding Social Studies Standards and Frameworks

When planning social studies instruction, teachers, teacher candidates, and higher education faculty should consider three different sources. The content standards, curriculum standards, and C3 (college, career, and civic life) framework are designed for teachers to draw from when deciding what content to teach and in what sequence. The teacher preparation standards outline pedogeological knowledge, skills, and dispositions needed for teacher candidates to become effective social studies educators. Because the audience of this book is teacher candidates, we will focus on the content needed to instruct K–12 students (i.e., content standards, curriculum standards, and C3 framework).

Content Standards

The content standards provide descriptions of concepts considered critical to content learning through four social studies disciplines: history, geography, civics, and economics. Although individual states decide exactly *what* to teach, educating students on each of the four disciplines is required. The individual standards are developed by committees of curriculum specialists, educators, and academics from each state and are typically revised every eight to 10 years. Because states have their own standards, the four disciplines are briefly discussed below in general terms.

History. To realize the goal of producing civically competent graduates, students must explore the past and understand how it has shaped the world they live in. Without historical knowledge and inquiry, we are not equipped to make sensible decisions or draw informed conclusions about political or social issues. Most importantly, history gives us the chance to examine past events that we do not want to repeat. This perspective directly contributes to the growth of a competent public citizen. Further, the University of California Los Angeles Public History Initiative (https://phi.history.ucla.edu/nchs/world-history-content-standards/) identifies two types of standards needed for students learning history: historical thinking skills and historical understanding. Historical thinking requires the student to evaluate and interpret historical evidence, draw sound conclusions, and generate historical arguments. While historical understanding involves the students recognizing the aspirations, strivings, accomplishments, and failures of people in their nation or around the world.

History instruction is focused on American history and world history. American history explores topics that have occurred within the United States and commonly include (but are not limited to) American colonization and settlement, the American Revolution, westward expansion, the Industrial Revolution, the Civil War and Reconstruction, the Great Depression, and World War II. Within this instruction, key people, places, and movements are also discussed. World history explores historically significant events around the world including (but not limited to) the beginning of human societies, early civilizations, the influence of religion and traditions around the world, global interactions and exchange, ancient Greece, ancient Egypt, and ancient China, among numerous other topics.

Geography. Geographically competent citizens do more than just point to a location on a map. According to the National Center on Geographic Education (NCGE), excellence in geography requires students to use geographical perspective, knowledge, and skills. Geographic perspective involves students using spatial and ecological knowledge to formulate questions and find the answers. Geographic knowledge is the mastery of the standards themselves (e.g., identifying the cardinal directions on a map, describing geographic characteristics of Italy, explaining how the climate and landscape contribute to a city's population). Finally, geographic skills include systematically conducting geographic investigations to generate solutions to problems.

The NCGE recognizes six "essential elements" and eighteen "standards." The essential elements are central ideas necessary to an understanding of geography and include (1) the world in spatial terms, (2) places and regions, (3) physical systems, (4) human systems, (5) environment and society, and (6) the uses of geography. Within these essential elements, students learn a breadth of skills and concepts: how to use maps and other geographic representations; how to analyze the spatial organization of people, places, and environments; how culture and experiences influence peoples' perceptions of places and regions; the physical patterns that's shape the Earth's surface; migration of human populations; patterns and networks of economic interdependence on the earth's surface; processes and patterns in human settlements; how human actions modify the physical environment; and how to apply geography to interpret the past and plan for the future.

Civics. Civics is defined as the study of the rights and duties of US citizens and how their governments work. Learning civics in the classroom helps students understand the essential principles and workings of their political system and that of others, as well as the relationship of American politics and government to world affairs. The goal of civics is to develop literate, informed, competent, and responsible citizens who are politically aware, active, and committed to the fundamental values and principles of American constitutional democracy (Oklahoma Department of Education, 2019).

The Center for Civic Education (https://www.civiced.org/standards?page=k4erica) explains in detail the five major content standards taught in K–4 public schools: (1) What is government and what should it do?; (2) What are the basic values and principles of American democracy?; (3) How does the government established by the Constitution embody the purposes, values, and principles of American democracy?; (4) What is the relationship of the United States to other nations and to world affairs?; and (5) What are the roles of the citizen in American democracy?

Economics. Although commonly thought of as a middle or high school–age academic subject, economic education in elementary grades is crucial in the development of economically literate citizens. After graduation (and even before), students enter a work force dictated by the state of our global economy. All citizens are expected to work, pay taxes, and buy (and sometimes sell) goods—all of which require an understanding of the economy.

The National Content Standards in Economics recognize multiple topics that should be taught starting in fourth grade. These topics include scarcity, decision-making, allocation, incentives, trade, specialization, markets and prices, role of prices, competition and market structure, institutions, money and inflation, interest rates, income, entrepreneurship, economic growth, role of government and market failure, government failure, economic fluctuations, unemployment and inflation, and fiscal and monetary policy.

Curriculum Standards

Originally published in 1994, the NCSS introduced a revised set of curriculum standards in 2010 (NCSS, 2010) to better reflect modern social studies topics. Curriculum standards differ from content standards in that they were created at the national level and can be thought of as topics that should be systematically interwoven within the four disciplines of social studies. These curriculum standards are meant to create a framework for teaching the four content standards while also offering rich exploration of the content from a holistic lens. The curriculum standards are organized by ten themes that not only structure ideas and concepts that should be woven into social studies programs but also represent prominent topics of the human experience: (1) culture; (2) time, continuity, and change; (3) people, places, and environments; (4) individual development and identity; (5) individuals, groups, and institutions; (6) power, authority, and governance; (7) production, distribution, and consumption; (8) science, technology, and society; (9) global connections; and (10) civic ideals and practices. Understanding these themes and intentionally threading them into everyday instruction allows students to consider social studies–related topics through multiple perspectives, creating a unique vantage point for students to generate questions and draw conclusions. See figure 11.1.

C3 Framework

Although there is not one single structure or tool used nationally to teach social studies, the C3 framework is among the most widely recognized and accepted teaching frameworks in the field. The college, career, and civic life (C3) framework was created to support states in producing social studies standards and introduced a new way of structuring social studies instruction. Recognizing the marginalization of social studies instruction, the authors of the framework sought to improve social studies teaching by introducing a more engaging and rigorous model for students of all grade levels. The C3 framework is a document created by leaders in social studies education with expertise in social studies disciplines and in partnership with many other professional organizations. At its heart, the C3 framework is meant to enhance

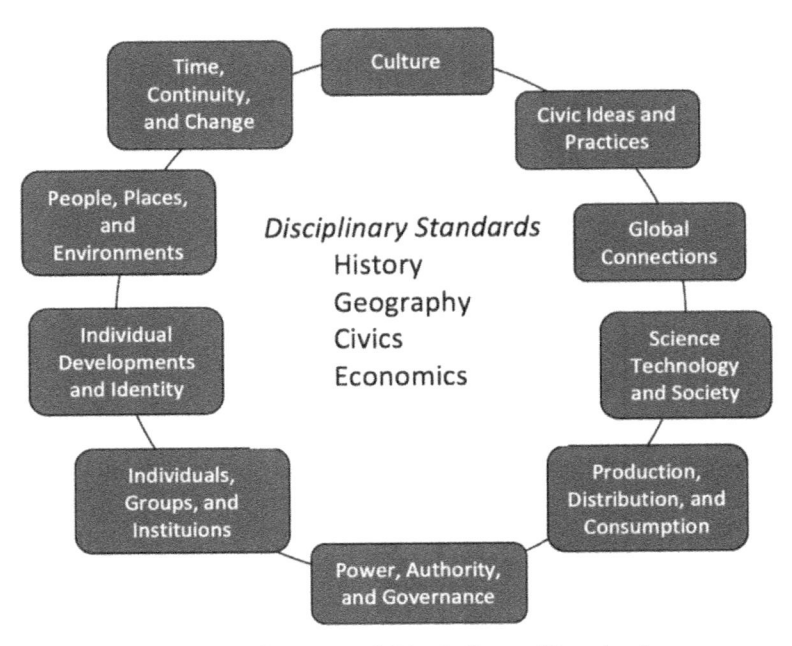

Figure 11.1. Social Studies Theme and Disciplinary Standards
Source: Created by the authors.

the rigor of civics, economics, geography, and history instruction for students of all grade levels by engaging them in inquiry-based learning. Unlike other social studies frameworks, the C3 includes an inquiry arc in the form of four dimensions that are meant to structure lessons and expectations of students during a lesson. Additionally, the C3 aligns the Common Core English language arts (ELA) standards in the areas of reading, writing, speaking, and listening to each dimension.

Disciplinary Inquiry Matrix. Although inquiry as a pedological method is not a new practice, using an inquiry model to teach social studies is a relatively new practice (Hughes & Marhatta, 2023; Thacker et al., 2018). The disciplinary inquiry matrix challenges students to investigate authentic social studies topics by working through the four inquiry dimensions: (1) developing questions and planning inquiries, (2) applying disciplinary concepts and tools, (3) evaluating sources and using evidence, and (4) communicating conclusions and taking informed action.

Dimension 1. Given the many disciplines at play in social studies, intentional questioning of ideas and concepts is imperative to drawing conclusions and making connections among information. Both student- and teacher-generated questions are acceptable for this dimension; however, student-generated questions should be encouraged when possible, as they could increase student buy-in. Students should also be encouraged to produce questions together. Students are naturally curious about the world and often ask compelling questions about their life and the world around them. For example, a compelling question a young child might ask could be: *Why do we have rules?* This is a relevant, honest, and intriguing question that the child has a personal stake in. Because the question is important and could be addressed in several diverse ways, helping students produce supporting questions is advised so the question is more focused. Examples of supporting questions for the compelling questions are: *What rules do we have in our classroom?* or *What are some rules that some families have at home?*

Generating a relevant and compelling question can be an advanced skill for some learners. Participating in the inquiry process can be accessible to all students with the appropriate support in place. Younger students and students with intellectual disabilities will need more support formulating their questions. One way to support students in question generation is to first introduce the topic that will be covered during the lesson with pictures or a video about the topic and then give students sentence starters such as: *I wonder why . . .?* or *Why do people . . .?* For students requiring more support, teachers (or even peers) can pre-make appropriate questions and have the students select the question they want to investigate. If a student receives special education services, all materials should align with adaptations described in the student's individualized education program (IEP) (e.g., picture supports, braille, high color contrast in printed materials, increased font size).

Dimension 2. Identifying which of the four major social studies disciplines (i.e., history, geography, economics, and civics) will be used to answer the question gives the investigation intellectual context. Investigating questions through these lenses at an early age can result in a much deeper understanding of the disciplines than just being taught the disciplines alone. Because states set their own content standards, the C3 framework does not attempt to list out exactly what the students are to learn within these disciplines but, rather, describes disciplinary skills and concepts. Dimension 2 is meant to provide guidance on organizing information to be taught—not prescribing what it is to be taught.

Note that there is no prescribed right or wrong discipline to choose when answering a compelling question. For example, the compelling question for a lesson, *What is freedom?* could be investigated through any of the disciplines. If students are investigating freedom through a history discipline, the question could be, *When did American gain its freedom?* Investigating freedom through a civics lens could look like answering the question, *What does freedom of speech mean?* Freedom could also be examined through a geography lens by asking, *Does freedom change from place to place?* Finally, freedom can be explored through an economics lens by asking, *Does having more freedom mean more prosperity?* Given that social studies is a combination of several disciplines, viewing these questions through different disciplinary lenses can help students make connections and draw informed conclusions.

Additionally, this dimension provides a pathway of skills that students should master by the end of grade levels 2, 5, 8, and 12. For example, in civics instruction, students should be able to describe roles and responsibilities of people in authority by the end of grade 2. This knowledge should deepen to the student being able to distinguish the responsibilities and powers of government officials at various levels and branches at different times and places by the end of grade 5. By the end of grade 8, students should be able to distinguish powers and responsibilities of citizens, political parties, interest groups, and the media in a variety of governmental and nongovernmental contexts. Finally, by the end of grade 12, students should be able to distinguish the powers and responsibilities of local, state, tribal, national, and international civic and political institutions. This progression of skills is continued through civics, history, geography, and economics.

Examining a topic through a civics lens invites students to think about topics through a framework of government and society. The C3 framework offers guidance in civics instruction through exploration of the areas of civic and political institutions, applying civic virtues and democratic principles through participation and deliberation, and examining processes, laws, and rules. Investigating a topic through an economics lens requires students to use economic reasoning. Economic reasoning involves consideration of the cost and benefit of making decisions. A large part of economics instruction is centered on a goal of making oneself and society "better off." The C3 framework supports economic reasoning by providing guidance in the areas of economic decision-making, exchange and markets, the national economy, and the global economy. Looking at a topic through a geography lens requires students to use spatial and environmental perspectives. Geography instruction can help students appreciate their place in the world and can lead to curiosity about the rest of the world. This can foster a sense of identity, belonging, and interconnectedness with the rest of the world. The C3 framework offers guidance in the areas of geographic representations; places, regions, and cultures; spatial patterns and movements of people; and global interactions. Finally, historical inquiry involves gaining knowledge about past events, people, documents, and ideas to learn more about the past. Historical knowledge assists students in gathering evidence from the past to make informed decisions about the future. Learning about the past can also support the development of individual identity and, by extension, facilitate a sense of belonging. For this discipline, the C3 framework challenges students to investigate topics such as change, continuity, and context; perspectives; historical sources and evidence; and causation and argumentation.

Dimension 3. Dimension 3 involves students evaluating sources and using evidence found to support conclusions. Although these skills sound advanced, many children understand the value of explaining why they think a certain way or oppose something. When gathering sources to support claims, students will need instruction on the types of sources available and where to find them. This skill could be taught in other subjects (e.g., researching an animal for science class or gathering sources to draft a persuasive essay in ELA) and social studies. Students should be exposed to a variety of sources from a variety of media. Consider including a variety of both print sources (books, maps, newspapers, printed articles [e.g., Scholastic]) and online sources (pictures, videos, interactive maps, online articles).

Like dimension 2, dimension 3 offers a progression of expected student skills through the grade levels. For example, by the end of grade 2, students should be able to evaluate a source by distinguishing between fact and opinion. By the end of grade 5, students should be able to use distinctions among fact and opinion to evaluate the credibility of multiple sources. By the end of grade 8, students should be able to evaluate the credibility of a source by determining its relevance and intended use. Finally, by the end of grade 12, students should be able to evaluate a source's credibility by examining how experts value it.

Dimension 4. Communicating a conclusion and taking informed action is the final dimension in the C3 framework. Communicating conclusions can prepare students to engage in civic tasks such as collaboratively making decisions, leading student organizations within and outside of school, and conducting research and communicating finds to stakeholders. Sharing conclusions can take many forms such as an oral presentation, written report, or a poster (or other media) presentation. Taking action is the second component of this dimension and the last step of the inquiry process. Taking action should be done once students have come to an informed conclusion and is grounded in their topic.

There are also skill-progression guidelines for both communicating conclusions and taking action. For example, to effectively communicate conclusions, by the end of grade 2, students should be able to construct an argument with reasons. By the end of grade 5, students should be able to construct an argument using claims and evidence from multiple sources. By the end of grade 8, students should be able to construct arguments using claims and evidence from multiple sources while acknowledging the strengths and limitations of the arguments. Finally, by the end of grade 12, students should be able to construct arguments using precise and knowledgeable claims, with evidence from multiple sources, while acknowledging counter claims and evidentiary weaknesses.

Social Studies Instruction for Students with Mild to Moderate Disabilities

While many teaching strategies exist for teaching academic content to students with mild to moderate disabilities, few have been applied to and researched in social studies. Because social studies has been traditionally taught using textbooks and expository texts, much of the research includes reading comprehension and writing instruction. For example, supporting students' comprehension of text (Capin & Vaughn, 2017; Vaughn et al., 2013) and collaborative reading strategy (Klingner et al., 2001) are both evidence-based practices in teaching reading comprehension that have been applied to social studies text. Aside from reading comprehension interventions, students with mild to moderate disabilities often benefit from the use of graphic organizers, mnemonic devices, and peer support.

Graphic organizers are used to support students with and without disabilities across grade levels and content areas. However, graphic organizers are especially helpful for students who have disabilities, who often benefit from visual displays to make meaningful connections. Ciullo and colleagues (2015) found that including graphic organizers in teaching social studies to elementary students with learning disabilities increased scores on social studies post-lesson tests. Additionally, students commented that the graphic organizer was "very helpful" to their learning. Schenning et al. (2013) taught students with autism social studies content using graphic organizers, structured inquiry, and explicit instruction. With each lesson, the research team also included adapted social studies text that included picture supports and highlighted vocabulary words. All students expect one demonstrated increased correct responding during the intervention and maintenance sessions when compared to baseline. Graphic organizers can also be adapted to meet student needs. See figure 11.2 for an example of a graphic organizer that includes picture supports. Graphic organizers are also useful in teaching historical perspective. Historical perspective is often a difficult concept for students with disabilities. Making sense of information that happened in the past can be supported by graphic organizers that represent a linear timeline.

Mnemonic devices are also an evidence-based practice in teaching many skills to students with mild to moderate disabilities. A mnemonic device is the organization and/or coding of information to make it easier to remember (Çolak & Aydın, 2022). Mnemonics can come in many forms including acronyms, songs, highlighting, keywords, and pictures (Taylor & Larson, 2000). This strategy lends itself well to social studies instruction because it not only makes concepts easier to remember but also allows for easier retrieval of information in the future (Lubin & Polloway, 2016). After sixth-grade students used the mnemonics strategy with pictures of

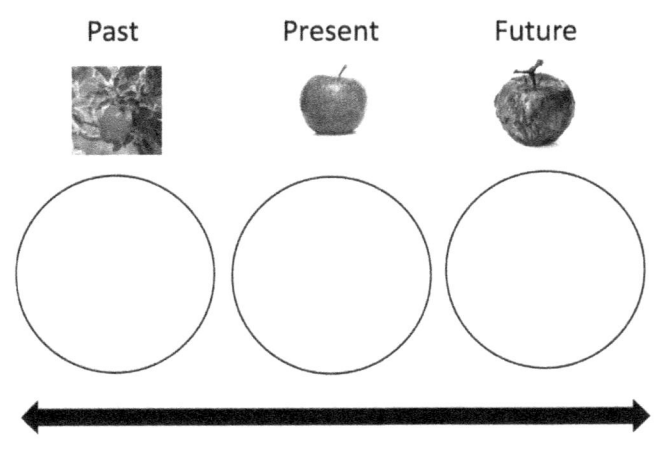

Figure 11.2. Graphic Organizer with Picture Supports
Source: Created by the authors.

historical topics to recall concepts during history instruction, students reported that they found the strategy entertaining and enjoyable. Students also reported that it helped them retain the information learned and helped them with "feeling the past" (Çolak & Aydın, 2022, p. 227). For young students, the incorporation of music and song into a lesson can be a powerful tool. There are numerous songs and rhymes that have stood the test of time in the social studies classroom that cover multiple topics including "The Pilgrims Sailed Far Across the Sea" (discovery of America), "Follow the Drinking Gourd" (slavery), "I'm Just a Bill" (government and law) by Schoolhouse Rock, "Yankee Doodle" (Revolutionary War), and "Fifty Nifty United States" (geography). Additionally, adding instruments to the singing of the songs may be especially engaging for younger students as it engages the sense of touch and sound.

Peer support across academic content areas is a commonly used evidence-based practice for students with mild to moderate disabilities. Although the research in peer support in social studies for students with disabilities is scant, a meta-analysis on peer support revealed that, regardless of student age or disability type, peer intervention had a statistically significant effect on student academic achievement outcomes (Moeyaert et al., 2021). Additionally, Dunn and colleagues (2017) found through a systematic review of peer-mediated interventions for students with emotional/behavioral disorders that the peers supporting the students also made meaningful gains in academic outcomes. A study by Carter and colleagues (2005) also revealed that the number of peers supporting a student can impact student achievement. Results indicated that students with two peers working with them relative to one, demonstrated better outcomes on both social interaction and general curriculum access.

Putting It All Together

Social studies instruction is multifaceted and requires intentional planning. Below is one example of how we use the content and curriculum standards as well as the C3 framework to create a comprehensive social studies lesson. First, start with a compelling question followed by aligning the inquiry to a standard. Next, choose a theme from the NCSS Curriculum Standards to supplement instruction and select primary and secondary sources for the students to investigate. Next, provide a graphic organizer to support student learning. Finally, include technology throughout the investigation or during reporting of findings.

Generate a Compelling Question

Mr. Hernandez is a second-grade teacher in a highly populated public school in the Bronx, New York. One day, Mr. Hernandez tells his students that he was born in Mexico and that it is a wonderful place to live because of the warm weather. The student teacher in the classroom states that he is from Indiana and Indiana is a wonderful place to live because the ground is good for growing crops for his family's farm. Mr. Hernandez explains that geography influences where people want to live. People live in different places around the world because of the way the land allows people to thrive. One student asks Mr. Hernandez, "Why do so many people live in New York?" Mr. Hernandez begins working on a comprehensive lesson for the next day to support students in answering the question. He follows the six steps below to create the lesson.

Note that a compelling question can be generated by students organically (like Mr. Hernandez's lesson) or the question can be teacher generated. Teacher-generated questions are appropriate when a social studies topic needs to be covered (based on curriculum sequence or state standards) within a certain time frame. Student buy-in may be increased with teacher-generated questions by allowing students to choose between two or three questions pre-made by the teacher on the topic that needs to be covered.

Target Your State's Discipline Learning Target or Standard

Mr. Hernandez uses the New York State K–8 Social Studies Framework (2017) to begin planning his instruction. The discipline of the lesson will be geography. He locates two standards that align with the topic to be taught. He also recognizes that the geography of the state of New York is emphasized as a learning target in fourth grade. While focusing on the second-grade learning targets for this lesson, Mr. Hernandez will also introduce and touch upon the fourth-grade target.

Second-Grade Learning Targets:

- 2.5a Geography and natural resources shape where and how urban, suburban, and rural communities develop and how they sustain themselves.
- 2.5b The location of physical features and natural resources often affects where people settle and may affect how those people sustain themselves.

Fourth-Grade Learning Target:

- 4.1 New York State has a diverse geography. Various maps can be used to represent and examine the geography of New York State.

Target a Theme

Mr. Hernandez wants his students to work in groups of three and create a poster displaying information on one reason people might choose to live in New York. Because students may choose different reasons (e.g., easy transportation due to being next to the ocean, the weather, convenience of the Hudson and East Rivers, good for businesses due to high trafficking), Mr. Hernandez targets the third theme of the NCSS Curriculum Standards: people, places, and environments.

Locate Sources

Mr. Hernandez gathers sources for his students to investigate potential reasons people move to New York. One source the students can use is their social studies textbook. There is a chapter about human migration that describes the reasons why people move at all. Another source he finds is an article from Scholastic that describes geographic features that lend themselves well to habitation. The article describes the many uses of water ways for the transportation of goods and human travel, ideal weather including temperatures and precipitation, and the benefits of living near mountain ranges. Another source is Google Maps. Each group of students will have access to a computer to look at the state of New York on the map. Google Maps allows students to see the ocean, rivers, mountains, highways, and other features. Another source is a list of YouTube videos Mr. Hernandez prepares for students to watch. The YouTube videos include reasons why people like living in or near New York through interviews, topics covered in the textbook (reasons why people migrate), and other videos about geographic features and prosperous societies.

Note that instruction on primary and secondary sources and their uses should be taught prior to students' investigation.

Provide a Graphic Organizer

Mr. Hernandez's students use graphic organizers in other content areas. Although there are many graphic organizers that are available online that would be appropriate for this investigation, he gives the students an organizer that states the compelling question (Why do so many people live in New York?) and has branches that connect to four boxes that are labeled "Reason 1," "Reason 2," "Reason 3," and "Reason 4." The students can also use a similar graphic organizer format to help organize what they are going to put on their poster.

There are many websites dedicated to graphic organizer use and have templates that are available for printing. Graphic organizers are also included in many curricula. If you cannot find an organizer that works for your students or lessons, they can be easily made using Microsoft Word. It is important to note that graphic organizer templates can be used across content areas and do not necessarily need to be social studies specific.

Include Technology

Mr. Hernandez knows his students learn best when information is presented in multiple formats. Using technology such as videos and applications also increases their engagement. The students will have access to laptops during their investigation to view videos and read online articles. Mr. Hernandez plans to put Google Earth on the projector in the classroom and have each group of students come up to the projector and zoom in to the state of New York. While the students look at the state, he will point out the different landscapes, bodies of water, and landmarks such as the Statue of Liberty. When wrapping up the lesson, Mr. Hernandez will also project a virtual field trip of video of New York City or Niagara Falls.

See table 11.1 for considerations pertaining to teaching across the C3 dimensions for students with intellectual disability.

Table 11.1. Example of Planning Across C3 Dimensions

C3 Dimension	Mr. Hernandez's First-Grade Class	Considerations for Students with ID
1. Developing questions and planning inquiries.	Students organically posed a question. • Teacher-generated questions are acceptable too. • Give students a selection of questions to choose from, if possible.	While the goal is for students to organically generate questions, many students will need support. • Give them sentence starters (verbally or in print) such as, *I wonder . . . , ?* or *Why do people . . . ?* • Give them choices of pre-made questions. • Include appropriate communication supports (e.g., picture supports, communication devices).
2. Applying disciplinary concepts and tools.	Refer to your state's discipline standards and the NCSS Curriculum Standards to integrate the disciplines with social studies themes.	• Consider pre-teaching discipline-specific vocabulary. • Apply systematic instructional strategies to teach discipline-specific concepts/ideas.
3. Evaluating sources and using evidence.	Students used Chromebooks to read online articles and watch videos. They also interacted with an interactive map on Google Maps and used a graphic organizer to organize information. • Remember to provide students with both primary and secondary sources. • Vary the media of sources offered (e.g., online articles, videos, books, maps).	• Consider using mnemonic devices to help students remember things learned (e.g., HOMES acronym to remember the Great Lakes). • Add visuals or other supports (sentence starters, e.g., *My first reason is . . .*). • Have students work with peers.
4. Communicating conclusions and taking informed action.	Students made posters in groups about one reason they found to explain why people live in New York and then presented them to the class. • Communicating ideas could be a written paper, PowerPoint presentation, or video. • Allow students to customize their presentation to make it unique and exciting. • Ensure that all students have the opportunity to speak during the presentation if it's an oral report.	• Allow students to present in the communication mode outlined in their IEP (e.g., communication device, text-to-speech technology, written response). • Consider ways to use peers as support for students with communication challenges.

Note: Supports suggested in the *Considerations for Students With ID* should be implemented in addition to general education strategies in "Mr. Hernandez's First-Grade Class" column. ID = intellectual disability; IEP = individualized education program.

CONCLUSION

According to the National Council for the Social Studies (NCSS, 2016), an excellent education in social studies is vital for students to grow into civically competent adults. Rich social studies instruction at an early age allows students to develop a deeper understanding of the world around them prior to participating in civic duties. It is our responsibility as teachers to take the task of shaping the future's adult civilians very seriously. Some key takeaways from this chapter include:

- Planning social studies instruction: teachers should consider content standards, curriculum standards, and the C3 framework.
- The disciplinary inquiry matrix challenges students to investigate authentic social studies topics by working through the four inquiry dimensions.
- Teaching tools for students with disabilities: graphic organizer, mnemonic devices, and peer support.
- Putting it all together: generate a compelling question, target a theme, locate sources, provide a graphic organizer, include technology, and embed HLPs.

REFERENCES

Browder, D. M., Spooner, F., & Courtade, G. R. (2020). *Teaching students with moderate and severe disabilities*. Guilford Publications.

Capin, P., & Vaughn, S. (2017). Improving reading and social studies learning for secondary students with reading disabilities. *Teaching Exceptional Children*, 49(4), 249–261.

Center for Civic Education. (n.d.). *Content standards*. Center for Civic Education. https://www.civiced.org/standards?page=k4erica

Center on Educational Policy. (2008). *Instructional time in elementary schools: A closer look at changes for specific subjects* (pp. 1–8). Center on Educational Policy.

Ciullo, S. (2015). Improving access to elementary school social studies instruction. *Teaching Exceptional Children*, 48(2), 102–109. https://doi.org/10.1177/0040059915605640

Ciullo, S., Falcomata, T., & Vaughn, S. (2015). Teaching social studies to upper elementary students with learning disabilities: Graphic organizers and explicit instruction. *Learning Disability Quarterly*, 38(1), 15–26. https://doi.org/10.1177/0731948713516767

Çolak, K., & Aydın, R. İ. (2022). The effect of using mnemonics on success in social studies? *Journal of Educational Research*, 115(3), 223–233. https://ideas.repec.org/a/taf/vjerxx/v115y2022i3p223-233.html

Dunn, M. E., Shelnut, J., Ryan, J. B., & Katsiyannis, A. (2017). A systematic review of peer-mediated interventions on the academic achievement of students with emotional/behavioral disorders. *Education & Treatment of Children* (West Virginia University Press), 40(4), 497–524. https://www.jstor.org/stable/44684181

Fitchett, P. G., Heafner, T. L., & Lambert, R. G. (2014). Examining elementary social studies marginalization: A multilevel model. *Educational Policy*, 28(1), 40–68. https://doi.org/10.1177/0895904812453998

Huck, A. (2019). Elementary social studies content integration in CCLS: An analysis of content integration. *Social Studies*, *110*(1), 1–16. https://doi.org/10.1080/00377996.2018.1524359

Hughes, R. E. & Marhatta, P. (2023). Learning to ask their own questions: How elementary students develop social studies inquiry questions. *Teaching & Teacher Education*, 127, https://doi.org/10.1016/j.tate.2023.104094

Klingner, J. K., Vaughn, S., Dimino, J., Schumm, J. S., & Bryant, D. (2001). *Collaborative strategic reading: Strategies for improving comprehension*. Sopris West.

Leming, J. S., Ellington, L., & Schug, M. (2006). The state of social studies: A national random survey of elementary and middle school social studies teachers. *Social Education*, 70, 322–327.

Levy, B. L. M., & Akiva, T., (2019). Motivating political participation among youth: An analysis of factors related to adolescents' political engagement. *Political Psychology*, *40*(5), 1039–1055.

Levy, B. L. M., Solomon, B. G., & Collet-Gildard, L., (2016). Fostering political interest among youth during the 2012 presidential election: Instructional opportunities and challenges in a swing state. *Educational Researcher, 45*(9), 483–495.

Lubin, J., & Polloway, E. A. (2016). Mnemonic instruction in science and social studies for students with learning problems: A review. *Learning Disabilities: A Contemporary Journal*, *14*(2), 207–224.

Moeyaert, M., Klingbeil, D. A., Rodabaugh, E., & Turan, M., (2021). Three-level meta-analysis of single-case data regarding the effects of peer tutoring on academic and social-behavioral outcomes for at-risk students and students with disabilities. *Remedial &Special Education, 42*(2), 94–106. https://doi.org/10.1177/0741932519855079

National Council for the Social Studies (NCSS). (2010). *National Curriculum Standards for Social Studies: A framework for teaching, learning, and assessment*. National Council for the Social Studies.

National Council for the Social Studies (NCSS). (2016). A vision of powerful teaching and learning in the social studies. *Social Education, 80*, 180–182.

Oklahoma Department of Education. (2019, May 15). *Oklahoma Academic Standards for Social Studies*. Oklahoma Department of Education. https://sde.ok.gov/sites/default/files/documents/files/Oklahoma%20Academic%20Standards%20for%20Social%20Studies%205.21.19.pdf

Schenning, H., Knight, V., & Spooner, F. (2013). Effects of structured inquiry and graphic organizers on social studies comprehension by students with autism spectrum disorders. *Research in Autism Spectrum Disorders, 7*(4), 526–540. DOI: 10.1016/j.rasd.2012.12.007.

Taylor, H. E., & Larson, S. M. (2000). Teaching elementary social studies to students with mild disabilities. *Social Education, 64*(4), 232.

Thacker, E. S., Friedman, A. M., Fitchett, P. G., Journell, W., & Lee, J. K. (2018). Exploring how an elementary teacher plans and implements social studies inquiry. *Social Studies*, *109*(2), 85–100. https://doi.org/10.1080/00377996.2018.1451983

Vaughn, S., Swanson, E. A., Roberts, G., Wanzek, J., Stillman-Spisak, S. J., Solis, M., & Simmons, D. (2013). Improving reading comprehension and social studies knowledge in middle school. *Reading Research Quarterly*, *48*(1), 77–93.

Vontz, T. S., Franke, J., Burenheide, B., & Bietau, L. (2007). Building bridges in social studies education: Professional development school partnerships. *The Journal of Educational Research*, *100*(4), 254–262.

Williams, J. K., & Maloyed, C. L. (2013). Much ado about Texas: Civics in the social studies curriculum. *The History Teacher*, *47*(1), 25–40.

Zakas, T.-L., Browder, D. M., Ahlgrim-Delzell, L., & Heafner, T. (2013). Teaching social studies content to students with autism using a graphic organizer intervention. *Research in Autism Spectrum Disorders*, *7*(9), 1075–1086. https://doi.org/10.1016/j.rasd.2013.06.001

12

Setting Up the Physical Environment for Elementary General Education Classrooms

Jasmine Justus, Julie Atwood, and Bre Martin

ONE WAY THAT SUPPORT can be offered to elementary-aged students is to provide them with a well-structured classroom environment. Setting up a physical environment to support the growth of academic and behavioral skills is more than just ensuring that the school conduct code is posted, and enough seats are provided for students. Setting up a classroom is an ongoing process that starts before the first day of school and continues with modification decisions made mid-school year (or more often) to accommodate changing student needs. To do this, a strong understanding of child development, professional standards, and federal guidelines (i.e., Every Student Succeeds Act) is needed.

This chapter describes evidence-based practices to create a safe and supportive learning environment. These universal concepts can be implemented and adapted based on the grade level of the students in the classroom. The following concepts will be described: (a) physical arrangement, (b) classroom design, and (c) choosing and organizing learning materials. Each section will provide a detailed description, an overview of research to support the practice, information on how to implement it, and relevant resources for reinforcement. This chapter also provides an overview of professional standards for elementary educators and an overview of policy, theory, and research surrounding the concepts discussed.

CHAPTER OBJECTIVES

At the conclusion of the chapter, readers will be able to:

1. Describe and identify the need for a well-structured classroom environment.
2. Understand the theoretical underpinnings and research supporting effective classroom management.
3. Recognize the professional standards that support educators in creating a positive learning environment.
4. Describe evidence-based classroom management practices that support positive student outcomes.

5. Determine developmentally appropriate
    - physical arrangements;
    - classroom design; and
    - learning materials.

Relevant Educational Policy

The Every Student Succeeds Act (ESSA, 2015) requires states to hold schools accountable for the education provided to students, and classroom management plays a large role. In addition, the National Commission on Social, Emotional, and Academic Development (SEAD) advocates for and supports public schools in providing a well-rounded education focused on the whole child by providing education professionals with guidance documents at no cost. The document titled "From a Nation at Risk to a Nation at Hope" (2014) provides information on how learning happens, recommendations for action, and how to work collaboratively to achieve the common goal of the commission. ESSA and SEAD set a precedent that an appropriate education requires more than an academic curriculum. Educators can provide a whole child–focused education through several actions, including setting up a positive learning environment based on evidence-based practices.

Foundational Learning Theory

It is important to consider the developmental stages in which children progress. Several learning theories support the need for a well-structured elementary classroom. Each learning theory presents a natural progression that children go through as they grow, aligning with developmental milestones. Adverse events (e.g., the COVID-19 pandemic, natural disasters, trauma) will likely impact the time frame within which children reach developmental milestones. Although entire books can be written on classroom management theory, three well-known theorists include Piaget, Vygotsky, and Montessori.

Piaget introduces the idea that children progress through four stages: sensorimotor (zero to two years old), preoperational (two to seven years old), concrete operational (seven to 11 years old), and formal operational (11 years old through adulthood) (Ediger, 2012). Elementary-aged students fall within the preoperational and concrete operational stages. Children begin to understand abstract concepts, gain the ability to recognize physical similarities across settings, and begin to understand the concept of categorization in the preoperational stage. Next, in the concrete operational stage, children develop stronger numeracy skills, spatial awareness, and an increased understanding of categorization. This information can assist educators in determining the best method for organizing learning materials, for determining which learning materials are appropriate for the classroom, and for ensuring that the physical space is appropriate for students' level of spatial awareness.

Vygotsky (1978) suggests that learning is a social concept and access to social interaction is vital to cognitive development. Further, the zone of proximal development (ZPD) is the gap between what a child has mastered and the skills they can obtain through the appropriate educational support (Podolskiy, 2012). When considering a child's ZPD, one might look at the physical environment of a classroom differently. The classroom should be structured to allow social interaction with students on different learning levels and access to needed materials and resources to complete a task.

Expanding on Piaget and Vygotsky, Montessori explores the idea that children develop best in a thoughtfully designed environment that promotes independence (Standing, 1962). The choice of learning materials and the student's ability to access those is a fundamental concept of the Montessori method. Children should have opportunities to explore materials before being expected to use them to complete learning tasks (Rosati, 2021). In addition, children need to be taught to care for materials, including accessing the items themselves and taking responsibility for putting them away when the task is complete. In the early stages of child development, Montessori emphasizes that children must explore their environment independently, and to do so safely, the environment must be designed with physical, psychological, and intellectual child development in mind. Understanding developmental stages and learning theory can be helpful when designing classrooms to meet student needs. The next section of our chapter focuses on professional standards.

SETTING UP THE PHYSICAL ENVIRONMENT

When designing the classroom environment, an effort should be made to link the environment to the purpose (Nazareno, 2014). The classroom space should accommodate multiple configurations for large and small groups, pairs, triads, and individuals to read, write, talk, listen, play, and engage (Roskos & Neuman, 2011). A well-structured classroom should maximize student–teacher interactions to foster positive student–teacher relationships, another foundational element for student growth in the classroom.

Often, the physical layout of the classroom is constrained to limitations within the room's design: the room's shape, size, any permanent fixtures such as a sink or built-in cabinets, locations of power outlets, and so on. However, some elements of the environment can be modified (e.g., furniture arrangement, classroom decorations, wall color, or lighting), which allows teachers to get creative in designing desk layouts, center locations, tables, technology, and traffic patterns. Most published work on altering the physical variables of the classroom offers practical suggestions for teachers rather than research on the various arrangements (Langford, 2017).

The physical layout of the classroom should be predictable and organized to ensure safety, production, and a conducive learning environment. Crowded classrooms can become disruptive and facilitate negative behavior, poor grades, a lack of motivation, and decreased school attendance (Cheryan et al., 2014; Langford, 2017). Fluid traffic patterns where students can move freely without bumping into other students or desks are ideal. When planning the furniture layout, consider how many students will be in the room, group meeting areas, and if there are any safety concerns. Also, remember to keep the furniture developmentally appropriate including correctly sized chairs, tables, and desks for the corresponding age group of students.

Research Support

When a classroom is organized in a manner that matches the mode of instruction, there is a positive impact on student behavior (Havik & Westergård, 2019).

210　Chapter 12: Setting Up the Physical Environment

Evidence also supports the inverse, that when classrooms are disorganized and cluttered, there are more significant problematic behaviors (Day et al., 2015; Lindstrom et al., 2017). Thus, adjusting the student's environment can be an effective tool in minimizing disruptive behaviors without the need for more intense intervention.

Three common seating arrangements have been studied: rows, clusters, and a horseshoe pattern (Langford, 2017). Figure 12.1 shows a sample pattern for the three main classroom seating arrangements. Simmons and colleagues (2015) found that while each of the three seating arrangements had positive effects on reducing disruptive behaviors and fostering learning, row seating produced the best results. This does not mean that row seating should be the only option employed. Given the evidence, seating arrangements should be aligned with tasks that students need to complete and should, therefore, be flexible. Adjusting the desks within a classroom can be an easier option than more restrictive options that may require students who are engaged in disruptive behavior to miss instruction.

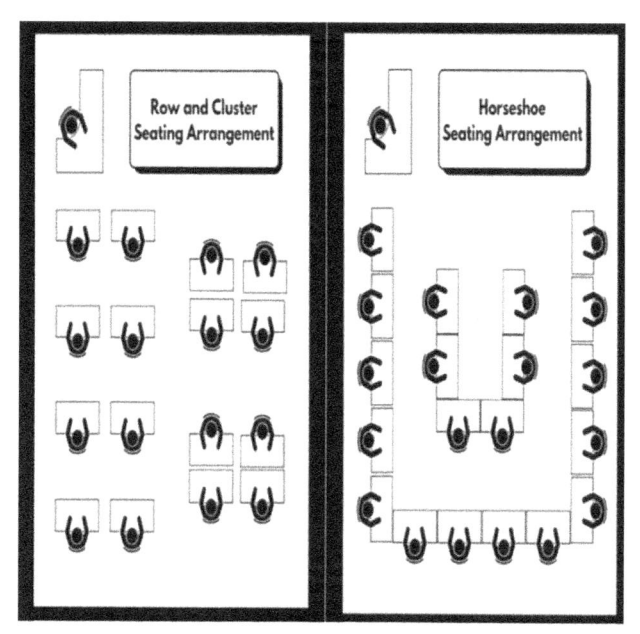

Figure 12.1. Classroom Examples for Seating Patterns
Source: Created by the authors on Canva.

How to Implement

According to Reinke (2023), there are four core elements to creating an effective classroom structure. It is important to (1) clearly define traffic patterns, (2) arrange student desks so all students can be visible to the teacher at all times, (3) clearly label and organize all classroom materials, and (4) create systems for turning in work. These elements do not require significant financial investment. They can be accomplished in a small modular learning unit as well as a classroom that is fully outfitted with the newest technology and equipment. The key is to set up a classroom that promotes focus and learning and is developmentally appropriate.

1. Clearly defined traffic patterns. Students and teachers should be able to move about the classroom easily, navigating to the desired location within the room while avoiding traffic congestion. Teachers move about the classroom as they provide instruction. This allows engagement with the students while describing, illustrating, and stimulating the class. For example, the teacher might start a lesson by standing at the front of the class, drawing on the whiteboard, and asking students to copy her work. As the lesson continues, the teacher will walk along the aisles, if the room is arranged in rows, doing accuracy checks and supporting students before moving along. If the room is designed in a horseshoe pattern, the teacher can walk along the inside of the horseshoe pattern or walk around the edges of a clustered pattern of desks. Likewise, students should be able to move about the classroom without distracting other students to meet their needs independently. If a student needs to get up to sharpen a pencil or approach the teacher's desk, the pathway should be as open as possible. Both the teacher and the students should be able to do so freely without bumping into furniture, having to squeeze through tight spaces, or tripping over supplies and materials. Creating a well-designed traffic pattern might take some trial and error. It is important to remember that a classroom's flow can change at any time. After analyzing the classroom's needs, teachers can rearrange the classroom in a way that meets the needs of both the students and the teacher.

2. Student visibility. During instructional time, the teacher is making eye contact with students, reinforcing answers, and encouraging participation, which makes sure all participants can feel seen. Allowing the physical environment to stimulate connections between the teacher and the students starts by arranging the room in a way that facilitates constant visibility. This includes arranging the furniture to optimize common instructional activities. When planning desk locations, it is helpful to keep in mind whether all students will be able to see the teacher during whole-group instruction or other presentations being delivered by students, what student arrangements will encourage student discussion and productive interaction, and if eye contact can be made with each student at any given time. Figure 12.2 provides an aerial view of how a room can be arranged so that each student can be seen at all times. Whether the room is designed in rows, clusters, or a horseshoe pattern, all of these options allow for student visibility while also accommodating easy traffic patterns.

3. Labeling and organization. The organization, availability, and access to materials needed within a classroom is another principle to consider when structuring a classroom. As previously stated, Montessori emphasizes the independent accessibility of all necessary supplies, which is accomplished by ensuring that all materials are at hand and at eye level for the students and within close proximity (Rosati, 2021). By arranging a thoughtfully designed classroom so that student supplies are at a level that allows them to be easily accessed, the teacher increases student independence, fosters the development of problem-solving skills, and teaches responsibility through the care of materials, as described by Montessori. Similarly, all classroom materials should be plainly labeled and organized. By leaning into child development theories and looking at classroom organization from a zone of proximal development lens, the classroom

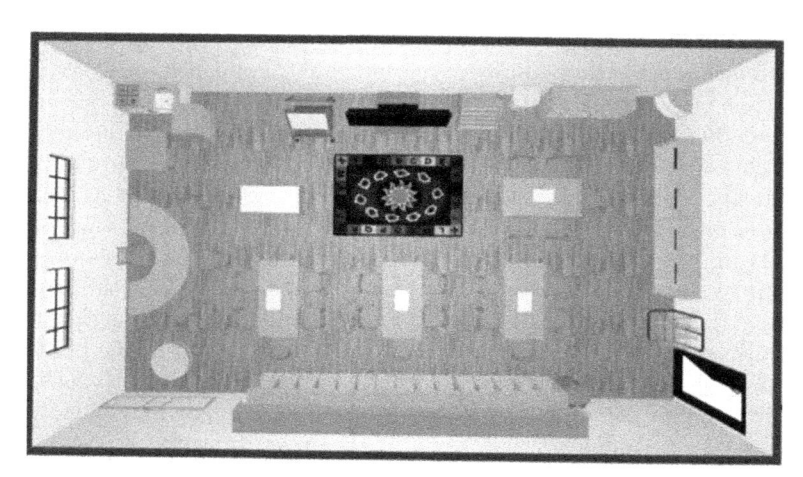

212   Chapter 12: Setting Up the Physical Environment

Figure 12.2.   Classroom Example Considering Traffic Patterns and Visibility
Source: Created using Kaplan Early Learner Floor Planner Version 2.

arrangement can not only foster independence but also meet social needs. When students can identify, locate, and access classroom supplies independently, it allows the teacher more time to provide instruction or assistance to other learners and emphasizes teacher–student relationships. Continuing the conversation on labeling and organizing, learning centers, technology, and equipment should be appropriately accessible. For example, certain centers should be conveniently located near specific books, materials, and other resources. It is also important to note whether certain materials require specific placement for safety reasons or accessibility. Educators should consider labeling supplies and classroom locations if possible. For example, pre-kindergarten and kindergarten classes need colors and pictures to help students identify the labels. Further, first graders may be able to pair a picture with a word for label identification, and all remaining grades can use words to identify the labels.

4. Turning in and retrieving student work. A well-structured classroom will allow students to turn in and retrieve work independently. For example, turn-in trays can be labeled near the teacher's desk so students can independently turn in completed work or retrieve graded work that has grades concealed to comply with the Family Educational Rights and Privacy Act (FERPA). For the higher grade levels, stackable trays can be labeled by subject (See figure 12.3, which provides a list of developmentally appropriate labels for upper elementary grades). When arranging a classroom, it is helpful to designate specific areas for students to complete these tasks without interrupting a lesson or disturbing other students. Another option for turning in or retrieving work is through digital programs. Technology is being increasingly integrated into the classroom, which opens the door for having students complete more assignments online. The labeling of a designated location still needs to be developmentally appropriate and easy to navigate, yet, a digital option allows for less use of school supplies and storage space within small settings. Whichever method is used for assignment completion, it might require some prompting and practice. Students will have to learn the procedure for how to turn in or retrieve assignments, both in the classroom and digitally, through practice. Having the designated area clearly and appropriately labeled will help students master the procedure.

Incorporating these four elements in the room's physical layout, classroom expectations and procedures can be taught and practiced without undue interference. Crowded and cluttered classrooms can foster chaos, while well-structured classrooms allow for established routines that align with classroom rules and expectations. A well-designed classroom facilitates efficiency, leaving more time for instruction and promoting positive academic and social behaviors among students, including student attention, peer interactions, and less disruptive behavior. This also fosters positive teacher–student interactions. Arranging the classroom to make it more accessible, both in the physical design and to the developmental and intellectual level of all students, makes students feel valued, important, and respected. These positive feelings can increase academic performance and student satisfaction with school, whereas students who do not feel valued and respected are more likely to disengage from the academic environment, resulting in more disruptive behaviors.

There will always be limitations to setting up a classroom, so flexibility must be maintained in how a classroom is structured. Classrooms will be limited in space, the types of desks and chairs available may not meet preconceived notions, content areas being taught may change yearly, and so on. When designing the classroom layout, it is helpful to make each area versatile. For example, the whole-group morning meeting rug in an early childhood classroom could double as an open space for students to sit while using electronics later in the day. Another example includes using an area outside of the classroom, such as the cafeteria or library, for group activities when space is limited inside the classroom. More options for flexibility include using the back of the classroom door or front of the classroom cabinets as space for magnet stations or art displays, open cabinets can have hanging pocket charts for activity centers, and so on. With this kind of flexibility, a well-structured classroom can still be established even with limited means, and students can feel supported. The key is setting up the room to enhance the ability to focus, teach, and learn. Regardless of how the classroom is designed with respect to the physical layout, teachers must remember to be flexible and are encouraged to change the layout as often as is necessary to ensure a logical, balanced arrangement that invites connection and active learning.

CLASSROOM DESIGN

Designing and decorating a classroom or educational space is often considered a fun and creative outlet for educators (Jacobs, 2023). Classroom design can transform a bare, cinderblock room into a space that is welcoming, engaging, and appealing to both educators and students, or it can cause disruption to the learning environment. Classroom design can include posters, anchor charts, student art, visual supports (e.g., visual schedules, material lists, choices), lighting, objects, classroom rules and expectations, social/emotional supports, and other items that are displayed in the classroom. These elements can and should serve an educational or organizational purpose. The items within a classroom communicate messages about what supports are available, the classroom culture, and the values held for students and classroom guests.

Cheryan et al. (2014) describe these items as the symbolic classroom, as décor can affect not only student performance and classroom culture but also help shape student aspirations (Cash & Twiford, 2010; Fisher & Kloos, 2016). The symbolic classroom is a powerful tool for helping others make inferences about the educational environment, supporting student understanding of expectations, improving social interactions, and increasing student curiosity (Cheryan et al., 2014). Teachers are often excited to share their interests with students, draw their attention, and excite them about learning (Roskos & Neumann, 2011). However, classroom décor should serve a purpose, and educators may need to exercise caution to avoid excessive stimuli and disruption of learning.

Visual bombardment (e.g., bright colors, items hanging from the ceiling, excessive posters, pictures, or other visual stimuli) (Bullard, 2010) and color are negatively related to student achievement in the classroom (Barrett et al., 2013) and may lead to student distraction, off-task behavior, and a reduction in attention to instructional tasks, which can decrease learning especially in younger students and students with disabilities (Fisher et al., 2016; Godwin et al., 2020; Hanley et al., 2017). A clean and orderly environment is not only impactful for positive student performance but teacher effectiveness as well (Cash & Twiford, 2010). Some educators may assume that all décor and visual stimuli harm student learning. However, that is not the case. What is more likely is that the moderation of visual stimuli and décor is the key, as both high and low levels of visual stimulation within the classroom may be unhelpful (Godwin et al., 2020). Environments with high levels of visual stimulation may result in competition between décor and instruction (Godwin et al., 2020), while environments with low levels of visual stimulation may feel less welcoming (Cheryan et al., 2014). Every classroom has unique educators, students, and needs. There is no "one size fits all" formula that will be effective for all classrooms, and educators should be aware of what works for their specific environment.

Visual supports are visual aids that provide students with information. A second-grade teacher may use a class-wide visual schedule with pictures and words to help students manage time. A kindergarten teacher may put pictures of a pencil, glue, and scissors on the whiteboard to show students what materials they need for the current activity. Visual supports are often lumped within the category of classroom design. However, they serve a very specific purpose as a preventative strategy that, combined with explicit instruction, can provide clear procedures and expectations for students to support learning (Cohen & Demchak, 2018). The low cost and versatility of this intervention are ideal, as it can be seamlessly interwoven into traditional classroom designs. Incorporating visuals can provide prompts/reminders of previously learned skills and increase student involvement in classroom routines (Foster-Cohen & Mirfin-Veitch, 2017). While most research addressing visual supports within the classroom focuses on students with disabilities, it should be noted that general educators will have students with various needs in their classrooms. Visual supports can be a helpful tool to support all students and can easily be incorporated while planning classroom design. Effective classroom design may seem simple, but there is a dearth of applied research on what variables and components of the classroom environment can impact student learning and to what extent (Godwin et al., 2020; Roskos & Neumann, 2011). What should be clear to educators is the need for deliberate planning of all aspects of the student learning environment, not just academic instruction.

Pencils	Scissors
Calculators	Crayons
Graph Paper	Markers
College Ruled Paper	Glue

Figure 12.3. Upper Elementary Developmentally Appropriate Labels
Source: Created by the authors using LessonPix.

How to Implement

Designing the classroom space can seem overwhelming, especially with the other demands on educator time at the start of the school year. The following five steps can assist with (e.g., general education teachers, special education teachers, paraprofessionals, administrators, etc.) planning and executing a classroom environment that is welcoming, individualized, and conducive to student learning.

Figure 12.4. Classroom Example Considering Appropriate Access to Materials
Source: Created using Kaplan Early Learner Floor Planner Version 2.

1. Assess the space. The first step in designing the educational environment is to assess the classroom space. Schools and classrooms come in a variety of shapes and sizes. A pre-kindergarten teacher may have a larger room with attached cubby spaces and bathrooms, while a reading specialist may work out of converted closet space. Both educators can impact learning with what is placed in their space. There are a variety of ways that educators can assess their classroom environment (e.g., draw a diagram, create a list of attributes, take a video or photos for later reference). Creating a physical document or visual of what is available within the classroom is an important step. Consider the classroom size, classroom setup, materials, and resources available. Figure 12.5 provides a brief checklist of questions to ask as classroom design is developed.

216   Chapter 12: Setting Up the Physical Environment

Newer buildings may restrict painting or posting items and visuals on the walls or have rules about *how* items can be affixed to the wall. Older buildings may have exposed brick, which makes hanging visuals more difficult. The guidelines or restrictions of the school site may ultimately restrict educators in how they design their space. A clear understanding of what is available and what is allowed will help to better plan what will be aesthetically pleasing in the environment as well as permitted by the district/school site.

2. Identify what is needed and important for the classroom space. After assessing the physical environment and determining what is available to work with, it is important to determine the priorities for the educators working in the classroom. If more than one educator is working in the space, collaboration and communication may be necessary to reach a consensus on needs. Careful consideration is key,

Room #: _____

Classroom Design Checklist

1. Classroom size: _____
2. How many students will be using the classroom? _____
3. How many walls are available for use? _____
4. How many bulletin boards, dry-erase boards, and/or smartboards are there?
   _____
5. Are there windows or natural light sources? _____
6. Where are the outlets located? _____
7. Is the hallway available for displays? _____
8. Are there any building rules on classroom design or the use of adhesives/push pins on the walls? _____

Classroom Outline

Figure 12.5.   Classroom Design Checklist
Source: Created by the authors using Microsoft Word.

as strategic classroom design planning can have a positive impact on everyone in the classroom (Cheryan et al., 2014). The design may reflect a topic or subject if a specific content area is taught in the environment (e.g., music; art; reading history; science technology engineering, art, and math [STEAM]). However, everything on display in the classroom should serve a purpose of some kind. For example, if an educator is considering putting a birthday chart on the wall. Consider its purpose—is the intention to practice days/months or to celebrate student birthdays? If not, the birthday chart does not serve a purpose and should be removed. Remember that excessive décor may distract students, even if it is on-theme or cute. Everything on display in the classroom should be working to enhance the success of those in the environment.

Consider how to light a space. There may not be many options if the environment has no windows. However, there may be other lighting choices available (e.g., stringing lights around the border of the classroom, lamps, partial overhead lights, light covers). Additional or overly decorative lighting may not be better if it distracts students. If natural light is preferred, be aware of the possibility of glare and temperature fluctuations, especially on sunny or cold days (Cheryan et al., 2014).

Effective classroom design can enhance the look of a classroom and communicate to students what is important to the educator/school site as well as what is expected within the classroom. If displaying student work is a priority, consider if it should only include completed work, or if show in-progress work as well is preferred. What visual supports will be displayed (e.g., visual schedules, classroom rules, visual choice boards, needed materials, feelings/emotions, classroom token economy systems, processes, procedure reminders)? Will a calm-down corner or a social/emotional area be used? Identifying what is important and practical for those working in the space is necessary for effective teaching.

3. **Identify the needs of the students**. When planning the design of a classroom, it can be easy to get caught up in what is aesthetically pleasing to the adults in the room. However, the design should meet the needs of educators *and* students. Consider the students who will be entering the classroom and what their specific needs are. It may be helpful to talk to teachers or staff who have previously worked with these students to gain their input on student needs to plan to maximum effect. If another educator is unavailable, parents can also be a valuable source of information. If there will be students who receive services or accommodations through an individualized education program (IEP) or a Section 504 plan, ensure that everyone responsible for setting up the educational environment has read these documents. Often, there is information about needed visual supports or ways to reduce distraction that may affect how educators plan to design the classroom.

Once the physical arrangement of the classroom is completed, it may be helpful to sit at each section to identify potential distractors. While eliminating distraction may not be a possibility, reducing distraction could be. However, it is important to remember that individual students may find different items, equipment, or décor distracting. Educators should ensure that their classroom design is not only functional for students but is age/ability appropriate. For example, posters or visual schedules that contain too many words may be too challenging

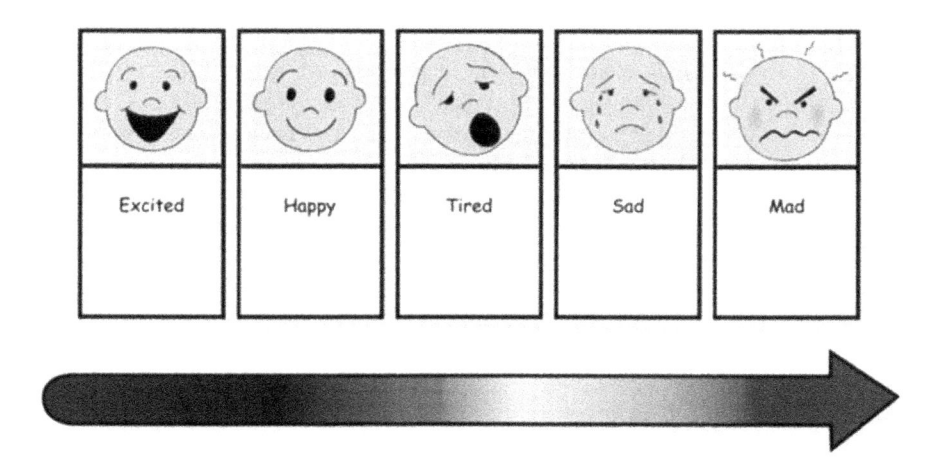

Figure 12.6. Purposeful Classroom Design Example: Emotion Chart
Source: Created by authors using LessonPix.

for younger students and may lead to less engagement or use. Visuals that are too simple or childish may be seen as beneath older elementary students and could lead to less engagement or use.

4. Create and implement. One of the most enjoyable parts of setting up a classroom is designing it to express individual styles and needs. While it can feel tedious to plan out classroom design at times, creating and implementing these items is something that many educators look forward to. Educators should consider what is controllable and practical for effective teaching—simplicity is fine. If visual supports will be used in the classroom, ensure the design is evidence-based. While websites like Pinterest or Teachers Pay Teachers can be wonderful sources of inspiration, they do not always contain content that has been thoroughly researched. For example, behavior clip charts highlighting classroom design and visual supports are commonly found on websites. However, this type of visual support is generally ineffective in creating lasting behavior change, and research has shown that it can potentially cause harm to students (Jung & Smith, 2018; McIntosh et al., 2020).

When implementing functional design in the classroom, teaching students how to use the items and supports is crucial. Visual schedules are an effective tool and can foster student independence (Foster-Cohen & Mirfin-Veitch, 2017), but students must be *taught* how to use them early on and often. Students can only be expected to use support with instruction and practice. Educators spend the first few weeks of the school year teaching students classroom procedures and expectations—ensuring the appropriate use of visuals and functional design is no different.

5. Review and make changes. One of the greatest skills that educators bring to the classroom is the ability to be flexible. Understanding when a lesson is going well

Morning Routine

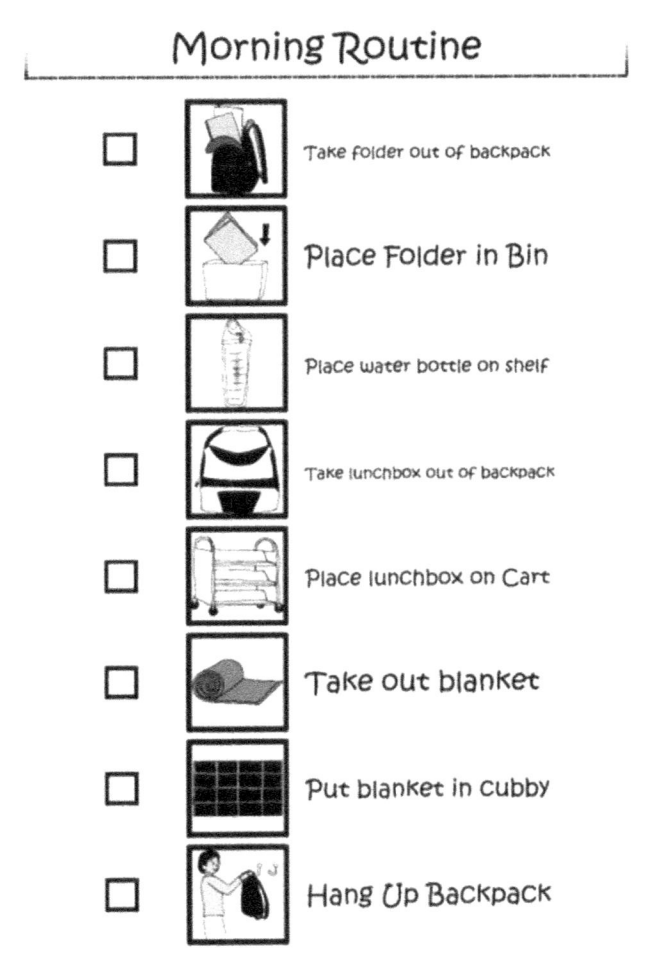

☐ [image] Take folder out of backpack

☐ [image] Place Folder in Bin

☐ [image] Place water bottle on shelf

☐ [image] Take lunchbox out of backpack

☐ [image] Place lunchbox on Cart

☐ [image] Take out blanket

☐ [image] Put blanket in Cubby

☐ [image] Hang Up Backpack

Figure 12.7. Purposeful Classroom Decor Example: Morning Routine
Source: Created by authors using LessonPix.

and when to make changes (even mid-lesson) is an essential trait of an effective educator. While this process tends to be obvious for academic instruction, it is often overlooked when environmental changes need to be made. Educators should ensure that their classroom design is assessed and reviewed regularly. Classroom dynamics can change as the school year progresses, and changes may need to be made to better support students. Basic data collection on student on-task/off-task behavior can be accomplished periodically throughout the day, and needed environmental changes can be implemented in real time. Visuals that relate to previous lessons (e.g., anchor charts) should be taken down when the class moves on to a new lesson, and educators should make adjustments, when needed, to remain relevant for classroom needs.

Careful consideration and planning appear to be crucial in effectively designing a classroom. Individualization and an aesthetically pleasing environment are important for student and educator comfort. That does not mean that the classroom design needs an overarching theme or that educators should spend significant money and effort creating and implementing it. Purposeful moderation appears to be the key when designing the classroom. Educators should ensure that if an item is on the wall or in the environment, it serves a purpose. Small changes can make a big impact, and classroom design is one of the easiest environmental variables to modify (Cheryan et al., 2014). Remember that needs may change yearly or week to week; educators should be aware of these changes and adjust support as needed. Students and school staff spend countless hours in the classroom environment throughout the school year. It would be ideal if educational spaces were comfortable so that effective learning could occur.

CHOOSING AND ORGANIZING LEARNING MATERIALS

Students can do amazing things in the classroom with the right resources. A typical day in any classroom will have varied activities. For example, while learning about the plant life cycle for science, one student could be near a sink, wetting a paper towel to wrap around a seed for an experiment in growing plants. Meanwhile, another student could be near a bin with soil, potting a sprouted seed. Across the room, three students could be grouped together using watercolors and colored pencils to paint and draw portraits of plants in various stages of the life cycle. In another area of the room, two other students are located at the whiteboard using dry-erase markers, rulers, and calculators to graph the growth changes of each student's plant experiment progress. The learning throughout the room is varied, focused, and substantial. Having the right materials is crucial to this type of learning environment.

It can be difficult to find guidance addressing how to set up materials within the classroom. The Montessori model, which has been used in classrooms for over a century, may be familiar to some elementary educators. This method allows access to classroom materials within a prepared environment, lends a focus on student choice in learning, and provides students with a relatively higher level of freedom than traditional classrooms (Thayer-Bacon, 2012). Activities and materials are arranged in locations that are easily and freely accessible for students to engage in a self-directed approach to learning (Marshall, 2017). While there are schools and classrooms dedicated to the Montessori method, there is limited research that addresses how students specifically engage with and access materials. Accessing classroom materials is a small but potentially important factor in effective classroom setup.

Another important piece of the environmental puzzle is which supplies to choose for a classroom. An exhaustive list of which school supplies and the quantity necessary to effectively teach at any grade level does not exist in the academic literature. Pencils, glue, various types of paper, scissors, erasers, tissues, and hand sanitizer are common needs. As the grade level increases, calculators and binders may be added. Since there is no best practice for selecting school supplies, different teachers choose different items for their respective classrooms.

As elementary-aged students fall within the preoperational and concrete operational stages of development (Ediger, 2012), it is important to remember that the chosen supplies should be age and ability appropriate. Early education children will use larger-sized crayons and blunt-tipped scissors that are small enough to fit in little hands. Primary grades may go through construction paper, glue, and crayons faster than intermediate students. Likewise, fifth- or sixth-grade students use more advanced supplies such as sharp scissors, notebooks, and calculators to complete their assignments. Educators ensure supplies are chosen from a "common-sense" lens and remain developmentally appropriate.

How to Implement

Assess the space. Consider what is available in the space (e.g., storage closet, shelving, cabinets, teacher desk, classroom furniture, tables, windowsills) and what activities will be done in the classroom. A treasure trove of supplies and materials will not be helpful if there is no place to store *and* easily access them.

Quality over quantity. The quality of the supplies matters just as much as having a varied and full stock in the classroom. Students need to feel empowered while learning and not be discouraged because of products that do not meet the needs of the activity. For example, certain crayons break easily, flake off while in use, leave chunks of crayon on the paper, are not cohesive in look, and are often requested not to be provided on school supply lists. When students are using supplies that produce disappointing results, it can diminish feelings about the finished product. Diminished feelings can result in a cyclical effect where students do not enjoy the learning process and are thus inclined to avoid task completion or participation altogether. Staplers should have the right size staples, smoothly staple papers, and be easy to use. Markers should have caps and remain moist for use.

Educators should consider where they will store supplies within the classroom (e.g., on a cabinet, table, shelf, in a bucket). Whatever method is chosen to organize materials, the arrangement should be purposeful and facilitate the activity (Stronge et al., 2011). For items used more frequently, plan to keep them in areas more easily accessible to educators and students. Less frequently used tools can be stored in areas out of the way of the ongoing lesson but still accessible if needed (e.g., in a cabinet, behind a curtain). Rarely used materials or materials that require supervision can be put away and brought out when appropriate. Materials that are more expensive, are a safety concern, or need higher staff support may require extensive planning and teaching before use.

Also, specific student needs should not be overlooked. There are differences between right-handed and left-handed supplies. Binders with the rings on the left are often more difficult to use for left-handed students. The same point could be made of left-handed scissors or even desks with built-in arm support on the right. For the left-handed students in the class, tables, left-handed scissors, and loose-leaf paper (as opposed to spiral bound) may be more comfortable, thus resulting in more successful focus and assignment completion. If some students require adapted materials (e.g., Rocket Pencils, adapted scissors), educators will need to know as soon as possible. Read IEPs and Section 504 plans and talk to the school occupational therapist or special education teacher to ensure that the required materials for *all* of the students who will be learning in the classroom will be available.

Implement. When allowing students access to materials in the classroom, educators should be realistic that things may not go according to plan. However, ensuring that students are taught how to access and use materials before being set loose will greatly increase the likelihood of success. Consider when and how it is appropriate to use each tool and explicitly teach these procedures to students. It may be necessary to do this many times at the start of the year and to incorporate procedure refreshers if problems arise. While it may be frustrating if students are not interacting with classroom tools appropriately, it is a learning opportunity. Taking that time to stop, instruct, model, practice, and provide praise for students who use materials appropriately can be helpful to the ongoing harmony of the classroom.

Another frequent concern for teachers is limited availability of classroom supplies. There are several ways to access needed supplies for any classroom so that teachers do not have to use personal funds to provide them. Donation requests via a quick note or newsletter can be sent to parents providing information about upcoming activities and the supplies that will be needed. Oftentimes, additional resources such as milk jugs, plastic bags, and cardboard rolls from paper towels can be brought in from students' homes without parents having to spend any money. Consider an Amazon wish list or other classroom needs list with easy-to-scan QR codes for those who may want to donate. If asking parents for additional resources has proven unfruitful, teachers can ask the school parent–teacher association (PTA) for classroom donations. The PTA often supports these endeavors for classrooms. Another option for requesting classroom donations is to contact local businesses for support. Churches sometimes sponsor a classroom for a year, or businesses with excess supplies such as paper and pencils will donate to schools. Last, another resource for requesting donations can be setting up a donors-choose list online and sharing it on social media platforms. Friends and family of teachers and students can view and purchase from the list, and by creating the list of various items, there is room for donations at any budget.

Teachers are discouraged from becoming wasteful with excessive supplies. Rationing items such as construction paper or pencils will ensure that students have what is needed throughout the entire school year. Hoarding and bickering can be avoided by sharing items where there is a plentiful stock. While we have addressed selecting and organizing materials in depth, designing activities that require fewer materials is also a perfectly valid option. Instruction does not always need "stuff" to be effective.

Review and revise. Once a clear method has been set up for students to access classroom materials, it is essential that educators observe if instruction has been successful. Are students using classroom materials appropriately? Do they know where and how to access what they need? If not, reteaching or even a change in procedure may be needed to meet student needs. Assess the flow of the classroom. Observe where students are congregating and where hiccups are happening. Are students in one area to access supplies for too long? If so, this may lead to distraction or other inappropriate behavior. Are students submitting work in the correct location? Count how many students follow classroom procedures to access materials during key transitions. This does not need to occur daily but every few weeks to ensure effective procedures. It may be necessary to make changes to procedures and plans frequently.

CONCLUSION

Elementary educators can provide effective support and instruction to promote student learning early in students' educational experience. While there are several instructional methods and individualized interventions that can be implemented in the classroom, a well-structured physical environment can provide students with support both academically and behaviorally. Ensuring that the classroom setting is set up to meet the class's needs as a whole can require some additional planning and effort on the part of educators. Child development and professional standards should be considered before setting up the physical space.

This chapter has highlighted several ways that educators can arrange and consider the use of their physical environment to address student needs and prevent many of the classroom management issues that can arise in an elementary classroom. Setting up the physical environment (e.g., spacing, traffic patterns), classroom design (e.g., decor, lighting, and visual supports), and the deliberate choice and organization of learning materials should be considered before student arrival. However, setting up the classroom environment is an ever evolving and ongoing process, and what was effective at the beginning of the year may not be so three months in. Educators should ensure that they continue to assess and update their setting based on student needs.

REFERENCES

Act, E. S. S. (2015). Every Student Succeeds Act (ESSA). *Pub. L*, 114–195.

Barrett, P., Zhang, Y., Moffat, J. & Kobbacy, K. (2013). A holistic, multi-level analysis identifying the impact of classroom design on pupils' learning. *Building & Environment*, 59, 678–689.

Bullard, J. (2010). *Creating environments for learning: Birth to age eight*. Prentice Hall.

Cash, C., & Twiford, T. (2010). Improving student achievement and school facilities in a time of limited funding. Connexions Project.

Cheryan, S., Ziegler, S. A., Plaut, V. C., & Meltzoff, A. N. (2014). Designing classrooms to maximize student achievement. *Policy Insights from the Behavioral and Brain Sciences*, 1(1), 4–12. https://doi.org/10.1177/2372732214548677

Cohen, A., & Demchak, M. (2018). Use of visual supports to increase task independence in students with severe disabilities in inclusive educational settings. *Education and Training in Autism and Developmental Disabilities*, 53(1), 84–99.

Custom materials. LessonPix. (n.d.). https://lessonpix.com/

Day, S. L., Connor, C. M., & McClelland, M. M. (2015). Children's behavioral regulation and literacy: The impact of the first-grade classroom environment. *Journal of School Psychology*, 53(5), 409–428. https://doi.org/10.1016/j.jsp.2015.07.004

Ediger, M. (2012). Recent leaders in American education. *College Student Journal*, 46(1),174–177.

Fisher, A. V., & Kloos, H. (2016). Development of selective sustained attention: The role of executive functions. In L., Freund, P. McCardle, & J. Griffin (Eds.), *Executive function in preschool age children: Integrating measurement, neurodevelopment and translational research* (pp. 215–237). American Psychological Association.

Foster-Cohen, S., & Mirfin-Veitch, B. (2017). Evidence for the effectiveness of visual supports in helping children with disabilities access the mainstream primary school curriculum. *Journal of Research in Special Educational Needs*, 17(2), 79–86.

From a nation at risk to a nation at hope: Recommendations from the National Commission on Social, Emotional, & Academic Development. (2019). The Aspen Institute.

Godwin, K. E., Seltman, H., Scupelli, P., & Fisher, A. V. (2020). *Attention competition in genuine classrooms: Analysis of the classroom visual environment.* Self-published.

Hanley, M., Khairat, M., Taylor, K., Wilson, R. Cole-Fletcher, R., & Riby, D. (2017). Classroom displays—attraction or distraction? Evidence of impact on attention and learning from children with and without autism. *Developmental Psychology, 53*(7), 1265–1275.

Havik, T., & Westergård, E. (2019). Do teachers matter? students' perceptions of classroom interactions and student engagement. *Scandinavian Journal of Educational Research, 64*(4), 488–507. https://doi.org/10.1080/00313831.2019.1577754

Jacobs, C. (2023). Teacher-approved decoration ideas. *Miss Jacob's Little Learners.* https://missjacobslittlelearners.com/blogs/blog/teacher-approved-decoration-ideas

Jung, L. A., & Smith, D. (2018). Tear down your behavior chart. *Educational Leadership, 76*(1), 12–18.

Kaplan Early Learning Floor Planner. (n.d.). Version (2). *Kaplan Early Learning.* Retrieved September 20, 2023, from https://www.kaplanco.com/

Langford, K. (2017). *The physical classroom environment and its effects on students.* (publication no. 10685517) [Doctoral dissertation, Eastern Oregon University]. ProQuest Dissertations & Theses Global.

Lindstrom Johnson, S., Waasdorp, T. E., Cash, A. H., Debnam, K. J., Milam, A. J., & Bradshaw, C. P. (2017). Assessing the association between observed school disorganization and school violence: Implications for school climate interventions. *Psychology of Violence, 7*(2), 181–191. https://doi.org/10.1037/vio0000045

Marshall, C. (2017). Montessori education: a review of the evidence base. Nature Partner Journals (NPJ) *Science of Learning, 2*(11), 2–9.

Martin, B. (2023, August 1). Classroom seating pattern examples. Canva. https://www.canva.com/design/DAFqsqXNn5c/2XE5aVmQozQ2JUWpZHDnxA/edit

McIntosh, K., Sugai, G., & Simonsen, B. (2020). Ditch the clip! Why clip charts are not a PBIS practice and what to do instead. Center on PBIS, University of Oregon. https://www.pbis.org/resource/ditch-the-clip-why-clip-charts-are-not-a-pbis-practice-and-what-to-do-instead

National Association for the Education of Young Children (NAEYC). (2023). https://www.naeyc.org/PBIS%20Practice%20and%20What%20to%20Do%20Instead.pdf

Nazareno, L. (2014, January 21). Form follows function in classrooms, too! *Education Week.* Retrieved August 5, 2023, from https://www.edweek.org/education/opinion-form-follows-function-in-classrooms-too/2014/01

Olson, L. (Ed.). (2019). (Report). *From a nation at risk to a nation at hope* (pp. 1–80). The Aspen Institute.

Preparing America's students for success. Home | Common Core State Standards Initiative. (n.d.). https://www.thecorestandards.org/

Podolskiy, A. I. (2012). Zone of proximal development. *Encyclopedia of the sciences of learning,* 3485–3487. https://doi.org/10.1007/978-1-4419-1428-6_316

Reinke, W. M. (2023). *Physical classroom structure: The classroom check-up*. Guilford Press. Retrieved July 24, 2023, from https://www.classroomcheckup.org/physicalclassroomstructure/#:~:text=The%20physical%20arrangement%20of%20the,transitions%2C%20and%20prevents%20disruptive%20ehavior

Rosati, N. (2021). Montessori method and universal design for learning: Two methodologies in conjunction for inclusive early childhood education. *Ricerche Di Pedagogia E Didattica*, 16(2), 105–116.

Roskos, K., & Neuman, S. B. (2011). The classroom environment: First, last, and always. *The Reading Teacher*, 65(2), 110–114.

Simmons, K., Carpenter, L., Crenshaw, S., & Hinton, V. (2015). Exploration of classroom seating arrangement and student behavior in a second-grade classroom. *Georgia Educational Researcher*, 12(1), 51–68. https://doi.org/10.20429/ger.2015.120103

Standing, E. (1962). *The Montessori method: A revolution in education*. Academy Library Guild.

Stronge, J. H., Ward, T. J., & Grant, L. W. (2011). What makes good teachers good? A cross-case analysis of the connection between teacher effectiveness and student achievement. *Journal of Teacher Education*, 62(4), 339–355.

Thayer-Bacon, B. (2012). Maria Montessori, John Dewey, and William H. Kilpatrick. *Education and Culture*, 28(1), 3–20.

Vygotsky, L. S. (1978). *Mind in society*. MIT Press.

13

Elementary Instruction and Intervention

Kathleen M. Randolph, Julie Atwood, Glenna Billingsley, and Kevin T. Muns

INCREMENTAL CHANGES IN A classroom environment can have a significant impact on both teacher and student success (Cheryan et al., 2014). While the previous chapter highlighted environmental changes that can be made to better support all students in the classroom (e.g., access to materials, classroom décor, classroom procedures, physical setup), these interventions are not always sufficient to change all student behavior. As educators assess and provide support in the classroom, they may need to provide more targeted and intensive interventions (i.e., Tier 2 or Tier 3) for students who are not progressing with universal (i.e., Tier 1) interventions (Scheuermann et al., 2022).

To review, universal interventions, referred to as Tier 1 or primary interventions, are designed for use with all students and prevent about 80% of challenging behavior from ever occurring. Appropriate for all students in Tier 1, explicit instruction (Archer & Hughes, 2010) of behavioral expectations, in addition to posting, reviewing, monitoring, and consistently reinforcing expectations with fidelity, can be incorporated within a schoolwide system (Simonsen et al., 2008b) and at the class level. Explicit instruction provides students with exactly what they need to meet the expectation, and can be coupled with behavior specific praise, often providing errorless learning opportunities for a student, which is the opportunity to perform the behavioral expectation without error, and with positive feedback. Teachers should continue to use explicit instruction for behavioral expectations as they increase the intervention intensity (i.e., Tier 2, Tier 3) provided to students beyond Tier 1.

Creating positive expectations and class routines and consistently praising and encouraging students to follow them are Tier 1 interventions. High-leverage instructional practices and behavior techniques are intertwined because quality instruction and appropriate behavior must occur simultaneously in a classroom where optimal learning occurs. When planning for students in the classroom, teachers typically focus only on academics, relying heavily on instruction to ensure students meet specific benchmarks. Behavior planning is equally as important as academic planning and should be planned in conjunction with academics. Evidence-based practices in classroom management can be applied to support students behaviorally, such as providing structure and predictability in the classroom environment (Simonsen et al., 2008a), which includes explicit instruction (Archer & Hughes, 2010) of schoolwide and classroom expectations. As well, providing judicious opportunities to respond to and interact with instructional material is an example of academic planning that will positively influence behavior (Common et al., 2020).

However, utilizing even the very best practices of Tier 1 may not be sufficient to address learning and behavioral needs for all students. And, yes, we must teach all students—not just those eager to learn and those adept in social and behavioral skills. Tier 2 and Tier 3 interventions are those that provide additional layers of academic and behavioral support without removing less intensive, individualized techniques. Specialized academic and behavioral strategies and principles are necessary to support students with significant learning and behavioral needs, and applying evidence-based practices increases the effectiveness of school-wide positive behavior programs. Advanced tiers (i.e., Tiers 2 and 3) support individual students with interventions prescribed specifically to address each student's unique challenges. This chapter will discuss interventions that are more comprehensive and matched with individual students' behavior.

It takes time and energy to determine which intervention(s) is appropriate for a specific student; however, teachers should resist the tendency to rely on more reactive strategies to address student behavior (Shook, 2012) as such strategies do not produce lasting change. Antecedent interventions provide proactive support to change student behavior, which includes instruction in replacement behaviors as effective alternatives (Cooper et al., 2020; Korpershoek et al., 2016). While the use of visual supports and environmental changes was introduced in chapter 12, this chapter discusses in more detail how to use these strategies to promote student success on an individualized level.

Chapter Objectives

Academic performance and appropriate behavior are closely related. Students learn when their behavior is consistent with school and classroom expectations. Similarly, students' behavior is better when they are actively engaged in the learning environment. The objectives in this chapter provide educators with the essential tools to help students succeed academically and behaviorally.

1. Identify evidence-based interventions for elementary classroom management to address challenging behavior when universal interventions have not sufficiently changed behavior.
2. Recognize that instructional practices and behavior techniques are intertwined because learning necessitates appropriate behavior.
3. Describe Tier 2 and Tier 3 strategies that prevent inappropriate behavior and promote improved behavior in elementary classrooms.
4. Select a behavioral strategy that effectively addresses a particular behavior challenge.
5. Describe ways to combine multiple strategies to increase appropriate behaviors that will promote learning.

Behavior Planning and Supports

According to the National Center for Intensive Intervention (NCII, 2021), many students with significant learning and behavioral needs are also those who have disabilities including autism spectrum disorder (ASD), emotional and behavior disabilities, and learning disabilities (NCII, 2021). Approximately 60% of students with disabilities are included with their peers in the general education classroom for more than 80% of the school day (Gilmour, 2018). Students displaying challenging behaviors often require behavior support and specialization that is outside the scope of performance of general or special education teachers, and these students require support in addition to those provided schoolwide (i.e., universal or Tier 1).

Once schoolwide strategies (i.e., universal, Tier 1) have been in place and consistently supported and reinforced, teachers can identify students who need more robust interventions to meet expectations. Some interventions designed as universal techniques can be used in advanced tiers by individualizing them for a particular student. For example, behavior-specific praise can be increased and targeted to address a particular behavior. Strategies that are successful at Tier 1 for larger groups of students can be intensified for individual students to help them meet success if they are used in a more targeted and intentional way, focused on the individual student's needs.

For resources, see table 13.1.

Changing the Physical Environment

Basic changes to the educational space may not be effective for all students; educators must rearrange and reorganize to meet the needs of their specific students. Rearranging a student's physical space can provide low-cost support and supervision prior to the occurrence of challenging behavior. This use of more proactive (i.e., antecedent) interventions is a powerful tool in reducing the reliance on reactive strategies and helps to focus efforts on preventing challenging behavior from occurring prior to reacting to the occurrence of such behavior (Korpershoek et al., 2016; Meadan et al., 2016).

Description. Rearranging a student's physical space can and should look differently for each student, as this intervention should be individualized to meet each student's needs. While one student may need their desk moved closer to instruction or adult supervision, another may need a visual boundary added to designate their area. There are many unpleasant or aversive stimuli in the environment that can be reduced to have an impact on student behavior, including noise level, lights, crowding, and overstimulating visuals (Meadan et al., 2016). Prior to considering more

Table 13.1. Resources

Center on PBIS	This website walks users through PBIS and its applications.	https://www.pbis.org/pbis/what-is-pbis
Explicit Instruction	This online resource provides background and video exemplars of explicit instruction.	https://explicitinstruction.org/

Note: PBIS = positive behavioral interventions and supports. *Source*: Compiled by the authors.

intensive intervention, educators should assess the target student's physical space to determine if minimal changes in the environment are appropriate (Banks, 2014).

Identify the Target Behavior. Educators should clearly identify and define behavior in order to change in the student's environment in a measurable way and collect data on how often and to what degree the behavior is occurring in each educational setting (Cooper et al., 2020). Data may show that the target behavior is only occurring in one area (e.g., P.E. or music) or during one activity (e.g., math). Ensuring that school staff have a clear understanding of what the behavior looks like and where it is happening will help in determining what impactful changes can be made to the student's physical space.

Find the Function. While modifying the student's environment may appear to be a relatively simple task, it should be approached with care. Before making any changes, educators should assess *why* the behavior is occurring, by determining the function of the behavior— escape, attention, tangible, or sensory (Cooper et al., 2020; Meadan et al., 2016). School staff should collect preliminary data and, if necessary, obtain consent for a functional behavior assessment (FBA) to guide development of a hypothesis, which helps to determine why the behavior is occurring or what the student is getting out of the behavior. If a student is engaging in a behavior to escape a task or demand, placing their desk at the back of the classroom is not ideal. However, if they are engaging in a behavior to access attention or a reaction from a specific peer, moving their desk to another area might help to prevent that behavior.

Plan and Implement Environmental Changes. Changes to a student's physical space will follow the needs of the student and the classroom and can be relatively simple. Adjustments to the way a student accesses materials, or where they sit in the classroom can have an impact on behavior (Banks, 2014). Teachers should ask several questions when determining such changes. Does the student need to be seated closer to the teacher or a positive peer model? Does the student need to sit further from a specific peer or item (e.g., computers or iPads)? Does the student need easy access to certain materials or areas in the classroom (e.g., bathroom or calm-down corner)? It may be easier to deliver reinforcement or to address inappropriate behavior when a student is seated closer to where instruction typically takes place (Banks, 2014; Gordon, 2001; Poole et al., 2019). First consider how a student can meet success in their current area, not only if the student needs to move to a different area within the classroom. If additional supports are needed, these supports can be easily paired with other interventions and strategies, including changes in the environment (McConomy et al., 2021).

Monitor Progress. Ongoing and consistent data collection is an important step in the behavior change process. Educators should continue to collect data during implementation and after interventions are in place (Cooper et al., 2020). School site teams should meet and review data regularly during the intervention process to determine if additional interventions are needed interventions need to be faded.

Research Support. Most of the research conducted that addresses the physical space of the classroom addresses the classroom as a whole rather than a specific student. However, research has shown that the way a classroom is arranged can impact student behavior (Zaheer et al., 2019). Black et al. (2016) investigated preservice teacher responses to student avatar behavior and noted higher levels of student rebellion when preservice teachers engaged in higher levels of retreatism (e.g., lack of proximity). While there is a significant lack of research that has investigated changes to student seating as it relates to behavior, Simmons et al. (2015) note that classroom arrangement should meet the needs of each student.

Case Study Example—Rearranging the Environment

Miss April is a first-year kindergarten teacher at Ocean View Elementary School. She carefully set up her classroom at the beginning of the school year but has noticed that Sanjay is struggling to remain in his seat throughout the school day and often wanders the classroom. Sanjay often takes things off other student's desks and tries to play with the toys put away on shelves. Miss April typically must interrupt her teaching to redirect Sanjay and prompt him to return to his seat. She decides that she would like to make some environmental changes before calling in the school resource team for help. Miss April collects data on how often and how long Sanjay is out of his seat along with how many disruptions he makes throughout the school day. Her data show that he is out of his seat most often during circle time and math, and that he sits an average of three minutes before he gets out of his seat.

Miss April decides to seat Sanjay closer to the SmartBoard so that he will be closer to her during these activities. She also talks with Sanjay about why he is getting out of his seat so often and he tells her that moving around helps him think better. Miss April and Sanjay decide to designate an area next to his desk where Sanjay can walk without disrupting others or instruction. They put a small sticker on the tile to remind Sanjay to identify his boundary and agree that this area is available if he follows the classroom rules (e.g., quiet voice, hands to himself). Miss April continues to collect data and notes a significant decrease in disruptive behavior. She also notices that with Sanjay so much closer to her, she can give him positive praise for remaining in his seat for longer periods of time. Sanjay and Miss April are happy with his progress.

For resources, see table 13.2.

Visual Supports

Visual supports can be used throughout the school day in all environments to support learning and positive behavior for all children (Cote et al., 2014). Visual supports require effort and buy-in from school staff to implement; parents and students report positive attitudes on the use of visuals and a long-term sustainable impact (Foster-Cohen & Mirfin-Veitch, 2017). While intensive implementation may

Table 13.2. Resources

IRIS Center	Case study on "Effective Room Arrangement: Elementary"	https://iris.peabody.vanderbilt.edu/wp-content/uploads/pdf_case_studies/ics_effrmarr_elementary.pdf
IRIS Center	Case study on "Effective Room Arrangement: Middle and High School"	https://iris.peabody.vanderbilt.edu/wp-content/uploads/pdf_case_studies/ics_effrmarr_middle_high.pdf

Source: Compiled by the authors.

initially be required, visual supports have been associated with improved outcomes for students in multiple environments (Zimmerman et al., 2017).

Description. Visual supports are described as concrete visual cues (e.g., pictures, icons) that provide the viewer with information that is also paired with a verbal description (Sam & Autism Focused Intervention Resources & Modules [AFIRM], 2015). While many educators may think of visual supports as simple visual schedules with laminated pictures and a strip of Velcro on the back, visuals have a variety of uses (Cote et al., 2014; Zimmerman et al., 2017). Visual supports can be used to teach and support multiple topics and skills (e.g., classroom expectations, academic skills, social skills, problem solving, and vocational skills), support the maintenance and generalization of previously learned skills, and help foster student independence (Aspiranti et al., 2019; Diamond, 2018; Knight et al., 2014; Zimmerman et al., 2017). Incorporating visual supports into daily classroom routines and instruction assists in reducing students' anxiety and helps serve as additional prompts while not requiring additional staff (Foster-Cohen & Mirfin-Veitch, 2017). While planning and prepping is necessary to set up the use of visual supports (i.e., printing, cutting, laminating), implementation of visual supports is simple (Zimmerman et al., 2017). Implementing visual supports can be done systematically using three easy steps—planning, implementation, and monitoring—which ensure effective creation, instruction, and use in any environment.

Planning. Visual supports look and function differently for each student. A crucial first step in the planning process is identifying the needs of the specific student using visual supports. Collect data on the challenging behavior school staff observe throughout the day. What are the student's strengths? What skills does the student need to be successful? Educators should assess the specific needs of each student for whom visual supports are being created to determine the most appropriate type of visual and how the student will interact with it. While a student with limited communication skills might benefit from a visual communication system, a student who struggles to play appropriately with peers may be better served with a visual prompting them to use specific social skills (e.g., ask to share a toy). Educators can then organize the needed materials and create the visual supports based on what works for their environment and student interests. This process does not involve extensive costs for educators; it can be done using available resources (Cote et al., 2014; Zimmerman et al., 2017).

Implementation. Sam and AFIRM (2015) identify three additional points in the effective implementation of visual supports: instruction, prompt fading, and consistency. Students should be taught *how* to use visual supports when the intervention is introduced and as needed throughout use (Gauvreau & Schwartz, 2013; Zimmerman et al., 2017). Students require instruction and prompting to begin and continue to use visual supports independently. However, to foster independent use of visual supports, educators should strive to fade visual prompts as quickly as possible. It is also important to remember that for an intervention to be effective, it must be used with consistency across environments. For example, if a student needs a visual schedule for the classroom, that schedule will likely need to travel with them for use in all school environments (e.g., physical education, music, lunch).

Monitoring. Educators should collect data on student behavior regularly to determine if an intervention has been successful, if changes, revisions, or adjustments need to occur (Sam & AFFIRM, 2015), or if visuals need to be paired with another individualized intervention (e.g., task analysis, the Premack principle, token economy) for maximum effect (Billingsley, 2016; Herrod et al., 2023; McConomy et al., 2021). As students begin to display more independent usage of visual supports, educators should assess whether a less intrusive visual is needed, or if the visual can be faded from use. For example, instead of a visual schedule that includes every activity, reduce the visual schedule to subject blocks.

Research Support. While there are several studies on visual supports in schools involving students with disabilities, there is a need for additional research on visual supports with early elementary students without disabilities. Zimmerman and colleagues (2017) emphasize the importance of teaching students to use visual supports prior to expecting independent use in an inclusive preschool setting. While visual activity schedules tested in their study resulted in a reduction in challenging behavior, the students were not able to use visual supports independently in environments other than their classroom. Foster-Cohen and Mirfin-Veitch (2017) provide an example where students may need additional interventions. Visual supports were used to successfully assist several children with disabilities in accessing the general education curriculum in primary schools. However, despite positive perceptions from parents and students, there were several students in this study who did not respond to the visual supports intervention and required additional intervention.

Case Study Example: Use of Visual Supports

Ms. Solis is a third-grade general education teacher at Meadow Creek Elementary School. She is concerned about a student in her class, Steven, who struggles with transition between activities. Steven will often stand in the middle of the classroom and refuse to move until Ms. Solis physically comes over to tell him what to do next. Ms. Solis collects data on Steven's behavior and notes that he is unable to independently follow multistep directions. Ms. Solis decides to implement a visual supports activity intervention for Steven to use during transitions that will help him know the expectations and what to do next without additional prompting. She creates a laminated task list for each key transition that allows Steven to cross tasks off a *to-do column* with a dry-erase marker. Ms. Solis teaches Steven how to use the visual support and prompts him through the process for the first few transitions. After Steven demonstrates that he can use the visual with minimal support, she slowly fades out her assistance until he is able to use the schedule independently and continues to collect data. Ms. Solis analyzes her data the next month and notices that with the use of a visual support, Steven can independently transition between activities successfully without additional prompting from staff.

For resources, see table 13.3.

Table 13.3. Resources

AFIRM Guide	Step-by-step guide in the implementation of visual supports.	https://afirm.fpg.unc.edu/sites/afirm.fpg.unc.edu/files/imce/resources/VS%20Step-by-Step.pdf
IRIS Center	Instructional modules on the use of evidence-based practices.	https://iris.peabody.vanderbilt.edu/module/asd2/

Source: Compiled by the authors.

POSITIVE REINFORCEMENT SYSTEMS

Environmental changes may not be enough to address more significant student behavior. It is common for students to need multiple, concurrent interventions at Tier 2 or Tier 3 to be successful (Klingbeil et al., 2019; Majeika, 2020). The following strategy addresses student behavior by increasing or modifying the schedule of reinforcement within the environment.

Token Economy

Token economies are simple, low-cost interventions that have been successfully used with students with and without disabilities (Jowett et al., 2016; Klein, 2020; Soares et al., 2016). Token economies are generally effective at addressing a wide range of student behavior (Grünke, 2019; Soares et al., 2016) and are associated with increases in student performance and self-esteem (Maggin et al., 2011; Smith et al., 2022).

Description. A token economy is a system that aims to increase pro-social, appropriate behavior through a structured reinforcement schedule that is meaningful to the student (Boerke & Reitman, 2014). The teacher provides tokens for identified pro-social behavior that are later exchanged for backup reinforcers or preferred items/activities (Cooper et al., 2020). Providing tokens immediately following an identified appropriate behavior allows educators to positively acknowledge student success without interrupting the flow of learning (e.g., nonvocally; Kazdin, 1977).

While token economies are relatively simple, they do require prior planning to ensure that they are correctly implemented (Soares et al., 2016). Heiniger and colleagues (2022) identify eight steps in the implementation of an effective token economy: (1) identifying target behaviors, (2) assessing student preferences, (3) determining a schedule of reinforcement and exchange rate, (4) creating a communication plan, (5) monitoring progress, (6) generalizing tokens, (7) fading tokens, and (8) shifting to self-monitoring.

Identify Target Behaviors. The first step in the creation of a token economy is to identify the behavior that needs to be addressed. Token economies yield positive results in addressing a wide variety of student behavior (Grünke, 2019; Soares et al., 2016). However, these behaviors should be defined in a way that is clear and measurable to all who may be interacting with the student and implementing the token economy and should include examples and non-examples of the target behavior (Cooper et al., 2020; Heiniger et al., 2022). Token economies generally focus on expected behaviors, those that educators would like to increase (e.g., using appropriate replacement behaviors), however, token economies have also been used to decrease inappropriate behavior (Klein, 2020).

Preference Assessment. Student preferences should be considered when designing the type of tokens and selecting backup reinforcers that the items tokens are exchanged for (Heiniger et al., 2022). Preference assessments can be used to identify students' interests and things students would like in exchange for earned tokens. Assessments can take many forms, including questionnaires, observation of play, formal trial assessments, or simple questions from the teacher. Preferences can change frequently with young children, and it may be necessary to conduct assessments regularly to ensure token economies remain effective (Cooper et al., 2020).

Determine Schedules of Reinforcement and Exchange Rate. Educators should create a schedule prior to implementing a token economy to ensure consistent token distribution (Heiniger et al., 2022). This includes giving a student a token for a predetermined number of identified appropriate behaviors (e.g., one token for every five completed math problems) or for engaging in a behavior for a specific time period (e.g., for remaining in their seat for five minutes). The schedule should be individualized to meet a student's needs. Expectations should be realistic and data based (Heiniger et al., 2022). For example, if data show that a student can remain in their seat for an average of three minutes at a time, it would be inappropriate to provide a token every five minutes, as the student would not access reinforcement often enough. The schedule of reinforcement can and should change based on data.

It is important to plan when and how the student will exchange tokens for backup reinforcers as well as the cost of those items/activities. Pairing token economies with a visual support, like a menu of reinforcers and their cost, is helpful to show students exactly how many tokens are required for each item or activity and when and how they can access them (Heiniger et al., 2022). Exchange times and cost should be realistic and individualized but can be changed based on student progress. Educators should take care when putting schedules and costs in place, as students can stop responding (i.e., reach satiation) if they reach a certain threshold, or may give up if they figure that they will never earn the predetermined number of tokens by exchange time (Cihon et al., 2019). The use of response cost (e.g., fines or fees paid with earned tokens for inappropriate behavior) should be done sparingly (Heiniger et al., 2022).

Communicate. Communication is a key factor in the success of any intervention. Incorporating the student and other stakeholders (e.g., teachers, administrators, paraprofessionals, and parents) into token economies planning could increase buy-in (Heiniger et al., 2022). Ensuring that everyone is on the same page will assist teams implementing token economies consistency as intended.

Monitor Progress. Ensuring that student progress is properly documented is an important component in any intervention (Heiniger et al., 2022; Soares et al., 2016). Educators should collect data on the number of tokens that are earned/exchanged throughout the day and how often the target behaviors occur. Collecting accurate data will help school teams identify if the intervention is working as intended or if adjustments need to be made in an area of implementation (e.g., schedules of reinforcement).

Generalization. Once the token economy is in place and has been used successfully, it should be generalized to other settings and with other individuals within the school environment (Cooper et al., 2020; Heiniger et al., 2022). This can look different depending on the student but could include other school staff providing tokens, or incorporating token economies in other classrooms (e.g., music, art, etc.). Ensuring that a clear plan is in place and that it has been communicated effectively to all staff will assist educators in implementing the token economies with consistency in all environments.

Fading. While token economies have been shown to be effective, educators should work toward fading this intervention when possible—systematically removing and replacing it with something more natural (Cooper et al., 2020; Heiniger et al., 2022). Educators should assess student progress regularly. Token economies can be faded in a number of ways: the cost of backup reinforcers can increase, exchange times can be altered, or the tokens themselves can be altered (Cooper et al., 2020; Heininger et al., 2022). Focusing on fading will help avoid student dependence on external reinforcement (Matson & Boisjoli, 2009). Without a fading procedure or plan, students can become reliant on tokens to engage in appropriate behavior (Anderman & Anderman, 2021; Kazdin, 1977; Matson & Boisjoli, 2009).

Shift to Self-Monitoring. Token economies offer a chance for students to practice monitoring their own behavior (Heininger et al., 2022). Incorporating students into the intervention process will allow them to see their progress by seeing how many tokens they have earned and helps them make behavioral changes as they go throughout their day. By encouraging students to be more independent and natural in monitoring their own behavior, educators will be better able to address the needs of their classroom rather than repeatedly addressing one student (Heiniger et al., 2022).

Research Support. While there have been many research studies conducted on the use of token economies in a variety of environments and ways (Kim et al., 2022; Soares et al., 2016; Smith et al., 2022), there has been less research on the use of token economies with individual students outside of a group system. For example, Williamson and McFadzen (2020) compared a virtual token economy tool to a traditional token economy, which was effective in an elementary setting. While an analysis of token economies research indicates that response-cost components are used in general education classrooms over other school environments (Kim et al., 2022), students report a preference for a traditional token economies system over response-cost (DeJager et al., 2020). Traditional token economies compared to a response-cost or combination system were observed to be the most effective in reducing problem behavior and increasing academic achievement (DeJager et al., 2020).

Case Study Example: Token Economy

Mr. Rogers is a teacher in an inclusive kindergarten classroom. One of his students, Hannah, struggles to remain in her seat and to keep her hands off her peers during classroom activities. Mr. Rogers decides that a token economy system would be an appropriate intervention for her. He collects data on the two behaviors and notes that Hannah is able to remain in her seat for about five minutes at a time and touches peers without prior permission an average of thirteen times per hour. Mr. Rogers completes a preference assessment questionnaire with Hannah and creates a list of backup reinforcers that she can earn with her tokens. Mr. Rogers and Hannah decide to use unicorn (Hannah's favorite animal) stickers on a token-board visual for her to track her tokens. Hannah will be allowed to turn her tokens in twice each day at times designated with Mr. Bennett, the school principal. Mr. Rogers decides that Hannah will earn tokens for every five minutes that she remains in her area and keeps her hands off others. She reviews these expectations with Hannah and the rest of the school team. While implementing the token economy, Mr. Rogers continues to collect data and gradually increases the time that Hannah successfully meets expectations to earn a token until Hannah is able to meet expectations for thirty minutes at a time before she earns a token and cashes them in at the end of the week with Mr. Bennett.

For resources, see table 13.4.

Table 13.4. Resources

IRIS Center	Instructional modules on the use of evidence-based practices.	https://iris.peabody.vanderbilt.edu/module/ecbm/cresource/q2/p07/
PBIS World	Tier 2 interventions and supports.	https://www.pbisworld.com/tier-3/reward-system/

INCREASING STRUCTURE OF TASKS

As educators implement Tier 2 and Tier 3 interventions in the classrooms with students, it may become necessary to add additional interventions and supports to assist students. The following interventions are examples of ways that school staff can layer structure into already-existing classroom routines and activities.

Premack Principle

The Premack Principle, or "Grandma's Law," is an established and often-applied strategy that has been used in a variety of settings and situations (Herrod et al., 2023). This intervention is especially *practitioner friendly*, as it takes advantage of already-established classroom activities and requires little effort from educators (Herrod et al., 2023).

Description. The Premack Principle focuses on pairing a high-probability activity with a low-probability activity so that the high-probability activity is contingent on the occurrence of a non-preferred or low-probability activity (Cooper et al., 2020). This pairing of high- and low-probability activities strengthens the likelihood that the student will engage in or attempt the less-preferred activity (Billingsley, 2016). While the Premack Principle is simple and straightforward, there are several steps to consider prior to implementation.

Educators should first identify preferred student activities. This can be accomplished in several ways, including questionnaires and preference assessments. However, Premack (1959) recommends observation of the student without demands to identify which activities are considered high probability. After high-probability activities have been identified, educators can determine what tasks those activities will be contingent upon, or the low-probability (i.e., non-preferred) activities (e.g., what the teacher wants the student to do). Educators can use first/then statements prior to placing demands on a student to specify the response requirements needed to access the high-probability activity (Trump et al., 2018). For example, a student who enjoys spending time with the custodian but does not typically engage in activities during math class may have a requirement to complete ten math problems successfully to earn five minutes of time with the custodian during lunch cleanup. While the Premack Principle may not be effective for all students, it has several benefits (Herrod et al., 2023). It is simple to use in classroom settings and can be easily paired with other interventions like visual supports (Billingsley, 2016; Herrod et al., 2023; Warren et al., 2021). Use of the Premack Principle can also help break activities into natural segments and can encourage engagement (Herrod et al., 2023).

Research Support. A significant amount of research exists on the use of the Premack Principle in a variety of settings and scenarios (Herrod et al., 2023). Noell and colleagues (2003) used the Premack Principle to increase the accuracy of responding on non-preferred academic tasks for preschool children. Herrod and colleagues (2023) examined 52 studies where the Premack Principle was implemented and although limitations were identified in some of the analyzed studies (e.g., majority of research was conducted prior to 1990), the Premack Principle was identified as promising and effective.

Case Study Example—Premack Principle

Sierra is a paraprofessional who assists a student, Jerica, in a fourth-grade general education classroom. She has noticed that when it is time for writing tasks, Jerica will push her paper away and refuse to complete the assignment. Sierra talks with Jerica about what she likes to do during the day at school and learns that she enjoys helping Mrs. Miller (the school secretary) deliver the mail to the teachers' boxes. The next day, before the writing task is presented, Sierra tells Jerica that if she completes her writing assignments, Sierra will take her to Mrs. Miller to help deliver the mail. Together they write out the first/then schedule, and Sierra draws a picture of Mrs. Miller on the page to remind Jerica. Jerica enthusiastically completes her writing assignment and earns a trip to help Mrs. Miller.

For resources, see table 13.5.

Task Analysis

Task analysis is a method used to teach a variety of multistep tasks (Gold, 1976). While task analysis does require some extra upfront effort from educators, it has been shown to be an efficient strategy that streamlines instruction in a visual way, can be tailored to meet the needs of a diverse group of students, and allows educators to monitor progress and independence during task completion (McConomy et al., 2021). This method is easily combined with other strategies including visual supports and video modeling.

Description. Task analysis is defined as a sequenced list of steps that comprise a task (Moyer & Dardig, 1978). While this may seem simple, care should be taken to ensure that steps are individualized to meet the skill and experience level of the selected student (Cooper et al., 2020). Task analysis breaks down any task that includes a series of logically ordered and discrete skills (McConomy et al., 2021) including daily living skills (e.g., making the bed, getting dressed, setting the table, etc.; Steinbrenner et al., 2020), academic skills (Browder et al., 2018), and social skills (Parker & Kamps, 2011). While similar, task analysis differs from simple checklists, as a checklist can be done in any order (e.g., grocery lists, to-do lists), but a task analysis must be completed in a specific sequence (e.g., brushing teeth; McConomy et al., 2021). Using task analysis is straightforward, as outlined by Gold (1976) in a three-phase cycle (i.e., identify the method for completing the task,

Table 13.5. Resources

Council for Exceptional Children	Simple and quick behavior management tips for the classroom.	https://exceptionalchildren.org/blog/3-simple-and-quick-behavior-management-tips-you-can-implement-your-classroom-tomorrow

define the content, determine the process for teaching) expanded upon by McConomy and colleagues (2021), and is described below.

Identify the Method. Task analysis is a method that should be implemented prior to the skill that educators would like to strengthen (Cooper et al., 2020). To do so, educators must first identify the task that they would like to teach. This can be done several ways (e.g., interview, assessment, or observation). Once a skill has been identified, educators should conduct observation to determine the necessary components of the skill. There are several methods that can be used to record the sequence including observation of the student engaging in the task, observation of a competent performer engaging in the task, executing the task yourself, or seeking expert input (Cooper et al., 2020). A combination of these options is recommended to fully understand the task sequence and to individualize the task analysis to meet the student's needs. If the skill is more difficult or complex (e.g., writing an essay), consultation with an expert like an English language arts teacher is appropriate. If the student struggles with social tasks like play, observation of the student as well as a peer model is necessary.

Define the Content. When a task has been identified and observed, educators should clearly document all steps included within the task into a logical sequential order (McConomy et al., 2021). Educators should ensure that every step is clearly documented within the task analysis. It should be noted that creating a task analysis for an elementary-aged student will look different than a task analysis for an older student (McConomy et al., 2021). Educators should ensure that steps are written in an appropriate and meaningful way for each student (e.g., consider the use of pictures, text, items, etc.). Icons can be moved from a *to-do* to *done* column, or items can be checked off a written list.

Determine the Process for Teaching. Simply creating the task analysis is not enough to provide support for the student; educators must plan how to explicitly teach the student to execute the task and use the task analysis as a guide. Consider if modeling, chaining, or another method is appropriate. Should this task be taught to the student in order from first to last? Or should the educator prompt the student through each step in the task and begin instruction with the last step in the sequence? Once a plan to teach the use of the task analysis has been created, a plan to assess progress should be next. While there are different methods of data collection, assessing independence at each step on the task analysis can be helpful in determining the place in the sequence where additional supports are needed (Kellems et al., 2020; McConomy et al., 2021). Educators should note the level of support (i.e., prompts) needed to perform the task (e.g., partial prompt, verbal prompt, gesture, etc.).

Prior to implementation, educators should ensure that the steps in the task have been appropriately identified (Cooper et al., 2020). Completing the task yourself by following the steps or reading the task out loud to a colleague can help to identify any issues or missing steps. When educators implement the task analysis with a selected student, consider how and when the task analysis should be used in other environments and how it will be faded upon student independence. For example, if a student requires a task analysis to assist with completing the steps of hand washing in the bathroom, should the task analysis be posted in all bathrooms that the student uses? When the student can follow the task analysis independently, the team should then decide how it will be systematically faded.

Table 13.6. Resources

AFIRM	Step-by-step guide for developing a task analysis.	https://afirm.fpg.unc.edu/sites/afirm.fpg.unc.edu/files/imce/resources/TA%20Step-by-Step.pdf
News2You	Overview of task analysis procedures.	https://www.n2y.com/blog/teach-life-skills-with-task-analysis/

Research Support. Research shows that task analysis can be used for a multitude of skills in a variety of environments and ways (McConomy et al., 2021). Cihak et al. (2016) used augmented reality with digital text and pictures to teach elementary-aged students with ASD to use a task analysis to successfully brush their teeth. Veazey and colleagues (2016) successfully used a task analysis with chaining to assist in the teaching of hygiene skills to young females with ASD. The literature shows that teaching steps of a task analysis is an important part of the process that is easily adopted by practitioners (Veazey et al., 2016).

Case Study Example: Task Analysis

Mr. Martin is a fifth-grade teacher at Plum Place Elementary School. He has observed that Sandra is struggling with correctly completing the heading components needed to turn in her writing papers (e.g., name, date, teacher, assignment, etc.). This is slowing down his grading, as he is not able to quickly identify to whom the work belongs. Mr. Martin decides to create a task analysis to help Sandra. He observes Sandra to see what steps she is currently completing and how he can best display the task analysis. Martin then creates a step-by-step sequence of each component needed and the order that they should appear on the paper. He practices with a colleague to make sure that the task is appropriately analyzed. Mr. Martin decides to place a small Post-it note at the top of her assignment page with each step in the sequence. As he introduces the task analysis to Sandra, he models each step in the sequence, in order, before having her complete the steps. The next time he presents the task analysis, he only models the first five steps and progressively removes the model as she becomes more independent. After a few days, Sandra is completing all of the steps in the task analysis independently and asks if she can bring a Post-it with her to her math class so that she can use the support there as well.

For resources, see table 13.6.

COMBINING INTERVENTIONS

While the above strategies have been shown to be effective in addressing student behavior, educators may encounter students who need more intensive intervention. The strategies in this section combine both an increase in structure with schedules of reinforcement to create a more robust support for students.

Check-In/Check-Out

Check-in/check-out (CICO) is one of the most implemented Tier 2 interventions in school settings (LaBrot et al., 2016; Majeika et al., 2022). While CICO does involve more steps and collaborative effort on the part of school staff, it has been shown to not only increase positive behavior but reduce challenging behavior as well (Maggin et al., 2015). CICO is unique, as it works to not only provide direct instruction in appropriate replacement behavior but also to cultivate positive student–teacher relationships (Majeika et al., 2022). This emphasis on relationships has led to high levels of acceptability from educators and other school staff (LaBrot et al., 2016).

Description. CICO is a multistep process that involves the communication of behavioral expectations, coaching, regularly scheduled feedback, and opportunities for earned rewards (Filter et al., 2007; LaBrot et al., 2016). CICO is ideal for students who engage in inappropriate behavior to access attention from adults (Wolfe et al., 2016). This process is designed to allow students to access more frequent and structured positive consequences for appropriate behavior (Maggin et al., 2015). The student has two scheduled meetings, once at the beginning of the day and again at the end of the school day, with a designated adult who facilitates feedback, coaching, and earned rewards. Crone et al. (2010) has outlined key steps in the implementation of CICO, which have been refined in research performed by Majeika et al., (2022) to a six-step daily cycle.

Select an Adult Mentor. The CICO process is designed to facilitate positive relationships between educators and the selected student (Majeika et al., 2022). Therefore, the selection of an appropriate adult mentor is an important step in this intervention. When designing a CICO program for a student, educators should determine which staff member is not only most appropriate to meet with the student but also available on the desired schedule. While a favorite coach may be an already-established trusted adult, if they are frequently out of the building to attend games or practices, they may not be the ideal adult mentor. Consider which staff members have a positive attitude about helping students who may engage in challenging behavior and ensure that a back-up adult is selected in case of absences. An adult mentor includes any appropriate staff member with the time and motivation including, administrators, school resource officers, media specialists, custodians, and more.

Morning Check-In with Mentor. Once an appropriate adult mentor has been selected, a morning check-in should be scheduled with the student (Crone et al., 2010; Majeika et al., 2022). During this meeting, the student receives positive attention that is not dependent on the student engaging in a specific behavior (i.e., noncontingent; Maggin et al., 2015). The mentor adult may provide words of encouragement or help the student set goals for the day.

Track Student Progress. Throughout the school day, teachers and school staff will collect data on the student's goals via the daily behavior tracking system (Crone et al., 2010; Majeika et al., 2022). The daily tracking system is typically a point or score card system that tracks student goals. This can be accomplished in several ways—a daily behavior chart that the student brings from activity to activity or an online tracker that is completed via a program like Google Sheets. This daily data tracker is crucial, as it allows educators to identify environments or activities where the student may be struggling and subsequently provide additional supports. It also allows both the student and educators a structured system to monitor progress toward established goals (Maggin et al., 2015).

Behavior Feedback. As teachers and staff track student progress throughout the school day, this data should be shared with the student at regular intervals (Crone et al., 2010; Maggin et al., 2015; Majeika et al., 2022). Both verbal and written communication (via the behavior tracking system) are important to ensure that the student receives positive feedback or can make adjustments to their behavior throughout the day (Maggin et al., 2015). Many educators have found that the use of the tracking system can serve as a reminder for themselves to ensure that this step is followed throughout the day (Sottilare & Blair, 2023).

Afternoon Check-Out With Mentor. At the end of the school day, the student checks out with their adult mentor. During this time, the student's daily behavior tracking system will be reviewed and the student and mentor will determine if the data show that they have earned a designated reward (Maggin et al., 2015; Majeika et al., 2022). The afternoon check-out is a good opportunity for the mentor adult to provide instruction, coaching, or additional feedback to the student based on teacher reports in the tracking sheet.

When implementing a CICO procedure, educators should remember that this level of support is not intended to be in place forever. While not identified by previous studies, a plan for fading should be in place and reviewed regularly (Cooper et al., 2020). This can look a number of ways including increasing the criteria for earning rewards at the end of the day (as discussed above with token economies), decreasing the number of times the student is provided feedback throughout the school day, or decreasing the number of CICOs for the week (e.g., from each day to every other day to once a week; Sottilare et al., 2023).

Parent Communication. A final component of an effective CICO program is regular communication between the student's home and school (Crone et al., 2010; Maggin et al., 2015, Majeika et al., 2022). This collaboration typically involves the student physically bringing their scorecard home, or the behavior tracker being sent home digitally to be signed by their parent or guardian (Maggin et al., 2015). This communication allows families to actively engage in the intervention at home as well and to provide additional feedback based on the student's behavior during the school day (LaBrot et al., 2016).

Research Support. CICO is an evidence-based and socially valid intervention for students with more significant behavioral needs in schools (Maggin et al., 2015). In an investigation by LaBrot and colleagues (2016) the effectiveness of a modified CICO procedure was evaluated in an early childhood setting. The CICO was determined to be feasible to implement in the early childhood setting and was successful in improving the behavior of participants. Majeika et al. (2022) compared the use of a traditional CICO with a modified CICO that included a system for taking breaks for five elementary students. For most students, there were indiscernible differences between the traditional CICO and modified CICO interventions. Wolfe et al. (2016) conducted a review of CICO literature and found CICO to be successful in improving behaviors that serve a variety of functions (purposes) but found it to be an evidence-based practice for problem behavior maintained by adult attention. In a review of the evidence of CICO and its effectiveness in reducing challenging behavior, Maggin et al. (2015) noted that research focused on individuals showed evidence of effectiveness, while group-based research did not. Further, while CICO has been shown to be effective, it may not be appropriate for all students. Student behavior that is maintained by attention was more likely to be successful with a CICO intervention than those maintained by escape.

Case Study Example: Check-In/Check-Out

Mitchell is a second-grade student at Pietzsch Elementary School. His school team has noticed that he is engaging in a significant number of callouts (i.e., verbal outbursts) throughout the school day and is frequently disrupting class. Mitchell's team collects some preliminary data and determines that the function of the behavior is to gain attention from school staff. They collaborate with Mitchell's mother and decide to put a CICO intervention in place for him. Mrs. Anderson, the principal, thinks that Mrs. Sanders, the PE teacher, should be Mitchell's mentor, as she has sufficient time in the day to conduct the check-ins and check-outs. However, Mrs. Sanders declines, as she thinks that Mitchell just needs more firm discipline and boundaries. Mrs. Anderson asks Mrs. Powell, the school custodian, if she could be the mentor adult for Mitchell, as she knows that Mitchell enjoys helping wipe down the tables after lunch.

The team creates a tracking sheet with each of Mitchell's daily activities in one column and two daily goals in the other. Mitchell can earn up to three points for each goal during each activity, and the team agrees to score him/provide feedback after each activity. Mitchell's team begins the CICO intervention and meets again after three weeks to assess his progress with his mother. When they meet, the team commends Mitchell on his progress. Mrs. Powell is especially impressed with how well he is doing, and the team has seen a significant decrease in callouts throughout the school day. They decide to decrease the number of times that Mitchell receives feedback throughout the day, but still have him continue to check-in and check-out daily.

For resources, see table 13.7.

Behavior Contracting

Behavior contracts (also called contingency contracts) clarify expectations, establish a reward, and provide structure for students who have not responded to Tier 1 supports (Majeika, 2020). These contracts can be used in a number of environments to support a variety of student needs (Alwahbi, 2020; Cooper et al., 2020; Grünke, 2019; Majeika, 2020). Behavior contracts have been shown to be effective in addressing both academic and non-academic skills (Alwahbi, 2020; Grünke, 2019). In addition to their versatility, behavior contracts are low cost and require minimal educator time to create or implement (Majeika, 2020).

Description. Cooper et al. (2020) describes a behavior contract as a document that defines a contingent relationship between the completion of a target behavior and access to a specified reward. Behavior contracts describe how individuals will interact, include student goals, and specify how the student will earn a reward. Behavior contracts have been used for decades in therapeutic environments (Bowman-Perrott et al., 2015; Janz et al., 1984), but have also been shown to be effective in school settings (Cooper et al.,2020; Majeika, 2020). Behavior contracts are

Table 13.7. Resources

Center on PBIS	PowerPoint describing the implementation of CICO.	https://www.pbis.org/resource/check-in-check-out-a-targeted-intervention

unique; they actively plan for educator and student collaboration, which has been shown to increase student engagement (Alwahbi, 2020). Contracts can be used as a stand-alone intervention or as a part of a treatment package (Alwahbi, 2020; Alwahbi & Hua, 2021; Simonsen & Myers, 2015) and typically include a task, a reward, and a way to record progress (Cooper et al., 2020). While this intervention has room for flexibility, Majeika (2020) outlines several crucial steps for not only the creation of effective behavior contracts but implementation as well.

Select Target Behaviors. Prior to determining if a behavior contract is an appropriate intervention for a student, educators should collect behavioral data and identify the behavior that they would like to address (Majeika, 2020). There are behaviors where a behavior contract may not be appropriate, such as high-risk or self-injurious behaviors. However, lower-intensity or higher-frequency behaviors are appropriate for targeting with behavior contracts (Majeika, 2020). Once an educator has identified a target behavior to address with a behavior contract, it is important to involve not only the school site team but the parent and student as well (Cooper et al., 2020). This could involve a full team meeting or a few individual meetings to gain input. Involving the student and other stakeholders in this process enhances buy-in and provides helpful information for teams as they move on to next steps in the behavior management process (Alwahbi, 2020).

Select Goals. After identifying target behaviors and assembling the team, educators can begin to collaborate with the student to create goals (Majeika, 2020). Cooper et al. (2020) suggest that each participant in the contract (e.g., teacher and student) complete a list of what each is already doing to meet this goal and what else they could do to meet the goal. Goals can include both daily and weekly targets and should be measurable (Majeika, 2020).

Set Up Rewards and Reteaching Opportunities. After establishing goals, educators and the student can work together to determine not only what rewards the student would like to earn but also how and when they will earn them (Majeika, 2020). This can be done several ways including simple interviews, lists, or a preference assessment (Cooper et al., 2020). This is also an opportunity to discuss and plan with the student regarding what should happen if daily or weekly goals are not met, and how the student will relearn or refresh their learning on the appropriate behavior.

Draft, Review, and Sign. Once the team has planned out the components of the contract, writing begins. Contracts should include the list of target behaviors, student responsibilities, teacher responsibilities, parent responsibilities (if appropriate), daily goals, rewards received when the goal is met, procedures for when the goal is not met, and a place for each party to sign (Majeika, 2020). It should be clear to everyone who is reading the behavior contracts what their roles and responsibilities are, along with when and how the student will access the reward (Cooper et al., 2020). Educators should consider the age and ability of the student and ensure that they are able to understand the behavior contracts clearly.

Implement the Behavior Contract. Teams should remember that implementing the behavior contract as intended with consistency and fidelity will produce a higher likelihood of success, as with any intervention. Majeika (2020) outlines several key steps in the effective implementation of behavior contracts with students: (1) educators must *teach* the student *how* to engage in the appropriate behavior(s) that are listed on the contract, (2) students should be reminded of the behavior contracts and their goals at specific times throughout the day, (3) data should be collected daily to track progress and assess if the student has met their goal/earned their reward, (4) rewards (or reteaching) should be provided immediately when earned, and (5) the intervention should be maintained with consistency until data indicate that the student is ready for the team to begin fading.

Research Support. Behavior contracts have been researched in a variety of environments, including schools, hospitals, homes, and clinics (Alwahbi, 2020; Alwahbi & Hua, 2021; Cooper et al, 2020). Alwahbi & Hua (2021) compare the use of peer training alone with a behavior contracts and peer training package on social interactions among students with ASD and their peers. While peer training alone was not effective, adding behavior contracts to the package resulted in a significant increase in social interactions from participants. Grünke (2019) used behavior contracts in the classroom to increase student's use of proper punctuation and found an immediate increase in the ratio of correct punctuation when a behavior contract was in place. Improvements were maintained over time, and participants reported that the behavior contracts helped them to attend while increasing their confidence.

Case Study Example: Behavior Contract

Ms. Juanita is a fourth-grade teacher who is working with her student, George, on attempting independent work before giving up or immediately asking for help. Juanita collects data on the behavior and notices that George typically waits an average of ten seconds before yelling to her for help or saying that he can't do the work. Juanita wants George to try at least one or two problems before he says he can't do it or asks for help. She sets up a meeting with George and his mother to discuss the issue. George and Juanita each make a list of what they are currently doing to address the problem as well as what else they could do. George notes that he could try to do one problem before asking for help, and Juanita notes that she could let George do a fewer number of problems on the page to ease his anxiety. They set a goal together that George will try one problem on each independent task before asking for help. George makes a list of things that he would like to work for, and Juanita makes him a choice board for if he meets his goal for the day and the week. They decide that if George does not meet his goal, he does not earn his choice board. They write the contract together and each sign it. George gets a copy for his binder. Before each independent task, Juanita does a review of the content, and quietly reminds George of his contract and goals. Juanita and George review his progress at the end of each day, and after three weeks, George has been able to attempt at least one question on every independent worksheet that week. Juanita and George decide to revise the contract and George agrees to attempt at least two questions for each worksheet moving forward.

For resources, see table 13.8.

Table 13.8. Resources

Intervention Central	Outline of the implementation of behavior contracts.	https://www.interventioncentral.org/behavioral-interventions/challenging-students/behavior-contracts

CONCLUSION

Elementary classrooms should rely on universal interventions to create a classroom where students can learn and feel supported. Such interventions promote appropriate behavior and prevent inappropriate behavior at a high rate. Creating high-quality lessons and having clear expectations and reinforcing students with praise and/or tangible rewards for demonstrating expected behavior are sufficient for most elementary students. Yet, because teachers are tasked with teaching all students, including those with the most challenging behaviors, additional layers of support may be needed. This chapter has provided supports that can be used independently or combined to promote more appropriate behavior that is necessary for learning.

Teachers need interventions that are accessible and require minimal resources (e.g. time and money) to implement. While the strategies presented require some front-end effort to create, they are not difficult or expensive and yield positive results. These strategies promote positive educator/student relationships because these techniques are not aversive or punitive. Further, as the student's behavior improves, their relationship with adults naturally improves (Patterson, 2016). Students learn more from those with whom they have a positive relationship (Košir & Tement, 2014).

All strategies presented in this chapter are rooted in the science of applied behavior analysis and are effective in school settings. Yet, none require a trained behavior analyst or specialist to implement them. All can be implemented by any general education practitioner (e.g., paraprofessional, teacher) who wishes to see positive changes in student behavior without applying punitive tactics like removing a student from the classroom.

A final key component in using interventions that yield the best results is fidelity of implementation. Interventions must be instituted exactly as described to have successful outcomes. These more advanced techniques cannot be administered in the absence of universal interventions. Often, in our haste for desired student behavior, teachers leap to robust techniques that create behavior change. However, Tier 2 and Tier 3 interventions are built upon the foundation of Tier 1 as additional layers and not substitutes for universal techniques.

REFERENCES

Alwahbi, A. (2020). The use of contingency contracting in educational settings: A review of the literature. *Educational Research and Reviews*, 15(6), 327–335. DOI: 10.5897/ERR2020.3949

Alwahbi, A., & Hua, Y. (2021). Using contingency contracting to promote social interactions among students with ASD and their peers. *Behavior Modifications*, 45(5), 671–694. http://doi.org/10.1177/0145445520901674

Anderman, E. M., & Anderman, L. H. (2021). *Classroom motivation: Linking research to teacher practice* (3rd ed.). Routledge.

Archer, A. L., & Hughes, C. A. (2010). *Explicit instruction: Effective and efficient teaching*. Guilford Publications.

Aspiranti, K. B., Bebech, A., Ruffo, B., & Skinner, C. H. (2019). Classroom management in self-contained classrooms for children with autism: Extending research on the color wheel system. *Behavior Analysis in Practice*, 12, 143–153. https://doi.org/10.1007/s40617-018-02646

Banks, T. (2014). Creating positive learning environments: Antecedent strategies for managing the classroom environment & student behavior. *Creative Education*, 5, 519–524. https://doi.org/10.4236/ce.2014.57061

Billingsley, G. M. (2016). Combating work refusal using research-based practices. *Intervention in School and Clinic*, 53(1), 12–16. https://doi.org/10.1177/1053451216630289

Black, J., Noltemeyer, A. L., Davis, D. R., & Schwartz, T. (2016). Pre-service teachers' responses to student behavior in a mixed-reality environment. *SAGE Open*, 6(1) January–March, 1–10. https://doi.org/10.1177/2158244016633494

Boerke, K. W., & Reitman, D. (2014). Token economies. In W. W. Fisher, C. C. Piazza, & H. S. Roane (Eds.), *Handbook of applied behavior analysis* (1st ed., pp. 370–376). Guilford Press.

Bowman-Perrott, L., Burke, M. D., de Marin, S., Zhang, N., & Davis, H. (2015). A meta-analysis of single-case research on behavior contracts: Effects on behavioral and academic outcomes among children and youth. *Behavior Modification*, 39, 247–269. https://doi.org/10.1177/0145445514551383

Browder, D. M., Spooner, F., Lo, Y.-y., Saunders, A. F., Root, J. R., Ley Davis, L., & Brosh, C. R. (2018). Teaching students with moderate intellectual disability to solve word problems. *The Journal of Special Education*, 51(4), 222–235. https://doi.org/10.1177/0022466917721236

Cheryan, S., Ziegler, S. A., Plaut, V. C., & Meltzoff, A. N. (2014). Designing classrooms to maximize student achievement. *Policy Insights from the Behavioral and Brain Sciences*, 1(1), 4–12. https://doi.org/10.1177/2372732214548677

Cihak, D. F., Moore, E. J., Wright, R. E., McMahon, D. D., Gibbons, M. M., & Smith, C. (2016). Evaluating augmented reality to complete a chain task for elementary students with autism. *Journal of Special Education Technology*, 31(2), 99–108.

Cihon, J. H., Ferguson, J. L., Milne, C. M., Leaf, J. B., McEachin, J., & Leaf, R. (2019). A preliminary evaluation of a token system with a flexible earning requirement. *Behavior Analysis in Practice*, 12, 548–556. https://doi.org/10.1007/s40617-018-00316-3

Common, E. A., Lane, K. L., Cantwell, E. D., Brunsting, N. C., Oakes, W. P., Germer, K. A., & Bross, L. A. (2020). Teacher-delivered strategies to increase students' opportunities to respond: A systematic methodological review. *Behavioral Disorders*, 45(2), 67–84.

Cooper, J. O., Heron, T. E., & Heward, W. L. (2020). *Applied behavior analysis* (3rd ed.). Pearson Education.

Cote, D. L., Jones, V. L., Barnett, C., Pavelek, K., Nguyen, H., & Sparks, S. L. (2014). Teaching problem solving skills to elementary age students with autism. *Education and Training in Autism and Developmental Disabilities*, 49, 189–199.

Crone, D. A., Hawken, L. S., & Horner, R. H. (2010). *Responding to problem behavior in schools: The behavior education pro-gram*. Guilford Press.

DeJager, B., Houlihan, D., Filter, K. J., Mackie, P. F. E., & Klein, L. (2020). Comparing the effectiveness and ease of implementation of token economy, response cost, and a combination condition in rural elementary school classrooms. *Journal of Rural Mental Health*, 44(1), 39–50. https://doi.org/10.1037/rmh0000123

Diamond, L. L. (2018). Problem solving using visual support for young children with autism. *Intervention in School and Clinic*, 54(2), 106–110. http://doi.org/10.1177/1053451218765234

Filter, K. J., McKenna, M. K., Benedict, E. A., Horner, R. H., Todd, A., & Watson, J. (2007). Check in/Check out: A post-hoc evaluation of an efficient, second-ary-level targeted intervention for reducing problem behaviors in schools. *Education and Treatment of Children*, 30, 69–84.

Foster-Cohen, S., & Mirfin-Veitch, B. (2017). Evidence for the effectiveness of visual supports in helping children with disabilities access the mainstream primary school curriculum. *Journal of Research in Special Education Needs*, 17(2), 79–86. http://doi.org/10.1111/1471-3802.12105

Gauvreau A. N., & Schwartz, I. S. (2013). Using visual supports to promote appropriate behavior in young children with autism and related disabilities. In M. M. Ostrosky & S. R. Sandall (Eds.), *Young exceptional children monograph series no. 15: Addressing young children's challenging behaviors* (pp. 29–44). The Division for Early Childhood of the Council for Exceptional Children.

Gilmour, A. F. (2018). Has inclusion gone too far? Weighing its effects on students with disabilities, their peers, and teachers. *Education Next*, 18(4), 8–16.

Gold, M. W. (1976). Task analysis of a complex assembly task by the retarded blind. *Exceptional Children*, 43(2), 78–84. https://doi.org/10.1177/001440297604300203

Gordon, D. G. (2001). Classroom management problems and solutions. *Music Educators Journal*, 88(2), 17–23.

Grünke, M. (2019). The effects of contingency contracts on the correct use of punctuation marks in elementary students with learning disabilities. *Insights into Learning Disabilities*, 16(1), 47–57.

Heiniger, S., Tucker, K. A., Hott, B. L., & Randolph, K. M. (2022). Classroom reinforcement systems: Using token economies to foster independence. *Beyond Behavior*, 31(3), 151–162. http://doi.org/10.1177/10742956221108359

Herrod, J. L., Snyder, S. K., Hart, J. B., Frantz, S. J., & Ayres, K. M. (2023). Applications of the Premack Principle: A review of the literature. *Behavior Modification*, 47(1), 219–246. http://doi.org/10.1177/01454455221085249

IRIS Center. (2016). *Autism spectrum disorder (part 2): Evidence-based practices*. https://iris.peabody.vanderbilt.edu/module/asd2/

Janz, N. K., Becker, M. H., & Hartman, P. E. (1984). Contingency contracting to enhance patient compliance: A review. *Patient Education and Counseling*, 5(4), 165–178.

Jowett Hirst, E. S., Dozier, C. L., & Payne, S. W. (2016). Efficacy of and preference for reinforcement and response cost in token economies. *Journal of Applied Behavior Analysis*, 49, 329–345. http://dx.doi.org/10.1002/jaba.294

Kazdin, A. E. (1977). *The token economy: A review and evaluation*. Plenum Press.

Kellems, R. O., Eichelberger, C., Cacciatore, G., Jensen, M., Frazier, B., Simons, K., & Zaru, M. (2020). Using video-based instruction via augmented reality to teach mathematics to middle school students with learning disabilities. *Journal of Learning Disabilities*, 53(4), 277–291. https://doi.org/10.1177/0022219420906452

Kim, J. Y., Fienup, D. M., Oh, A. E., & Wang, Y. (2022). Systematic review and meta-analysis of token economy practices in K–5 educational settings, 2000 to 2019. *Behavior Modification*, 46(6), 1460–1487. http://doi.org/10.1177/01454455211058077

Klein, L. (2020). Comparing the effectiveness and ease of implementation of token economy, response cost, and a combination condition in rural elementary school classrooms. *Journal of Rural Mental Health*, 44(1), 39–50. http://dx.doi.org/10.1037/rmh0000123

Klingbeil, D. A., Dart, E. H., & Schramm, A. L. (2019). A systematic review of function modified check-in/check-out. *Journal of Positive Behavior Interventions*, 21(2), 77–92. https://doi.org/10.1177/10983007187780

Knight, V., Spriggs, A., & Sartini, E. (2014). Evaluating visual activity schedules as evidence-based practice for individuals with autism spectrum disorder. *Journal of Autism and Developmental Disorders*. DOI: 10.1007/s10803-014-2201-z.

Korpershoek, H., Harms, T., DeBoer, H., VanKuijk, M., & Doolaard, S. (2016). A meta-analysis of the effects of classroom management strategies and classroom management programs on students' academic, behavioral, emotional, and motivational outcomes. *Review of Educational Research*, 86(3), 643–680. http://doi.org/10.3102/0034654315626799

Košir, K., & Tement, S. (2014). Teacher–student relationship and academic achievement: A cross-lagged longitudinal study on three different age groups. *European Journal of Psychology of Education*, 29, 409–428. https://doi.org/10.1007/s10212-013-0205-2

LaBrot, Z. C., Dufrene, B., Radley, K., & Pasqua, J. (2016). Evaluation of a modified check in/check-out intervention for young children. *Perspectives on Early Childhood Psychology and Education*, 1(1), 144–165.

Maggin, D. M., Chafouleas, S. M., Goddard, K. M., & Johnson, A. H. (2011). A systematic evaluation of token economies as a classroom management tool for students with challenging behavior. *Journal of School Psychology*, 49(5), 529–554. https://doi.org/10.1016/j.jsp.2011.05.001

Maggin, D. M., Zurheide, J., Pickett, K. C., & Baillie, S. J. (2015). A systematic evidence review of the check-in/check-out program for reducing student behaviors. *Journal of Positive Behavior Interventions*, 17(4), 197–208. DOI: 10.1177/1098300715573630.

Majeika, C. E. (2020). Supporting student behavior through behavioral contracting. *Teaching Exceptional Childreni* 53(2), 132–139. http://doi.org/10.1177/0040059920952475

Majeika, C. E., Wehby, J. H., & Hancock, E. M. (2022). Are breaks better? A comparison of breaks are better to check-in check-out. *Behavioral Disorders*, 47(2), 118–133. https://doi.org/10.1177/01987429211001816

Matson, J. L., & Boisjoli, J. A. (2009). The token economy for children with intellectual disability and/or autism: A review. *Research in Development Disabilities*, 30, 240–248. https://doi.org/10.1016/j.ridd.2008.04.001

McConomy, M. A., Root, J., & Wade, T. (2021). Using task analysis to support inclusion and assessment in the classroom. *Teaching Exceptional Children*, 54(6), 414–422. DOI: 10.1177/00400599211025565

Meadan, H., Ayvazo, S., & Ostrosky, M. M. (2016). The ABCs of challenging behavior: Understanding basic concepts. *Young Exceptional Children*, 19(1), 3–15. https://doi.org/10.1177/1096250614523969

Moyer, J. R., & Dardig, J. C. (1978). Practical task analysis for special educators. *Teaching Exceptional Children*, *11*(1), 16–18. https://doi.org/10.1177/004005997801100105

National Center for Education Statistics (NCES). (2022). Students with disabilities. Condition of education. US Department of Education, Institute of Education Sciences. Retrieved July 8, 2022, from https://nces.ed.gov/programs/coe/indicator/cgg

National Center for Intensive Intervention (NCII). (2021). Data-based individualization. https://intensiveintervention.org/data-based-individualization

Noell, G. H., Whitmarsh, E. L., VanDerHeyden, A. M., Gatti, S. L., & Slider, N. J. (2003). Sequencing instructional tasks: A comparison of contingent and noncontingent interspersal of preferred academic tasks. *Behavior Modification*, *27*(2), 191–216. https://doi.org/10.1177/0145445503251577

Parker, D., & Kamps, D. (2011). Effects of task analysis and self-monitoring for children with autism in multiple social settings. *Focus on Autism and Other Developmental Disabilities*, *26*(3), 131–142. https://doi.org/10.1177/1088357610376945

Patterson, G. R. (2016). Coercion theory: The study of change. In T. J. Dishion & J. J. Snyder (Eds.), *The Oxford handbook of coercive relationship dynamics* (pp. 7–22). Oxford University Press.

Poole, I., Evertson, C., & The IRIS Center. (2019). *Effective room arrangement: Elementary*. https://iris.peabody.vanderbilt.edu/wp-content/uploads/pdf_case_studies/ics_effrmarr_elementary.pdf

Premack, D. (1959). Toward empirical behavior laws: I. Positive reinforcement. *Psychological Review*, *66*(4), 219–233. https://doi.org/10.1037/h0040891

Sam, A., & Autism Focused Intervention Resources & Modules (AFIRM). (2015). *Visual supports*. National Professional Development Center on Autism Spectrum Disorder, FPG Child Development Center, University of North Carolina. http://afirm.fpg.unc.edu/visual-supports

Scheuermann, B., Billingsley, G. M., & Hall, J. A. (2022). *Positive behavioral supports for the classroom* (4th ed.). Pearson.

Shook, A. C. (2012). A study of preservice educators' dispositions to change behavior management strategies. *Preventing School Failure*, *56*, 129–136. https://doi.org/10.1080/1045988X.2011.606440

Simmons, K., Carpenter, L., Crenshaw, S., & Hinton, V. (2015). Exploration of classroom seating arrangement and student behavior in a second-grade classroom. *Georgia Educational Researcher*, *12*(1), 51–68. DOI: 10.20429/ger.2015.120103.

Simonsen, B., & Myers, D. (2015). *Classwide positive behavior interventions and supports: A guide to proactive classroom management*. Guilford Press.

Simonsen, B., Fairbanks, S., Briesch, A., Myers, D., & Sugai, G. (2008a). Evidence-based practices in classroom management: Considerations for research to practice. *Education and Treatment of Children*, *31*(3), 351–380. DOI: 10.1353/etc.0.0007.

Simonsen, B., Sugai, G., & Negron, M. (2008b). Schoolwide positive behavior supports: Primary systems and practices. *Teaching Exceptional Children*, *40*(6), 32–40. https://doi.org/10.1177/004005990804000604

Smith, J., Guimond, F. A., Amand, J. Olivier, E., & Chouinard, R. (2022). "Keep calm and earn more points": What research says about token economy systems.

Theory into Practice, 61(4), 384–394. https://doi.org/10.1080/00405841.2022.2107808

Soares, D. A., Harrison, J. R., Vannest, K. J., & McClelland, S. S. (2016). Effect size for token economy use in contemporary classroom settings: A meta-analysis of single-case research. *School Psychology Review*, 45(4), 379–399. https://doi.org/10.17105/SPR45-4.379-399

Sottilare, A. L., & Blair, K. C. (2023). Implementation of check-in/check-out to improve classroom behavior of at-risk elementary school students. *Behavioral Sciences*, 13, 1–16. https://doi.org/10.3390/bs13030257

Steinbrenner, J. R., Hume, K., Odom, S. L., Morin, K. L., Nowell, S. W., Tomaszewski, B., Szendrey, S., McIntyre, N. S., Yücesoy-Özkan, S., & Savage, M. N. (2020). *Evidence based practices for children, youth, and young adults with autism*. The University of North Carolina, Frank Porter Graham Child Development Institute, National Clearinghouse on Autism Evidence and Practice Review Team.

Trump, C. E., Pennington, R. C., Travers, J. C., Ringdahl, J. E., Whiteside, E. E., & Ayres, K. M. (2018). Applied behavior analysis in special education: Misconceptions and guidelines for use. *Teaching Exceptional Children*, 50(6), 381–393. https://doi.org/10.1177/0040059918775020

Veazey, S. E., Valentino, A. L., Low, A. I., McElroy, A. R., & LeBlanc, L. A. (2016). Teaching feminine hygiene skills to young females with autism spectrum disorder and intellectual disability. *Behavior Analysis in Practice*, 9(2), 184–189.

Warren, T., Cagliani, R. R., Whiteside, E., & Ayres, K. M. (2021). Effect of task sequence and preference on on-task behavior. *Journal of Behavioral Education*, 30(1), 112–129. https://doi.org/10.1007/s10864-019-09358-1

Williamson, R. L., & McFadzen, C. (2020). Evaluating the impact of token economy methods on student on-task behaviour within an inclusive Canadian classroom. *International Journal of Technology and Inclusive Education*, 9(1), 1531–1541.

Wolfe, K., Pyle, D., Charlton, C. T., Sabey, C. V., Lund, E. M., & Ross, S. W. (2016). A systematic review of the empirical support for check-in check-out. *Journal of Positive Behavior Interventions*, 18(2), 74–88. https://doi.org/10.1177/1098300715595957

Zaheer, I., Maggin, D., McDaniel, S., McIntosh, K., Rodriguez, B. J., & Fogt, J. B. (2019). Implementation of promising practices that support students with emotional and behavioral disorders. *Behavioral Disorders*, 44(2), 117–128. https://doi.org/10.1177/0198742918821331

Zimmerman, K. N., Ledford, J. R., & Barton, E. E. (2017). Using visual activity schedules for young children with challenging behavior. *Journal of Early Intervention*, 39(4), 339–358. https://doi.org/10.1177/1053815117725693

14

Technology

A Tool to Unify and Include

Theresa Cullen

THERE ARE VERY FEW things that can equally be woven into content instruction or have the potential to invite learners to the table like technology. Technology offers ubiquitous tools and is constantly changing to allow teachers new ways to teach, include, and create. With its constant evolution, to make meaningful use of technology, educators must stay knowledgeable and be willing to change with it.

TECHNOLOGY IS EVERYWHERE

Technology is ubiquitous. In 2011, Chris Dede from Harvard made several predictions about technology in education. He pointed out that given that technology is everywhere, technology encourages learning to leave traditional settings, which are highly based on industrial education models, to more contextualized settings (Dede, 2011). For example, the mobile phone is a powerful computer and is a wonderful aid during a nature visit to identify both plants and animals with apps like Leaf Snap, which serve to replace book based dichotomous keys for plant identification. These tools can be readily available on a phone or a smartwatch, can connect via Bluetooth to headphones, and can be adding annotation to a student experience. For example, many museums have added QR codes and Augmented Reality tokens that encourage visitors to learn more about the site and its history by using these devices (to see an example visit: https://www.greenwoodrising.org/mobile-app)

The most important part is that technology with its reduced costs, offer many affordances both to the teachers and the students. It can change how teachers plan and assess lessons and offer students multiple ways of communicating (e.g., audio, video, text). To support access, educators must make sure that all students have at least one internet connected device available to them to be able to engage and create (Dede, 2011). In a recent conversation by the Pew Research Center, experts were asked about the future of technology (Anderson & Rainie, 2023). Their vision continued to see technology as more integrated in our lives from our devices to how we solve problems and do work. The experts stressed the amazing opportunity for people to learn how to make technology more human centered by learning how to navigate these technologies while still keeping people and their needs in mind (Anderson & Rainie, 2023). Helping students develop these kinds of skills often falls to teachers and presents an opportunity to use technology to engage students in higher order thinking and problem solving.

Technology as an Invitation to Engage

Learning does not occur passively but instead thrives when students are engaged. Kearsley and Shneiderman (1998) explain that engagement is best supported in a group context where students can *relate*, *create*, and *donate*: *relate* means that students working on group-based projects learn through explaining and clarifying their ideas; a project allows them to *create* something new; and *donate* allows them to apply their ideas to a real-world context and solving a real-world problem. The authors suggest that these processes are enhanced by using technology. Current trends in education published after the pandemic reinforce these ideas and stress that student learning must include student voice and emotional engagement (Hanover Research, 2023). Henrie et al. (2015) unpack engagement via technology. They discuss the overall definition of engagement that varies from interaction of students with the content they are learning to much broader definitions of student engagement with school, including emotional and cognitive constructs. In their goal to assess engagement with technology, the researchers' definition focused on relationships, the interactions with teachers, other students, and the technology itself. This definition is applicable to all kinds of learning settings—hybrid, online, and face to face—where technology serves to assist in the instruction and student learning processes. Student lives are filled with technology, so teachers must acknowledge that educational use of technology also competes with the technology that fills every day for students. To engage students in meaningful technology enhanced learning, the activities must be active and different than common technologies like social media or streaming services. Teachers, with their training in how people learn and build knowledge, have the opportunity to be different by engaging students and designing activities that support them in learning increasingly complex content. Techniques such as scaffolding and the use of formative assessment are not void in technology integration and, as in regular instruction, serve to enhance the learning and support of students. Modern approaches to scaffolding value student voice and encourage structures to promote problem-solving and the development of affective skills for personal and professional success (Hanover Research, 2023; Yelland & Masters, 2007).

Choosing technology to engage can be a difficult task. But just like in content areas such as math, science, and language arts, there are standards to help guide the process. The International Society for Technology in Education (ISTE) offers standards for everyone in school, in their given roles. Standards for educational leaders, educators, and students are aligned. The adult standards focus on professional learning and teachers or administrators improving their ability to do their jobs and modeling appropriate technology use for students. When considering professional learning, the educator standards (https://iste.org/standards/educators) can help guide your choices, and the student standards (https://iste.org/standards/students) can help guide how you plan to have students use technology. These standards emphasize student voice, media literacy skills, critical thinking, and problem-solving. Remembering that content is always key, using the student technology standards can help identify ways students engage using technology while still teaching content that is specific to other areas. For example, given a traditional classroom task like making a report on a state, technology can enhance the task beyond writing an essay. The assignment can be designed to emphasize students as "knowledge constructors," and the assignment can guide them in valuing online information and sources. Educators can also use a choice board to allow students to show creativity in designing a different way of showing information and communicating their new knowledge in different ways. By designing the task with the technology standards in mind, educators can touch upon the "empowered learner," "innovative designer," and "creative communicator." These are all learning roles that are supported by the standards and further broken down into academic and problem-solving skills that can be fostered in students (ISTE, 2017). Probably one of the most important parts of designing a technology-rich assignment for students is not underestimating what students can do. Students are hungry to show their creativity and often approach technology without the same fear that adults often do. When embracing the technology standards for both students and teachers, educators should be willing to be co-learners and let students show them what they can do. The IPSE standards website provides project examples and notes on how the standards can be applied.

Technology as Private Differentiation

Technology offers privacy in a lot of ways, with the exception of, perhaps, social media. Technology can level the playing field for students will all kinds of learning differences without anyone else in the classroom knowing. Students are often seen wearing headphones while they work, but do we really know what purpose those headphones are serving? For some students, their device could be playing calming music to help them self-regulate. For other students, their device could be reading text aloud. For some, their device could be reading alternative text to explain pictures or graphics or allowing them to hear visual captions to aid in comprehension. Other students could be using the headphones' noise-cancelling feature to help them focus. These technology uses are valid and assist students in being successful, and they can all occur without other students in the classroom knowing. This privacy also offers students the power to be able choose how they will adjust tasks to their needs without embarrassment.

Differentiation with technology can, and should, be a student-empowering experience. As engagement requires student voice, so does differentiation. Students engage with technology daily and learn what works for them. In a 2022 study, researchers interviewed students and teachers and about their views on differentiated instruction. The results were very compelling. Students knew how they wanted to do things, and wanted to be heard in the process of learning and asked how they learn best. Students acknowledged that they enjoyed learning more when they were challenged, but that different students had different abilities and so their challenges would look different. In their conclusion, Scarparolo and MacKinnon (2022), summed it up well, "The students' responses revealed that they were more engaged, motivated, and interested in this differentiated inquiry unit of work because they were consulted and had choice and flexibility regarding elements of their learning" (p. 12).

So how can a teacher start using technology to differentiate? There are a few important steps. First, teachers must be constantly learning, themselves, about both technology and pedagogy so that they can be aware of what tools may best serve them and their students. Second, they need to learn about how their students are naturally using technology. Before giving students choice, learning about how their students approach problems offers an opportunity for differentiation. Finally, teachers must provide opportunities for students to co-design the interventions. As Scarapolo and MacKinnon (2022) found, giving students voice and allowing them to be heard promotes motivation and engagement and may extend the effectiveness of all other teaching interventions.

Technology as a Window into Work Skills

Work and learning have become intertwined in the modern information-age workplace. Workers are expected to adapt to a changing world and show critical thinking and discernment skills. There is less emphasis on what workers know (content) and more on how they can learn. As the skills needed to succeed in a modern workplace are ever changing, so must their skills to adapt and learn be. There is a movement away from jobs that can be easily automated and a need for new workers that have had opportunities to develop effective soft skills such as collaboration and problem-solving. Trends show that these kind of work skills, more cognitive in nature, are also more difficult to fill and therefore offer premium wages (Ra et al., 2019). Increased pay can create a significant difference in a learner's quality of life.

Students with disabilities have lower employment rates than their typical counterparts (Lombardi et al., 2017). When planning to use technology, keeping a constant eye on college and career readiness is key to providing maximum benefit to the students. In a study of transition programs across two states, researchers found that students with disabilities benefitted when their learning was paired with information technology (IT)–literacy content. Through this learning, they developed the ability to think critically about technology and the information that it provides and had greater statistically significant academic gains than their counterparts (Lombardi et al., 2017).

Therefore, considering the changing needs of the workforce and acknowledging where some students may face employment challenges, it is important for content instruction to also integrate technology and the skills needed to use it effectively. Technology is a great support to group projects and collaboration. Students can contribute to multiple modalities (e.g., graphics, writing, video) to communicate their content knowledge. Meanwhile, through the process, they are given opportunities to navigate the social landscape of the workplace to develop collaboration and problem-solving skills. Given the decreasing number of students attending college (Binkley, 2023) and the increasing number of students entering the workforce right after high school, as educators, we have new opportunities to prepare them for the challenges ahead.

Technology Trends in Education

To find out what new technologies will affect teaching and learning, there are a few resources that might aid teachers in staying aware of new technologies and help move students toward desirable job skills. The Department of Education (DOE)

Office of Educational Technology, all state departments of education, and even local school districts may offer insights and, often, funding for prioritized technologies. Professional organizations and their conferences provide both publications and professional learning opportunities in cutting-edge innovations.

The DOE offers publications to help educators identify technology trends. The National Educational Technology Plan (https://tech.ed.gov/netp/), which will release an update in 2024, is normally published every four to six years and lays out the national priorities for technology. It also provides a rich collection of case studies of schools that are leading the way in meaningful technology integration. How are these priorities realized? This resource is often paired with information about grant programs available through the DOE or individual state departments of education to help fund innovation to match the federal priorities. State education departments also publish reports on technology priorities, and these are often set by business stakeholders in the state and linked to employment data. For example, in Arkansas, they publish a digital learning guide (https://dese.ade.arkansas.gov/Offices/learning-services/digital-learning-guide). Within your state, there may be tools that are free to use and opportunities for professional learning. Each state offers its own guidance, especially in how teachers can decide what technology to use.

Professional organizations like ISTE can provide additional context as to where technology is going. Each year at their annual conference, ISTE showcases innovative technology uses both by individual teachers and companies to help educators envision how technology can be incorporated into their own practice. This conference is organized by the ISTE standards to help educators navigate the skills they want to learn. Since the pandemic, conferences like ISTE offer virtual attendance options to reduce barriers to attendance. If attending a conference is not an option, then these organizations also publish many books and journals to assist educators in staying up to date while illustrating best practices in integrating technology. A final source of trends in technology use in learning is higher-education focused; Educause, a professional organization for technology in education, releases a report each year that is called the "Horizon Report" (https://library.educause.edu/resources/2023/10/2023-educause-horizon-report-holistic-student-experience-edition). This report discusses what technology is currently being used for things such as engagement and accessibility, but it also looks ahead to the technology that will be used in the near future. As you are deciding which tools will be best to use with your students, the "Horizon Report" may help you make choices about what tools your students should be using and what experiences your students should be having in order to be college and career ready.

An Example

Often, it is difficult to envision what a new technology looks like in classroom practice. Let's use one technology example to work through the value of technology in education and understand its value to learners. Given its rapid growth, we will explore generative artificial intelligence (AI) in education. People are both intrigued and scared about using AI in learning, but the technology offers so many opportunities. AI can be simply defined as the use of automation to do work based on associations. Computers can see patterns and aggregate data, which allows them to "write" summaries and suggest patterns that humans can apply to problems (DOE, 2023). *Generative* means that a computer can take these patterns and apply them to create content. Generative AI depends on the user giving the AI prompts to which it can respond. This means that while the computer is generating content, the content it generates is in response to human interaction.

To gain insight on this technology, go to the DOE Office of Educational Technology and access their report, *Artificial Intelligence and the Future of Teaching and Learning*. This document outlines the advantages of using AI. These advantages include engaging students in new ways, having tools to adapt to different learning needs, providing feedback, and making educators' jobs easier. These are all benefits of technology, but the report also cautions us that many negatives are unknown and have yet to emerge through thoughtful use and application of the tools (DOE, 2023). This coincides with some of what the 2023 Horizon Report shares that generative AI can help student performance and improve the overall learning experience; however, it will require both students and educators to develop new literacies to be able to value and assess the information gained from AI (Horizon, 2023).

Now that we have framed why this trend was chosen as an example, let's talk specifically about how AI offers advantages to all learners, but especially those with exceptionalities. AI is incorporated in many of the tools we use. For example, the red lines in grammar check or the way that new content is pushed at us in social media, are generated by AI (Horizon, 2023). A simple Google search of AI for teaching will give you a long list of the latest tools. Different tools offer different affordances. Just as with any technology, it is important for teacher to first experiment with a new tool, check to make sure that it is appropriate for children and compliant with the Child Online Protection and Privacy Act (COPPA, 1998), if you are not familiar with COPPA, you might be familiar with warnings on websites that ask if you are over the age of 13. COPPA keeps companies from collecting information from children under the age of 13. Any website that asks for age is likely collecting information. Since AI depends on the human-offered prompt, many AI applications are collecting all of those prompts so it can better generate responses in the future.

AI can demonstrate how technology can be an invitation to engage. AI can take student work to the next level. We often focus on writing or math skills when talking about education, but students have different ways of communicating and creating. Going back to fundamental teaching frameworks like Bloom's taxonomy, we know that student engagement increases as students complete more complex tasks approaching creation (Hover & Wise, 2022). AI can help students create and provide them support and scaffolding to achieve it. Young learners often draw, and an AI tool like Animated Drawings (https://sketch.metademolab.com/) allows students to animate their own drawings before they are even able to read and write. The students are motivated by seeing their drawings dancing on the screen and by having their work recognized and shared. By using a tool like this, teachers are given the opportunity to encourage and motivate students. Not to mention, it might motivate teachers too.

AI can demonstrate how technology can provide private differentiation. Students with exceptionalities often benefit from technology supports to be successful in the classroom and AI is especially designed for this. For example, a tool called goblin.tools (http://goblin.tools) will break tasks down into steps. The level of breakdown is customizable. Students who have a project to complete or a task to learn can use a tool like goblin.tools to break down its complexity and better understand what is being asked of them. The checkboxes allow teachers to work with students to develop strategies in self-monitoring for managing tasks. This can all be done using a Chromebook, tablet, computer, or smartphone. The individual device does not matter, but learning how to access data in the cloud and write effective prompts are important skills for students to develop.

Finally, the innovative use of AI is a highly valued work skill. *Forbes* published an article in 2023 discussing what the work world is looking for related to generative AI (Bannon, 2023). The article points out that we need to think about technology differently. Humans will be helping technology do the work, which will allow for greater efficiency (i.e., one person doing multiple people's jobs), which will change some jobs and their value. For example, as generative AI becomes more able to write computer code, the role of the human in computer science will become more focused on assessing the efficiency and accuracy of code that is generated. So as educators, we are called on to help students identify AI tools that help them do their work, while still instilling the critical thinking skills needed to assess the value of work that computers contribute. This opens doors to many engaging lessons where we help students develop these skills. Such lessons could include collaborative work and other activities could emphasize human skills while harnessing the power of AI. Since there seems to be new AI tools emerging daily, students can participate in co-learning about new technologies with their teachers, giving them agency and voice, which reflects the trends suggested by the DOE (2023) and Pelletier et al. (2023). In doing so, teachers will not only be preparing students for college but also their future careers.

As educators, with any technology, AI included, we have the responsibility and the skills to help our schools and classrooms make decisions about what technology to use. This goes beyond our own classroom decisions, to leading our teams to make decisions by weighing the pros and cons of any technology with benefit of students in mind. Since AI is a new and highly sought after technology, many organizations offer insights on how to approach it adoption into the educational environment. One of the best resources available is the "AI Guidance for Schools Toolkit" (http://teachai.org/toolkit). This toolkit is written by Code.org—an educational and technology company consortia that helps students learn how to code and promotes the ethical use of technology. They provide both technical guidance and sample lesson plans to help teachers integrate AI in meaningful ways.

CONCLUSION

Technology is one of the tools that helps to keep teaching interesting. Its constant change mirrors the constant change of our society, workplaces, and schools. However, technology, when paired with meaningful content instruction, has the potential to engage, motivate, and include students as they are being prepared for college and career. Students want to develop these skills, and their engagement increases when they are allowed to participate in the process and solve problems with their teacher. Planning to use technology in meaningful ways in instruction may require professional learning but has the potential to keep teachers engaged throughout their career while providing individualized support and care for the students in their classroom.

REFERENCES

Anderson, J., & Rainie, L. (2023, June 21). *As AI spreads, experts predict the best and worst changes in digital life by 2035.* Pew Research Center. https://www.pewresearch.org/wp-content/uploads/sites/20/2023/06/PI_2023.06.21_Best-Worst-Digital-Life_2035_FINAL.pdf

Bannon, M. T. (2023, June 22). How AI is changing the future of work. *Forbes.* https://www.forbes.com/sites/marenbannon/2023/06/22/how-ai-is-changing-the-future-of-work/?sh=22c74e3672e0

Binkley, C. (2023, March 9). The labor shortage is pushing American colleges into crisis, with the plunge in enrollment the worst ever recorded. *Fortune.* https://fortune.com/2023/03/09/american-skipping-college-huge-numbers-pandemic-turned-them-off-education/

Children's Online Privacy Protection Act (COPPA) of 1998, 15 U.S.C. 6501–6505. https://uscode.house.gov/view.xhtml?req=granuleid%3AUSC-prelim-title15-section6501&edition=prelim

Dede, C. (2011). Emerging technologies, ubiquitous learning, and educational transformation. In *Towards ubiquitous learning: Sixth European conference of technology-enhanced learning*, EC-TEL 2011, Palermo, Italy, September 20–23, 2011. Proceedings 6 (pp. 1–8). Springer Berlin Heidelberg.

Hanover Research. (2023, January 25). 2023 trends in K–12 education. Hanover Research. https://www.hanoverresearch.com/reports-and-briefs/2023-trends-in-k-12-education/

Henrie, C. R., Halverson, L. R., & Graham, C. R. (2015). Measuring student engagement in technology-mediated learning: A review. *Computers & Education*, 90, 36–53. DOI: 10.1016/j.compedu.2015.09.005.

Hover, A., & Wise, T. (2022). Exploring ways to create 21st century digital learning experiences. *Education 3–13, 50*(1), 40–53.

International Society for Technology in Education (ISTE). (2017). ISTE standards for students. ISTE. https://iste.org/standards/students

Kearsley, G., & Shneiderman, B. (1998). Engagement theory: A framework for technology-based teaching and learning. *Educational Technology, 38*(5), 20–23.

Lombardi, A., Izzo, M. V., Gelbar, N., Murray, A., Buck, A., Johnson, V., & Kowitt, J. (2017). Leveraging information technology literacy to enhance college and career readiness for secondary students with disabilities. *Journal of Vocational Rehabilitation*, 46(3), 389–397.

Pelletier, K., Robert, J., Muscanell, N., McCormack, M., Reeves, J., Arbino, N., & Grajek, S. (2023). *2023 EDUCAUSE Horizon report, teaching and learning edition.* EDUCAUSE23.

Ra, S., Shrestha, U., Khatiwada, S., Yoon, S. W., & Kwon, K. (2019). The rise of technology and impact on skills. *International Journal of Training Research*, 17(sup1.), 26–40.

Scarparolo, G., & MacKinnon, S. (2022). Student voice as part of differentiated instruction: students' perspectives. *Educational Review*, 1–18. https://doi.org/10.1080/00131911.2022.2047617

US Department of Education. (2023). *Artificial intelligence and future of teaching and learning: Insights and recommendations.* Office of Educational Technology. https://www2.ed.gov/documents/ai-report/ai-report.pdf

Yelland, N., & Masters, J. (2007). Rethinking scaffolding in the information age. *Computers & Education*, 48(3), 362–382.

15

Executive Functioning Skills

Organizing Attention for Learning

Pamela Williamson

EXECUTIVE FUNCTION (EF) SKILLS are the mental processes that make it possible for people to sustain attention, maintain goals and information in mind, delay response, and ignore distractions (Zelazo et al., 2016). It also supports the ability to reflect on previous experiences, tolerate frustration, and plan. EF differences are characteristic of a range of disabilities including attention deficit hyperactivity disorder (ADHD), autism spectrum disorder (ASD), emotional and behavioral disorders (EBD), and specific learning disabilities (SLD). EF includes a specific set of attention regulation skills that support conscious goal direction and problem solving. These three skills are cognitive flexibility, working memory, and inhibitory control. Notably, EF skills can be influenced by education and practice (Zelazo & Lee, 2010). Reading this chapter will help you address the following questions:

1. How are the three EF skills defined and how are they related to academic performance?
2. How can EF skills be developed through instruction?
3. How can EF skills be taught?

FOUNDATIONAL THEORY

Historically, EF was a nebulous theoretical construct that loosely included all things related to planning, directing attention, and self-regulation (Zelazo et al., 1997). Although the matter is still not settled (e.g., Landi, 2023), Zelazo and his colleagues (2016) suggest that there are three distinct executive functioning skills: cognitive flexibility, working memory, and inhibitory control. The three EF skills are characterized as neurocognitive skills (Zelazo et al., 1997). EF is the bridge from knowledge to practice, or what Zelazo et al. refer to as "the adaptive use of one's knowledge in the service of one's goals" (p. 4).

Cognitive flexibility is the ability to consider ideas from more than one perspective. During reading, for example, cognitive flexibility allows students to understand that characters in a story have more than one point of view or that words can have more than one meaning (Carnahan & Williamson, 2010). Cognitive flexibility is also critical in all other academic subjects that require problem solving (e.g., mathematics, science). Similarly, working memory is heavily implicated in all academic tasks. It allows more than one idea to be held in mind at a time, such as when a student is trying to determine the main idea of an expository text or which aspects of a word problem need to be considered to arrive at the solution. Finally, inhibitory control includes students' ability to ignore unrelated or distracting/competing information to stay with a task. This could be ignoring details in a word problem that are not relevant to solving it or ignoring noise in their environment. Together, these skills allow individuals to make predictions, identify patterns, and draw logical conclusions (Zelazo et al., 2016).

EF overlaps with other educationally important concerns, including self-regulation and social-emotional learning (Zelazo et al., 2016). Self-regulation relies upon effortful executive function, or purposefully modifying behavior in service of a goal. EF skills support or enable goal-directed behaviors, including reflection, planning, persistence, emotional regulation, and deliberate problem solving. Noncognitive skills also have underpinnings in EF. This refers to constructs that are not academic in nature but are critical for academic success, such as persistence, social-emotional learning, and determination.

Guiding Research

EF and Academics

Jacob and Parkinson (2015) conducted a metanalysis of published studies to examine the relationship between EF and achievement in reading and mathematics. They concluded that there was an unconditional association between EF and achievement across different ages, EF skills, subject area, and measurement types (naturalistic versus laboratory-based research). They did not find these relationships to be causal. In other words, the research did not prove that better EF skills directly improved academic achievement in reading and mathematics. Further, results on transfer effects from global EF interventions to broader academic domains is limited (e.g., Titz & Karbach, 2014). Investigations that pair EF intervention with academics are equivocal, with some studies reporting that EF accounts for little in the variation of outcomes (e.g., Church et al., 2019), while others report positive associations between EF and academic outcomes (e.g., Lovett et al., 2017).

Although the relationship remains unsettled, some scholars continue to suggest that EF has the potential to support academic response to intervention (e.g., Burgess & Cutting, 2023; Dekker et al., 2016). This suggestion is partly based upon the fact that there is an established link between EF and performance in a variety of areas (e.g., academics), strong underpinnings inferred from relevant educational theories and concerns that research attempting to establish direct links needs to continue to evolve and be explored. For example, brain studies suggest that to better understand how cognitive control and domain knowledge work together, additional research is needed that manipulates lower-level task features of an academic task in relation to higher-order cognitive constructs (Wilkey, 2023). Willoughby and his colleagues (2019) suggested designing interventions that examine academic and EF outcomes by targeting only one or the other but measuring both to look for effects. Thus, largely because of the promising nature of the relationship of EF to other educational concerns, the role of EF and academics continues to be of interest to policymakers and teachers (Willoughby et al., 2019). In this next section, we will explore research on self-regulation and social-emotional learning as they are connected to developing executive function skills.

Self-Regulation

Self-regulation is the idea that learners initiate and maintain active control over their cognition, emotions, and behavior to achieve a goal (Zimmerman, 1994). Zimmerman's (2008) model of self-regulation includes three phases: plan it, practice it, and evaluate it. The idea is that when students become more engaged, they take responsibility for learning, which leads to improved performance. There are multiple opportunities for feedback during each phase. Provided feedback is reflected upon and used to iterate the learning cycle. Interventions in a wide variety of academic areas, including reading, mathematics, and social-emotional learning, have included self-regulation as components of intervention.

Berkeley and Larsen (2018) evaluated reading comprehension interventions for students with learning disabilities that included components of self-regulation. They concluded that across studies, large effects were reported immediately after instruction and many studies had effects after a time delay. Self-regulation components used in the studies they reviewed included the use of strategy sheets and checklists and questions to promote reflection, alongside other support to learn the strategy. They concluded that if teachers wish to foster students' use of strategies, embedding components of self-regulation is warranted.

In writing, self-regulation strategy development (SRSD) is an approach where students learn to be goal directed to purposely achieve their writing goals. SRSD includes six connected and iterated stages designed to support and empower the writing abilities of students with disabilities (Graham & Harris, 2003). Instructional routines include (a) developing background knowledge, (b) discussing skills and strategies, (c) modeling skills and strategies, (d) memorizing strategies using mnemonics, (e) guided practice of skills and strategies, and (f) independent practice. These practices are designed to help students practice intentional self-regulation during writing. The What Works Clearinghouse (WWC) evaluated available studies of SRSD and found "strong evidence of positive effects with no overriding contrary evidence" (WWC, 2017, p. 6). SRSD was deemed to have "potentially positive effects," which means that additional high-quality studies are needed to deem it an evidence-based practice.

SRSD has also been tested in mathematics to teach problem solving (e.g., Popham et al., 2018). The SOLVE strategy leans on self-regulation. SOLVE is a mnemonic that stands for (a) study the problem, (b) organize the facts, (c) line up a plan, (d) verify your plan with action, and (e) evaluate your results (Freeman-Green et al., 2015). As with writing interventions, evidence is still emerging that potentially supports the use embedding self-regulation in mathematics strategy instruction. Schema-based instruction (SBI) is another (e.g., Hott et al., 2021). Features of SBI include building a rich schema for word-problem structures (e.g., total, difference, change), which is supported by a mnemonic to recall steps that students can use to monitor their own behavior, and graphic organizers to elaborate mapping word problems to schema type. Given the potential effectiveness of embedding

SRSD with mathematics strategy instruction, Popham et al. (2018) concluded that practitioners should consider implementing them.

Social Emotional Learning

Social emotional learning (SEL) is about developing social competence and sometimes EF skills (Zelazo et al., 2016). McKown et al. (2009) define SEL as "the ability to encode, interpret, and reason about social and emotional information" (p. 858). In a meta-analysis of 213 school-based, universal social- emotional learning programs, participants in SEL programs compared to controls had significantly improved social-emotional skill outcomes and an 11-percentile-point gain in academic achievement (Durlak et al., 2011). Hagarty and Morgan (2020) conducted a systematic review of social-emotional learning for children with learning disabilities. While they found that programs were feasible, they found little evidence they were consistently effective for students with learning disabilities. The authors cited the need for additional research with more rigorous designs to enable robust recommendations to be made.

For early learners, Burchinal and colleagues (2022) recommend regular, intentional, engaging instruction and practice focused on developing social-emotional skills. This recommendation comes with the highest evidence rating from the What Works Clearinghouse. To address this recommendation, a systematic, incremental approach is suggested. Setting aside 10 to 20 minutes to teach social-emotional skills one to two times weekly is recommended. Opportunities for practice should include prepared, scripted activities. Appropriate social behaviors should be noticed and reinforced in naturalistic settings (e.g., centers, snack time). Burchinal et al.'s final recommendation is to share what is happening at school with families so that they can reinforce learning at home.

Together, explicitly embedding self-regulation as part of academic and social skills development is warranted. Although the extant base of literature does not meet the requirements to deem SRSD and SEL interventions to be evidence-based practices for students with learning disabilities, the emerging evidence is strong enough to be included in practice recommendations developed by the Institute of Education Science (IES) (e.g., Burchinal et al., 2022).

Assessment and Instruction

Zelazo and his colleagues (2016) suggest there are numerous ways EF might contribute to academic challenges, including behaviors such as poor planning skills and time management, problems with working memory, or performance anxiety that suppresses use of EF skills. Although teachers are unlikely to assess EF alone, they might receive EF assessment information as part of individual student evaluations. Assessment of EF includes performance-based assessments and commercially available standardized measures. EF measures are included in many intelligence tests (e.g., working memory).

There is evidence that high-quality educational programming does support the development of EF skills (Zelazo et al., 2016). Burchinal and colleagues (2022) reviewed the evidence around EF for early childhood and preschool and concluded that there is moderate support for strengthening children's executive functioning skills using specific games and activities. They suggest that games should include features aimed at encouraging children to listen, remember, and follow directions. Games should also promote flexible thinking and self-control. They suggest that games should last from 10 to 20 minutes and be played multiple times per week, and that the complexity of games should increase over time (e.g., add more rules to the game). They also suggest embedding EF within content lessons. For example, following directions, which addresses working memory, can be included in outdoor play or during art, remembering items on a list can be a feature of read-alouds that feature repetitive information, and planning and problem solving can be featured as part of math lessons. Academic interventions that include components of self-regulation are supported by research (e.g., SRSD).

SUMMARY AND RECOMMENDATIONS FOR PRACTICE

EF skills are attention-regulation skills and include cognitive flexibility, working memory, and inhibitory response (Zelazo et al., 2016). Many disabilities point to underlying executive function differences that are well documented in the literature (Zelazo et al., 2016). These skills are malleable, which means that with instruction, they can be learned and used to support learning in other domains. Theoretical underpinnings that are used to guide research efforts connect neurocognitive skills, including executive functioning skills and reflection, to overall goal-directed behavior that supports effective learning (e.g., Buss & Spencer, 2014; Munakata et al., 2013). These connections extend to the role of EF for self-regulation (e.g., Blair & Raver, 2014). At the same time, the evidence on interventions related to EF is still emerging with much of the work in this area conducted recently (e.g., Gunnars, 2023).

As with all educational practices, teachers are encouraged to keep abreast of advances in knowledge about the effects of EF for learning in the areas of academic and social behavior. For example, Gunnars (2023) conducted a systematic review of educational interventions that included EF and digital technology. His search found more than half of all studies were published after 2020. He also found that scholars explored game-based solutions for EF for students with disabilities that included supporting explicit goals for students. For teachers, he found EF skills training (e.g., mindfulness training) and classroom management with digital monitoring devices were studied and potentially useful. Thus, the results of his review were equivocal but promising. Direct approaches that include self-regulation and social-emotional learning currently have the strongest research support (e.g., Berkeley & Larsen, 2018; Graham & Harris, 2003) but have still not been recognized as an evidence-based practice, primarily because additional high-quality studies are needed. Given the totality of the evidence, the following recommendations related to EF and instruction are warranted.

1. Direct students' attention to what is important. For students with disabilities, inhibiting their attention to distracting information supports learning. Explicit instruction identified as a high-leverage practices (HLPs) identified as the Big Ideas in special education support this recommendation (McLeskey et al., 2017). Through explicit instruction, students are focused on what they will be learning by teachers who deliver unambiguous information. Examples and non-examples are also a feature of explicit instruction (Archer & Hughes, 2011). This aligns with promoting cognitive flexibility.

Graphic organizers are frequently featured as part of instructional interventions (e.g., Williamson et al., 2016). While they are used to direct students' attention to what's important, they can also be used to support planning. For example, Williamson and her colleagues (2016) taught students to use graphic organizers during reading to support reading comprehension. Next, students were taught to use the graphic organizers to plan and write summaries about what they read. This suggestion is also a feature of scaffolded instruction, which is an HLP (McLeskey et al., 2017).

2. Provide positive and constructive feedback as part of self-regulation strategy instruction. The feedback loop is central to self-regulated learning strategies (Zimmerman, 2008). McLeskey et al. (2017) emphasize the importance of providing feedback when learners need ways to improve their performance. Feedback can support reflection and direct attention as students learn strategies.

3. Teach strategies to support planning. Often, strategies that are supported by research include components that emphasize one or more EF skills. For example, SRSD for writing uses mnemonics to support planning what to write (Graham & Harris, 2003). The SBI and SOLVE strategies involve creating a plan to solve problems in mathematics (Hott et al., 2021; Freeman-Green et al., 2015.

REFERENCES

Berkeley, S., & Larsen, A. (2018). Fostering self-regulation of students with learning disabilities: Insights from 30 years of reading comprehension intervention research. *Learning Disabilities Research & Practice, 33*(2), 75–86. https://doi.org/10.1111/ldrp.12165

Blair, C., & Raver, C. C. (2014). Closing the achievement gap through modification of neurocognitive and neuroendocrine function: Results from a cluster randomized controlled trial of an innovative approach to the education of children in kindergarten. *PLoS ONE, 9*(11), e112393. https://doi.org/10.1371/journal.pone.0112393

Burchinal, M., Krowka, S., Newman-Gonchar, R., Jayanthi, M., Gersten, R., Wavell, S., Lyskawa, J., Haymond, K., Bierman, K., Gonzalez, J. E., McClelland, M. M., Nelson, K., Pentimonti, J., Purpura, D. J., Sachs, J., Sarama, J., Schlesinger-Devlin, E., Washington, J., & Rosen, E. (2022). *Preparing young children for school* (WWC 2022009). National Center for Education Evaluation and Regional Assistance (NCEE), Institute of Education Sciences, US Department of Education. https://ies.ed.gov/ncee/wwc/PracticeGuide/30

Burgess, A. N., & Cutting, L. E. (2023). The behavioral and neurobiological relationships between executive function and reading: A review of current and preliminary findings. *Mind, Brain, and Education, 17*(4), 267–278. https://doi.org/10.1111/mbe.12378

Buss, A. T., & Spencer, J. P. (2014). The emergent executive: A dynamic field theory of the development of executive function. *Monographs of the Society for Research in Child Development, 79*(2), vii.

Carnahan, C., & Williamson, P. (2010). *Quality literacy instruction for students with autism spectrum disorders*. Autism Asperger Publishing Company.

Church, J. A., Cirino, P. T., Miciak, J., Juranek, J., Vaughn, S., & Fletcher, J. M. (2019). Cognitive, intervention, and neuroimaging perspectives on executive function in children with reading disabilities. *New Directions for Child and Adolescent Development*, 2019(165), 25–54. https://doi.org/10.1002/cad.20292

Dekker, M. C., Ziermans, T. B., & Swaab, H. (2016). The impact of behavioural executive functioning and intelligence on math abilities in children with intellectual disabilities. *Journal of Intellectual Disability Research*, 60, 1086–1096. DOI: 10.1111/jir.12276.

Durlack, J. A., Dymnicki, A. B., Taylor, R. D., Weissberg, R. P., & Schelling, K. A. (2011). The impact of enhancing students' social and emotional learning: A meta-analyses of school-based universal interventions. *Child Development*, 82(1), 405–432. https://jstor.org/stable/29782838

Freeman-Green, S. M., O'Brien, C., Wood, C. L., & Hitt, S. B. (2015). Effects of the SOLVE strategy on the mathematical problem solving skills of secondary students with learning disabilities. *Learning Disabilities Research & Practice*, 30(2), 76–90. DOI:10.1111/ldrp.12054

Graham, S., & Harris, K. R. (2003). Students with learning disabilities and the process of writing: A meta-analysis of SRSD studies. In H. L. Swanson, K. R. Harris, & S. Graham (Eds.), *Handbook of learning disabilities* (pp. 323–344). The Guilford Press.

Hagarty, I., & Morgan, G. (2020). Social-emotional learning for children with learning disabilities: A systematic review. *Educational Psychology in Practice*, 36(2), 208–222. https://doi.org/10.1080/02667363.2020.1742096

Hott, B. L., Peltier, C., Heiniger, Palacios, M., Le, M. T., & Chen, M. (2021). Using schema-based instruction to improve the mathematical problem solving skills of a rural student with EBD. *Learning Disabilities: A Contemporary Journal*, 19(2), 127–142. https://eric.ed.gov/?id=EJ1314840

Jacob, R., & Parkinson, J. (2015). The potential for school-based interventions that target executive function to improve academic achievement: A review. *Review of Educational Research*, 85(4), 512–552. https://doi.org/10.3102/003465431456133

Lovett, M. W., Frijters, J. C., Wolf, M., Steinbach, K. A., Sevcik, R. A., & Morris, R. D. (2017). Early intervention for children at risk for reading disabilities: The impact of grade at intervention and individual differences on intervention outcomes. *Journal of Educational Psychology*, 109(7), 889–914.

McLeskey, J., Barringer, M-D., Billingsley, B., Brownell, M., Jackson, D., Kennedy, M., Lewis, T., Maheady, L., Rodriguez, J., Scheeler, M. C., Winn, J., & Ziegler, D. (2017). *High-leverage practices in special education*. Council for Exceptional Children & CEEDAR Center.

Munakata, Y., Snyder, H. R., & Chatham, C. H. (2012). Developing cognitive control: Three key transitions. *Current Directions in Psychological Science*, 21(2), 71–77. DOI: 10.1177/0963721412436807.

Popham M., Counts J., Ryan J. B., & Katsiyannis, A. (2018). A systematic review of self-regulation strategies to improve academic outcomes of students with EBD. *Journal of Research in Special Educational Needs*, 18(4), 239–253. https://doi.org/10.1111/1471-3802.12408

Titz, C., & Karbach, J. (2014). Working memory and executive functions: Effects of training on academic achievement. *Psychological Research*, 78(6), 852–868. https://doi.org/10.1007/s00426-013-0537-1

What Works Clearinghouse, Institute of Education Sciences, & US Department of Education. (2017, November). *Students with a specific learning disability intervention report: Self-regulated strategy development*. What Works Clearinghouse. https://whatworks.ed.gov/

Wilkey, E. D. (2023). The domain-specificity of domain-generality: Attention, executive function, and academic skills. *Mind, Brain, and Education*, 17(4), 219–406. https://doi.org//10.1111/mbe.12373

Willoughby, M. T., Wylie, A. C., & Little, M. H. (2019). Testing longitudinal associations between executive function and academic achievement. *Developmental Psychology*, 55(4), 767–779. http://dx.doi.org/10.1037/dev0000664

Zelazo, P. D., Blair, C. B., & Willoughby, M. T. (2016). *Executive function: Implications for education* (NCER 2017–2000). National Center for Education Research, Institute of Education Sciences, US Department of Education. http://ies.ed.gov/.

Zelazo, P. D., Carter, A., Reznick, J. S., & Frye, D. (1997). Early development of executive function: A problem-solving framework. *Review of General Psychology*, 1, 198–226.

Zelazo, P. D., & Lee, W. S. C. (2010). Brain development: An overview. In W. F. Overton (Ed.), *Handbook of life-span development* (Vol. 1, pp. 89–114). Wiley.

Zimmerman, B. J. (1994). Dimensions of academic self-regulation: A conceptual framework for education. In D. H. Schunk & B. J. Zimmerman (Eds.), *Self-regulation of learning and performance: Issues and educational applications* (pp. 3–21). Lawrence Erlbaum Associates.

Zimmerman, B. J. (2008). Goal setting: A key proactive source of academic self-regulation. In D. H. Schunk & B. J. Zimmerman (Eds.), *Motivation and self-regulated learning: Theory, research and applications* (pp. 267–295). Lawrence Erlbaum Associates.

Index

abstract concepts, 17, 54–56, 59–60, 76–77, 132–33, 137
academic performance, 132, 175–76, 179, 213; behavior and, 227; COVID-19 and, 48, 208; EF skills and, 260
academic standards, 89, 144, 169, 187; for reading instruction, 5–6
accommodations, 28, 102, 144, 148, 187; curriculum and, 174
acquisition, of knowledge, 54–56, 69–70, 153
action and expression, UDL and, 10, 97–99, 152, 180
active learning, 169–71, 252
activities, 36–37, 88–90, 142, 220–22, 232–36; extension, 134, 137; focus on, 54–55; writing, 97–100
adaptive reasoning, mathematics and, 52, 71
AI. *See* generative artificial intelligence
algebra competence, mathematics and, 50–52, 69
alternative teaching, 120–21, 154
applied knowledge, 6, 49, 57, 171, 196–97
ASD. *See* autism spectrum disorder
assessment: of behavior, 229; can't do/won't do, 81; of classroom environment, 215–16, 219; data and, 32, 62–63, 78–81, 155–56, 176, 178; EF skills and, 262–63; engagement and, 172; evidence-based, 32–34, *33*, 79, 112–13, 146; FBA, 178, 229; formative, 112–13, 118–19, 146, 172–73, 252; IEP and, 102; language, 34–35, 37; mathematics instruction and, 62–63; in mathematics intervention, 78–85, *80*, *83*; MTSS and, 30–31, 145; of MTSS Tier 1instruction, 43, 63–64; NAEP, 48, 108; ORF, 38–39; precision teaching and, 143; preference, 122–23, 233–34, 236; of progress, 146–47; of reading, 8–12, 22–23, 176; research and, 82; scaffolded instruction and, 102–3; science instruction and, 133, 138–39, 153–55; scientific models and, 133; of self, 113, 153–54; social studies and, 172–73; student work and, 147, 156, 172; summative, 146, 172; tests and, 115–16; writing instruction and, 102–3
assistive technology, 181, 186, 252, 254, 256–57
autism spectrum disorder (ASD), 72, 199, 228, 239, 244, 259

background knowledge. *See* prior knowledge
behavior: academic performance and, 227; assessment of, 229; classroom environment and, 176–77, 209–10;

267

disabilities and, 228, 259; EI and, 123; FBA, 178, 229; feedback on, 240–41; focus and, 181–86; goals for, 243–44; group work and, 122–23; peers and, 229; progress and, 229, 234–35; supports for, 228, *228*; well-being and, 179
behavioral interventions, 2–3, 245; behavior contracts and, 242–44, *244*; case studies and, 230, 232, 235, 237, 239, 242, 244; CICO, 177–78, 239–42; classroom environment and, 226–32; combined, 239–44; data and, 229–32, 234–35, 238, 240, 243–44; fading of, 229, 231–35, 238, 241; HLPs and, 226–27; positive reinforcement and, 178, 233–35; structure in, 236–39; token economies and, 178, 233–35, *236*; visual supports and, 230–32
behavior contracts, 242–43; case study and, 244, *244*; research and, 244
behaviorism, 142, *143*
behavior-specific praise, 3, 32, 122, 226, 228, 230, 245
bias, 33–34, 103, 113
Big Ideas: in writing instruction, 89–90, 102–4; writing intervention and, 91–92, 97, 100, 108, 115–23. *see also* high-leverage practices
blocked practice, 60–61, 76
Booth, J. L., 52
Bradley-Levine, J., 171

C3. *See* college, career, and civic life framework
can't do/won't do assessment, 81
case studies: behavioral intervention and, 230, 232, 235, 237, 239, 242, 244; behavior contracts and, 244, *244*; CICO, 242, *242*; classroom environment and, 230, *230*; MTSS and, 179; Premack Principle and, 237, *237*; reading intervention and, 176; of science instruction, 133–38, *135*, *137*, 155–59; of scientific models, 133–38, *135*, *137*; social studies intervention and, 181–87; in task analysis, 239, *239*; on token economies, 235, *236*; UDL and, 181–82; on visual supports, 232, *232*

CAST. *See* Center for Applied Special Technologies
CCSS. *See* Common Core State Standards
CEC. *See* Council for Exceptional Children
CEEDAR. *See* Collaboration for Effective Educator Development, Accountability, and Reform
Center for Applied Special Technologies (CAST), 10, 90, 179–80. *See also* universal design for learning
chained procedures, in mathematics instruction, 78
change: to physical space, 228–30; technology and, 251, 257
check-in/check-out (CICO), 177–78; case study on, 242, *242*; collaboration and, 239–40; research and, 241; routines and, 240–41
Child Online Protection and Privacy Act (COPPA), 256
choice, 209, 233, 253–54; engagement and, 10–11
choice boards, 10, 217, 244, 253
choral reading, 17–18, 118, 121
chunking, of information, 142, 184–86
CICO. *See* check-in/check-out
Ciullo, S., 199
civic competencies, social studies and, 171, 191–94, 204
civics, in social studies instruction, 168, 191–92, 194–95, 197
classroom design, *216*, 218–19, 220; collaboration and, 215–17; distractions in, 214–15, 217–18, 222; IEP and, 217, 221; needs of students and, 207, 211, 217–18, 222–23; revision in, 218–19, 222–23; visual supports in, 214–15, 217–18
classroom environment, 2–3, 213–14; assessment of, 215–16, 219; behavioral interventions and, 226–32; behavior and, 176–77, 209–10; case study and, 230, *230*; discussion and, 211; EBPs and, 207–8, 210, 218, 227; groups and, 209, 220; inclusivity and, 141, 144; needs of students and, 221, 227; policies and, 207–8; research on, 209–10, 229–30; social interaction and,

208–9, 214; as support, 207, 222–23, 229; theories and, 208–9
classroom materials: development and, 211–12, *212*, 220–21; organization of, 210–12, *212–13*, 220–22; quality of, 221
classrooms: flexibility in, 213–15, 218–19; seating arrangements in, *210*, 210–14; student-centered, 50, 170–71, 208; student work and, 210, 212–13; traffic patterns in, 209–11, *212*; visibility in, 210–11, *212*; visual stimulation in, 214–15, 228–29
cognitive flexibility, 259–60, 263
cognitive load, 9, 56, 73
cognitive strategies, for writing, 92–97, *93–94*, 100–101
collaboration, 31, 100, 254; CICO and, 239–40; classroom design and, 215–17; engagement and, 138, 242–43; flexible grouping, 99; groups and, 101–2; parent, 115, 178–79, 217, 222, 234, 241–44; science instruction and, 133; teachers and, 154, 172–73, 188
Collaboration for Effective Educator Development, Accountability, and Reform (CEEDAR), 112, 149–50
college, career, and civic life framework (C3), 195–98, 200–204, *203*
combined interventions, 239–44
Common Core State Standards (CCSS), 5–6, 49–50, 73, 91, 112, 192, 196
competencies: algebra, 50–52, 69; civic, 171, 191–94, 204; mathematics instruction and, 51–53; social studies instruction and, 192; strategic, 53, 71; writing, 107–8
comprehension: fluency and, 38; prior knowledge and, 12–13, 21, 41; reading, 6–8, 20–21, 40–43; reading instruction and, 20–22; reading intervention and, 40–43; RSF and, 29; visual supports and, 183–84; vocabulary and, 18–20, 39–40
conceptual knowledge, 54; mathematics and, 52, 56, 68–69, 71; science and, 128–30
concrete examples, in instruction, 55–56, 132, 135, 150–51, 231

concrete-representational-abstract framework (CRA), 55–56, 76–77
construction, of knowledge, 130–31, 142
constructivism, 59, 169; science instruction and, 128–30, *129*, 142–43, *143*; social studies instruction and, 170–71, 187; Socratic seminars and, 170, 181
context: mathematics instruction and, 50; mathematics intervention and, 81–82; reading instruction and, 12, 19–20; of students, 177
COPPA. See Child Online Protection and Privacy Act
core instruction, 1–2, 61–64; physical environment and, 207–23
co-teaching: alternative teaching, 120–21, 154; inclusive science instruction and, *154*, 154–60; instruction plans and, 154–55; special education and, 154–56, 160; station teaching, 120
Council for Exceptional Children (CEC), 108, 111, 113, 148–50
COVID-19 pandemic, 252; academic performance and, 48, 208
CRA. See concrete-representational-abstract framework
cross-content learning, 3, 19, 141, 148, 150–51, 156–60, 202. See also interdisciplinarity
curriculum: accommodations and, 174; knowledge-rich, 13; mathematics instruction and, 68–69; social studies, 191–95

data, 22–23; assessment and, 32, 62–63, 78–81, 155–56, 176, 178; behavioral interventions and, 229–32, 234–35, 238, 240, 243–44; goals and, 115–16; groups and, 11–12; on mathematics, 48–49; MTSS and, 30, 145, 147–48; progress and, 81–84, *83*; universal screening and, 62–63, 78–81; writing and, 119–20
data-based decision-making (DBDM), instruction plans and, 8–9
DCI. See disciplinary core ideas
declarative facts, in mathematics, 53, 69
decoding skills, 6–7, 15, 21, 34, 37–38, 151; phonics and, 8, 16–17

Department of Education (DOE), 1, 254–57
design: of classrooms, 214–23, *216*, *218–19*; instructional, 4, 143–45, 147, 153; intervention, 73; students and, 135–36, 253–54. *See also* universal design for learning
development, 1; classroom materials and, 211–12, *212*, 220–21; of language skills, 13–14, 29–30, 34–35; mathematics and, 68–69; science and, 142; ZPD and, 208–9, 211–12
DI. *See* direct instruction
dialogic reading, 34–35
DIBELS. *See* Dynamic Indicators of Basic Early Literacy Skills
differentiated instruction, 10, 23, 141–42, 160, 179; technology and, 253–54, 256–57
difficulty factors, mathematics intervention and, 71–73
direct instruction (DI), 2, 20, 240; science intervention and, 142, 150
disabilities, 1, *51*; behavior and, 228, 259; dyscalculia, 72; dyslexia, 6, 72–73; educational environments and, 144; EF skills and, 263; EI and, 50; LRE and, 174; manipulatives and, 54; mathematics and, 60; reading comprehension and, 7, 40; RTI and, 174–75; science instruction and, 141–43, 148; social studies intervention and, 198–200; writing instruction and, 90. *See also* students with disabilities
disciplinary core ideas (DCI), 130, 133, 136
discussion, 98–101, 136–38, 170, 181–82; classroom environment and, 211; read-aloud and, 12–14, 17–18, 21, 34, 41–42, 152, 263
distractions, 259; in classroom design, 214–15, 217–18, 222
distributed practice, 62
DOE. *See* Department of Education
driving questions, 138, 171
Dynamic Indicators of Basic Early Literacy Skills (DIBELS), 9, *155*
dyscalculia, 72
dyslexia, 6, 72–73

EBPs. *See* evidence-based practices
economics, in social studies instruction, 194, 197
educational environments, 70–72, 128; disabilities and, 144; LRE, 154, 173–74; technology and, 251. *See also* classroom environment
EF. *See* executive function
EI. *See* explicit instruction
ELAR. *See* English language arts reading
Elementary and Secondary Education Act (ESEA), 5
Elkonin boxes, literacy and, 15–17, 35, 37
engagement, 19–20, 97–98, 143; assessment and, 172; choice and, 10–11; collaboration and, 138, 242–43; groups and, 252; self-regulation and, 261; supports and, 200; technology and, 252–53, 256; UDL and, 152–54, 180
engineering instruction, 128, 132, *132*
English language arts reading (ELAR), 155–59
ESEA. *See* Elementary and Secondary Education Act
Every Student Succeeds Act (ESSA), 5–6, 50, 144, 178, 208
evidence-based assessment, 32–34, *33*, 79, 112–13, 146
evidence-based instruction, 1–3, 22, 89–90, 175–76; reading interventions and, 30–34, *33*; writing and, 108
evidence-based practices (EBPs): classroom environment and, 207–8, 210, 218, 227; in inclusive science instruction, 148–50, *149*, 154, 160; mnemonic devices, 60, 77, 99, 120, 199–200, 261; research and, 148–49
examples: concrete, 55–56, 132, 135, 150–51, 231; worked, 56–59, *57*, 77
executive function skills (EF): academic performance and, 260; assessment and, 262–63; disabilities and, 263; graphic organizers and, 264; HLPs and, 263–64; problem solving and, 259, 261–62; reading comprehension and, 41; research on, 260–61, 263;

self-regulation and, 260–62; theories and, 259–63; working memory, 8, 56, 73, 89, 259–60, 262–63
explicit instruction (EI), 2–3, 9–10, 13, 31, *36*, 226, 263; behavior and, 123; disabilities and, 50; group work and, 117–18; mathematics intervention and, 69–70; phonics and, 16; reading and, 176; science intervention and, 142–43, 150; social studies intervention and, 183; task analysis and, 238; of vocabulary, 40; writing intervention and, 111, 117–19
extension activities, in instruction plans, 134, 137

fading: of behavioral interventions, 229, 231–35, 238, 241; of supports, 56, 64, 69–71, 97–98, 100, 142
FAPE. *See* free and appropriate public education
FBA. *See* functional behavior assessment
feedback, 180, 261, 264; on behavior, 240–41; mathematics and, 77–78; from peers, 99–101, 112–13, 138; phonics and, 37–39; practice and, 183; reading and, 31–32, 34–35, 155; writing instruction and, 100–102, 117–19
flexibility: in classrooms, 213–15, 218–19; cognitive, 259–60, 263
flexible grouping, 97–98, 100; collaboration, 99; writing intervention and, 119–23
fluency, 107–8; comprehension and, 38; procedural, 52–53, 56, 69, 71; in reading instruction, 8, 17–18; reading interventions for, 29, 38–39, 155–56, 176
focus, of students, 8, *56–57*, 259; on activities, 54–55; behavior and, 181–86
formative assessment, 146, 172–73, 252; writing intervention and, 112–13, 118–19
frameworks, 2–3, 10, 12; C3, 195–98, 200–204, *203*; CEC toolkit and, 108, 111, 113, 148–49; CRA, 55–56, 76–77; for mathematics intervention, 73, *74–75*; RSF, 7, 28–29; SVR, 6–7, 28, 70. *See also specific frameworks*
Frayer models, 20, 40
free and appropriate public education (FAPE), 144, 173–74
functional behavior assessment (FBA), 178, 229

generative artificial intelligence (AI), 255–57
Gentry, R., 8
geography, in social studies instruction, 168, 193–94, 197, 200–202
goals, 240; behavior, 243–44; data and, 115–16; EF and, 259; instruction plans and, 102–3; science intervention and, 144, 147–48; SRSD and, 261; writing intervention and, 115–16, 119–20
graphic organizers, 136–38, *137*, 151; EF skills and, 264; Frayer models, 20, 40; literacy and, 181; reading and, 40–42, 183–84; social studies and, 185–86, 199, *199*, 202, 204; writing and, 95–99, 119
groups: classroom environment and, 209, 220; collaboration and, 101–2; data and, 11–12; engagement and, 252; flexible, 97–100, 119–23
group work, 8, 12, 15–16, 182–83; behavior and, 122–23; dialogic reading in, 34–35; EI and, 117–18; PBIS and, 177; peers and, 119; reading interventions and, 29–30, 176; science instruction and, 137–38; science intervention and, 145–48; supports for, 186

high-leverage practices (HLPs), 204; behavioral interventions and, 226–27; EF skills and, 263–64; inclusive science instruction and, 148–50, *149*, 154, 160; reading intervention and, 31, 34; special education and, 111; writing instruction and, 91–92; writing intervention and, 108, *109–10*, 111, 115–17, 119, 123
history, in social studies instruction, 168, 193, 197, 199–200
HLPs. *See* high-leverage practices

IDEA. *See* Individuals with Disabilities Education Act
IDEIA. *See* Individuals with Disabilities Education Improvement Act
IEP. *See* individualized education program
IES. *See* Institute of Education Sciences
inclusive science instruction, 151, *159*; co-teaching and, *154*, 154–60; EBPs in, 148–50, *149*, 154, 160; HLPs and, 148–50, *149*, 154, 160; UDL and, 152–54
inclusive social studies instruction, 198–204
inclusivity: classroom environments and, 141, 144; standards and, 148–49
independence, of students, 209, 211–12, 220, 231
independent practice: reading and, 17–19, 31–32, 39; writing and, 97–100, 118, 121
individualized education program (IEP), 121, 173–74; assessment and, 102; classroom design and, 217, 221; long-term goals and, 115–16, 119; science intervention and, 144, 147–48, 160; social studies intervention and, 196
Individuals with Disabilities Education Act (IDEA), 50, 144, 173
Individuals with Disabilities Education Improvement Act (IDEIA), 50, 144–45, 148, 173–74
inhibitory control, 259–60
inquiry-based learning: science instruction and, 151–52; social studies instruction and, 195–98, 200–204, *203*
Institute of Education Sciences (IES), 90, 112, 262
instructional design, 4; SDI, 143–45, 147; UDL and, 153
instruction plans, 156–60; co-teaching and, 154–55; DBDM and, 8–9; extension activities in, 134, 137; goals and, 102–3; reading instruction and, 6; social studies intervention and, 182–83, 185–87, 200–204, *203*
interactive literacy framework, 12
interdisciplinarity, 146; in science instruction, 129–30, 141, 150–51; social studies and, 191, 196–97
interleaving practice, 61–62

International Society for Technology in Education (ISTE), 252, 255
intervention blocks, in MTSS, 11–12, 35
intervention dimensions, for reading, 31–32
ISTE. *See* International Society for Technology in Education

knowledge, 50; acquisition of, 54–56, 69–70, 153; applied, 6, 49, 57, 171, 196–97; conceptual, 52, 54, 56, 68–69, 71, 128–30; construction of, 130–31, 142; representation of, 10, 95, 98–99, 152–53, 180–81; social studies and, 168–69; teachers and, 95–96; technology and, 253–54. *See also* prior knowledge
knowledge-rich curriculum, 13

language, 16–17; assessments of, 34–35, 37; ELAR, 155–59; oral, 13–14, 29, 34–35; in reading instruction, 13–14
language skills, development of, 13–14, 29–30, 34–35
learning: active, 169–71, 252; chunking of information and, 142, 184–86; cross-content, 3, 19, 141, 148, 150–51, 156–60, 202; inquiry-based, 151–52, 195–98, 200–204, *203*; PBL, 171, 187; SEL, 262; writing and, 88
least restrictive environment (LRE), 154, 173–74
literacy, 4, 12, 27; decoding skills in, 6–8, 15–17, 21, 34, 37–38, 151; Elkonin boxes and, 15–17, 35, 37; graphic organizers and, 181; morphology and, 7, 17, 20, 29, 39–40, 151; multisensory approaches and, 19–20, 35–37; oral language and, 13–14; orthography and, 7, 13, 28–29; phonology and, 2, 7, 13–15, 29, 73; policies and, 5–6; science and, 150–51; social studies and, 168; whole language strategy for, 5–6
long-term goals, 120; IEP and, 115–16, 119
LRE. *See* least restrictive environment

MacKinnon, S., 253
Majeika, C. E., 240–43

Index 273

manipulatives, 17, 35–37, 76–77; disabilities and, 54; in mathematics instruction, 54–56, *55*
mathematics: adaptive reasoning and, 52, 71; algebra competence and, 50–52, 69; conceptual knowledge and, 52, 56, 68–69, 71; data on, 48–49; declarative facts in, 53, 69; development and, 68–69; disabilities and, 60; feedback and, 77–78; motivation and, 69–70; multilingual students and, 72; practice and, 60–62, *61*, 76; problem solving in, 49, 59–60; procedural fluency and, 52–53, 56, 69, 71; productive disposition in, 53, 71; reading and, 59–60, 72–73; strategic competence and, 53, 71; teacher modeling and, 55, 58–60
mathematics instruction, 48; assessment and, 62–63; chained procedures in, 78; competencies and, 51–53; context and, 50; curriculum and, 68–69; manipulatives in, 54–56, *55*; MTSS and, 62–64; policies for, 49–51, *51*; prior knowledge and, 50, 59; research on, 68–69; vignettes of, 54–55, 58–59; word problems in, 59–60, 73; worked examples in, 56–59, *57*, 77
mathematics intervention, 68; assessment in, 78–85, *80*, *83*; context and, 81–82; difficulty factors and, 71–73; EI and, 69–70; frameworks for, 73, 74–75; methods for, 73–84, *74–75*; prior knowledge and, 69–70, 73–76; scaffolded instruction and, 70–71, 76–77; self-regulation and, 261; systematic instruction in, 73–77, 84; theories and, 70–71; vocabulary in, 73–76
math rope, of NRC, 50–53, *51*, 58, 71, *71*
meanings, 142; vocabulary and, 13, 20, 28–29, 39–40
meta-cognitive strategies, for writing, 92–97, *93–94*
methods, for mathematics intervention, 73–84, *74–75*
mnemonic devices, 60, 77, 99, 120, 199–200, 261
modes, of writing, 102
Montessori, M., 208–9, 211–12, 220

morphology, literacy and, 7, 17, 20, 29, 39–40, 151
Mosier, G., 171
motivation, 181; mathematics and, 69–70; for reading, 8
MTSS. *See* multi-tiered system of supports
multilingual students, 8, 19, 135; mathematics and, 72; vocabulary and, 151
multimodality, 251; in science instruction, 131, 153; in social studies instruction, 181, 186–87, 198, 201–2
multisensory approaches, 143; literacy and, 19–20, 35–37
multi-tiered system of supports (MTSS), 178; assessments and, 30–31, 145; data and, 30, 145, 147–48; intervention blocks in, 11–12, 35; mathematics instruction and, 62–64; reading instruction and, 9, 11–12; science intervention and, 145–48, *146*, *149*, 155–56, 160; Tier 1 of, 27, 43, 63–64, 228; Tier 2 of, 3, 30, 32–39, 63–64, 148, 155–56, 239–40; Tier 3 of, 3, 31, 34–36, 148, 245; tiers of, 2, 11, 28, 30, 43, 145–47, 179, 226–27. *See also* universal screening

National Assessment of Education Progress (NAEP), 48, 108
National Center for Intensive Intervention (NCII), 33, 228
National Center of Response to Intervention (NCRTI), 175
National Center on Geographic Education (NCGE), 193–94
National Council for the Social Studies (NCSS), 168, 171–72, 191, 194–95, 200–201
National Council of Teachers of Mathematics (NCTM), 49
National Mathematics Advisory Panel (NMAP), 50–53, 68, 71
National Reading Panel, 4–6, 8, 68
National Research Council (NRC), math rope of, 50–53, *51*, 58, 71, *71*
National Science Teaching Association (NSTA), 128
NCGE. *See* National Center on Geographic Education

NCII. *See* National Center for Intensive Intervention
NCLB. *See* No Child Left Behind Act
NCRTI. *See* National Center of Response to Intervention
NCSS. *See* National Council for the Social Studies
NCTM. *See* National Council of Teachers of Mathematics
needs, of students, 12; classroom design and, 207, 211, 217–18, 222–23; classroom environment and, 221, 227; diverse, 10, 90, 123, 141, 153, 183; UDL and, 97; visual supports and, 231
Newton, K. J., 52
Next Generation Science Standards (NGSS), 128–30, 134; scientific models and, 132–33
NMAP. *See* National Mathematics Advisory Panel
No Child Left Behind Act (NCLB), 5, 50, 143–44, 192
NRC. *See* National Research Council
NSTA. *See* National Science Teaching Association

Obama, Barack, 5
oral language, 29; literacy and, 13–14; reading interventions and, 34–35
oral reading fluency assessment (ORF), 38–39
organization, of classroom materials, 210–12, *212–13*, 220–22
orthography, 7, 13, 28–29
Ouellette, G., 8

PA. *See* phonemic awareness
parent collaboration, 115, 178–79, 217, 222, 234, 241–44
PBIS. *See* positive behavior interventions and supports
PBL. *See* project-based learning
peers, 187; behavior and, 229; feedback from, 99–101, 112–13, 138; group work and, 119; support from, 200
Pershan, Michael, 56
phonemic awareness (PA), 14–15; reading intervention and, 35–36, *36*
phonics, 5–6, 15; decoding skills and, 8, 16–17; feedback and, 37–38; reading intervention and, 36–38; scaffolded instruction and, 37
phonology, 2, 7, 13, 29, 73; reading instruction and, 14–15
physical environment: change to, 228–30; core instruction and, 207–23. *See also* classroom environment
Piaget, J., 131, 208–9
PLC. *See* professional learning community
policies: classroom environment and, 207–8; literacy and, 5–6; for mathematics instruction, 49–51, *51*; science intervention and, 143–45; social studies, 173–74; special education and, 173; technology and, 255; tests and, 5, 192; writing instruction and, 90–91; writing intervention and, 112
positive behavior interventions and supports (PBIS), 176–79
positive reinforcement, behavioral interventions and, 178, 233–35
practice, 151; distributed, 62; feedback and, 183; independent, 17–19, 31–32, 39, 97–100, 118, 121; interleaving, 61–62; mathematics and, 60–62, *61*, 76
praise, behavior-specific, 3, 32, 122, 226, 228, 230, 245
precision teaching, 71–72, 142; assessment and, 143
preference assessment, 122–23, 233–34, 236
Premack Principle: case study and, 237, *237*; research and, 236–37
preskills. *See* prior knowledge
pre-teaching, 13, 18–19, 76, 147, 150–51
preventative interventions, 62–63, 120, 215, 227–29, 245
primary interventions. *See* Tier 1, of MTSS
prior knowledge, 7–9, 169–70; comprehension and, 12–13, 21, 41; mathematics instruction and, 50, 59; mathematics intervention and, 69–70, 73–76; reading instruction and, 12–13; reading intervention and, 32; science instruction and, 131–33, 145, 151; writing intervention and, 117, 121
privacy, technology and, 253–54, 256

problem solving: EF and, 259, 261–62; in mathematics, 49, 59–60; skills for, 168–69; technology and, 252–53; in writing instruction, 92
procedural fluency, mathematics and, 52–53, 56, 69, 71
productive disposition, in mathematics, 53, 71
professional development, for teachers, 144–45, 147, 154–55, *159*, 255
professional learning community (PLC), 172–73
progress, 148; assessment of, 146–47; behavior and, 229, 234–35; data and, 81–84, *83*; RTI and, 175–76
project-based learning (PBL), 171, 187

quality, of classroom materials, 221

read-aloud, 12–14, 17–18, 21, 34, 41–42, 152, 263
reading, 5, 29, 33; assessments of, 8–12, 22–23, 176; EI and, 176; feedback and, 31–32, 34–35, 155; graphic organizers and, 40–42, 183–84; independent practice and, 17–19, 31–32, 39; mathematics and, 59–60, 72–73; motivation for, 8; science and, 147, 151–52; social studies and, 181–82, 186, 198–99; spelling and, 15–17, 37–38; SVR, 6–7, 28, 70; teacher modeling and, 16–18, 20, 32, 36, 39–40, 156; writing and, 107
reading comprehension, 6, 8; disabilities and, 7, 40; story grammar and, 20–21, 40–41; text structures and, 42–43
reading instruction, 4, 30; academic standards for, 5–6; comprehension and, 20–22; context and, 12, 19–20; fluency in, 17–18; instruction plans and, 6; MTSS and, 9, 11–12; phonics and, 15–17; phonology and, 14–15; prior knowledge, 12–13; reading intervention and, 28; research and, 7–8; theories for, 6–7; UDL and, 9–10, 17, 23; vignettes for, 9–21; vocabulary and, 18–20
reading intervention, 27; case studies and, 176; comprehension and, 40–43; evidence-based instruction and, 30–34, *33*; for fluency, 29, 38–39, 155–56, 176; group work and, 29–30, 176; HLPs and, 31, 34; intervention dimensions for, 31–32; oral language and, 34–35; PA and, 35–36, *36*; phonics and, 36–38; prior knowledge and, 32; reading instruction and, 28; research for, 29–30; self-regulation and, 261; special education and, 30–31; theories and, 28–29; vignettes for, 32, 35–39, 41–43; vocabulary and, 39–40
reading systems framework (RSF), 7, 28–29
reciprocal teaching, science instruction and, 152
reinforcement, 56, 58–59, 63–64, 262; positive, 178, 233–35; teachers and, 122
representation of knowledge, UDL and, 10, 95, 98–99, 152–53, 180–81
research, 50–51, 176–77; assessment and, 82; behavior contracts and, 244; CICO and, 241; on classroom environment, 209–10, 229–30; EBPs and, 148–49; on EF skills, 260–61, 263; mathematics instruction, 68–69; Premack Principle and, 236–37; reading instruction and, 7–8; for reading intervention, 29–30; on task analysis, 239; technology and, 252, 255–56; token economies and, 235; on visual supports, 232; writing instruction and, 89–90, 108; writing intervention and, 111–12
response to intervention (RTI), 177–79; disabilities and, 174–75; progress and, 175–76
revision: in classroom design, 218–19, 222–23; science instruction and, 133–34, 136, 138–39; writing instruction and, 100, 107–8, 112, 119–21
reward systems, 122–23, 240–45; token economies as, 178, 233–35, *236*
risk factors, for students, 1, 27, 72–73, 78–79, 148
routines, 184, *219*; CICO and, 240–41; for study, 58–59
RSF. *See* reading systems framework
RTI. *See* response to intervention

SBI. *See* schema-based instruction
scaffolded instruction, 12–13, 121, 252, 264; assessment and, 102–3; mathematics intervention and, 70–71, 76–77; phonics and, 37; science and, 141–43; worked examples and, 57–59; writing and, 98
scaffolded silent reading (ScSR), 18, 21–22
Scarparolo, G., 253
schema-based instruction (SBI), 59–60, 142, 261, 264
science, 5, 33; conceptual knowledge and, 128–30; development and, 142; instructional design and, 143; literacy and, 150–51; reading and, 147, 151–52; scaffolded instruction and, 141–43; special education and, 143–44, 148; standards for, 128–30, 138; systems thinking and, 130–32, 138–39
science instruction, *131*; assessment and, 133, 138–39, 153–55; case studies of, 133–38, *135*, *137*, 155–59; collaboration and, 133; constructivism and, 128–30, *129*, 142–43, *143*; disabilities and, 141–43, 148; group work and, 137–38; inclusive, 148–60, *149*, *154*, *159*; inquiry-based learning and, 151–52; interdisciplinarity in, 129–30, 141, 150–51; multimodality in, 131, 153; prior knowledge and, 131–33, 145, 151; reciprocal teaching and, 152; revision and, 133–34, 136, 138–39; science intervention and, 148–52; scientific models in, 130–38, *132*, *135*, *137*; theories and, 131–32, 142–43, *143*; vocabulary and, 148, 150–51
science intervention: DI and, 142, *150*; EI and, 142–43, 150; goals and, 144, 147–48; group work and, 145–48; IEP and, 144, 147–48, 160; MTSS and, 145–48, *146*, *149*, 155–56, 160; policies and, 143–45; precision teaching and, 143; science instruction and, 148–52; SDI and, 143–45, 147
scientific models: case studies of, 133–38, *135*, *137*; NGSS and, 132–33; theories and, 130–33, *132*
ScSR. *See* scaffolded silent reading

SDI. *See* specially designed instruction
seating arrangements, in classrooms, *210*, 210–14
SEL. *See* social emotional learning
self-assessment, 113, 153–54
self-regulated strategy development (SRSD), 95–96, 263; goals and, 261; problem solving and, 261–62
self-regulation, 29–30, 40–41, 178; EF skills and, 260–62; SOLVE strategy and, 261–62, 264
short-term goals, 115–16, 119–20
simple view of reading (SVR), 6–7, 28, 70
skills, 12, 238; decoding, 6–8, 15–17, 21, 34, 37–38, 151; EF, 8, 41, 56, 73, 89, 259–64; language, 13–14, 29–30, 34–35; PA, 14–15; practice and, 60–62; for problem solving, 168–69; social studies, 193–94, 197–98; work, 254, 257
social emotional learning (SEL), 262
social interaction, classroom environment and, 208–9, 214
social studies: assessment and, 172–73; civic competencies and, 171, 191–94, 204; curriculum of, 191–95; graphic organizers and, 185–86, 199, *199*, 202, 204; interdisciplinarity and, 191, 196–97; knowledge and, 168–69; literacy and, 168; NCSS and, 168, 171–72, 191, 194–95, 200–201; policies, 173–74; reading and, 181–82, 186, 198–99; skills in, 193–94, 197–98; standards, 171–72, 192–98, *195*, 201; writing and, 198
social studies instruction, 172, 188, *195*; civics in, 168, 191–92, 194–95, 197; competencies and, 192; constructivism and, 170–71, 187; economics in, 194, 197; geography in, 168, 193–94, 197, 200–202; history in, 168, 193, 197, 199–200; inclusive, 198–204; inquiry-based learning and, 195–98, 200–204, *203*; multimodality in, 181, 186–87, 198, 201–2; social studies interventions and, 181–86; theories and, 169–71; vignettes and, 200–202
social studies intervention: case studies and, 181–87; disabilities and, 198–200; EI and, 183; IEP and,

196; instruction plans and, 182–83, 185–87, 200–204, *203*; social studies instruction and, 181–86; supports and, 185–87
Socratic seminars, 170, 181
SOLVE strategy, 261–62, 264
special education, 1, 9; co-teaching and, 154–56, 160; HLPs and, 111; policies and, 173; reading intervention and, 30–31; science and, 143–44, 148; supports and, 187–88; writing and, 108–11
specially designed instruction (SDI), 143–45, 147
spelling, 15–17, 37–38
SRSD. *See* self-regulated strategy development
SSR. *See* sustained silent reading
standards: inclusivity and, 148–49; science, 128–30, 138; social studies, 171–72, 192–98, *195*, 201; SWDs and, 144–45; for technology, 252–53; for writing instruction, 91
station teaching, 120
story grammar, reading comprehension and, 20–21, 41–42
strategic competence, mathematics and, 53, 71
structure, in behavioral interventions, 236, 239; task analysis and, 237–38
student-centered classrooms, 50, 170–71, 208
students: cognitive load and, 9, 56, 73; context of, 177; design and, 135–36, 253–54; focus of, 8, 54–57, 181–86, 259; independence of, 209, 211–12, 220, 231; multilingual, 8, 19, 72, 135, 151; risk factors for, 1, 27, 72–73, 78–79, 148. *See also* needs, of students
students with disabilities (SWDs): SDI and, 143–45, 147; standards and, 144–45; work skills and, 254; writing intervention and, 107–8, 111–13, 117–18, 120
student work, 222; assessment and, 147, 156, 172; classrooms and, 210, 212–13; technology and, 213, 256
study, routines for, 58–59
summative assessment, 146, 172

supports, 196; behavior, 228, *228*; choice boards, 10, 217, 244, 253; classroom environments as, 207, 222–23, 229; engagement and, 200; fading of, 56, 64, 69–71, 97–98, 100, 142; for group work, 186; mnemonic devices, 60, 77, 99, 120, 199–200, 261; from peers, 200; social studies intervention and, 185–87; special education and, 187–88; verbal, 76–77, *77*. *See also* multi-tiered system of supports; visual supports
sustained silent reading (SSR), 18
SVR. *See* simple view of reading
SWDs. *See* students with disabilities
systematic instruction, in mathematics intervention, 73–77, 84
systems thinking, 130–32, 138–39

task analysis, 237–38; case study in, 239, *239*; research on, 239
teacher modeling, 252; mathematics and, 55, 58–60; reading and, 16–18, 20, 32, 36, 39–40, 156; think-alouds as, 21, 29–30, 40, *95*–98, 118; writing and, 95, 118–19
teachers: collaboration and, 154, 172–73, 188; knowledge and, *95*–96; professional development for, 144–45, 147, 154–55, *159*, 255; reinforcement and, 122
technology: assistive, 181, 186, 252, 254, 256–57; change and, 251, 257; differentiated instruction and, 253–54, 256–57; engagement and, 252–53, 256; privacy and, 253–54, 256; problem solving and, 252–53; research and, 252, 255–56; student work and, 213, 256; work skills and, 254, 257
tests: assessment and, 115–16; policies and, 5, 192
textbooks, 50, 201–2
text structures, reading comprehension and, 42–43
theories: classroom environment and, 208–9; EF skills and, 259–63; mathematics intervention and, 70–71; for reading instruction, 6–7; reading intervention and, 28–29; science instruction and, 131–32, 142–43, *143*;

scientific models and, 130–33, *132*; social studies instruction and, 169–71; writing instruction and, 88–89
think-alouds, 21, 29–30, 40, 95–98, 118
Tier 1, of MTSS, 27, 228; assessment of, 43, 63–64
Tier 2, of MTSS, 3, 32–39, 63–64, 148, 155–56, 239–40; skills and, 30
Tier 3, of MTSS, 3, 31, 34–36, 148, 245
tiers, of MTSS, 2, 11, 28, 30, 43, 145–47, 179, 226–27
tiers, of PBIS, 177–78
tiers, of RTI, 175–76
token economies, 178; behavioral interventions and, 233–35; case study on, 235, *236*; research and, 235
traffic patterns, in classrooms, 209–11, *212*

UDL. *See* universal design for learning
UFLI. *See* University of Florida Literacy Institute
universal design for learning (UDL), 3, 179; action and expression and, 10, 97–99, 152, 180; case studies and, 181–82; engagement and, 152–54, 180; inclusive science instruction and, 152–54; reading instruction and, 9–10, 17, 23; representation of knowledge and, 10, 95, 98–99, 152–53, 180–81; writing activities and, 97–100; writing instruction and, 90–92, 94, 95, 97–100, 102–4
universal interventions. *See* Tier 1, of MTSS
universal screening, MTSS and, 69, 72, 84–85, *146*, 146–48, 175–76; data and, 62–63, 78–81
universal screening, of RTI, 175–76
University of Florida Literacy Institute (UFLI), 34

verbal supports, 76–77, *77*
vignettes: mathematics instruction and, 54–55, 58–59; reading instruction and, 9–21; for reading intervention, 32, 35–39, 41–43; social studies instruction and, 200–202; writing instruction and, 96–99, 101–2; writing intervention and, *109–10*, 115–19, 121–22, 179. *See also* case studies
visibility, in classrooms, 210–11, *212*
visual stimulation, in classrooms, 214–15, 228–29
visual supports, 76–77, *77*, 199, *199*, 236; behavioral interventions and, 230–32; case study on, 232, *232*; in classroom design, 214–15, 217–18; comprehension and, 183–84; needs of students and, 231; research on, 232
vocabulary, 8; comprehension and, 18–20, 39–40; in mathematics intervention, 73–76; meanings and, 13, 20, 28–29, 39–40; multilingual students and, 151; science instruction and, 148, 150–51
Vygotsky, L. S., 131, 208–9

well-being, behavior and, 179
What Works Clearinghouse, 22, 33–34, 90, 149, 261–62
whole language strategy, for literacy, 5–6
word problems, in mathematics instruction, 59–60, 73
worked examples, in mathematics instruction, 56–59, *57*, 77
working memory, 8, 56, 73, 89, 259–60, 262–63
work skills, technology and, 254, 257
writers-within-community (WWC) instructional method, 3, 88–90, 92, 97, 111–13; collaboration and, 101
writing: cognitive strategies for, 92–97, *93–94*, 100–101; competencies for, 107–8; data and, 119–20; evidence-based instruction and, 108; graphic organizers and, 95–99, 119; independent practice and, 97–100, 118, 121; learning and, 88; meta-cognitive strategies for, 92–97, *93–94*; modes of, 102; reading and, 107; in reading instruction, 13–14; scaffolded instruction and, 98; social studies and, 198; special education and, 108–11; teacher modeling and, 95, 118–19
writing activities, UDL and, 97–100
writing instruction, *93*; assessment and, 102–3; Big Ideas in, 89–90, 102–4; disabilities and, 90; feedback and, 100–102, 117–19; HLPs and, 91–92;

policies and, 90–91; problem solving in, 92; research and, 89–90, 108; revision and, 100, 107–8, 112, 119–21; standards for, 91; theories and, 88–89; UDL and, 90–92, 94, 95, 97–100, 102–4; vignettes and, 96–99, 101–2
writing intervention, 114; Big Ideas and, 91–92, 97, 100, 108, 115–23; EI and, 111, 117–19; flexible grouping and, 119–23; formative assessment and, 112–13, 118–19; goals and, 115–16, 119–20; HLPs and, 108, 109–10, 111, 115–17, 119, 123; policies and, 112; prior knowledge and, 117, 121; research and, 111–12; SWDs and, 107–8, 111–13, 117–18, 120; vignettes and, 109–10, 115–19, 121–22, 179
WWC. See writers-within-community

Zelazo, P. D., 259–60, 262
zone of proximal development (ZPD), 208–9, 211–12

About the Authors

Julie Atwood, MEd, BCBA, LBA, is a board certified behavior analyst (BCBA) and special educator supporting rural school districts in Oklahoma. Ms. Atwood is currently a research scientist and doctoral student at the University of Oklahoma, where she is exploring behavior intervention plan fidelity in schools, educator buy-in of evidence-based behavior intervention, and professional development models for rural districts.

Glenna M. Billingsley, PhD, is associate professor at Texas State University in San Marcos, Texas. She is currently chair of the Department of Curriculum and Instruction in the College of Education. Dr. Billingsley's research primarily focuses on schoolwide and individual application of positive behavior interventions and supports as well as academic and behavioral interventions for students with emotional, mental, and behavioral health needs.

David A. Brunow, PhD, is a middle school assistant principal in Norman, Oklahoma. His research interests include assistive technology, universal design for learning (UDL), and students with learning disabilities. Dr. Brunow has served as an adjunct professor at the University of Oklahoma and has taught individuals with exceptionalities in middle school and high school settings.

Stephen Ciullo, PhD, is associate professor of special education in the Department of Curriculum and Instruction at Texas State University. Dr. Ciullo's interests include intervention and instructional methods in the area of written expression for students with learning disabilities, observational research, and professional development for co-teachers.

Alyson A. Collins, PhD, CALT, is associate professor of special education in the Department of Curriculum and Instruction at Texas State University. Her program of research focuses on exploring writing instruction for students with and without disabilities, effective interventions for elementary students, and professional development models that support teacher implementation of evidence-based practices.

Theresa A. Cullen, PhD, is professor at and director of the Center for Faculty LIFE. She is an Apple Distinguished Educator and is currently director of the Arkansas Tech University Online Teaching Academy to help educators learn how to teach remotely and online.

About the Authors

Scott Dueker, PhD, BCBA-D, is assistant professor of special education and applied behavior analysis at Ball State University. He is also a board certified behavior analyst—doctoral level. His interests include mathematics instruction and language development for learners with moderate to severe intellectual and developmental disabilities as well as using technology for instruction in both clinical and classroom settings. He has experience providing applied behavior analysis (ABA) services in clinical, home, institutional, and classroom settings. Dr. Dueker uses a verbal behavior approach to behavior change and has been successful in both teaching new behavior and reducing unwanted behavior by increasing a learner's communication ability. He often works with learners exhibiting more intense behavioral issues.

Kelly Feille, PhD, is associate professor of science education at the University of Oklahoma. Her teaching and research emphasize the support and development of elementary science teachers who engage learners in authentic science experiences inside and outside of the classroom.

Caroline Fitchett, PhD, is assistant professor at California State University San Bernardino. Her research interests include academic interventions for students with extensive support needs, social studies education for students with intellectual disabilities, high-leverage practices (HPLs) for special education teachers, and teacher preparation and development.

Garrett Hall, PhD, is assistant professor in the School Psychology Program at Florida State University. His research focuses primarily on the development of academic skills (especially mathematics). This includes examining predictors of academic development (such as language and linguistic diversity as well as executive functions) and equitable methods to assess, prevent, and intervene on academic difficulties. He is also interested in quantitative methods in school psychology research and practice (such as causal inference, measurement, and longitudinal methods) and how these methods can inform school-based prevention and intervention within a multi-tiered system of support (MTSS). Last, he is interested in how "ecological" factors within MTSS promote students' academic, social, emotional, and behavioral functioning, such as implementation fidelity and family–school involvement.

Stephanie Hathcock, PhD, is associate professor of science education at Oklahoma State University. Her research agenda is influenced by place as a key starting point for change and creativity as a necessary component and by-product of change.

Casey Hord, PhD, is professor in the Department of Special Education at the University of Cincinnati. His primary research interest is developing mathematics interventions for students with learning disabilities and students with mild intellectual disability. Other research interests include the role of visual representations and strategic questioning in mathematics teaching, the training of preservice teachers to teach mathematics to students with mild disabilities, and the potential role of mathematics tutors for students with mild disabilities in urban, suburban, and rural settings.

Jasmine Justus, MEd, BCBA, LBA, earned a bachelor's degree in early childhood education and a master's degree in special education from the University of Oklahoma. For the past five years, she has taught in an elementary setting as a general and special education teacher. Currently, she serves students and educators within a public school system as an academic resource coordinator. Currently, she is pursuing a doctoral degree in special education at the University of Oklahoma, where she focuses her research on classroom management and Individuals with Disabilities Education Act (IDEA) compliance within rural public education.

Randa G. Keeley, PhD, is associate professor of special education at Texas Woman's University in Denton, Texas, with a research concentration in classroom interventions that promote inclusive learning environments for students with special educational needs and disabilities. Her research interests include the application of quantitative and qualitative measures to analyze the effects of inclusive practices, culturally responsive teaching, and co-teaching as they relate to the teacher and student.

Sagarika Kosaraju, EdD, is a project coordinator in the Department of Curriculum and Instruction at Texas State University. She manages research focused on elementary general and special education writing instruction, and she coaches teachers on intervention strategies for students at risk or with disabilities in writing.

Bre Martin, MEd, BCBA, LBA, serves students and educators within a public school system as an academic resource coordinator. She earned a bachelor's degree in sociology and a master's degree in special education, both from the University of Oklahoma. She is currently a doctoral student at the University of Oklahoma, where she is pursuing research in behavior intervention plan fidelity in schools, the impact of trauma on behavior, and trauma-informed practices within public education.

John William McKenna, PhD, is associate professor of special education at the University of Massachusetts Lowell and is an affiliate of the Center for Autism Research and Education (CARE). His research interests include evidence-based academic and behavioral interventions for students with emotional and behavioral disabilities, responsible inclusion, and school–family partnerships. His service interests center on improving student access to empirically based instruction and intervention and the full continuum of placement options.

Hanna Moore, PhD, is multi-tiered system of support (MTSS) coordinator in Guilford County, North Carolina, where she supports the development and implementation of MTSS in a secondary setting. Dr. Moore also serves as a special education adjunct professor; her research and teaching interests include teacher preparation and development, the research-to-practice gap, and teaching reading to students with disabilities.

Kevin T. Muns, MEd, BCBA, LBA, is a board-certified behavior analyst (BCBA) who predominantly works within clinical applications for dissemination and intervention related to behavior analysis. He is currently a doctoral student at the

University of Oklahoma studying evidence-based practices for individuals on the autism spectrum both within and outside of the school system to reduce challenging behavior that serves as a barrier for placement in lower restrictive environments.

Jodi Arroyo Nagel, MEd, is a special education teacher and multi-tiered system of support (MTSS) coordinator in Levy County, Florida. She earned her bachelor's degree in elementary education from the University of Florida and her master's degree in curriculum and instruction with focuses in special education and trauma-informed education from Concordia University. Nagel is currently a doctoral student at the University of North Florida, focusing her research on special education policy in rural communities, MTSS in secondary settings, and inclusive teaching practices.

Corey Peltier, PhD, is associate professor of special education in the Department of Educational Psychology at the University of Oklahoma. His research interests include (1) identifying effective interventions and assessment procedures to improve the mathematical outcomes for students identified or at-risk for disabilities, (2) methodological considerations when using single-case research designs, and (3) the use of systematic reviews and meta-analyses to inform the fields' understanding of effective interventions under specific contexts.

Maria B. Peterson-Ahmad, PhD, is associate professor of special education and the associate dean for research, inclusion, and innovation at Texas Woman's University. Her research focuses on teacher effectiveness, particularly for general and special education teachers of students with mild/moderate disabilities with a focus on educational technology and high-leverage practices (HLPs).

Jacquelyn Purser, MEd, is a special education teacher in a life skills/adaptive skills classroom (grades 6–12) for Blanchard Public Schools in Blanchard, Oklahoma. Her interests are coaching paraprofessionals and teachers, inclusive teaching practices for students with extensive support needs, and preservice teacher training.

Kathy M. Randolph, EdD, BCBA-D, is assistant professor at Texas State University, and a board-certified behavior analyst at the doctoral level. Her research focuses on supporting teacher implementation of evidence-based practices using iCoaching, where teachers receive a packaged intervention to learn and implement evidence-based practices in classroom management to ensure successful inclusion of students with challenging behavior in the general education classroom.

Hope Rigby-Wills, EdD serves as lecturer and doctoral completion coach in the Department of Educational Leadership and Policy Studies within the College of Education at the University of Houston. She previously served as a K–12 special educator and special populations director in Houston and New York City. Her primary area of interest is the use of evidence-based practices—specifically explicit instruction and data-based individualization of instruction—to improve student outcomes.

Andrea K. W. Smith, MEd, is a teacher and instructional coach in Baker County, Florida. She earned a BA and MEd in special education from the University of Florida where she focused on supporting students with learning disabilities, behavioral disorders, and reading challenges. Andrea is a doctoral student and OSEP Scholar at the University of North Florida where her research interests include multi-tiered system of support (MTSS), literacy education, special education, and teacher preparation.

Bailey D. Smith, BSEd, is an early childhood teacher at Riverside Public Schools in El Reno, Oklahoma. She has earned a bachelor of science in elementary education from the University of Science and Arts of Oklahoma. Bailey is currently a graduate student at the University of Oklahoma working to obtain a master's degree in special education with an emphasis in applied behavior analysis.

About the Editors

Brittany L. Hott, PhD, BCBA-D, is associate director of the Institute for Community and Society Transformation (ICAST) and professor of special education at the University of Oklahoma. She is an author of *Teaching Students with Emotional and Behavioral Disabilities*. Dr. Hott is the editor of *Quality Instruction and Intervention: Strategies for Secondary Educators* and coeditor of *Research Methods in Special Education*. Dr. Hott currently serves as an associate editor for *Rural Special Education Quarterly* and *Intervention in School and Clinic*. Her recent work appears in prominent journals including *Behavior Modification*, *Learning Disabilities Research and Practice*, *Learning Disability Quarterly*, and *The Journal of Special Education*. Dr. Hott is a past president of the Council for Learning Disabilities.

Pamela Williamson, PhD, is professor at the University of North Florida. She is coeditor of *Teaching Exceptional Children* and coeditor of an award-winning textbook, *Quality Literacy Instruction for Students with Autism Spectrum Disorder*. Williamson prepares preservice teachers to provide effective literacy instruction and intervention and research methods to graduate students. The work of Williamson together with her colleagues has been published in well-respected journals, including *Exceptional Children*, *The Journal of Special Education*, *Remedial and Special Education*, and *Focus on Autism and Other Developmental Disabilities*.